Fusion

Integrated Reading and Writing
North Carolina Community College System DRE 097

Dave Kemper | Verne Meyer | John Van Rys |
Pat Sebranek

CENGAGE
Learning·

Australia • Brazil • Japan • Korea • Mexico • Singapore • Spain • United Kingdom • United States

CENGAGE
Learning·

Fusion: Integrated Reading and Writing North Carolina Community College System DRE 097

Senior Project Development Manager:
Linda deStefano

Market Development Manager:
Heather Kramer

Senior Production/
Manufacturing Manager:
Donna M. Brown

Production Editorial Manager:
Kim Fry

Sr. Rights Acquisition Account Manager:
Todd Osborne

Fusion: Integrated Reading and Writing, Book 1
Dave Kemper, Verne Meyer, John Van Rys, Pat Sebranek
© 2013 Cengage Learning. All rights reserved.

Fusion: Integrated Reading and Writing, Book 2
Dave Kemper, Verne Meyer, John Van Rys, Pat Sebranek
© 2013 Cengage Learning. All rights reserved.

For product information and technology assistance, contact us at
Cengage Learning Customer & Sales Support, 1-800-354-9706
For permission to use material from this text or product,
submit all requests online at **cengage.com/permissions**
Further permissions questions can be emailed to
permissionrequest@cengage.com

This book contains select works from existing Cengage Learning resources and was produced by Cengage Learning Custom Solutions for collegiate use. As such, those adopting and/or contributing to this work are responsible for editorial content accuracy, continuity and completeness.

Compilation © 2013 Cengage Learning

ISBN-13: 978-1-285-88932-0

ISBN-10: 1-285-88932-0

Cengage Learning
5191 Natorp Boulevard
Mason, Ohio 45040
USA

Cengage Learning is a leading provider of customized learning solutions with office locations around the globe, including Singapore, the United Kingdom, Australia, Mexico, Brazil, and Japan. Locate your local office at:
international.cengage.com/region.
Cengage Learning products are represented in Canada by Nelson Education, Ltd.
For your lifelong learning solutions, visit **www.cengage.com /custom.**
Visit our corporate website at **www.cengage.com.**

Printed in the United States of America

Brief Contents

Part I: Reading and Writing for Success   1

1 The Reading-Writing Connection   3
2 Academic Reading and Learning   11
3 The Traits of Academic Reading   29
4 The Traits of Academic Writing   87
5 Academic Writing and Learning   65

Part II: Reading and Writing Paragraphs   109

6 Classification   111
7 Cause-Effect   135
8 Comparison   159
9 Argumentation   183
10 Summarizing   207
11 Reading and Writing Essays   223

Part III: Sentence Workshops   243

12 Sentence Basics   243
13 Simple, Compound, and Complex Sentences   261

14 Agreement   275
15 Sentence Problems   291

Part IV: Word Workshops   311

16 Noun   313
17 Pronoun   327
18 Verb   341
19 Adjective and Adverb   361
20 Conjunction and Preposition   375

Part V: Punctuation and Mechanics Workshops   387

21 Capitalization   389
22 Comma   399
23 Quotation Marks and Italics   409
24 Other Punctuation   415

Appendix and Glossary   426

To the Student

Our mission with **Fusion: Integrated Reading and Writing, NC DRE 097 Edition**, is to help you function, and even flourish, as a college reader and writer. This book was designed to meet all the requirements of the North Carolina Community College DRE 097 course, with a focus on reading and writing paragraphs and essays for professional and academic purposes. As you work through the chapters in this book, you will learn skills that take the mystery out of understanding reading assignments and developing effective writing assignments. And by providing just the right amount of practice and enrichment, we make sure that you can remember and apply these skills in all your classes.

It's important for you to understand the special connection between reading and writing. Both help you learn and improve your communication skills. Reading gives you ideas for writing, and writing helps you understand your reading more fully. The connections go on and on. Studying reading and writing together, or in an integrated way, makes perfect sense. For the first time, you may truly connect to the written language—and do so much more quickly and effectively than if you had to take separate reading and writing courses. What is more exciting is this: Your work in this book will give you the confidence and motivation to learn in any setting.

Your instructor may have chosen to include **Aplia™ for Fusion: Integrated Reading and Writing** to accompany this book. This online program was written to provide interactive and engaging assignments that offer practice needed to build fundamental reading, writing, and grammar skills.

- Diagnostic tests offer a good picture of your overall strengths and weaknesses, and allow you to focus your efforts on strengthening areas of weakness.
- Assignments are automatically scored, and include immediate and constructive feedback to allow you to reinforce key concepts.

Part I:

Reading and Writing for Success

1

> "There's nothing more exciting to me than to read books."
> —Toni Morrison

The Reading-
Writing Connection

Professional writers know all about the special connection between reading and writing. Stephen King says, "Reading is the creative center of a writer's life." Joan Aiken says, "Read as much as you possibly can." William Faulkner said, "Read, read, read. Read everything. . . ." Writers know that reading helps them write, and that writing influences them to read more.

As a student, you need to make your own special connection between reading and writing. To begin, it is important to understand how academic reading and writing work together to help you learn. Then you'll need strategies for improving your academic reading and writing. The next four chapters in this section will introduce you to these strategies.

Learning Outcomes

LO1 Understand reading and writing assignments.

LO2 Use the traits for reading and writing.

LO3 Use graphic organizers for reading and writing.

LO4 Review the reading-writing connection.

What do you think?

In the above quotation, why might author Toni Morrison find reading so exciting? How do Morrison's feelings about reading compare to your own?

Adrin Shamsudin, 2011 / Used under license from Shutterstock.com

LO1 Understanding Reading and Writing Assignments

> "It's good to rub and polish our brain against that of others."
> —Michel de Montaigne

Being prepared is an important part of making good choices. You would, for example, want to know the basics about a job or an internship before you applied for it. The same holds true for each of your college reading and writing assignments. You should identify the main features before you get started on your work.

The STRAP Strategy

You can use the STRAP strategy to analyze your writing and reading assignments. The strategy consists of answering questions about these five features: *subject, type, role, audience,* and *purpose.* Once you answer the questions, you'll be ready to get to work. This chart shows how the strategy works:

For Reading Assignments		For Writing Assignments
What specific topic does the reading address?	**S**ubject	What specific topic should I write about?
What form (*essay, text chapter, article*) does the reading take?	**T**ype	What form of writing (*essay, article*) will I use?
What position (*student, responder, concerned individual*) does the writer assume?	**R**ole	What position (*student, citizen, employee*) should I assume?
Who is the intended reader?	**A**udience	Who is the intended reader?
What is the goal of the material?	**P**urpose	What is the goal (*to inform, to persuade*) of the writing?

The STRAP Strategy in Action

Suppose you were given the following reading assignment in an environmental studies class.

Assignment: Read the essay "The ABC Daily To-Do List." (See Appendix.) Then write a blog entry comparing the advice in the essay with the way you have managed your time in the past. (Below are answers to the STRAP questions for this assignment.)

Subject:	Keeping a daily to-do list
Type:	Process essay
Role:	An educator helping students achieve
Audience:	Students
Purpose:	To inform students about time-management skills

Respond for Reading   Analyze the following reading assignment by answering the STRAP questions below.

Assignment: Read the personal narrative "Codes of Conduct" in Appendix. Then in your notebook, respond to the reading noting its key features and your reactions to them.

Subject: What specific topic does the reading address?

Type: What form (*essay, narrative, text chapter*) does the reading take?

Role: What position (*concerned individual, observer, participant,* etc.) does the writer assume?

Audience: Who is the intended audience?

Purpose: What is the goal of the text (*to inform, to persuade, to share*)?

Additional Practice: Use the STRAP questions above to analyze the following assignment.

- Read the definition essay "What Is Emotional Intelligence?" in Appendix. Identify the main features of this essay.

Respond for Writing   Analyze the writing assignment by answering the STRAP questions that follow it.

Assignment: In a posting on the class blog, reflect on the importance of a specific school-related experience. Consider who was involved, what happened, and why it is significant.

Subject: What specific topic does the writing assignment address?

Type: What form (*essay, report, blog posting*) should my writing take?

Role: What position (*student, citizen, family member*) should I assume?

Audience: Who is the intended audience?

Purpose: What is the goal of my writing (*to inform, to persuade, to reflect*)?

Additional Practice: Use the STRAP questions above to analyze this assignment.

- The ability to work in groups is important in college and in the workplace. Write an essay explaining three or four group skills that students should learn and practice.

LO2 Using the Traits for Reading and Writing

Using the traits of writing can help you gain a full understanding of reading assignments, and they can help you develop your own paragraphs and essays. The traits identify the key elements of written language, including ideas, organization, voice, word choice, sentence fluency, and conventions.

INSIGHT

Using the traits helps you answer these two questions: "What elements should I look for in each of my reading assignments?" and "What elements should I consider when developing my writing assignments?"

The Traits in Action

This chart shows the connection between using the traits for reading and writing assignments.

Read to identify . . .	The Traits	Write to shape . . .
▪ the topic. ▪ the thesis (main point). ▪ the key supporting details.	**Ideas**	▪ a thesis or focus. ▪ your thoughts on the topic. ▪ effective supporting details.
▪ the quality of the beginning, middle, and ending parts. ▪ the organization of the supporting details.	**Organization**	▪ an effective beginning, middle, and ending. ▪ a logical, clear presentation of your supporting details.
▪ the level of the writer's interest in and knowledge about the topic.	**Voice**	▪ a voice that sounds interesting, honest, and knowledgeable.
▪ the quality of the words. (Are they interesting and clear?)	**Word Choice**	▪ words that are specific, clear, and fitting for the assignment.
▪ the effectiveness of the sentences. (Do they flow smoothly, and are they clear?)	**Sentence Fluency**	▪ smooth-reading, clear, and accurate sentences.
▪ to what degree the writing follows conventions (and why or why not).	**Conventions**	▪ paragraphs or essays that follow the conventions or rules.

Note Design, or the appearance of a text, is sometimes included in a list of the traits. The key consideration of design is readability: Does the design add to or take away from the reading of a text?

Respond for Reading To get a feel for using the traits for reading, answer the questions below for the essay "Herbivore, Carnivore, or Omnivore?" (see Appendix).

Questions to Answer for Reading

Ideas: What is the topic of this essay?

What main point is made about the topic? (Look for a thesis statement.)

What details stand out? Name two.

Organization: How does it start?

What happens in the middle?

How does it end?

What part do you like best and why?

Voice: Does the writer seem interested in and knowledgeable about the topic? Why or why not?

Respond for Writing To get a feel for using the traits for writing, answer the questions below for this assignment:

- In a posting on the class blog, reflect on the importance of a specific school-related experience. Consider who was involved, what happened, and why it is significant.

Questions to Answer for Writing

Ideas: What topic will you write about?

What main point about the topic could you focus on? (Did the experience help you, change you, etc.?)

What types of details could you include (explanations, examples, descriptions, personal thoughts, conversations, etc.)? Name two.

Organization: How might you start your writing?

What happens in the middle?

How might you end your writing?

What part do you like best and why?

Voice: What kind of writing voice and language will best fit this assignment?

Extra Practice: Answer the questions above for this writing assignment:

- The ability to work in groups is important in college and the workplace. Write an essay explaining three or four group skills that students should learn and practice.

LO3 Using Graphic Organizers with Reading and Writing

Graphic organizers help you map out your thinking for writing and reading assignments. You can, for example, use a Venn diagram or a T-graph to arrange your thoughts for a comparison essay assignment, or to take notes about an essay you have just read. Other common graphics help you organize your thinking for problem-solution, cause-effect, and narrative writing and reading assignments.

Using a Time Line

Provided below is a time line charting the main actions in a narrative essay. (A time line identifies the key actions and events, without the related details and explanations.)

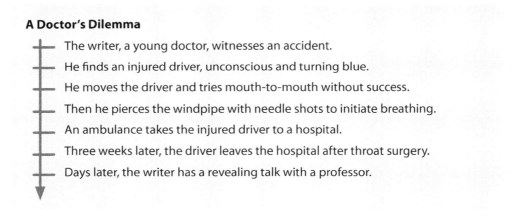

A Doctor's Dilemma

The writer, a young doctor, witnesses an accident.

He finds an injured driver, unconscious and turning blue.

He moves the driver and tries mouth-to-mouth without success.

Then he pierces the windpipe with needle shots to initiate breathing.

An ambulance takes the injured driver to a hospital.

Three weeks later, the driver leaves the hospital after throat surgery.

Days later, the writer has a revealing talk with a professor.

Respond for Reading Use a time line to list the main actions from the essay "Remembering Gramps" (see Appendix).

Respond for Writing Use a time line to list the main actions for an essay about an important school-related experience.

Sample Graphic Organizers

Time Line Use for personal narratives to list actions or events in the order they occurred.

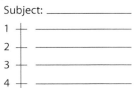

Line Diagram Use to collect and organize details for informational essays.

Cause-Effect Organizer Use to collect and organize details for cause-effect essays.

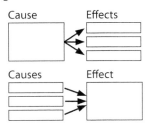

Evaluation Chart Use to collect supporting details for essays of evaluation.

Subject: _____

Points to Evaluate	Supporting Details
1	
2	
3	
4	

Process Diagram Use to collect details for science-related writing, such as the steps in a process.

Venn Diagram Use to collect details to compare and contrast two topics.

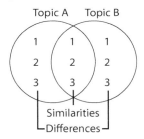

Problem-Solution Web Use to map out problem-solution essays.

Cluster Use to collect details for informational essays.

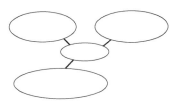

LO4 Reviewing the Reading-Writing Connection

Complete these activities as needed to help you better understand the reading-writing connection.

Understand the STRAP Strategy   Answer these questions about the STRAP strategy.

- What is the STRAP strategy? _____
- What does each letter in STRAP stand for? _____

Assignment: Use the STRAP strategy to analyze the essay "Remembering Gramps" (see Appendix).

Subject: _____

Type: _____

Role: _____

Audience: _____

Purpose: _____

Use the Traits   Answer these questions about the traits of writing.

- What traits of writing should you identify in reading and writing assignments?

  _____

- Which trait deals with the writer's level of interest in the writing?

  _____

- Which trait deals with the rules for using the language correctly?

  _____

Assignment: Write an essay explaining how to do or make something. Choose a topic that you know well, and be sure to include all of the necessary steps. Answer the "Questions to Answer for Writing" on page 7 for the following assignment:

Ideas: _____

_____

Organization: _____

_____

Voice: _____

_____

2

Academic Reading and Learning

Technology is "simply irresistible," especially with the immediate connections that it allows you to make. One minute you are texting a friend, and the next minute you are watching something on YouTube. Because of electronic gadgetry, the world truly is at your fingertips. Unfortunately, this fast action can be a problem, especially when it comes to college-level reading and learning.

Rather than skimming and surfing, your instructors will expect you to become thoughtfully involved in each reading assignment. In other words, they want you to be a critical reader, entirely focused on the material in front of you. The guidelines and strategies presented in this chapter will help you do just that for all types of reading assignments, from textbook chapters to published articles and essays.

Learning Outcomes

LO1 Read to learn.
LO2 Understand the reading process.
LO3 Use basic reading strategies.
LO4 Read critically.
LO5 Improve vocabulary.
LO6 Read graphics.
LO7 Review reading and learning.

What do you think?

What does the quotation at the top of the page have to say about the connection between reading, thinking, and learning?

What books make you think the most?

> "Meaning doesn't reside ready-made in the text . . . , it happens during the transaction between reader and text."
> —Louise Rosenblatt

LO1 Reading to Learn

Reading and learning logically go hand in hand. You read to learn about new concepts and ideas; you read to learn how to do something; and you read to understand the past, the present, and the future. In college, reading is an essential learning tool, and you will learn the most by becoming an active reader.

CONSIDER THE TRAITS

In effective text, the reader will find strong ideas, logical organization, a clear voice, precise words, and smooth sentences. These traits are the working parts of a text.

Effective Academic Reading

Follow the guidelines listed below for all of your reading assignments.

1. **Divide the assignment into doable parts.** Don't try to read long texts all at once. Instead, try to read for 15-30 minutes at a time.

2. **Find a quiet place.** You'll need space to read and write without distractions. (Quiet background music is okay, if it helps you stay on task.)

3. **Gather your materials.** Have on hand a notebook, related handouts, Web access, and so on.

4. **Approach your reading as a process.** Academic reading requires that you do a number of things, usually in a certain order.

5. **Use proven reading strategies.** For example, taking notes and annotating a text gets you actively involved in your reading.

6. **Know what to look for when you read.** There are key ideas or elements that you need to identify in order to understand a text.

7. **Summarize what you have learned.** Also note any concepts or explanations that you don't understand.

8. **Review your reading from time to time.** Doing this will help you internalize the information so you can apply it in your writing and class work.

Practice Choose the star below that best describes your academic reading skills. Then, in a brief paragraph, explain your choice. In your paragraph, consider which of the guidelines above you do or do not follow.

Weak ★ ★ ★ ★ ★ Strong

LO2 Understanding the Reading Process

Reading a sport or fashion magazine can be quick and easy because you are reading for enjoyment. Reading an academic text is entirely different because you are reading to gain information. Always approach your academic reading carefully, following the steps in an effective process, so you don't miss important facts and details.

Think about it.

Reading allows you to discover what other people are thinking about important subjects.

The Steps in the Process

The process described below helps you pace yourself and read thoughtfully.

Process	Activities
Prereading	First become familiar with the text and establish a starting point for reading.
Reading	Read the assignment once to get a basic understanding of the text.
Rereading	Complete additional readings and analysis as needed, until you have a clear understanding of the text's key elements or traits.
Reflecting	Evaluate your reading experience: *What have you learned? What questions do you have about the material? How has this reading changed or expanded what you know about the topic?*

The Process in Action

This graphic presents the reading process in action. The arrows show how you may move back and forth between the steps. For example, after beginning your reading, you may refer back to something in your prereading.

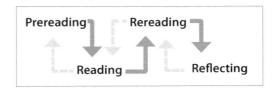

Practice   What observations can you make about the reading process after reviewing the information above? One observation is provided below; list three or four additional ones on your own paper.

Academic reading can't be done quickly.

A CLOSER LOOK at the Process

Each step in the reading process requires a special type of thinking and planning. Following these steps will help you become a more confident reader and learner.

Prereading addresses what you should do *before* your actual reading. A cook reviews a recipe in order to have everything in place before starting; prereading serves a similar purpose. Here are the basic prereading tasks.

- **Review the title.** Many readers give the title very little thought. Bad move. The title often identifies the topic of the reading and helps you understand the author's attitude or feeling about it.

- **Learn about the author.** Read the brief biography about the author if it is provided with the text. Otherwise, check online for information about the writer. This information may help you appreciate the author's approach or point of view taken in the text.

- **Preview the text.** Complete the following actions:
  - Read the first paragraph or two to get a general idea about the topic, the level of language used, the writer's tone, and so on.
  - Next, skim the text for headings, bold words, and graphics.
  - Then read the final paragraph or two to see how the text ends.
  - Finally, consider the author's purpose and audience.

- **Establish a starting point for reading.** Once you have done all of these things, write down your first thoughts about the text. Consider what you already know about the topic, what questions you have, and what you expect to learn.

CONSIDER ————————————————————————

Prereading is more important when you are assigned to read essays, articles, and other longer texts, and less important when you are assigned to read an individual paragraph.

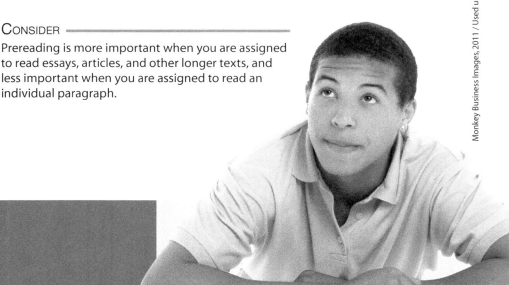

Monkey Business Images, 2011 / Used under license from Shutterstock.com

Reading a text requires your undivided attention. These are your goals during the first reading.

- **Confirm the author's purpose and audience:** Is the material intended to explain, describe, or persuade? And does it address general readers, college students, professionals, or so on?
- **Identify the thesis or the main idea** of the text.
- **Locate the evidence**—the facts and details that support the main idea.
- **Consider the conclusion**—the closing thoughts of the writer.

Rereading a text helps you to better understand its main points. These are your goals during your rereading.

- **Confirm your basic understanding of the text.** Are you still sure about the thesis and support? If not, adjust your thinking as needed.
- **Analyze the development of the ideas.** Is the topic timely or important? Does the thesis seem reasonable? What types of support are provided—facts, statistics, or examples? Does the conclusion seem logical?
- **Consider the organization of the material.** How does the writer organize his or her support?
- **Check the voice and style of the writing.** Does the writer seem knowledgeable about the topic and interested in it? Are the ideas easy to follow?

Reflecting helps you fine-tune your thinking about the material. Writing about your reading is the best way to reflect on it. These are your goals during this step.

- **Explain what you have learned.** What new information have you gained? How will you use it? Does this new information change your thinking in any way? Explain.
- **Explore your feelings about the reading.** Did the reading surprise you? Did it disappoint you? Did it answer your questions?
- **Identify what questions you still have.** Then try to answer them.

CONSIDER ───
Try summarizing the text. Doing so will help you determine how well you understand it.

Apply Use this process for your next reading assignment. Afterward discuss the experience with your classmates.

Other Reading Processes

Two other reading processes—KWL and SQ3R—are variations on the reading process described on the previous pages.

KWL

KWL stands for what I *know*, what I *want* to know, and what I *learned*. Identifying what you know (K) and want to know (W) occurs during prereading. Identifying what you learned (L) occurs after your reading, rereading, and reflecting.

Using a KWL Chart

1. Write the topic of your reading at the top of your paper. Then divide the paper into three columns and label them **K, W,** and **L.**
2. In the **K** column, identify what you already know.
3. In the **W** column, identify the questions you want answered.
4. In the **L** column, note what you have learned.

Topic:		
K	W	L
Identify what you **KNOW.**	Identify what you **WANT** to know.	List what you **LEARNED.**

SQ3R

SQ3R is a thorough reading process, very similar to prereading, reading, rereading, and reflecting. The letters SQ3R stand for *survey, question, read, recite,* and *review.*

Using SQ3R

Survey: When you survey, you skim the title, headings, graphics, and first and last paragraphs to get a general idea about the text.

Question: During this step, you ask questions about the topic that you hope the text will answer.

Read: While you do the reading, you take careful notes, reread challenging parts, and so on.

Recite: At the end of each page, section, or chapter, you should state out loud what you have learned. (This could involve answering the 5 W's and H—*who? what? when? where? why?* and *how?*) Reread as necessary.

Review: After reading, you study your notes, answer questions about the reading, summarize the text, and so on.

LO3 Using Basic Reading Strategies

To make sure that you gain the most from each reading assignment, carry out the reading strategies on the next few pages.

Forming Personal Responses

To thoughtfully interact with a text, you need to write about it. Reserve part of your class notebook for these personal responses. Personal responses to a text help you think about it—to agree with it, to question it, to make connections with it. The following guidelines will help you do this:

> **INSIGHT**
>
> If you are a visual person, you may understand a text best by clustering or mapping its important points.

- **Write several times,** perhaps once before you read, two or three times during the reading, and one time afterward.
- **Write freely and honestly** to make genuine connections with the text.
- **Respond to points of view** that you like or agree with, information that confuses you, connections that you can make with other material, and ideas that seem significant.
- **Label and date your responses.** You can use these entries to prepare for exams or complete other assignments.
- **Share your discoveries.** Your entries can provide conversation starters in discussions with classmates.

Types of Personal Responses

Here are some specific ways to respond to a text:

Discuss Carry on a conversation with the author or a character to get to know her or him and yourself a little better.

Illustrate Create graphics or draw pictures to help you figure out parts of the text.

Imitate Continue the article or story line, trying to write like the author.

Express Share your feelings about the text, perhaps in a poem.

Practice Follow the guidelines on this page to explore your thoughts about one of your next reading assignments. Afterward, assess the value of forming personal responses to a text.

Annotating a Text

To annotate means "to add comments or make notes in a text." Annotating a text allows you to interact with the ideas in a reading selection. Here are some suggestions:

- Write questions in the margins.
- Underline or highlight important points.
- Summarize key passages.
- Define new terms.
- Make connections to other parts.

> **NOTE:**
> Annotate reading material only if you own the text or if you are reading a photocopy.

Annotating in Action

Los Chinos Discover el Barrio
by Luis Torres

contrasting images, interesting

There's a colorful mural on the asphalt playground of Hillside Elementary School, in the neighborhood called Lincoln Heights. Painted on the beige handball wall, the mural is of life-sized youngsters holding hands. Depicted are Asian and Latino kids with bright faces and ear-to-ear smiles.

The mural is a (mirror) *reflection* of the makeup of the neighborhood today: Latinos living side by side with Asians. But it's not all smiles and happy faces in the Northeast Los Angeles community, located just a *contrast* couple of miles up Broadway from City Hall. On the surface there's harmony between Latinos and Asians. But there are indications of simmering ethnic-based tensions.

The writer makes a personal connection.

That became clear to me recently when I took a walk through the old neighborhood—the one where I grew up. As I walked along North Broadway, I thought of a joke that comic (Paul Rodriguez) *Who?* often tells on the stage. He paints a picture of a young Chicano walking down a street on L.A.'s East Side. He comes upon two Asians having an animated conversation in what sounds like

Ha! This shows how two different immigrant groups struggle to fit in.

babble. "Hey, you guys, knock off that foreign talk. This is America—speak Spanish!"

Annotate Carefully read the excerpt below from an essay by Stephen King. Then, if you own this book, annotate the text according to the following directions:

- Circle the main point of the passage.
- Underline or highlight one idea in the first paragraph that you either agree with, question, or are confused by. Then make a comment about this idea in the margin.
- Do the same for one idea in the third paragraph and one idea in the final paragraph.
- Circle one or two words that you are unsure of. Then define or explain these words.

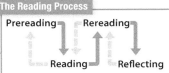

Why We Crave Horror Movies

I think that we're all mentally ill; those of us outside the asylums only *1* hide it a little better—and maybe not all that much better, after all. We've all known people who talk to themselves, people who sometimes squinch their faces into horrible grimaces when they believe no one is watching, people who have some hysterical fear—of snakes, the dark, the tight *5* place, the long drop . . . and, of course, the final worms and grubs that are waiting so patiently underground.

When we pay our four or five bucks and seat ourselves at tenth-row center in a theater showing a horror movie, we are daring the nightmare.

Why? Some of the reasons are simple and obvious. To show that we *10* can, that we are not afraid, that we can ride this roller coaster. Which is not to say that a really good horror movie may not surprise a scream out of us at some point, the way we may scream when the roller coaster twists through a complete 360 or plows through a lake at the bottom of the dip. And horror movies, like roller coasters, have always been the special *15* province of the young; by the time one turns 40 or 50, one's appetite for double twists or 360-degree loops may be considerably depleted.

We also go to re-establish our feelings of essential normality; the horror movie is innately conservative, even reactionary. Freda Jackson as the horrible melting woman in *Die, Monster, Die!* confirms for us that no *20* matter how far we may be removed from the beauty of a Robert Redford or a Diana Ross, we are still light-years from true ugliness.

And we go to have fun.

Ah, but this is where the ground starts to slope away, isn't it? Because this is a very peculiar sort of fun, indeed. The fun comes from seeing *25* others menaced—sometimes killed. One critic suggested that if pro football has become the voyeur's version of combat, then the horror film has become the modern version of the public lynching. . . .

Taking Effective Notes

Taking notes helps you to focus on reading material and understand it more fully. Notes change information you have read about to information that you are working with. Of course, taking effective notes makes studying for an exam much easier.

Note-Taking Tips

- Use your own words as much as possible.
- Record only key points and details rather than complicated sentences.
- Consider **boldfaced** or *italicized* words, graphics, and captions as well as the main text.
- Employ abbreviations and symbols to save time (vs., #, &, etc.).
- Decide on a system to organize or arrange your notes so they are easy to follow.

An Active Note-Taking System

To make your note taking more active, use a two-column system. One column (two-thirds of the page) is for your main notes, and the other column (one-third of the page) is for comments, reactions, and questions.

INSIGHT

Note taking should be more than writing down what you read. It should also be connecting with and questioning new information.

Two-Column Notes

In Africa, AIDS Has a Woman's Face
by Kofi A. Annan   March 3

Main notes
- women backbone of African societies

Annan-UN Secretary General thru 2008

Comments, reactions, questions

- UN work depends on building partnerships with African women and their husbands

- studies show that strong development strategies must involve women

← interesting idea

Is this true only in Africa?

- famine and AIDS threatening any development movements

- famine and AIDS linked

- 30 million at risk of starvation

← How was this statistic determined?

Summarizing a Text

Summarizing a reading assignment will tell you how well you understand the information. Summarizing means "to present the main points in a clear, concise form using your own words." Generally speaking, a summary should be about one-third as long as the original.

Summarizing Tips

- Start by clearly stating the main point of the text.
- Share only the essential supporting facts and details (names, dates, times, and places) in the next sentences.
- Present your ideas in a logical order.
- Tie all of your points together in a closing sentence.

Example Summary

The example below summarizes a two-page essay by Kofi A. Annan concerning the suffering caused by AIDS and famine in southern Africa.

The Face of AIDS

Main points
(underlined)

Essential
supporting
facts

Closing
sentence
(underlined)

Famine and AIDS are threatening the agricultural   *1*
societies in southern Africa. Tragically, women, the
main unifying force in African societies, make up 59% of
individuals worldwide infected by the HIV virus. With so
many women suffering from AIDS, the family structure   *5*
and the agricultural infrastructure are suffering severely.
These conditions have significantly contributed to the famine
conditions and resulting starvation. Any traditional survival
techniques used by African women in the past won't work for
these twin disasters. International relief is needed, and it   *10*
must provide immediate food and health aid. A key focus of
health aid must be the treatment of women infected with HIV
and preventative education to stop the spread of the disease.
The future of southern Africa depends on the health and
leadership of its women.   *15*

LO4 Reading Critically

Critical reading involves a lot of analyzing and evaluating. Analyzing refers to, among other things, classifying and comparing ideas as well as looking for cause-effect relationships. Evaluating refers to weighing the value of a text and considering its strengths and weaknesses.

INSIGHT ———————————————————————————————————————

When you analyze or evaluate a text, you are involved in higher-level thinking. At the same time, other types of thinking like remembering and understanding also come into play.

Bloom's New Taxonomy

Whenever you are asked to . . .	Be prepared to . . .
Remember ———————————	collect basic information, identify key terms, and remember main points.
Understand ———————————	explain what you have learned, give examples, and restate information.
Apply ———————————	identify crucial details, organize key points, and model or show understanding.
Analyze ———————————	carefully examine the topic, classify the main points, show cause-effect relationships, and make comparisons.
Evaluate ———————————	judge the value of information, identify strengths and weaknesses, and argue for or against the ideas.
Create ———————————	develop something new from what you have learned.

Practice Study the chart above. Then explain in a brief paragraph how many of these thinking skills you apply to your own academic reading.

A CLOSER LOOK at Critical Reading

When reading critically, you are, in effect, asking and answering thoughtful questions about a text. Here are some thoughtful questions that a critical reader may ask about a nonfiction text:

Asking Critical Questions

- What is the purpose of the reading (to inform, to entertain, to persuade)?
- Who is the intended audience (general readers, students, professionals)?
- What parts does the text include (title, headings, graphics, introduction, etc.)?
- What logical pattern of reasoning does it follow? (See below.)
- What is the thesis or main idea in the reading?
- How is the thesis supported or developed (facts, examples, definitions, etc.) ?
- What parts of the text seem especially important and why?
- What questions do you still have about the topic?
- How will you use this information?

Logical Patterns of Reasoning

Almost all texts that you read will follow either deductive or inductive patterns of reasoning. **Deductive thinking** moves from a general thesis to specific supporting details. Most texts follow this form of thinking. **Inductive thinking** moves from specific facts and details to a general conclusion.

Use these questions to check for deductive thinking.

- Does the text start with a thesis (main point or major premise)?
- Do the details logically support or follow from the thesis?
- Does the conclusion logically follow the ideas that come before it?

Use these questions to check for inductive thinking.

- Does the text start with a series of facts, examples, and explanations?
- Do they logically lead up to the general conclusion?
- Does the general conclusion make sense in terms of the preceding evidence (facts, examples, etc.)?

Apply Use the "critical questions" on this page as a general guide for your next information reading assignment. Afterward, share your reading experience with your classmates.

LO5 Improving Vocabulary

To understand and benefit from your academic reading, you need to understand the words used in each text.

Keeping a Vocabulary Notebook

Proactive means "acting in advance" or "acting before." Keeping a vocabulary notebook is proactive because you are taking control of your vocabulary building. The note card to the right shows the kinds of information to include for words you list in your notebook.

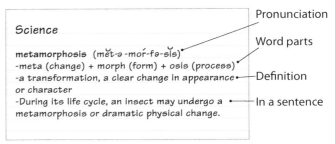

Pronunciation

Word parts

Science

metamorphosis (mĕt-ə-mor-fə-sĭs)
-meta (change) + morph (form) + osis (process)
-a transformation, a clear change in appearance —Definition
or character
-During its life cycle, an insect may undergo a —In a sentence
metamorphosis or dramatic physical change.

Create In your vocabulary notebook, list two or three challenging words from one of your next reading assignments. For each word, include the types of information shown above. Continue adding new words from your reading selections.

Using Context

Avoid the temptation to skip new words in your reading. Instead, try to figure out what the new words mean in *context*—looking for clues in the other words and ideas around them. Use these examples of context clues as a guide:

- **Cause-effect relationships:** Suggesting the use of seat belts didn't work, so the state officials made seat-belt use *mandatory.*
- **Definitions built into the text:** Dr. Williams is an *anthropologist,* a person who scientifically studies the physical, social, and cultural development of humans.
- **Comparisons and contrasts:** Lynn Dery lives in New York, so she is used to a fast-paced life; Mandy Williams lives in the country, so she is used to a more *serene* lifestyle.
- **Words in a series:** Spaghetti, lasagna, and *ziti* all have their own special shape.
- **Synonyms (words with the same meaning):** Hector's essay contains too many *banal,* overused phrases.
- **Antonyms (words with the opposite meaning):** Mrs. Wolfe still seemed strong and energetic after the storm, but Mr. Wolfe looked *haggard.*
- **The tone of the text:** The street was filled with *bellicose* protesters who pushed and shoved their way through the crowd. The scene was no longer peaceful and calm, as the marchers promised it would be.

Define Define each italicized word above using the clues in the sentences. Afterward, check your definitions in a dictionary.

Understanding Word Parts

You may have heard of the following terms: *roots* (base words), *prefixes*, and *suffixes*. Many words in our language are made up of combinations of these word parts.

- **Roots** like *liber* (as in liber̲a̲t̲e) or *scope* (as in tele s̲c̲o̲p̲e) are the starting points for most words.
- **Prefixes** like *anti* (as in a̲n̲t̲i̲biotic) or *un* (as in u̲n̲real) are word parts that come before roots to form new words.
- **Suffixes** like *dom* (as in bore d̲o̲m̲) or *ly* (as in hour l̲y̲) are word parts that come after roots to form new words.

Sample Words

The following examples show how multiple word parts can be combined to form words.

Transportation **combines . . .**
- the prefix *trans* meaning "across" or "beyond,"
- the root *port* meaning "carry,"
- and the suffix *tion* meaning "act of."

So, *transportation* means "the act of carrying across or beyond."

Biographic **combines . . .**
- the root *bio* meaning "life,"
- the root *graph* meaning "write,"
- and the suffix *ic* meaning "nature of" or "relating to."

So, *biographic* means "relating to writing about real life."

Micrometer **combines . . .**
- the root *micro* meaning "small"
- and the root *meter* meaning "measure."

So, a *micrometer* is "a device for measuring small distances."

Identify   Using the examples above as a guide, analyze and define the words below.
- nominate (*nomin + ate*)
- hemisphere (*hemi + sphere*)
- senile (*sen + ile*)
- translucent (*trans + luc + ent*)

LO6 Reading Graphics

In many of your college texts, a significant portion of the information will be given in charts, graphs, diagrams, and drawings. Knowing how to read these types of graphics, then, is important to your success as a college student. Follow the guidelines below to help you understand graphics.

- **Scan the graphic.** Consider it as a whole to get an overall idea about its message. Note its type (bar graph, pie graph, diagram, table, and so forth), its topic, its level of complexity, and so on.
- **Study the specific parts.** Start with the main heading or title. Next, note any additional labels or guides (such as the horizontal and vertical guides on a bar graph). Then focus on the actual information displayed in the graphic.
- **Question the graphic.** Does it address an important topic? What is its purpose (to make a comparison, to show a change, and so on)? What is the source of the information? Is the graphic out of date or biased in any way?
- **Reflect on its effectiveness.** Explain in your own words the main message of the graphic. Then consider its effectiveness, how it relates to the surrounding text, and how it matches up to your previous knowledge of the topic.

Analysis of a Graphic

Review the bar graph below. Then read the discussion to learn how all of the parts work together.

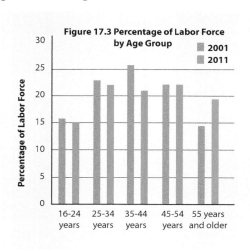

Discussion: This bar graph compares the labor force in 2001 to the labor force in 2011 for five specific age groups. The heading identifies the subject or topic of the graphic. The horizontal line identifies the different age groups, and the vertical line identifies the percentage of the labor force for each group. The key in the upper right-hand corner of the graphic explains the color-coded bars. With all of that information, the graphic reads quite clearly—and many interesting comparisons can be made.

React Read and analyze the following graphics, answering the questions about each one on your own paper. Use the information on the previous page as a guide.

Graphic 1

1. This graphic is called a pictograph rather than a bar graph. What makes it a "pictograph"?

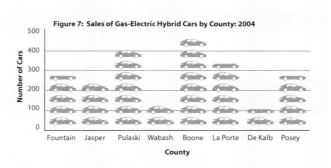

Figure 7: Sales of Gas-Electric Hybrid Cars by County: 2004

sabri deniz kizil, 2011 / Used under license from Shutterstock.com

2. What is the topic of this graphic?

3. What information is provided on the horizontal line? On the vertical line?

4. What comparisons can a reader make from this graphic?

Graphic 2

1. This graphic is called a line diagram, and it maps a structure. What structure does this diagram map?

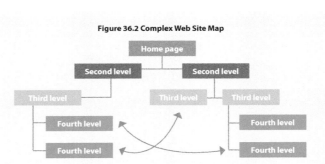

Figure 36.2 Complex Web Site Map

2. From the following items, choose the two working parts in this diagram: *words, lines, symbols.*

3. How are the different navigational choices on a complex Web site shown on this graphic?

LO7 Reviewing Reading and Learning

On your own paper, respond to each set of directions to review the concepts covered in this chapter.

Reading to Learn Explain in a few sentences how you should approach your academic reading to get the most out of each assignment.

_____

_____

_____

Understanding the Reading Process List the four steps in the reading process. Identify two things that you should do during each step.

1. _____

2. _____

3. _____

4. _____

Using Reading Strategies Answer the following questions about reading strategies.

- What does it mean to respond personally to a text? _____

- What does it mean to annotate a text? _____

- What are two-column notes?_____

Improving Vocabulary Explain what it means to use context clues to figure out the meaning of new words.

_____

_____

Reading Graphics Explain why it is important to know how to read graphics.

_____

_____

3

> "Reading is a basic tool of the living of a good life."
> —Joseph Addison

The Traits of Academic Reading

Here's one thing you know for sure: As a college student, you will do a lot of reading. Because reading is so important, you need to know the best way to understand and learn from each assignment. The last chapter, "Academic Reading and Learning," provided a starting point by discussing important skills such as note taking and vocabulary building. This chapter takes a closer look at reading.

You will learn about the traits or building blocks of a reading assignment. The basic traits include ideas, organization, voice, word choice, and sentences. Knowing how to identify and analyze these traits will make you a better reader. And becoming a better reader will help you succeed in all of your classes.

Remember: Reading may be your most important learning tool in college, so you need to know how to learn from your reading assignment.

Learning Outcomes

LO1 Ideas
LO2 Organization
LO3 Voice
LO4 Word choice and sentences
LO5 Review

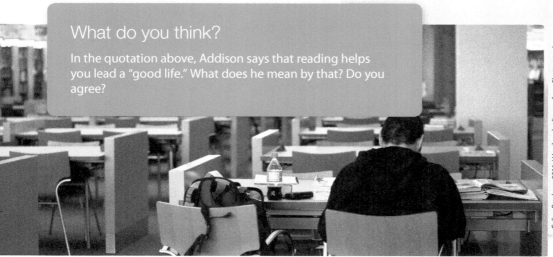

What do you think?

In the quotation above, Addison says that reading helps you lead a "good life." What does he mean by that? Do you agree?

Galina Barskaya, 2011 / Used under license from Shutterstock.com

LO1 Ideas

Ideas are the key trait in everything that you read. Every other trait—organization, voice, word choice—depends on the ideas. In this section you will learn about identifying the main idea and supporting details in a text.

Identifying the Main Idea

Almost every thing that you read—be it an essay, an article, or a textbook chapter—develops a main idea. This idea is usually stated in the topic sentence in paragraphs and in the thesis statement in essays or other longer texts.

There are times, however, when the main idea comes later in the text, perhaps as a concluding or closing statement. You may also read some essays or articles where the main idea is only implied, rather than stated directly. You may even read some longer texts that have more than one main idea or a main idea and one or two secondary ideas.

What the Main Idea Tells You

In a *narrative* text, the main idea will tell you what experience the writer is going to share:

- "My final moments on stage during the musical *Grease* are ones I'll never forget."

In an *informational* text, the main idea will tell you what the author is going to explain or discuss:

- "One word in medical reports strikers fear into people everywhere, and that word is pandemic."

In a *persuasive* text, the main idea will tell you what claim or opinion the writer is going to argue for:

- "Text messaging should be banned in all states because it is making U.S. roads dangerous."

INSIGHT

Every piece of writing needs a spark to ignite or start a piece of writing. A main idea serves this purpose.

SPECIAL NOTE: The way that a sentence is worded might tell you that it states the main idea: "It has been more than two years since my telephone rang with the news . . . ," "There are several steps . . . ," or "All the flavors a person can taste are made up of . . . ."

Vocabulary

implied
suggested rather than stated directly

secondary
lesser, not primary

Steps to Identifying the Main Idea

Follow the steps below to help you identify the main idea in a text. In paragraphs, you usually need to look no further than the first sentence—the topic sentence. In an essay, you usually will find the main idea stated in the thesis in one of the opening paragraphs. These steps will help you identify the main idea.

Steps to Follow

1. Study the title, and the first and last sentences of paragraphs. For essays, study the title and first and last paragraphs.

2. Then read the paragraph from start to finish. For an essay read the opening few paragraphs to gain a general understanding of the topic.

3. Next, in a paragraph, look for a sentence (usually the first one) that directs the writing. In an essay, look for this sentence at the end of one of the opening paragraphs.

4. Write this statement down, or underline it if you own the text or are reading a copy. (If you can't find such a statement, try to state it in your own words.)

5. Read the paragraph again (or the essay completely) to make sure that this statement makes sense as the main idea. In a paragraph, each new sentence should support or develop this idea. In an essay, each new paragraph should support or develop it.

6. If your thinking changes, identify or write down what you now believe to be the main idea.

INSIGHT ——

A paragraph is really an essay in miniature. That is, it should contain the same traits or working parts. Essays, of course, provide more information because the support comes in the form of paragraphs rather than sentences.

The Structure of a Topic Sentence or Thesis Statement

A topic sentence or thesis statement usually consists of two parts: (1) a specific topic plus (2) a particular feeling or idea about it. Here are three examples:

- "The United States must invest in wind power *(topic)* to resist our dependence on fossil fuel *(feeling/opinion)*."
- "Captain Chesley 'Sully' Sullenberger *(topic)* performed an emergency landing in the Hudson River *(idea)*."
- "The Don Quixote statuette my dad gave me *(topic)* isn't worth much to other people *(feeling)*."

In Context

Example 1

Study the following paragraph in which the writer explains Braille.

Communicating by Braille

<u>Braille is a system of communication used by the blind. It was</u>   *1*
<u>developed by Louis Braille, a blind French student, in 1824.</u> The code
consists of an alphabet using combinations of small raised dots. The
dots are imprinted on paper and can be felt, and thus read, by running
the fingers across the page. The basic unit of the code is called a "cell,"   *5*
which is two dots wide and three dots high. Each letter is formed by
different combinations of these dots. Numbers, punctuation marks, and
even a system for writing music are also expressed by using different
arrangements. These small dots, which may seem insignificant to the
sighted, have opened up the entire world of books and reading for the   *10*
blind.

Discussion: A paragraph, by definition, is a group of sentences sharing ideas about a main point, which is usually stated in the topic sentence. The topic sentence in the above paragraph is underlined. It identifies the topic *(Braille)* and an important idea about it *(is a system of communication used by the blind)*. The sentences in the body of the paragraph give facts about the topic.

Example 2

Read the following paragraph, in which the writer recalls a memorable gym teacher.

Duck-Walking

<u>Mr. Brown, my middle school gym teacher, did not allow any fooling around in his classes</u>. Unfortunately, two of my friends learned this the hard way. At the end of the first day of flag football, Mr. Brown blew his whistle. Most of us knew enough to stop and fall in line. He had made it very clear on the first day of class that when he blew his whistle, we had to stop our activity. Immediately. Kerry Schmidt and Jesse Johnson ignored the whistle and continued throwing a football. With fire in his eyes, Mr. Brown quickly sent the rest of us in. We all watched from the locker room doorway while Mr. Brown made Kerry and Jesse duck-walk on the football field. By the time they went 20 yards, they were really struggling. He sent them in after another 10 yards when their duck-walk had turned into more of a crawl. We couldn't help giving a few duck calls when they limped into the locker room, but we didn't quack too loudly because we didn't want Mr. Brown to make us walk like a duck or another other type of animal.

1

5

10

Piotr Tomicki, 2011 / Used under license from Shutterstock.com

Discussion: The topic sentence, which is underlined above, identifies the topic (*Mr. Brown*) and a feeling about him (*did not allow any fooling around in his classes*). The sentences in the body describe one experience that supports the topic sentence.

Example 3

Read the title, opening paragraph, and numbered main points in an essay from a book entitled *Focus on College and Career Success.*

Be Advised! Advising Mistakes Students Make

One of the most important relationships you'll have as a college   *1*
student is the one you build with your academic advisor. In your college
this person may be an advisor, a counselor, or a faculty member who can
steer you toward courses you can handle and instructors you can learn
best from. An advisor can keep you from taking classes that bog you down   *5*
academically or unnecessary ones that take you extra time to earn your
degree. <u>Here's a list of advising mistakes students make from real advisors
who work with college students every day.</u>

1. Not using the campus advising office or your faculty advisor. . . .   *10*

2. Not planning ahead. . . .

3. Procrastinating. . . .

4. Skipping prerequisites. . . .

"Be Advised! Advising Mistakes Students Make," from STALEY/STALEY. *FOCUS on College and Career Success,* 1E. © 2012 Wadsworth, a part of Cengage Learning, Inc.

Discussion: The title and general comments in the opening paragraph about the topic lead up to the thesis statement (underlined). Each of the numbered points that follow identifies an advising mistake. So clearly, the underlined statement is the thesis of the essay.

Vocabulary

procrastinating
putting off doing
something

prerequisites
courses that are
needed

Supri Suharjoto, 2011 / Used under license from Shutterstock.com

Example 4

Read the title and opening part of a section from *Sociology: Your Compass for a New World* in which the authors discuss clothing as a symbol of status.

Status and Style

Often rich people engage in conspicuous displays of consumption, waste and leisure not because they are necessary, useful, or pleasurable but simply to impress their peers and inferiors (Veblen, 1899). <u>This is evident if we consider how clothing acts as a sort of language that signals one's status to others</u> (Lurie, 1981).   *1*   *5*

For thousands of years, certain clothing styles have indicated rank. In ancient Egypt, only people in high positions were allowed to wear sandals. The ancient Greeks . . .

European laws governing the dress styles of different groups fell into disuse after about 1700. That is because a new method of control emerged   *10* as Europe became wealthier. . .

Today we have different ways of using clothes to signal status. Designer labels loudly proclaim the dollar value of garments. . . .

"Status and Style" from BRYM/LIE. *Sociology: Your Compass for a New World, 2E.* © 2006 Thompson, a part of Cengage Learning, Inc.

Discussion: The underlined statement in the opening paragraph essentially restates the claim made in the title—which suggests that it is the main point or thesis of the text. The start of the next three paragraphs show that the underlined idea will be explored in the main part of the text.

Vocabulary

conspicuous consumption
wasteful spending to show off

lev radin, 2011 / Used under license from Shutterstock.com

Practice   Identify the topic sentence in the two paragraphs that follow. For the essay on the following page, identify the thesis statement. Then explain each of your choices (how the statement relates to the other sentences in the text).

Practice 1

Defying Gravity

Unlike race cars or trains, roller coasters do not rely on powerful engines for speed. Instead, roller coasters let gravity do much of the work. (Gravity is the force that constantly pulls objects of mass toward the ground.) When a roller-coaster track slopes down, the passenger cars accelerate forward because gravity pulls the front car downward. When the track tilts up, the cars decelerate because gravity pulls the back car downward. But gravity is not the only factor in maintaining speed. Another factor is momentum. On most roller coasters, the first drop is the tallest and steepest. Coasters are designed this way to create enough momentum to carry the forward through the rest of the track. Momentum is especially needed to make it up hills and through loops, as gravity pulls the cars in the opposite direction. This tug-of-war between gravity and momentum makes for exciting rides.

1

5

10

Topic sentence: _____

_____

_____

Explain your choice: _____

_____

_____

_____

Practice 2

The Value of Serving

Community service requirements give students life-changing   *1*
experiences not available in the classroom. First, they learn the
importance of basic job skills such as being on time, teamwork, and
completing tasks. Volunteer Anna Hernandez said, "I had to be at the
senior center right at 3:00 p.m. when the board games started. The   *5*
residents expected me to be there." Community service work also helps
students appreciate the problems and challenges facing Burlington. Scott
Thompson, part of a clean-up crew, never realized how thoughtless people
can be until he started cleaning up after them. As he stated, "Some people
really trash the parks." Most importantly, students learn about giving   *10*
back. For many students, community service is the first time they have
helped people in the community. According to Ms. Sandra Williams, the
community service advisor, "Working in the community shows students
that a lot of people need help." Critics feel that this requirement seems
almost like a punishment. However, participants quickly discover the   *15*
value of their efforts. Essentially, community service gives students a taste
of real life at just the right time.

Topic sentence: _____

_____

_____

Explain your choice: _____

_____

_____

_____

Practice 3

Dietary Diversity

Whatever your cultural heritage, you have probably sampled Chinese, Mexican, Indian, Italian, and Japanese foods. If you belong to any of these ethnic groups, you may eat these cuisines regularly. Each type of ethnic cooking has its own nutritional benefits and potential drawbacks.   *1*

Mediterranean Diet Several years ago epidemiologists noticed something unexpected in the residents of regions along the Mediterranean Sea: a lower incidence of deaths from heart disease. . . .   *5*

Ethnic Cuisines The cuisine served in Mexico features rice, corn, and beans, which are low in fat and high in nutrition. However, the dishes Americans think of as Mexican are far less healthful. . . .   *10*

African American cuisine traces some of its roots to food preferences from west Africa (for example, peanuts, okra, and black-eyed peas). . . .

The mainland Chinese diet, which is plant-based, high in carbohydrates, and low in fats and animal protein, is considered one of the most healthful in the world. . . .   *15*

Many Indian dishes highlight healthful ingredients such as vegetables and legumes (beans and peas). However, many also use ghee (a form of butter) or coconut oil; both are rich in saturated fats. . . .

"Dietary Diversity" from HALES. *An Invitation to Health,* 7E. © 2012 Brooks/Cole, a part of Cengage Learning, Inc.

Thesis statement: _____

_____

_____

Explain your choice: _____

_____

_____

_____

Vocabulary

cuisines
manners or styles of preparing food

epidemiologists
medical professionals who study the causes and control of diseases

Recognizing and Analyzing Supporting Details

The main idea serves as the starting point for writing. The supporting details explain or develop this idea. To gain a complete understanding of a reading assignment, you must be able to identify and understand the supporting information.

Recognizing the Types of Support

The next two pages demonstrate different types of supporting details that you will find in informational texts. The examples come from an article about the Crazy Horse Memorial in South Dakota.

> "The great gift we can bestow in others is a good example."
> —Thomas Morrell

- **Facts and statistics** give specific details about a main point or topic.

  The head of Crazy Horse will be 87 feet high, which is 20 feet higher than any of the heads of the presidents at Mount Rushmore.

- **Explanations** move the discussion along.

  There is no verifiable photograph of Crazy Horse. What will be captured in the carving is the spirit of this man.

- **Examples** show or demonstrate something.

  Crazy Horse was that last leader to surrender to the U.S. military, and he did so because the people who followed him were suffering so much. *(This example shows that Crazy Horse tried to stay true to the Lakota ways of life as long as he could.)*

- **Descriptions** or observations show how something or someone appears.

  Crazy Horse will be seen leaning over his horse's head, pointing his left hand toward his sacred lands.

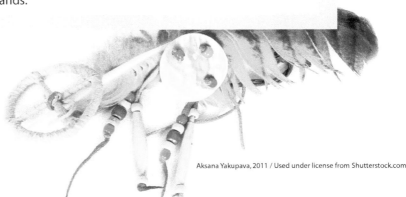

- **Reasons** answer the question "Why?" about something.

  Crazy Horse is being memorialized because he was known as a courageous fighter, a humble man, a giver and provider, and someone true to the Lakota way of life.

- **Quotations** share the specific thoughts of people knowledgeable about the main point.

  "The development of this memorial is not without controversy. For example, descendants of Crazy Horse feel that the family wasn't properly consulted at the outset of the project," stated local historian Marcie Smith.

- **Reflections** offer the writer's personal thoughts and feelings.

  Because of Crazy Horse's private nature, one can only assume that he would have had little interest in such a memorial.

- **Analysis** shows the writer's critical thinking about the topic.

  The memorial seems like a good idea, a way to honor a great man. Unfortunately, it is also a reminder of the difficult history of Native Americans.

Additional Support

Listed below are other types of support that you may find in your reading assignments.

- **Analogies** often compare something unfamiliar with something familiar.
- **Definitions** explain complex terms.
- **Experiences** share events in the writer's life, sometimes in the form of flashbacks.
- **Anecdotes** provide a slice of life (a brief story) to illustrate something.
- **References** to experts or studies add authority to an essay.

INSIGHT

A text may contain any combination of supporting details, and in any number. Knowing this will help you follow its development.

Supporting Details in Context

Here is a paragraph from a student essay in which the writer identifies an unusual plant, the banyan tree. The writer uses *facts, explanations,* and *examples* in his explanation.

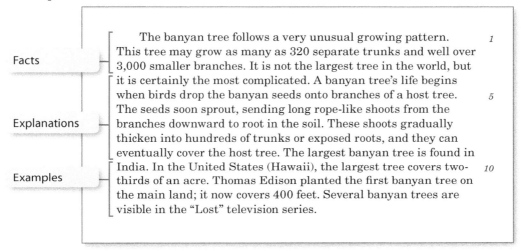

Facts

Explanations

Examples

> The banyan tree follows a very unusual growing pattern. 1
> This tree may grow as many as 320 separate trunks and well over
> 3,000 smaller branches. It is not the largest tree in the world, but
> it is certainly the most complicated. A banyan tree's life begins
> when birds drop the banyan seeds onto branches of a host tree. 5
> The seeds soon sprout, sending long rope-like shoots from the
> branches downward to root in the soil. These shoots gradually
> thicken into hundreds of trunks or exposed roots, and they can
> eventually cover the host tree. The largest banyan tree is found in
> India. In the United States (Hawaii), the largest tree covers two- 10
> thirds of an acre. Thomas Edison planted the first banyan tree on
> the main land; it now covers 400 feet. Several banyan trees are
> visible in the "Lost" television series.

Here is another paragraph from a textbook, *Sociology: Your Compass for a New World.* The writer discusses religious sects using *explanations, examples,* and *analysis.*

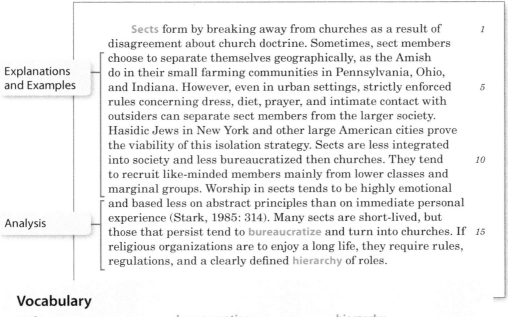

Explanations
and Examples

Analysis

> Sects form by breaking away from churches as a result of 1
> disagreement about church doctrine. Sometimes, sect members
> choose to separate themselves geographically, as the Amish
> do in their small farming communities in Pennsylvania, Ohio,
> and Indiana. However, even in urban settings, strictly enforced 5
> rules concerning dress, diet, prayer, and intimate contact with
> outsiders can separate sect members from the larger society.
> Hasidic Jews in New York and other large American cities prove
> the viability of this isolation strategy. Sects are less integrated
> into society and less bureaucratized then churches. They tend 10
> to recruit like-minded members mainly from lower classes and
> marginal groups. Worship in sects tends to be highly emotional
> and based less on abstract principles than on immediate personal
> experience (Stark, 1985: 314). Many sects are short-lived, but
> those that persist tend to bureaucratize and turn into churches. If 15
> religious organizations are to enjoy a long life, they require rules,
> regulations, and a clearly defined hierarchy of roles.

Vocabulary

sects
groups forming distinct units within larger groups

bureaucratize
to make into a group of governing officials

hierarchy
a group of people with authority

Lastly, here is a personal essay in which student writer Eric Dawson explains his fascination with car racing. He uses *reflections, explanations, descriptions,* and *analysis* to share his story.

The Thrill of Victory

My fascination started the first time I saw my dad race. That was back in 1982. Ever since then, racing has been my main interest. I will never forget the afternoon when my dad told me I could drive, and that he would build a race car for me. That was probably the most exciting day of my life. That was the day my dad passed down the legacy of racing to me.

Reflections

You wouldn't believe the feeling that I had the first day I hit the track with my brand-new Buick stock car. I was a 13-year-old kid with absolutely no driving experience, being strapped into a 400-horsepower stock car. It was a very scary but exciting experience. All it took was one afternoon at the track, and I was hooked. I became the youngest driver ever to race at the Lake Geneva Raceway.

Explanation and Description

I guess you could say that my first year racing was a big learning experience. Driving race cars was not as easy as it appeared. I finished 18th overall out of 70 cars. It was a rough year. Because of my age and inexperience, many people had little or no faith in me, and I was sponsorless all season. Racing is a very expensive sport. Without some type of sponsorship or financial backing, it is almost impossible to maintain a race team. After that year, my future looked grim. I had no money and no sponsorship offers, but I did have some respectable finishes.

I managed to get enough funds together to build a new and more competitive car for the following season. The racing year started off great. I pulled off two second-place finishes in the first two races. Then disaster struck. I was leading the final race of the night, when my brand-new Monte Carlo hit an oil slick and slid headfirst into the wall, at just over 100 miles per hour. My car was destroyed. I was sent to the hospital with a broken wrist and a separated shoulder. I thought my racing career was over. I had spent every nickel I had on this car, and I was still sponsorless.

Analysis

Just when I thought I was through with racing, a miracle happened. When I returned from the hospital, there were two men waiting to speak to me. The men were from B. F. Goodrich. They not only wanted to sponsor me, but also wanted to give me a new race car. My future did a 180-degree turnaround.

This year will be my third year with B. F. Goodrich, and everything looks great. This year I have switched from Dodge to Jeep, and I am getting backing from Mopar Performance. Jeep Motorsports is another of my sponsors. It looks like all my hard work and dedication is starting to pay off.

Practice   Identify the type of support used in the underlined information. Use the previous pages as a guide. (The first one is done for you.)

1. By the 1800s, there were believed to be between 3,000 and 5,000 wolves living in the state. (Wydeven). Around the same time, many European settlers arrived in the area.

   fact/statistic

2. When I was in first grade, our circus field trip was one huge disappointment. First of all, I couldn't see much of anything because we were sitting in one of the last rows. I could barely make out tiny figures scurrying around the three rings.

3. Rent control is a main factor in determining the number of homeless a city will have. For example, the number of homeless in Santa Monica, California, is so great that the city has been called "The Homeless Capital of the West Coast."

4. The emotional outburst known as road rage is a factor in as many as two-thirds of nonfatal accidents. . . . Psychologist Arnold Nerenberg of Whittier, California, a specialist in motorway mayhem, estimates 1.78 billion episodes of road rage occur each year. . . . (Adapted from *An Invitation to Health*, p422.)

5. Webster's defines "eclectic" (i-klek'-tik) as selecting elements from different sources or systems. Eclectic suggests variety. But what a great way to say variety. Variety sounds so plain, so Brand X. But eclectic is rich with imagination.

6. My grandmother's rose garden was a symphony of color, and she was the conductor. Shears in hand, she would step confidently toward the rose trellis and spread her hands. With a quick downbeat, her sheers sliced through the sharp thorns.

Practice   Here is part of an essay by Lois Krenske in which she discusses an unusual happening in nature, whale strandings. Try to identify different types of support used in each paragraph. Work on this activity with one or more of your classmates if your instructor allows it.

Suicide by Strandings

Mass whale suicides, or "strandings," as they are called, occur with   1
disturbing consistency. Many men have tried to understand these bizarre
suicides. Even Aristotle, the ancient Greek philosopher, considered
them. Although he decided the suicides may indeed happen "without any
apparent reason," modern biologists are not so easily convinced.   5

One researcher has pointed out that the whales are descended
from land-dwelling animals. He decided the whales may simply be
"remembering" their ancient roots and beach themselves to go home. This
habit, however, would have put the whales close to extinction years ago.
The idea had to be dismissed.   10

A newer theory suggests that the whales blindly follow the earth's
magnetic forces. The whales travel wherever these forces lead, almost as
if they were following a road map. Unfortunately, the magnetic flow will
sometimes intersect the shore and guide the whales along a collision course
with the beach.   15

Biologists realize, of course, that none of these findings are complete
explanations. They feel that the strandings must have a number of causes.
To make this point, they compare beached whales to crashed planes. One
theory will never explain them all.

Vocabulary

strandings	intersect
occurrences of swimming onto a beach	cut across, form a cross

Analyzing the Support

Identifying the different details in a reading assignment is the first step. You should also decide how effective they are. Reading without analyzing the details is like attempting to play soccer without defining the boundaries of the field: One of the key elements is missing.

A Guide to Careful Analysis

Use the following questions as a guide when you analyze the support in a paragraph or an essay that you read. Your answers will help you better understand the text and judge its value.

Questions to Ask

1. What supporting evidence seems especially strong? Why?

   _____

2. Does this information seem reliable and well researched? Explain.

   _____

3. What evidence, if any, does not seem that effective? Explain?

   _____

4. How would you rate the overall quality of the supporting information and why?

   Weak ★ ★ ★ ★ ★ Strong

   _____

5. What have you learned from this text?

   _____

6. What questions do you still have about it?

   _____

INSIGHT ——————————————————————————————————
Answering questions like these helps you connect with your reading assignment and remember the key points in it.

> "The book to read is not the one which thinks for you, but the one which makes you think."
> —Harper Lee

Analysis in Action

Here is a paragraph that shares a story about coming to America. The topic sentence is underlined. The supporting information includes explanations and descriptions. The analysis follows the paragraph.

<u>I saw the pain in Frances Opeka's eyes when she talked about fleeing</u>   *1*
<u>Yugoslavia when the Russian and communist troops were moving in.</u>
Sometime, in May of 1945, at 4:00 a.m., my grandfather's brother knocked
on the window of Frances' home and said, "If you're coming with us,
we're leaving in a half an hour." So my grandma, who was seven months   *5*
pregnant, and my great-aunt (Frances) woke up my grandma's three
children and left. They didn't have time to say good-bye to their parents,
relatives, or friends. They just left. Their first stop was a camp in Austria
and then they went to Italy where they lived for five difficult years in a
refugee camp. Living conditions were primitive, to say the least. At times,   *10*
they slept on the cold ground or if they were lucky, they slept on a thin
covering of hay. At night, France would often go without her coat because
she wanted to cover her pregnant sister to keep her warm. For food, they
usually received bread and soup. They would cup their hands around the
bread so they would not lose even a crumb. To get a potato was a treat.   *15*
Germs and colds spread easily in the camp, so they all went through their
sick times. My great-uncle Greg had the measles and being so young, he
thought he was going to die. My grandma and great-aunt had high fevers
multiple times. Well, my grandmother had her child, my mother, and her
family was the first one that was allowed to come to America.   *20*

Sample Analysis

Main point as stated in the topic sentence (underlined): Fleeing her
homeland was a painful experience for the writer's great-aunt.

1. What supporting information is especially strong? Why?

    The information held my interest because it showed what the
    family had to do to remain free. One detail that stands out
    is this one: The family left early in the morning without saying
    goodbye to anyone. Also, not wasting even a crumb of bread
    showed how hungry they were.

2. Does this information seem reliable and well-researched?

This information comes from one of the refugees, so it should be reliable. But Frances Opeka is recalling something that happened a long time ago, so some of the details might be fuzzy. The experience of people fleeing communist rule could be checked on the Internet to learn more about this time.

3. What evidence, if any, does not seem that effective? Why?

For the most part, the story seems realistic and believable. There were no really questionable ideas shared. Anyway, why would anyone try to make this up?

4. How would you rate the overall quality of the supporting information and why?

Weak ★   ★   ★ (★) ★   **Strong**

The supporting information got my attention because the story is so dramatic. But at times, more details would have made it better. For example, how did the family actually get to Austria and Italy?

5. What have you learned from this text?

The end of World War II did not bring an end to the suffering of people in Europe. For this family, the suffering continued for at least five more years.

6. What questions do you still have about it?

Two questions were identified in question 4. Also, I would like to know how many people attempted to flee Yugoslavia, and how many actually succeeded.

Practice Analyze the following paragraph. To get started, carefully read the paragraph; then underline the topic sentence and consider the different types of support that it includes. Next, answer the analysis questions that follow the paragraph.

Drug Deal

    I was an eyewitness to a drug deal, and the smoothness and quickness   *1* of the transaction will be in my mind forever. I was busy at work when I happened to observe the deal. My work place, a restaurant, opens onto an alley. About 25 feet from the rear of the restaurant is a dumpster. I was taking a break and glanced out the back door. I saw a well-dressed   *5* man come from the left and a raggedy-looking man come from the right. They both met by the dumpster in clear view of me. The both looked around, watching for anyone who might be in the alley. Then they quickly exchanged packages and checked what they received. The slick man flipped through the roll of bills he received and nodded. The raggedy   *10* man checked his package and gave a quick nod. Both men slipped their packages in their pockets and after a few quick glances, each went the way he had come. The whole incident took about 45 seconds.

Analysis

1. What main point is stated in the topic sentence or thesis statement?

   _____

2. What supporting evidence seems especially strong? Why?

   _____

3. Does this information seem reliable and well-researched? Explain.

   _____

4. What evidence, if any, does not seem that effective? Why?

   _____

5. How would you rate the overall quality of the supporting information and why?
   Weak ★ ★ ★ ★ ★ Strong

   _____

6. What have you learned from this text? What questions do you have about it?

   _____

LO2 Organization

When you read, remember that the ideas and organization work together to create meaning. Unless the ideas are organized, it would be almost impossible to follow them.

Common Patterns of Organization

Factual texts may follow one of these basic patterns. Knowing how these patterns work will help you follow the ideas in a text.

- **Chronological** – Paragraphs that recall experiences or explain how something works or how to do something usually follow chronological or time order.

- **Spatial** –Paragraphs that describe something or someone are often organized spatially or by location, working from top to bottom, right to left, and so on.

- **Logical** –Paragraphs that simply present supporting ideas in a sensible or reasonable order are organized logically.

- **Cause-effect** – Paragraphs that explain the relationship between causes and effects usually explore the causes first, then the effects.

- **Comparison-contrast** – Paragraphs that compare show the similarities and differences between two ideas. Comparative essays may discuss one subject first, then the next subject; they may discuss all of the similarities between the two and then their differences; or they make a point-by-point comparison.

- **Problem-solution** – Paragraphs that explore a particular problem often begin with a summary of the problem, follow with possible solutions, and then focus on the best solution.

- **Order of importance (argumentative)** – Paragraphs that support a claim or an opinion may be organized from the most important argument to the least important or the other way around. Objections to the claim or arguments often come first or last.

INSIGHT ————————————————————————————————

While a text usually follows one main pattern, other patterns may be used in a few specific parts.

The Patterns in Action

Each paragraph that follows shows how a writer uses a common pattern of organization to arrange his or her ideas.

Chronological Order

This paragraph narrates an interesting historical story about growing up in the American frontier. (The words and phrases in italics show that time order is used.)

Francis Anne Slocum

Francis Anne Slocum was born in Rhode Island in March of 1773. The *1* next year her family moved to Pennsylvania. There, *until she was five,* she lived a happy childhood. But *on November 2, 1778,* Delaware Indians raided her home during the absence of the father. No one was hurt, but Francis was taken from the family and lost for 57 years. Then *in January of 1835,* a fur *5* trader named Colonel Ewing stopped at the house of a widow of the Chief of the Miami Indians. Colonel Ewing became interested in the mistress of the house because her features and coloring seemed different to him. Ewing *later* learned she was born of white parents and that her father's name was Slocum. He announced this discovery in a Lancaster, Pennsylvania, newspaper. *10* *Eventually*, one of Francis's brothers read the article and was *soon* reunited with his long-lost sister.

Comparison-Contrast

This paragraph compares and contrasts two main types of lightbulbs by first identifying their similarities and then discussing their differences.

See the Light

To select a lightbulb, you need to understand the differences between the *1* traditional incandescent bulb and the new compact fluorescent ones. Both bulbs are similar in that they come in many shapes, sizes, and brightnesses. But they are different in many important ways. For example, the new compacts have some limitations in their usability. Because of their odd shape, *5* they may not fit in the bulb sockets on some lamps. Compacts also may not work well in very cold temperatures , and they can't be used with a dimmer switch. On the other hand, compact bulbs are four times more efficient than incandescent ones. A 15-watt compact bulb produces as many lumens of light as a 60-watt incandescent bulb. Cost is another factor to consider. A compact *10* may cost about $15.00 while an incandescent can be purchased for a dollar. However, the compact burns less electricity and lasts seven to ten times longer. So in the long run, it should be less expensive. This information may help you decide what bulbs to choose in your own room or apartment.

Cause-Effect

This paragraph identifies the causes and effects of job opportunities in journalism. (The words in italics identify the cause-effect order used.)

Wanted: Newspaper Jobs

Students interested in journalism may want to consider other professions.   *1*
The *cause* is simple: Fewer and fewer people are buying newspapers. Many
individuals, especially young people, are getting their news on the Internet.
Fewer buyers of newspapers and magazines mean less income from sales.
Fewer readers also mean fewer ad dollars, which is a major source of revenue.   *5*
As a result, newspapers are going out of business or cutting back and
magazines are folding. This situation has forced publishers to re-form their
companies. Newspapers are now offering electronic alternatives to their print
products, but readers get this news for free or pay a small fee that in no way
offsets the huge losses the companies are facing. The *effect* of this situation   *10*
on journalists is predictable: There are not enough jobs for experienced
journalists, let alone college graduates. However, not all is lost. The Internet
may offer exciting new career choices in the Information Age, especially for
people who understand and appreciate the power of electronic communications.

Problem-Solution

This problem-solution paragraph discusses a serious issue in older urban dwellings, lead poisoning. (The words in italics show the pattern of organization used.)

Dangers of Lead Poisoning

Young children unprotected from almost any amount of lead may   *1*
suffer serious health problems. Lead poisoning can lead to everything from
headaches to periods of confusion to learning problems. Inner-city dwellings
built before 1960 may contain lead-based paints, the major source of the
problem. If the lead paint is peeling, very young children will eat the paint   *5*
chips. Even the dust from this paint can be harmful. Unfortunately, once
someone suffers from lead poisoning, there are no complete cures. The best
solutions for families are preventative, such as daily house cleaning and
regularly washing of hands. Long-term solutions include painting over the old
lead paint, but without sanding beforehand. The Mayo Clinic Web site on lead   *10*
poisoning reminds renters that they have rights protecting their health and
safety. Landlords are required by law to find and address sources of lead.

Vocabulary

preventative
a remedy that prevents something

Practice   Label the main pattern of organization used in the following paragraphs.

Those Were the Days

1. The old man grumbled a bit as he wiped his eyes with the back of his gnarled hand. From his perch above the crowd, he watched the proceeding. He then glanced at his wife standing a short distance away. She, too, was old, but he still saw her as a much younger woman. His thoughts went back. He recalled the black and white dishes on which she had so proudly served him home-cooked meals. The chairs, the tables, the curtains, things that had made their home—all raced before his eyes. Then the auctioneer's voice brought his thoughts back to the present. He shifted in the seat of his old John Deere tractor. It was now being auctioned off and would soon be plowing someone else's field. Then the other machinery was to be sold, piece by piece. Within the next hour or so, the things he had worked for all his life would be gone. A half century of thoughts and feelings went with everything on display.

Pattern of organization:

Religion and School

2. Americans have the right to practice the religion of their choice, but practicing religion in public schools touches on sensitive ground. Religion in public schools goes against the Constitution of the United States. Most specifically and importantly, the First Amendment clearly states its desire to leave religion out of public schooling. The establishment clause in this amendment says there can be no official religion. The free-exercise clause states how one people can practice whatever religion they choose. If religious education were mandated in public schools, both of these rights would be violated. In addition, the Fourteenth Amendment contains an equal protection clause that makes clear the separation of church and state. The Supreme Court has also voiced its opinion that having religion affiliated with public schooling is unconstitutional. So it is clear that the writers of the Constitution wanted to keep religion separate from public institutions such as the education system.

Pattern of organization:

TV and Your Health

3. Regardless of where they live, Americans spend most of their leisure time watching television: on average, more than 30 hours a week. Yet the more time spent in front of the TV, the greater the risk of obesity and related chronic diseases. Compared with other sedentary activities, such as reading, writing, or driving, watching TV lowers metabolic rate, so people burn fewer calories. Every hour spent watching television may increase your risk of dying prematurely from any cause by 11 percent, from cardiorespiratory disease by 18 percent, and from cancer by 9 percent, according to recent research. Compared with those who watched less than two hours per day, individuals who watched more than four hours had an 80 percent greater risk of premature death from heart-related causes.

"TV and Your Health" from HALES. *An Invitation to Health,* 7E. © 2012 Brooks/Cole, a part of Cengage Learning, Inc.

Pattern of organization:

About Race

4. Race is often the first thing people think of when they hear the word diversity. But some experts say race is a relatively modern idea. Centuries ago people tended to classify other people by status, religion, or language, for example, not by race. Actually, most of us are a blend of enthnicities, and how we perceive ourselves may be different from the way others see us. People may assume that a Pacific Islander with light-brown skin, dark hair, and dark eyes, for example, is Hispanic. And a classmate you may assume is White may think of himself as black. Or consider this: If you have a Chinese mother and a White father, you may not know which "race box" to check on standard forms. Should you choose Mom or Dad? Biologists tell us that there's more variation within a race than there is between races. Race isn't biological, they say, but *racism* is real.

"About Race" from STALEY/STALEY. *FOCUS on College and Career Success,* 1E. © 2012 Wadsworth, a part of Cengage Learning, Inc.

Pattern of organization:

Vocabulary

mandated
required or commanded by

sedentary
requiring much sitting

metabolic
dealing with the chemical processes occurring within an organism to sustain life

cardiorespiratory
of or relating to the heart and the respiratory system

enthnicities
ethnic character and background

Another Approach to Organization

The patterns of organization refer to the main part of a text, in which the supporting evidence is presented. There are, of course, beginning and ending parts to a text as well. When analyzing a text, keep this three-part structure in mind.

Three-Part Structure

Paragraph Structure

Topic Sentence

- Names the topic and focus

Body Sentences

- Provide supporting sentences
- Follow a pattern of organization

Closing Sentence

- Wraps up the paragraph

Essay Structure

Beginning Part

- Introduces the topic
- Provides background information
- Identifies the main point or thesis

Middle Part

- Supports or develops the main point
- Follows one or more patterns of organization

Ending Part

- Summarizes the key ideas
- Restates the thesis
- Provides final thoughts or analysis

Considering the Three Main Parts

Use these questions as a guide when considering the beginning, middle, and ending parts in a paragraph or an essay. Your answers will contribute to your overall understanding of the text.

Questions to Ask

1. What type of information is given in the topic sentence or opening paragraph (in an essay)? Consider naming the topic, giving background information, starting the main point.

2. What types of supporting details are included?

3. How are the details in the main part organized?

4. What type of information is given in the closing sentence or ending part—summary of key ideas, restatement of the main point, final thoughts, and so on.

5. Does the organization make the text easy or hard to follow? Explain.

Practice   Answer the above questions for each of these paragraphs. (Work on this activity with a classmate if your instructor allows it.)

- "Drug Deal" (LO1)

- "See the Light" (LO2)

LO3 Voice

Another main trait of a text is voice—the special way in which the writer speaks to the reader. It may help to think of voice as the personality in a piece of writing. Most informational texts will speak to you in one of three ways:

- **Academic voice:** Writers of professional materials use a serious academic voice.
- **Personal voice:** Writers of essays, articles, and blog postings often use a casual personal voice.
- **Satiric voice:** Occasionally, writers sometimes use a satiric voice when they want to criticize or make fun of someone or something.

> "Voice is the aspect of writing closest to the writer."
> —Dan Kirby

A Basic Guide to Voice

Academic Voice

An academic voice is used in most textbooks, professional journals, and in thoughtful, serious research. An academic uses **formal English** and sounds serious and objective (sticking to the facts). The following informational text uses an academic voice.

According to the Sierra Club, pollutants from farm run-off are   *1*
steadily seeping into streams, lakes, reservoirs, and wells. Because much
of the drinking water comes from these sources, warnings are posted in
a number of U.S. and Canadian communities, and many more postings
might be needed in the future (Sierra Club, 2005). As the Sierra Club   *5*
argues, the pollution and related warnings are serious, and failure to heed
them could be deadly. . . .

SPECIAL NOTE: Serious texts may contain brief personal introductions or brief passages containing the writer's personal thoughts and feelings and still be academic in voice.

formal English
a serious, straightforward style used in most academic writing including textbooks; characterized by objectivity (sticking to the facts)

Arkorn, 2011 / Used under license from Shutterstock.com

Personal Voice

A personal voice used in personal essays, articles in popular magazines, and personal blog postings uses informal English and sounds somewhat relaxed and subjective (including the writer's personal thoughts and feelings). The following description uses a personal voice.

> One Capewell photograph is proudly displayed in our house. It' a black-and-white photograph of two people neatly attired in their best military uniforms, and it was taken during World War II in a small studio in Leicester, England. . . . What makes this photograph so special to our family is the occasion that prompted it. It's my great-grandparents' wedding picture. They were both on leave to get married. Their honeymoon had to wait until after the war. This photograph is one of the few keepsakes that we have left from their military experience and wedding day, and we take very special care of it.   *1*   *5*

Satiric Voice

A satiric voice is used in essays and commentaries in which the writer speaks humorously or sarcastically about someone or something. A satire may be objective or subjective. The following passage from a personal blog posting uses a satiric voice. (King Arne refers to Arne Duncan, the Department of Education Secretary.)

> ### All Hail to the King
>
> King Arne made a visit to Milwaukee, and at one point during his visit, he toured a downtown public high school. A photograph in the newspaper shows the king marching down a hall with his attendants following close behind.   *1*
>
> The king was impatient with his subjects here because in his estimation, they weren't making enough school improvements. And of course, when the king speaks, everyone listens because the king controls the coffers (stimulus money). He has $10 billion to invest in education, and this is only part of the money for education that he controls. (Talk about a power high).   *5*

informal English	satiric	sarcastically
a relaxed style used in most personal essays; characterized by subjectivity (the writer's personal thoughts and feelings)	the use of humor, fake praise, or sarcasm to make fun of someone or something	the act of making critical comments

Practice Carefully read the following passages. Then identify the voice used in each one—academic, personal, or satiric.

1. I recently sat in on a meeting that made my eyes droop and my toes curl. The purpose of the meeting was clear, but it dragged on and on without anything getting accomplished. And here's why: One person wouldn't stop talking. . . .

   Voice: _____

   _____

2. Several factors contributed to the tragedy in Walkerton, Ontario, including human error. First, according to *The Edmonton Journal,* a flaw in the water treatment system allowed water to enter Walkerton's well (Blackwell, 2001). Even after the manure washed in Walkerton's well, the chlorine should have killed the bacteria. . . .

   Voice: _____

   _____

3. Then there comes an odor in the cafeteria. No more than an odor. It is a heavy choking presence that overpowers the senses and settles on the skin leaving a thin greasy film. The food line lurches forward once more and doomed students mover closer to their noon meal. . . .

   Voice: _____

   _____

4. On a cold August morning, the stars blanketed the night sky over the outskirts of Quito, Ecuador. I stood on the street corner, shaking underneath my wool sweater, waiting for a guide to show me around this massive market. . . .

   Voice: _____

   _____

5. The major danger associated with texting is the distraction it causes to the driver. When a driver's eyes are concentrating on a phone instead of the road, he or she is more likely to get in an accident. Some critics say teenage drivers are the problem, but 20 percent of adults in a recent AAA study admitted regularly texting while driving. . . .

   Voice: _____

   _____

LO4 Word Choice and Sentences

Two other important traits are word choice and sentences.

Word Choice

Word choice is closely connected to voice, in that the words used help create the writer's voice. For example, textbook writers will naturally use many specific words associated with the topic. These content-specific words help create the academic voice in the text. Personal essayists, on the other hand, usually rely on more familiar words, which helps create a more personal or conversational voice.

Academic passage with content-specific words (underlined)

> Wind farms are a clean energy source. Unlike power plants, which   *1*
> emit dangerous pollutants, wind farms release no pollution into the air,
> meaning less smog, less acid rain, and fewer greenhouse emissions. The
> American Wind Energy Association reports that running a single wind
> turbine has the potential to displace 2,000 tons of carbon dioxide, or the   *5*
> equivalent of one square mile of forest trees.

Passage from a personal essay with mostly familiar words:

> There was this old guy I used to know. His name was Jimmy, but I   *1*
> called him "Admiral" because he had been in some war. He was about five
> feet tall and smelled of cigar smoke mixed with coffee and other scents I
> didn't recognize. He had smoke-stained teeth that were crooked. His white
> hair always looked like it needed to be washed, and he wore the same   *5*
> wrinkled clothes. But he had beautiful blue eyes, the deepest blue I've ever
> seen.

Practice   Team up with a classmate to find one passage (two or three sentences) in a paragraph in this book that uses many content-specific words. Write the passage down and underline these words. Then write down a passage from a paragraph that seems more personal and uses very familiar terms. Be prepared to discuss your findings.

Sentences

Sentences come in all shapes and sizes. Some of them are very brief and direct. Others flow along very smoothly like a lazy country stream. Then, of course, there are sentences that are very complex that require multiple readings to understand.

Academic Sentences

The sentences in most textbooks are often long and complex, sometimes containing many ideas. These sentences suggest that the writer has been very careful her or his thinking. This makes sense because textbooks must share information thoroughly and accurately. Here are some longer sentences from academic texts. In each one, the core sentence is underlined. Notice all of the additional information added to each one.

> <u>Public housing was built in Chicago because of the Great Migration</u>, the name given to the movement of African Americans from the South to the North.

> Over time, <u>the first musical instruments</u>, which were stone and clay sound-producing objects, <u>evolved into wind instruments</u> including flutes and windpipes.

> While North American wealth grew out of the Industrial Revolution, <u>today's capitalism is a system largely based on consumerism</u>—an attitude that values the purchase of goods in the belief that it is necessary.

> In the past couple of decades, <u>the status of the stewardess</u> (i.e., the position of the stewardess in relation to others) <u>has changed</u>. In the era of shoe searches, deep discount no-frill service, and packaged peanut snacks, <u>little of the glamour remains</u>.

Sentences in Personal Essays

The sentences in personal essays are usually simpler than the ones that you will find in academic texts. As such, they are easier to follow and move along rather quickly. As a general rule, you will find more variety in the sentence length and structure. Notice how easy it is to read the following passages from personal essays.

The burnt smell of oil was the first thing I would notice in my grandfather's garage. On the right wall, he had pictures of the Smith Family. Some days, I would study all of the smiling faces on the pictures.

I had locked myself in the walk-in freezer. I knew I would get out. Someone *had* to open the door. But when? All around me, I saw frozen shrimp, crab legs, and lobsters. I couldn't even eat any of it.

My Indian culture is important to me, but that doesn't mean that I don't value my independence. During this semester, I have had a chance to think about my life. And I realize that I am an Indian and an American.

Have questions about your love life? Wonder what fashions to wear this fall? Want to know about the latest in hip food? Trendy magazines geared for young women address "deep" issues like these. Am I the only female that is both embarrassed and offended by these magazines?

Practice   Carefully read the following sets of sentences. Then identify each set as either academic or personal in structure. (Word choice, of course, plays a role in the level of difficulty or complexity in these sentences.)

1. The fourth type of Latin American music known as urban popular music combines a dynamic sound with calls for social change that appeals to many young listeners.

   Sentence style: _____

   _____

2. It's laundry night for me, and the Laundromat is buzzing, thumping, whirring. All the seats by the window are taken, as usual. The vending machines are doing overtime. A very pregnant young woman is folding clothes. Her toddler son is trying to climb into a dryer.

   Sentence style: _____

   _____

3. Waking up is hard. I'd rather dream I've won the tournament than get up and face the scale. But I'm hopeful. I've been strict and focused, in the gym and at the table. This tournament is the toughest one for the year, by far.

   Sentence style: _____

   _____

4. The Dutch fear of Islamic extremism has also increased, brought on in part by international attacks such as September 11 (2001) and later attacks in Madrid and London. This fear was further intensified when two well-know Dutch politicians were assassinated.

   Sentence style: _____

   _____

5. Sethe lives in house number 124, a house generally believed to be haunted and "full of baby venom" (Morrison 3). The child's ghost living in the house throws things around, shakes the floor, and stomps up the stairs.

   Sentence style: _____

   _____

Special Challenge   Find two sentences in the models in this book that are clearly academic because of their length and complexity. Then find two sentences that are personal in structure. Share your work with your classmates.

LO5 Reviewing the Traits of Reading

Respond to each set of directions to review the concepts covered in this chapter.

Ideas Answer the following questions about the ideas in writing.

1. What is the first step to follow to find the main idea in a paragraph? The last step?

2. What is the name of the sentence that contains the main idea in a paragraph?

3. What two parts does this sentence usually contain?

4. What is the purpose of supporting details in a paragraph?

5. What are four types of supporting details?

6. What type of support includes the writer's personal thoughts and feelings?

Organization Explain the following patterns of organization.

Chronological _____

Spatial _____

Comparison-contrast _____

Order of importance _____

Organization Explain the three-part structure in a paragraph.

_____

Create a graphic that will help you remember these three parts.

_____

Voice Answer the following questions about voice.

   1. What is voice in writing?

_____

_____

   2. What is meant by academic voice? (Find an example in one model.)

_____

_____

   3. What is meant by a personal voice? (Find an example in one model.)

_____

_____

   4. What is meant by a satiric voice?

_____

_____

Word Choice and Sentences Answer the following questions about word choice and sentences.

   1. What are the main features of academic word choice and sentences?

_____

_____

   2. What are the main features of personal word choice and sentences?

_____

_____

4

"Good writing is also about making good choices when it comes to picking the tools you plan to work with."
—Stephen King

The Traits of Academic Writing

Writing is basically forming your thoughts on paper. Since you have plenty of thoughts and feelings, shouldn't writing then be an easy and natural thing to do? After all, how difficult can it be to record what you are thinking? Well, as you know, it can actually be quite a challenge. The problem that you and many others may face is understanding how to form your thoughts on paper.

This chapter introduces you to the traits or working parts of academic writing. The traits include ideas, organization, voice, word choice, sentences, and conventions.

Together, the writing process and the traits of writing will help you develop your best thoughts on paper.

Learning Outcomes

LO1 Ideas
LO2 Focus
LO3 Organization
LO4 Voice
LO5 Word choice and sentences
LO6 Conventions
LO7 Review

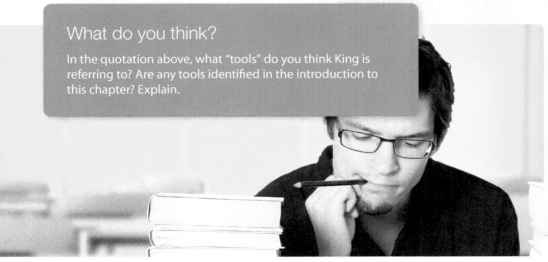

What do you think?

In the quotation above, what "tools" do you think King is referring to? Are any tools identified in the introduction to this chapter? Explain.

Rido, 2011 / Used under license from Shutterstock.com

LO1 Ideas

Ideas are the first and most important trait to consider when you are writing. Without ideas you have nothing to work with. Just as a cook needs ingredients to make something, a writer needs ideas to develop a piece of writing. When choosing ideas, you need to consider a topic first, then details to support it.

> "As soon as you connect with your true subject, you will write."
> —Joyce Carol Oates

Selecting a Topic

Always try to select a topic that attracts you; otherwise, you will have a hard time working with it through the steps in the writing process. Granted, your choices may be limited for many of your writing assignments. Even so, do your best to select a topic that truly has some meaning to you.

Limiting Your Choices

In most cases, a writing assignment will identify a general subject area, and your first job is to find a specific writing idea related to this subject. This graphic shows how the selecting process should work from the general subject area to a specific topic.

Assignment: Write a paragraph explaining a stress-related condition.

INSIGHT ————
A topic for a research report must be broad enough to offer plenty of information. For a more limited assignment (a one- or two-page essay), the topic should be more specific.

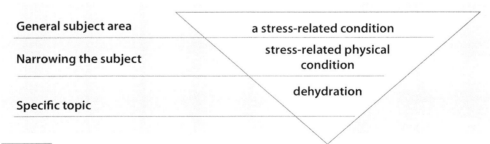

General subject area — a stress-related condition

Narrowing the subject — stress-related physical condition

Specific topic — dehydration

Select Identify a specific topic for the following assignment.

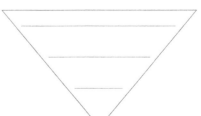

Assignment: Write a paragraph explaining an important environmental problem.

1. General subject area
2. Narrow this subject
3. Specific topic

Selecting Strategies

Always review your class notes, textbook, and Web sites for possible topics. You may also want to try one of the selecting strategies that follow.

- **Clustering** Begin a cluster (or web) with a nucleus word or phrase related to the assignment. (The general subject area or narrowed subject would work.) Circle it and then cluster related words around it. As you continue, you will identify possible writing ideas.

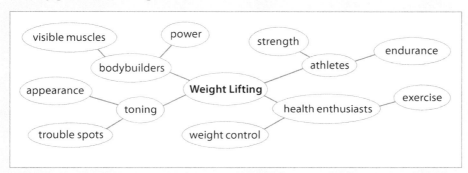

- **Listing** Freely list ideas as you think about your writing assignment. Keep going as long as you can. Then review your list for possible topics.
- **Developing a Dialogue** Write nonstop for 5–10 minutes about your assignment to discover possible topics. Begin by writing down a particular thought about the assignment.

Practice   Use one of the strategies explained above to identify possible topics related to one of the following general subject areas:

exercise   popular music   careers   freedom/rights   technology

Gathering Details

To write about a topic, you need plenty of supporting details. Some of these details may come from your own thoughts about the topic. Other details will come from reading and learning about the topic.

Identifying What You Already Know

To learn what you already know about a topic, try one of these strategies.

- **Clustering** Create a cluster with your topic as the nucleus word. (see the previous page.)
- **Listing** List your thoughts and ideas about your topic as well as questions that come to mind. Keep your list going as long as you can.
- **Freewriting** Write nonstop for 5-8 minutes to see what ideas you can discover about your topic. Go where your thoughts take you, one after another.
- **Discussing** Create a dialogue (written conversation) about your topic. In this dialogue, talk about your topic. Keep the dialogue going as long as you can. Here's one way to get started:

  (Your name): Luis, do you know anything about (your topic)?

  Luis: I know a little bit. How about you?

Collect   Use one of the strategies above to gather your thoughts about a topic you identified on the last page. (Select an activity different from the one you used on the previous page.)

_____

_____

_____

_____

CONSIDER THE TRAITS

Remember that at this stage, the most important trait is ideas. Gather them, discover them, hunt them down. More is better.

> "Knowledge is of two kinds. We know subjects ourselves, or we know where we can find information about it."
> —Samuel Johnson

Learning More About a Topic

Your own thoughts will not be enough for many writing assignments. You will need to collect addition information through research. You can read about a topic or learn about it some other way. You can also try one of these strategies.

Answering Key Questions Create a list of questions about the topic that you would like to answer during your research. Let's say that you are writing about an event. You could list questions based on the 5 W's and H to answer.

- **When** did the event take place?

  _____

- **What** exactly happened?

  _____

- **Who** was involved?

  _____

- **Why** did it occur?

  _____

- **Where** did it take place?

  _____

- **How** did everything go? (Were there any problems?)

  _____

Analyzing You can explore your topic from different angles by answering these questions.

- What parts does my topic have? _(Break it down.)_

  _____

- What do I see, hear, or feel when I think about my topic? _(Describe it.)_

  _____

- What is it similar to and different from? _(Compare it.)_

  _____

- What value does it have? _(Evaluate it.)_

  _____

- How useful is it? _(Apply it.)_

  _____

Collect Use either of the above strategies to discover more about the topic you worked with on the last page. (Answer at least three of the questions after doing some quick research.)

_____

_____

Understanding Supporting Details

When you collect information, you need to know that there are different types of details that you can use in your writing. These details will help you explain or support your topic.

Types of Details

The following list identifies the common types of details.

- **Facts and statistics** give specific information that can be checked.

  Peregrine falcons have the same mate for life and produce three or four eggs each season.

- **Examples** demonstrate or show something.

  Main point: Americans responded in many ways during the latest oil crisis.

  Example: Many homeowners in the Northeast voluntarily turned down their home thermostats.

- **Definitions** explain new terms.

  A pandemic is an "infectious disease covering a wide geographic area and affecting a large part of the population."

- **Quotations** provide the thoughts of people knowledgeable about the topic.

  Chris Woolston of the Consumer Health Interactive says, " Fatty, unbalanced, and oversized. That, in a nutshell, is the American diet."

- **Reasons** answer the question "Why?" about an idea.

  Huck and Jim both escaped from civilization. They were both fleeing from an unbearable situation.

Identify List two or three different types of details that you could use to support the topic you have been working with in this chapter.

_____

_____

_____

Levels of Details

List two or three different types of details that you could use to support the topic you have been working with in this chapter.

- **Level 1:** A **controlling sentence** names a topic (usually a topic sentence) or makes a main point.
- **Level 2:** A **clarifying sentence** explains a level 1 sentence.
- **Level 3:** A **completing sentence** adds details to complete the point.

Details in Action

In the passage that follows, the level 1 sentence (a topic sentence) is supported by two level 2 sentences. Each level 2 sentence is supported by two level 3 sentences.

> **(Level 1)** Cartoons helped to shape the way I think. **(Level 2)** Most   *1*
> of them taught me never to take life too seriously. **(Level 3)** Many of the
> characters made their way through life with smirks on their faces. **(Level
> 3)** And all but a few of them seized the day, living for the moment. **(Level
> 2)** In an offhanded way, cartoons also provided me with a guide on how   *5*
> to act. **(Level 3)** Good versus evil was usually clearly defined. **(Level 3)**
> Other cartoons stressed the importance of loyalty.

Identify Identify After reading the following passage, label its levels of detail. Work on this activity with a partner if your instructor allows it.

> (_____) Jim Thorpe was one of the star athletes   *1*
> representing the United States in the 1912 Summer Olympics in Sweden.
> (_____) Thorpe, a Native American, was an extremely versatile
> athlete, but he was especially skilled in track and field. (_____)
> He won a gold medal in the pentathlon, a track-and-field event of five   *5*
> parts. (_____) He also won a gold medal in the decathlon, a ten-
> part track-and-field event.

Special Challenge Write a brief paragraph describing a favorite television show. Label your sentences with a 1, 2, or 3, depending on the level of detail they include. (Your paragraph may or may not have level 3 details.)

LO2 Focus or Thesis

Focus is not one of the basic traits of writing, but it is included here because it helps you plan how to use the ideas that you collect.

Choosing a Focus

A focus is a particular feeling or part of the topic that you want to emphasize.

Let's say you are writing about the food in your school's union. More specifically, you want to complain about the huge amount of food that goes to waste. Your feelings about the waste could serve as the focus for your writing.

Topic: food in your school union

Focus: amount of food that is wasted

Your writing will be hard to follow if it lacks focus. So it's important to identify a clear and reasonable focus. To try to describe everything about the food in the union would be unreasonable, because there would be too much to say.

Evaluating a Focus

Your writing will hard to follow if it lacks focus. As a result, it's important to identify a clear and reasonable focus. To try to describe every activity related to an annual community event would be too general; whereas, focusing on one or two unique activities would seem reasonable.

Review   Rate the effectiveness of each focus below by circling the appropriate star. Consider whether the focus is clear, reasonable, and worth developing. Explain each of your choices.

1. **Topic:** sports drinks **Focus:** the best choice during long workouts
   weak ★ ★ ★ ★ ★ strong _____

2. **Topic:** society's view of beauty **Focus:** seems good
   weak ★ ★ ★ ★ ★ strong _____

3. **Topic:** cultural comparisons between Korea and the United States **Focus:** contrasting views on cleanliness
   weak ★ ★ ★ ★ ★ strong _____

Forming a Topic Sentence

State your focus in a topic sentence for a paragraph and in a thesis statement in an essay. The following formula can be used to write a topic sentence or thesis statement. The following example is for an informational paragraph.

A specific topic	A particular feeling, feature, or part	An effective topic sentence or thesis statement
arrival of Hernán Cortés in Mexico	**+** marked the beginning of the end of the Aztec empire	**=** The arrival of Hernán Cortés in Mexico marked the beginning of the end of the Aztec empire.

Create Identify a focus and then write a topic sentence or thesis statement for each of the following assignments. The first one is done for you.

1. **Writing assignment:** Paragraph describing a specific style of clothing

   Specific topic: Zoot suit

   Focus: _Popular during the swing era_

   Topic sentence: _The zoot suit (specific topic) became a popular fashion symbol in the swing era (a particular feature)._

2. **Writing assignment:** Paragraph explaining how to do something

   Specific topic: Using chopsticks

   Focus: _____

   Topic sentence: _____

   _____

3. **Writing assignment:** Paragraph analyzing a popular type of cooking

   Specific topic: Cajun cooking

   Focus: _____

   Thesis statement: _____

   _____

4. **Writing assignment:** Paragraph exploring technology and education

   Specific topic: Electronic textbooks

   Focus: _____

   Thesis statement: _____

   _____

Vocabulary

topic sentence
the controlling idea in paragraph

thesis statement
the controlling idea in an essay

LO3 Organization

You should next think about the pattern of organization that you plan to use to develop your topic sentence (or thesis statement). Here's one way to do this:

1. **Study your topic sentence or thesis.** It will usually indicate how to organize your details. Consider the following topic sentence

   Eating locally grown produce will improve the local economy.

   This topic sentence suggests arranging the information by order of importance (see below) because the writer is trying to prove a point.

2. **Then review the details you have gathered.** Decide which details support your topic sentence; also decide on the best pattern of organization to arrange them. For the example topic sentence, the writer would arrange his or her details (reasons) from most important to least important or the other way around.

Patterns of Organization

Listed below are some of the common patterns that you will use in your writing.

- Use **chronological order** (time) when you are sharing a personal experience, telling how something happened, or explaining how to do something.
- Use **spatial order** (location) for descriptions, arranging information from left to right, from top to bottom, from the edge to the center, and so on.
- Use **order of importance** when you are taking a stand or arguing for or against something. Arrange your reasons either from most important to least important or the other way around.
- Use **logical order** if you want to follow your topic sentence or thesis statement with supporting details (reasons, examples, and so on) that naturally and logically follow one another.
- Use **compare-contrast organization** when you want to show how one topic is different from and similar to another one.

CONSIDER THE TRAITS

Think about your purpose as you choose a pattern of organization. Often, your working thesis statement will suggest how you should organize details.

Choose Study each of the following topic sentences and thesis statements. Then choose the best method of organization to develop it. The first one is done for you. (Work on this activity with a classmate if your instructor allows it.)

1. **Topic sentence:** The bottom of the hill in my childhood neighborhood offered everything young boys wanted.

    Appropriate method of organization: _spatial order_

    Explain: _The topic sentence suggests that the writer will describe the area_

    at the bottom of the hill, so using spatial order seems appropriate.

2. **Topic sentence:** In most cases, people involved in recreational fishing should use barbless hooks.

    Appropriate method of organization: _____

    Explain: _____

3. **Topic sentence:** To become an effective leader, a person must develop three main traits.

    Appropriate method of organization: _____

    Explain: _____

4. **Thesis statement:** Meeting my grandmother for the first time rates as one of my most important personal encounters.

    Appropriate method of organization: _____

    Explain: _____

5. **Thesis statement:** (Choose one that you wrote in LO2.)

    Appropriate method of organization: _____

    Explain: _____

Arranging Your Details

Here are three basic strategies for arranging the supporting details after selecting a pattern of organization.

- **Make a quick list** of main points.
- **Create an outline**—an organized arrangement of main points and subpoints.
- **Fill in a graphic organizer,** arranging main points and details in a chart or diagram.

Using a Quick List

A quick list works well when you are writing a short piece or when your planning time is limited. Here is a quick list for a descriptive paragraph about zoot suits. (The list organizes details in spatial order, from top to bottom.)

Sample Quick List

Topic sentence: The zoot suit became a popular fashion symbol in the swing era.
   – begins with a stylish wide-brimmed hat turned down
   – follows with an oversized, tapered long jacket
   – under jacket, a dress shirt with a tie
   – pleated pants taper to narrow bottoms
   – ends with two-tone, thin-soled shoes

Create Write a topic sentence and a quick list for a narrative paragraph about a funny, scary, or otherwise significant personal experience. Include four to six details in your list, organized chronologically.

Topic sentence:

_____

_____

Quick list:

_____

_____

_____

_____

Using an Outline

An outline shows how ideas fit together for your writing. Topic and sentence outlines follow specific guidelines: If you have a "I," you must at least have a "II." If you have an "A," you must at least have a "B," and so on. You can also change or simplify an outline to meet your needs. Outlines are often used to arrange the ideas in essays and other longer pieces of writing.

Simplified Outline

Here is the first part of a simplified outline that includes main points stated in complete sentences and supporting details stated as phrases.

Thesis statement: Humpback whales are by far the most playful and amazing whale species.

1. Most observers note that humpbacks appear to enjoy attention.
   - lift bodies almost completely out of water (breaching)
   - slap huge flippers against the water
   - thrust their flukes (tail portion) straight out of water

2. Humpback whales "sing" better than other whales.
   - song lasts up to 30 minutes
   - head pointed toward ocean floor when singing
   - seem to engage in group singing

Develop Create a simplified outline for an essay about becoming a leader. A thesis statement and three main points are provided. Put the main points in the most logical order, and make up two or three details to support each one. (Work on this activity with a classmate if your instructor allows it.)

Thesis statement: To become an effective leader, a person must develop three main traits.

Main points: Leaders must earn the respect of others. Leaders must display good work habits. Leaders must be confident..

1. _____
   - _____
   - _____
   - _____

2. _____
   - _____
   - _____
   - _____

LO4 Voice

Voice is the personality in writing—how the writer speaks to the reader. Your college instructors will expect you to use an academic voice for most of your writing. In some cases, however, you will be able to use a more personal voice.

■ **Academic voice:** An academic voice sounds serious, and it is the one that you should use for informational essays and reports. This passage is written using an academic voice.

> Wisconsin farmers and hunters have serious concerns about the large number of wolves in the state. While wolves are extremely shy and don't pose a threat to humans, they do threaten livestock. With wolf populations on the rise since the mid-1990s, wolf attacks on livestock have been increasing.

INSIGHT

Generally speaking, an academic voice speaks in the third person *(he, she, it, they, and so on)*. It follows the rules for Standard English, it is objective (meaning that it sticks to the facts), and it chooses words that sound more formal *(he would* rather than *he'd)*.

■ **Personal voice:** A personal voice sounds more relaxed and conversational. It is generally used for narratives and personal essays. This passage is written using a personal voice.

> I was generally a brave little kid, but there were two things that scared me: storms and spiders. The storms that scared me were the ones when tornado warnings were issued and everybody would have to go in the basement. I'd always go to the bathroom, partly because of my nervous reaction, and partly because I thought it was the safest place.

INSIGHT

A personal voice speaks in the first-person *(I, my, we,* etc.). It generally follows the rules for Standard English, it is subjective (meaning it includes personal thoughts and feelings), and it is more relaxed with word choice *(they're* instead of *they are)*.

Create   Write two or three sentences about school or a job that sound academic. Then rewrite these sentences to make them sound more personal. Afterward, share your writing with your classmates.

_____

_____

_____

Working with Voice

Your individual writing voice, or special way of saying things, will develop through practice and experience. In other words, you won't write with "voice" just by learning about it. You must work on it. Here are a few things that you can do.

- **Practice writing.** Write nonstop for at least 10 minutes a day. Write about anything and everything. This practice will help you feel more comfortable with writing, which will help you write with more voice.

- **Become a regular reader.** Read newspapers, magazines, blogs, books. As you read, you will learn about different ways of expressing yourself.

- **Watch for good models.** If you really like the sound of something you read, try to write a brief passage like it.

- **Know your topics.** If you know a lot about a topic, it's easier to sound interested and knowledgeable.

- **Know your purpose and assignment.** For informational paragraphs and essays, you will need to sound more formal and academic. For narratives and personal essays, you should sound more conversational and personal.

- **Be honest.** And keep things simple. This may be easier said than done. As editor Patricia T. O'Conner says, "Simplicity takes practice."

Practice Write nonstop for 5 to 10 minutes (time yourself) about any topic or topics, but be sure not to stop. (If you draw a blank, write "I'm stuck" until some new ideas come to mind.) Afterward, count the number of words you have written. Continue this practice daily or every other day and the number of words that you can write will increase dramatically. In the process, your individual writing voice will begin to develop.

OLJ Studio, 2011 / Used under license from Shutterstock.com

LO5 Word Choice and Sentences

The words and sentences that you use carry the meaning in your writing. So it is important that they are clear, interesting, and honest. Also be sure that they fit the type of writing that you are doing. As you learned on the last two pages, the language you use for an informational paragraph will be different from the language you use in a narrative recalling a personal experience.

Using the Best Words

Generally speaking, specific words *(LeBron soars)* are better to use than general ones *(the basketball player jumps)*. And fresh words (a *drop-dead* beauty) are usually better to use than overused ones (a *real* beauty).

Specific Nouns and Verbs

It's especially important to use specific nouns and verbs because they carry the most meaning in your sentences. The charts below show different examples of general versus specific nouns and verbs.

General nouns:	personal computer		adventure		performer
Specific nouns:	iMac		bungee jumping		Jennifer Lopez

General verbs:	laugh	run	look	build
Specific verbs:	giggle	sprint	inspect	erect

 Study List examples of specific nouns and verbs that come to mind when you inspect the photograph to the right. Afterward, compare lists with your classmates.

Specific Nouns	Specific Verbs

Samot, 2011 / Used under license from Shutterstock.com

What to Watch For with Words

If the words you use help to create clear and interesting paragraphs, essays, and reports, then you have probably used the right ones. The following information discusses word-related issues to consider:

Watch for . . .

- **Vague adjectives** (modifiers of nouns) such as *neat, big, pretty, small, cute, fun, bad, nice, good, great,* and *funny.* Use more specific adjectives instead.

    Vague adjective: Josie makes a good pizza crust.

    Specific adjective: Josie makes a thin and crisp pizza crust.

- **Too many adjectives in general.** Being "adjective happy" detracts from rather than adds to writing.

    Too many adjectives: Part-time help can complete high-profile, high-impact workplace tasks without adding full-time employees.

    Fewer adjectives: Part-time help can complete important tasks without adding full-time employees. (simpler and clearer)

- **Too many "be" verbs** (*is, are, was, were, and so on*). Instead, use specific action verbs.

    "Be" verb: Laura is a powerful diver.

    Specific action verb: Laura dives powerfully.

- **The same word used over and over.** Such repetition calls undo attention to the word.

    Overuse of a word: I noticed a woman dressed in a crisp, navy blue suit. The woman appeared to be in charge. I soon realized that the woman was the owner.

    Variety added: I noticed a woman dressed in a crisp, navy blue suit who appeared to be in charge. I soon realized that she was the owner.

- **Words used incorrectly.** Words such as *their, they're,* and *there* and *it* and *it's* are commonly misused.

    Most engineers get their (not they're or there) training on the job.

    Jogging has its (not it's) most impact if it's (not its) done regularly.

Create   Write your own example for at least three of the problems discussed above. For each one, provide a new sentence with improved word choice. Afterward, share your work with your classmates.

Writing Clear Sentences

To write strong, clear sentences, you must first understand the basics. By definition, a simple sentence expresses a complete thought and contains a subject and a verb. But not all sentences are "simple." There are compound sentences, complex sentences, as well as other types.

The most common sentence errors include fragments *(incomplete sentences)*, comma splices *(two sentences connected only with a comma),* and run-on sentences *(two sentences joined without punctuation).* The examples that follow show what is and what isn't a sentence.

A Basic Guide to Sentences

Correct sentences

Simple sentence:	Jackson chews his fingernails. (*one complete idea*)
Compound sentence:	Max watches the presentation, but his mind is really somewhere else. (*two complete ideas*)
Complex sentence:	Sonja takes quick notes, while Connie sketches tiny flowers. (*one main idea and one subordinate or lesser idea*)

Sentence errors

Fragment:	Popcorn all over the floor. (*no verb*)
	Popcorn *spilled* over the floor. (*verb added*)
Fragment:	Couldn't help laughing. (*no subject*)
	We couldn't help laughing. (*subject added*)
Comma Splice:	Josie and I ordered coffee, we decided to split a cookie. (*missing a connecting word or end punctuation*)
	Josie and I ordered coffee, *and* we decided to split a cookie. (*connecting word added*)
Run-on:	Taking my dog for a walk frustrates me he has to sniff every tree and shrub in front of him. (*no punctuation*)
	Taking my dog for a walk frustrates me. He has to sniff every tree and shrub in front of him. (*punctuation added*)

Develop   Write for 5 minutes about your favorite late night snack (or snacks). Then use the information above to check your sentences for correctness. Ask a classmate to check them as well. Correct any sentence errors that you find.

Checking Your Sentences for Style

There are other issues to consider when it comes to writing effective sentences. The information that follows identifies four of them.

Watch for . . .

■ **Short, choppy sentences.** Too many short sentences in a row will sound choppy. To correct this problem, combine some of the ideas.

> **Choppy sentences:** A Harley roared past us. The cycle was jet black. It stopped in front of a food stand. The food stand sells fresh fish tacos.

> **Combined sentences:** A jet-black Harley roared past us and stopped in front of a food stand that sells fresh fish tacos.

■ **Sentences with the same beginning.** (This problem often creates choppy sentences.) To correct this problem, vary some of your sentence beginnings and lengths.

> **Sentences with no variety:** Keeping a daily planner is important. It keeps track of your schedule. It lists your assignments. It helps you plan your time during the day.

> **Varied sentences:** Keeping a daily planner is important. In addition to keeping track of your schedule, it lists your assignments and helps you plan your time.

■ **Sentences with passive verbs.** With a passive verb, the subject is acted on rather than doing the action. To fix this problem, change the passive verbs into active ones.

> **Passive verb:** The 16-ounce porterhouse steak was *attacked* by the Chihuahua.

> **Active verb:** The Chihuahua *attacked* the 16-ounce porterhouse steak.

Check Use the following strategy to evaluate the sentences that you used in the activity on the previous page.

1. List the opening words in your sentences. Decide if some sentence beginnings need to be varied.

2. List the number of words in each sentence. Decide if some sentence lengths need to be varied.

3. List the main verbs used. Decide if you need to replace any overused "be" verbs (*is, are, was, were*) with action verbs.

LO6 Conventions

The conventions are the rules for grammar, usage, and mechanics that you need to follow in your writing. But be sure to focus on the correctness of your writing at the best time, when you have completed the revising of your writing. Once all of your ideas are in place, then checking for the conventions becomes important.

Getting Started

If you're working on a computer, do your correcting on a printout of your work. Then enter the changes on the computer. Be sure to save the edited printout so you have a record of the changes you've made.

If you're working with pen and paper, do your editing on a neat copy of your revised writing. Then make a new copy of your writing and save the edited copy. Once you develop a final copy, be sure to proofread it for correctness before you submit it.

Strategies for Editing

When checking for errors, examine your writing word for word and sentence by sentence. The following strategies will help you edit thoroughly and effectively.

- Work with a clean copy of your writing, one that includes your revising changes.
- Check one element at a time—spelling, punctuation, and so on.
- For spelling, start at the bottom of the page to force yourself to look at each word. (Remember that your spell-checker will not catch all errors.)
- For punctuation, circle all the marks to force yourself to look at each one.
- Read your work aloud at least once, noting any errors as you go along.
- Refer to a list of common errors.
- Have an editing guide
- Ask a trusted classmate to check your work as well.

Using Editing Strategies

You can use editing symbols to mark errors in your writing. Listed below are some of the most common symbols.

C̲chicago	Capitalize a letter.	firstmy∧speech	Insert here.
Fall	Make lowercase.	∧ ∧ ∧	Insert a comma, a colon, or a semicolon.
Mr⊙Ford	Insert (add) a period.	⌄ ⌄ ⌄	Insert an apostrophe or quotation marks.
Sp. or (recieve)	Correct spelling.	? !∧ ∧	Insert a question mark or an exclamation point.
Mr. Lott he	Delete (take out) or replace.	(possible worst)	Switch words or letters.

Edit Use the editing symbols above to mark the errors in the following piece and show how they should be corrected.

> When we lived on Maple street, we had a neighbor who seemed to   *1*
> have two personalities his name was Mr. Bunde. I worked for him one
> Summer while I was in grade school, cutting his lawn and doing other yard
> work. After a few months of working for him I'd had more than enough. In
> general, he was a nice enough guy and he likes to joke around some of the   *5*
> time. Unfortunately, it was hard to tell if he was really kidding or if his
> mood was suddenly changing. When he was in one of his moods I couldn't
> do anything rite. Sometimes he would complain about other neighbors and
> he would expect me to agree with him, even though he new they were my
> friends. I not only have to concentrate on my work but I also had to be on   *10*
> my guard, trying to predict Mr. Bunde's mood. Why did I have to work for
> him

LO7 Reviewing the Traits of Writing

Respond to each set of directions to review the concepts in this chapter.

Ideas Answer the following questions about this section.

■ What does it mean to narrow a subject?

_____

■ What are four different types of supporting details?

_____

Identifying a Focus Explain the importance of a topic sentence in a paragraph.

_____

_____

Organization List the first four patterns listed in this section. Explain each one.

1. _____
2. _____
3. _____
4. _____

Voice Explain the following two types of writing voices.

■ Academic Voice: _____

_____

■ Personal Voice: _____

_____

Word Choice and Sentences Answer the following questions about this section.

■ Why is it important to use specific nouns and verbs? _____

_____

■ Why should you vary some of your sentence beginnings and lengths? _____

_____

Conventions Explain when in the writing process you should check for conventions and why the "timing" is important.

_____

_____

5

Academic Writing and Learning

> "Writing became such a process of discovery that I couldn't wait to get to work in the morning."
> —Sharon O'Brien

In college, all of the new information coming your way can seem overwhelming. To succeed, you must be able to retain this new knowledge, connect it to other ideas, and share conclusions with your peers and instructors. Writing can help you do all of these things.

Writing is a tool that can help you become a better, more efficient learner. In fact, no other activity can improve your learning and communication skills as well as writing can. And you'll be happy to know that these skills translate directly to the workplace. Today's employers place a premium on effective writing skills.

The guidelines and strategies presented in this chapter will help you meet the demands of your academic writing. You will learn about writing to learn, the writing process, as well as many helpful writing strategies.

Learning Outcomes

LO1 Write to learn.
LO2 Write to share learning.
LO3 Understand the writing process.
LO4 Use writing strategies.
LO5 Think critically and logically.
LO6 Review

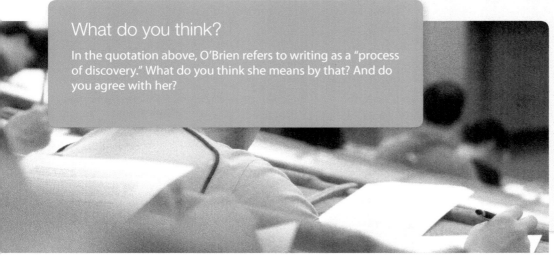

What do you think?

In the quotation above, O'Brien refers to writing as a "process of discovery." What do you think she means by that? And do you agree with her?

Cristian M, 2011 / Used under license from Shutterstock.com

"Don't think and then write it down. Think on paper."
—Harry Kemelman

LO1 Writing to Learn

Gertrude Stein made one of the more famous and unusual statements about writing when she said, "To write is to write is to write is to write. . . ." The lofty place that writing held in her life echoes in the line. As far as she was concerned, nothing else needed to be said on the subject.

What would cause someone to become so committed to writing? Was it a desire for fame and recognition? Not really. The real fascination that experienced writers have with writing is the frame of mind it puts them in. The act of filling up a page triggers their thinking and leads to meaningful learning.

Changing Your Attitude

If you think of writing in just one way—as an assignment to be completed—you will never discover its true value. Writing works best when you think of it as a way to learn. A series of questions, a list, or a quick note can be a meaningful form of writing if it helps you think and understand. If you make writing an important part of your learning routine, you'll change your attitude about writing (for the better), and you'll become a better thinker and learner.

Keeping a Class Notebook

Keeping a class notebook or journal is essential if you are going to make writing an important part of your learning routine. Certainly, you can take notes in this notebook, but it is also helpful to reflect on what is going on in the class. These writing activities will help you think about your course work.

- Write freely about anything from class discussions to challenging assignments.
- Explore new ideas and concepts.
- Argue for and against any points of view that came up in class.
- Question what you are learning.
- Record your thoughts and feelings about an extended project.
- Evaluate your progress in the class.

Reflect Write freely for 5 to 10 minutes about your writing experiences. Consider how you feel about writing, your strengths and weaknesses as a writer, if you have ever used writing to learn, and so on. Then share your thoughts with your classmates.

LO2 Writing to Share Learning

The other important function of writing is to share what you have learned. When you write to learn, you are your only audience. But when you write to share learning, your audience expands to include your instructor, your classmates, and others.

All writing projects (paragraphs, essays, blog entries) actually begin with writing to learn as you collect your thoughts and feelings about the topic. But with a first draft in hand, you must make the writing clear, complete, and ready to share with others.

A Learning Connection

As this graphic shows, improved thinking is the link between the two functions of writing. Writing to learn involves exploring and forming your thoughts, and writing to share learning involves clarifying and fine-tuning them.

| Writing to Learn | Improved Thinking | Writing to Share Learning |

INSIGHT

Following the steps in the writing process is the best way to develop writing to share. This process helps you pace yourself so you don't try to do everything all at once.

The Range of Writing

The forms of writing to share cover a lot of territory, as you can see in the chart to the right. As a college student, your writing will likely cover the entire spectrum, with a focus on the more formal forms, such as essays and reports.

React Answer these questions about the chart: What forms of writing do you most often engage in? How does your writing approach change at different points along the spectrum?

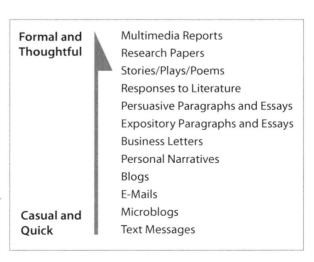

Formal and Thoughtful
- Multimedia Reports
- Research Papers
- Stories/Plays/Poems
- Responses to Literature
- Persuasive Paragraphs and Essays
- Expository Paragraphs and Essays
- Business Letters
- Personal Narratives
- Blogs
- E-Mails
- Microblogs
- Text Messages

Casual and Quick

LO3 Understanding the Writing Process

When facing an extended writing assignment, most students ask the same question: How will I ever get this done? Even professional writers sometimes labor for the right answer. But have no fear. A writing project is much less imposing when you approach it as a process rather than as an end product. This section will introduce you to the steps in the writing process.

The Steps in the Process

You cannot change a flat tire with one simple action. It takes a number of steps to get the job done right. The same goes for writing. If you expect to complete a paper in one general attempt, you (and your instructor) will be disappointed in the results. On the other hand, if you follow the writing process, you'll complete the job in the right way—one step at a time.

Process	Activities
Prewriting	Start the process by (1) selecting a topic to write about, (2) collecting details about it, and (3) finding a focus or thesis to direct your writing.
Writing	Then write your first draft, using your prewriting plan as a general guide. Writing a first draft allows you to connect your thoughts about a topic.
Revising	Carefully review your first draft and have a classmate read it as well. Change any parts that need to be clearer, and add missing information.
Editing	Edit your revised writing by checking for style, grammar, punctuation, and spelling errors.
Publishing	During the final step, prepare your writing to share with your instructor, your peers, or another audience.

Reasons to Write

Always use the writing process when you are writing to share learning and when you are writing certain personal forms. You don't need to use it when you are simply writing to learn.

Reason	Forms	Purpose
Writing to share learning	Summaries, informational essays	To show your understanding of subjects you are studying
Personal writing	Personal essays, blog postings, short stories, plays	To share your personal thoughts, feelings, and creativity with others

Reflect Explain how the writing process explained above compares with your own way of completing assignments. Consider what you normally do first, second, third, and so on.

> "A writer is not so much someone who has something to say as he is someone who has found a process that will bring about new things he would not have thought of if he had not started to say them."
> —William Stafford

The Process in Action

As the chart to the right indicates, there can be forward and backward movement between the steps in the writing process. For example, after writing a first draft, you may decide to collect more details about your topic, which is actually a prewriting activity.

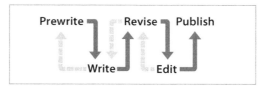

Points to Remember

When using the writing process, you need to understand the following points.

1. All the steps require some type of writing. Prewriting (planning), revising, and editing are as much writing activities as composing the first draft is.

2. It is unlikely that the process will work the same for any two writing assignments. For one assignment, you may struggle with gathering details. For another, you may have trouble starting the first draft. For still another, you may move from step to step with little difficulty.

3. No two writers develop their writing in the same way. Some writers need to talk about their writing early on, while others would rather keep their ideas to themselves. Some writers need to step away from their writing at times to let their thoughts percolate. Other writers can't stop until they produce a first draft. Your own writing personality will develop as you gain more writing experience.

4. All the information about the writing process won't make you a better writer unless you make a sincere effort to use it. You wouldn't expect to play the piano just by reading about it—you must follow the instructions and practice. The same holds true for writing.

INSIGHT —————

When you respond to a writing prompt on a test, use an abbreviated form of the writing process. Spend a few minutes gathering and organizing your ideas; then write your response. Afterward, read what you have produced and quickly revise and edit it.

Create Make a chart that shows your own process—the one you described on the previous page. Share your chart with your classmates.

A CLOSER LOOK at the Process

Each step in the writing process requires a special type of thinking. Following these steps will help you become a more confident writer and learner.

Prewriting is the first step in the writing process. In many ways, it is the most important step because it involves all of the decisions and planning that come before writing a first draft. If you plan well, you will be well prepared to work through the rest of the process. These are the basic prewriting tasks.

- **Identify a meaningful writing idea.** Choose a topic that meets the requirements of the assignment and that truly interests you. Otherwise, you will have a hard time writing about it. Begin your topic search by writing freely about the assignment or by simply listing your ideas.

- **Collect plenty of details.** Explore your own thoughts and feelings about the topic. Then gather additional information, either through firsthand experience (observations, interviews, and so on.) or by reading about the topic in books, magazines, and on the Internet.

- **Establish a focus.** Just as a skilled photographer focuses or centers the subject before taking a photograph, you must identify a special part or feeling about the topic before writing your first draft. This focus, or emphasis, is usually expressed in a thesis statement.

- **Choose a pattern of arrangement.** Once you have established a focus, decide what details to include in your writing and how to organize them. You can arrange your details chronologically (by time), logically, by order of importance, and so on.

- **Organize your information.** With a pattern of arrangement in mind, you can organize your details in one of three basic ways:
  - Make a quick list of main points and support.
  - Create an outline—a more formal arrangement of main points and subpoints.
  - Fill in a graphic organizer—arranging main points and details in a chart or diagram.

INSIGHT

Thorough prewriting is critical when you are writing essays, articles, and reports. It is not as important when you are writing personal blogs and narratives.

Drafting is the next step in the writing process. You have one important task during this step—to connect your thoughts and ideas about your topic. Just put these thoughts on paper so you have something to work with. They do not have to be perfectly worded. Here is a basic guide to drafting.

- **Strike while you're hot.** Write your first draft while your planning is still fresh in your mind.

- **Refer to your prewriting.** Use all of your planning and organizing as a basic writing guide. But also be open to new ideas as they come to mind.

- **Write as much as you can.** Keep writing until you get all of your ideas on paper, or until you come to a natural stopping point. Concentrate on forming your ideas rather than on making everything correct.

- **Form a meaningful whole.** A meaningful whole for a paragraph means a topic sentence, body sentences, and a closing sentence. For an essay, it means an opening paragraph (with a thesis statement), multiple middle paragraphs, and a closing paragraph.

Paragraph   **Essay**

Topic sentence ⟶ Opening paragraph (with thesis statement)

Body ⟶ Middle paragraphs

Closing sentence ⟶ Closing paragraph

- **Pay special attention to each part.** All three parts—the opening, the middle, and the closing—play important roles in your writing. Give each part special attention.
  - The opening gets the reader's interest and states your thesis.
  - The middle supports your thesis.
  - The closing offers important final thoughts about the topic.

- **Look back to move forward.** Sometimes it helps to stop and reread what you have written to help you add new ideas.

- **Write naturally and honestly.** "Talk" to your readers, as if a group of classmates were gathered around you.

- **Remember, it's a draft.** A first draft is your first look at a developing writing idea. You will have plenty of opportunities to improve upon it later in the process.

A CLOSER LOOK at the Process (continued)

Revising is the third step in the process. During this step, you shape and improve the ideas in your first draft. You would never expect a musician to record a song after putting lyrics and music together for the first time. The same holds true with your writing. You still have a lot of work ahead of you. Here is a basic guide to revising.

- **Step away from your draft.** Your time away will help you see your first draft more clearly, and with a fresh outlook.

- **Revisit your purpose.** Are you writing to explain, to persuade, to describe, or to share?

- **Read your draft many times.** Read it silently and out loud to get an overall impression of your work.

- **Have peers read it.** Their comments and questions will help you decide what changes to make.

- **Check your overall focus.** Decide if your thesis still works and if you have provided enough support for it.

- **Review each part.** Be sure that the opening sets the proper tone for your writing, the middle part supports your thesis, and the closing provides worthy final thoughts about the topic.

- **Know your basic moves.** There are four basic ways to make changes— adding, cutting, rewriting, or reordering information. Each change or improvement that you make will bring you closer to a strong finished paper.

Add information to . . .
- make a main point more convincing.
- complete an explanation.
- improve the flow of your writing.

Cut information if it . . .
- doesn't support the thesis.
- seems repetitious.

Rewrite information if it . . .
- seems confusing or unclear.
- appears too complicated.
- lacks the proper voice.

Reorder information if it . . .
- seems out of order.
- would make more sense in another spot.

- **Plan a revising strategy.** Decide what you need to do first, second, and third, and then make the necessary changes.

Editing is the fourth step, when you check your revised writing for style and correctness. Editing becomes important *after* you have revised the content of your writing. Editing is like buffing out the smudges and scratches on a newly painted car. The buffing is important, but only after the main work—the actual painting—is complete. Here is a basic guide to editing.

■ **Start with clean copy.** Do your editing on a clean copy of your revised writing; otherwise, things get too confusing.

■ **Check first for style.** Make sure that you have used the best words, such as specific nouns and verbs and smooth-reading sentences.

■ **Then check for correctness.** Start by checking your spelling, then move on to end punctuation, and so on.

■ **For spelling, read from the last word to the first.** This strategy will force you to look at each word. (A spell checker will not catch every error.)

■ **Circle punctuation.** This strategy will force you to look at each mark.

■ **Refer to an editing checklist.**

■ **Use editing symbols.** These symbols provide an efficient way to mark errors.

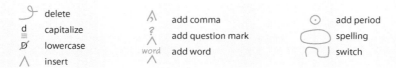

■ **Get help.** Ask a trusted classmate to check for errors as well. You are too close to your writing to notice everything.

Publishing is the final step in the writing process. During this step, you prepare your writing before submitting or sharing it.

■ **Prepare a final copy.** Incorporate all of your editing changes.

■ **Follow design requirements.** Format your final copy according to the requirements established by your instructor.

■ **Proofread the text.** Check your writing one last time for errors.

LO4 Using Writing Strategies

The writing strategies and instruction on the next 10 pages will help you write strong essays and reports.

Creating an Effective Opening

In many situations, first impressions are important—say, for instance, when you're interviewing for a job or introducing yourself to a roommate or coworker. First impressions are important in writing, too, because the first few ideas help set the tone for the rest of the piece. (Tone refers to the writer's attitude toward her or his topic.) The information that follows will help you make a positive first impression in your essays.

The Basic Parts

The opening paragraph should (1) identify the topic, (2) gain the reader's interest, and (3) state the thesis. You may also include a sentence or two of background information.

Listed here are strategies to help you gain the reader's interest.

- Begin with a surprising or little-known fact about the topic.

   Thousands of babies are born each year with alcohol-related defects, making fetal alcohol syndrome one of the leading causes of mental retardation.

- Ask an interesting or challenging question about the topic.

   What exactly do the signs held up by homeless people tell us?

- Start with a revealing quotation.

   "We live here and they live there," Bigger Thomas says in *Native Son*. "We black and they white. They got things and we ain't. They do things and we can't."

- Share a brief, dramatic story.

   It was May 1945. World War II had just ended and Yugoslavia had been overtaken. The town of Vrhnika, Yugoslavia, was no longer safe. Russian and communist troops would break into houses, take what they wanted, and even kill.

- Open with a bold statement.

   Barbie's boobs and spacious mansion helped cause the decay of today's youth, or so say some experts.

Example Opening Paragraph

Analyze Carefully read the following opening paragraph from an essay about a degenerative bone disease called Legg-Calve-Perthes (pronounced leg-cal-VAY-PER-theez). Then answer the questions below.

Allie Mason acted like a typical high school freshman. She was   *1*
bubbly, energetic, and extremely friendly. She was also a conscientious
student, belonged to the Honors Art Club, and enjoyed golfing. What set
Allie apart was a debilitating physical condition that caused one of her
legs to be noticeably shorter than the other one and forced her to limp.   *5*
As a result, she had to endure endless medical procedures and missed
out on typical school activities such as gym and dances. She also had to
endure more than her share of insensitive remarks. She remembered, "My
classmates would tease me and call me names." Their comments obviously
hurt, especially those made by her friends. The reason for Allie's suffering   *10*
was Legg-Calve-Perthes, a painful bone disease that truly challenges the
sufferer.

1. What strategy does the writer use to introduce the topic and engage the reader? (See the previous page.)

   _____

2. What, if any, background information is provided about the topic?

   _____

3. What is the thesis statement in this paragraph?

   _____

4. What special part or feeling about the topic is identified in this statement?

   _____

5. How would you rate this opening and why?

   Weak ★ ★ ★ ★ ★ Strong

   _____

Developing the Middle Part

In the middle paragraphs, you develop all of the main points that support your thesis statement. Use your planning (quick list, outline, graphic organizer) as a general guide when you develop this part of an essay. Here are a few tips for getting started.

- **Keep your thesis statement in mind as you write.** All of your main points should support or explain this statement.
- **Develop each main point in a separate paragraph (or two).** State the main point in the form of a topic sentence and follow with detail sentences that support it.
- **Use plenty of details** to fully explain your ideas.
- **Use your own words,** except on those few occasions when you employ a quotation to add authority to your writing.
- **Be open to new ideas that occur to you,** especially if they will improve your essay.
- **Try any of the basic writing moves** that are appropriate to your topic.

Basic Writing Moves

The paragraphs in the middle part of an essay should, among other things, *explain, describe, define, classify,* and so on. What follows is a list and definitions of these basic writing moves.

Narrating ———	sharing an experience or a story
Describing ———	telling how someone or something appears, acts, or operates
Explaining ———	providing important facts, details, and examples
Analyzing ———	carefully examining a subject or breaking it down
Comparing ———	showing how two subjects are similar and different
Defining ———	identifying or clarifying the meaning of a term
Reflecting ———	connecting with or wondering about
Evaluating ———	rating the value of something
Arguing ———	using logic and evidence to prove something is true

Special Challenge Read two different essays in this book. On your own paper, list the different moves that the writers use in the middle paragraphs of the essays. For example, a writer may *explain* in one or more paragraphs, *reflect* in another, and so on.

Example Middle Paragraph

Analyze   Carefully read the following middle paragraph from an essay on Legg-Calve-Perthes. Then answer the questions below.

Legg-Calve-Perthes is both rare and mysterious. The disease affects only 5 of every 100,000 children, usually when they are between the ages of five and twelve. While boys suffer from the disease far more frequently than girls do by a ratio of 4 to 1, when girls do develop Legg-Calve-Perthes, they tend to suffer more severely from it. At this point, researchers are not really sure of the cause of the disease. They are, however, fairly certain that it is not genetic. They also know that a reduction of blood flow at the hip joint contributes to the disease and causes the bone tissue to collapse or react in other strange ways. Usually, the rounded part of the femur bone that fits into the hip joint becomes deformed. In Allie's case, the top of her femur bone grew to double its normal size, a condition that produced extreme pain when she tried to walk. It's hard to imagine how Allie or anyone else is able to deal with this condition during the active childhood years.

1. What is the topic sentence in this paragraph?

   _____

2. What special feature about the topic is emphasized in this sentence?

   _____

3. What basic writing move (or moves) does the writer use in this paragraph? (See the previous page.)

   _____

4. How would you rate this paragraph and why?

   Weak ★ ★ ★ ★ ★ Strong

   _____

Writing a Strong Closing

While the opening part of your writing offers important *first* impressions, the closing part offers important *final* impressions. More specifically, the closing helps the reader better understand and appreciate the importance of your topic or thesis.

The Basic Parts

Consider the strategies below when writing your closing. In most cases, you will want to use more than one of these strategies; but whatever you choose to do, your closing must flow smoothly from your last middle paragraph.

- Remind the reader of the thesis.

   Legg-Calve-Parthes is like a cancer in how it affects an individual and her or his family.

- Summarize the main points or highlight one or two of them.

   Ultimately, both Alan and Bigger (two literary characters) fail to gain real control over the outside forces in their lives. Alan forfeits his interest in life, and Bigger forfeits life itself.

- Reflect on the explanation or argument you've presented in the middle part.

   It would be a shame to lose these amazing creatures (humpback whales). We don't want their mysterious song to be a thing of the past. And we can't turn to zoos when the numbers shrink to a precious few.

- Offer a final idea to keep the reader thinking about the topic.

   If the country waits until an agroterrorist attack happens, people may become ill, the overall economy could be damaged, and the agricultural economy may never recover.

INSIGHT ────────────

You may need to write two or three versions of your closing before it says exactly what you want it to say.

Example Closing Paragraph

Analyze   Carefully read the following closing paragraph from an essay on Legg-Calve-Perthes. Then answer the questions below.

> Legg-Calve-Perthes is like a cancer in how it affects an individual *1*
> and her family. In Allie's case, the debilitating effects started with her
> painful efforts to walk and has continued with attempts to address the
> condition with operations, therapy, and braces. Through all of this, she
> and her family have missed out on so much. Her mother had to quit her *5*
> job, and her sister felt ignored. As Allie recalled, "My sister has always felt
> jealous of all of the attention I get from my parents." But knowing that the
> condition should, in time, resolve itself certainly must help sufferers like
> Allie meet each new challenge. It must also help them to know that young
> people suffering from Legg-Calve-Perthes usually do quite well in the long *10*
> term. Unfortunately, the chance of permanent hip damage exists as well.

1. In what way does the first sentence remind the reader of the thesis statement?

   _____

2. What other strategy or strategies does the writer use?

   _____

3. How would you rate this paragraph and why?
   Weak ★　★　★　★　★ Strong

   _____

Understanding Strong Writing

The traits (ideas, organization, voice, and so on) are the key ingredients in writing. Each one contributes to a successful essay or report.

The traits-based checklist below serves as a guide to strong writing. Your writing will be clear and effective when it can "pass" each point. This checklist is especially helpful during revising, when you are deciding how to improve your writing.

> "There is no such thing as good writing, only good rewriting."
> —Louis Brandeis

INSIGHT

Word choice and sentence fluency are not as important early on in the revising process, when you are focused on content. But they do become important later on, during editing.

A Guide to Strong Writing

Ideas

- [ ] **1.** Does an interesting and relevant topic serve as a starting point for the writing?
- [ ] **2.** Is the writing focused, addressing a specific feeling about or a specific part of the topic? (Check the thesis statement.)
- [ ] **3.** Are there enough specific ideas, details, and examples to support the thesis?
- [ ] **4.** Overall, is the writing engaging and informative?

Organization

- [ ] **5.** Does the writing form a meaningful whole—with opening, middle, and closing parts?
- [ ] **6.** Does the writing follow a logical pattern of organization?
- [ ] **7.** Do transitions connect ideas and help the writing flow?

Voice

- [ ] **8.** Does the writer sound informed about and interested in the topic?
- [ ] **9.** Does the writer sound sincere and genuine?

Word Choice

- [ ] **10.** Does the word choice clearly fit the purpose and the audience?
- [ ] **11.** Does the writing include specific nouns and verbs?

Sentence Fluency

- [ ] **12.** Are the sentences clear, and do they flow smoothly?
- [ ] **13.** Are the sentences varied in their beginnings and length?

React Carefully read the following paragraphs from a persuasive essay. Then answer the questions below.

Learn to Earn

Lack of student motivation is a main topic of discussion when it comes   *1*
to today's underachieving schools. The experts ask, how can we motivate
our students to learn? And how can we keep them in school long enough
to prepare for the twenty-first century workplace? These questions are
especially important in urban areas, where the drop-out rate is alarming,   *5*
especially among nonnative English students. One answer appears quite
logical: Give them money. In other words, if we want our students to
succeed in school, we should pay them.

Students, in one way, are already bribed to attend school. The whole
point of academic scholarships is based on receiving a monetary reward for   *10*
being a good student. Calling a cash award a "scholarship" doesn't alter the
fact that what's being offered is money. Presently, only the best students or
the best athletes pick up all the cash. That does not seem fair. What about
the student that doesn't want to go to college? Why not pay everyone for
going to school the same way they would get paid for doing any other job?   *15*

Many students drop out of school because they are forced to work to
help support their families. When it comes to choosing between going to
school or going to work, the latter usually wins out for practical reasons.
If these same students were paid a minimum wage for attending school,
they wouldn't have to worry about choosing between education and keeping   *20*
their jobs. In the long run, it would probably be less expensive to keep
these students in school by paying them than to have them drop out of
school with no skills.

Ideas

☐ **1.** Is the topic relevant and interesting?

☐ **2.** Is the focus, or thesis, of the essay clear?

☐ **3.** Does the essay contain a variety of specific details?

Organization

☐ **4.** Does the first paragraph include the key elements of an effective opening?

☐ **5.** Do these paragraphs follow a logical pattern of organization?

Voice

☐ **6.** Does the writer sound informed and interested in the topic?

☐ **7.** Does the writer sound sincere and honest?

Using Standard English

Standard English (SE) is English that is considered appropriate for school, business, and government. You have been learning SE throughout your years in school. The chart that follows shows the basic differences between non-Standard English (NS) and SE.

Differences in . . .	NS	SE
1. Expressing plurals after numbers	10 mile	10 miles
2. Expressing habitual action	He always be early.	He always is early.
3. Expressing ownership	My friend car . . .	My friend's car . . .
4. Expressing the third-person singular verb	The customer ask . . .	The customer asks . . .
5. Expressing negatives	She doesn't never . . .	She doesn't ever . . .
6. Using reflexive pronouns	He sees hisself . . .	He sees himself . . .
7. Using demonstrative adjectives	Them reports are . . .	Those reports are . . .
8. Using forms of *do*	He done it.	He did it.
9. Avoiding double subjects	My manager he . . .	My manager . . .
10. Using *a* or *an*	I need new laptop. She had angry caller.	I need a new laptop. She had an angry caller.
11. Using the past tense of verbs	Carl finish his . . .	Carl finished his . . .
12. Using *isn't* or *aren't* versus *ain't*	The company ain't . . .	The company isn't . . .

"Standard English is not a language—
but a variety of English among many."
—Peter Trudgill

Read   Carefully read the following descriptive essay. As you will see, it contains underlined examples of non-standard variations of American English (NS).

My grandparents they used to baby-sit for me when my mom had to   *1*
work weekends. They were never too busy to have me. Whenever I be bored
with playing outside, I would head into the two-car garage and "help"
Grandpa. His garage was really just a collection place for all of his old
machines. He be always putzing around with something in there. I think   *5*
Grandpa saw hisself as a master repairman.

When I walked into that old garage, the burnt smell of oil were the
first thing I would notice. Once my eyes adjusted to the gloom, I could
start making out different parts of the collection. On the right wall, he had
picture of everyone in the Smith family. On certain days I had to stand   *10*
four inch from the picture to see the grinning faces. Glaring sunbeams
would shoot through them dusty, yellowish curtains covering the one
window.

In one corner, there were a dirty old refrigerator load up with cans of
soda and new canisters of snuff, just in case he run out while working on   *15*
a project. You see, Grandpa he always had a pinch of snuff in his mouth.
Because of that nasty habit, he would sometimes spit into an old coffee
can. I didn't never touch that can for sure. Other than that, he was a great
person to be around because he be so patient and interested in working
with me.

Discuss   In small groups or as a class, identify the number that describes each underlined NS form, using the chart on the previous page as a guide. Then explain how to express each one using Standard English (SE).

LO5 Thinking Critically and Logically

Critical thinking is careful, logical thinking—the kind of thinking that you should use for your academic essays and reports. Here are some questions that will help you to think critically and logically about your writing projects.

Asking Critical Questions

- What is the purpose of my writing (to inform, to entertain, to persuade)?
- Who is my intended audience (general readers, my instructor, my peers)?
- Can my topic be separated into parts? If so, what are they?
- How well do I know my topic?
- What will the reader gain from reading about this topic?
- What logical pattern of thinking should I follow? (See below.)
- What will be the focus, or thesis, of my writing?
- How will I support my thesis?

Logical Patterns of Thinking

Most of your academic writing will follow either a deductive or an inductive pattern of thinking. **Deductive thinking** moves from a general thesis to specific supporting details. This is the most common pattern of thinking that you will use. **Inductive thinking** moves from specific facts and details to a general conclusion.

Use these questions to check for deductive thinking.

- Do I include a thesis in my opening part?
- Do the details logically support or follow from my thesis?
- If the writing is persuasive, do I address any obvious limitations or opposing points of view?
- Does the conclusion logically follow the ideas that come before it?

Use these questions to check for inductive thinking.

- Do I start with a series of facts, examples, and explanations?
- Do the details logically lead up to a general conclusion?
- If the writing is persuasive, do I address any obvious limitations or opposing points of view?
- Is the general conclusion reasonable?

Apply For your next writing assignment, use the questions on this page as a general guide to critical and logical thinking.

A CLOSER LOOK at Logic

Logic is the science of reasonable and accurate thinking. Your writing will be logical if it contains relevant and provable evidence.

Reliable and Logical Evidence

If you were writing a paper about the aurora borealis, the following types of evidence would be provable:

Observation: I saw the northern lights for the first time last week.

Quotation: "Carl Sagan once said . . ."

Statistic: It takes the solar wind _____ number of hours to reach earth.

Comparison: The aurora borealis works much like the excited gases in a fluorescent light bulb.

Explanation: According to the latest reports from NASA . . .

Inference: For the aurora borealis to appear, there must have been solar flares within the previous 24 hours.

Faulty Logic

The opposite of logical evidence is evidence that is illogical or exaggerated like the examples below. Be sure to avoid these types of faulty logic in your own writing.

Exaggerating the Facts: Eating chocolate can cause all kinds of diseases, even if you only eat one or two pieces a day.

Distracting the Reader: Chocolate is not only bad for your health, but it also costs a lot of money and the wrappers add to the problem of littering.

Offering Extremes: Either people should give up chocolate, or we are going to face incredible increases in heath-care costs.

Telling Only Part of the Truth: The new increase in tuition is a good idea because it will lower taxes for county residents.

Appealing to a Popular Position: The new tuition increase is a good idea because it passed unanimously at the last board meeting.

Practice   Write two or three of your own examples of faulty logic (without naming the type). Then exchange your work with a partner and discuss each other's examples.

LO6 Reviewing Academic Writing and Learning

Writing to Learn   Answer the following questions about writing to learn.

1. How is writing to learn different from traditional writing assignments?

   _____

2. What are some ways you can write to learn using a class notebook? Name two.

   _____

Understanding the Writing Process   Answer the following questions about the writing process.

1. What are the steps in the writing process?

   _____

2. Explain the forward and backward movement of this process?

   _____

3. Which step deals with planning to write? With improving the first draft?

   _____

Using Writing Strategies   Answer the following questions about the writing strategies and instruction covered in this chapter.

1. What are the three main parts of an academic essay?

   _____

2. What is Standard English?

   _____

3. How can the guide to strong writing help you?

   _____

Thinking Critically and Logically   Answer the following questions about critical and logical thinking.

1. What is critical thinking?

   _____

2. What is meant by faulty logic? Give one example.

   _____

Part II:

Reading and Writing Paragraphs

6

> "You ask what is the use of classification . . . ?
> I answer you: order and simplification are the
> first steps toward the mastery of a subject."
> —Thomas Mann

Classification

Music is a popular subject. It is loved and enjoyed around the world. However, *music* covers a lot of territory. Think of the many styles, artists, and genres out there. It could take someone years to become an authority on a single era of classical music. At the same time, that music expert would probably know very little about the latest trends in hip-hop.

When you encounter a topic as large or as complex as music, it is helpful to break it down into manageable categories or parts. Then you can examine the parts separately. This organizational strategy is called classification. You will often encounter classification in your college reading and writing.

In this chapter, you will read a number of classification paragraphs and then develop one of your own. Doing so will help you better understand the individual parts of a topic and how they relate to one another.

Learning Outcomes

LO1 Understand classification.
LO2 Learn about reading strategies.
LO3 Read and react to a professional paragraph.
LO4 Read and react to a student paragraph.
LO5 Practice reading skills.
LO6 Plan a classification paragraph.
LO7 Write the first draft.
LO8 Revise the writing.
LO9 Edit the writing.

What do you think?
How might you use classification in your daily life?

Mark Atkins, 2011 / Used under license from Shutterstock.com

LO1 Understanding Classification

Look up at the sky on a clear night, and you will realize how challenging it can be to classify a topic. At first glance the stars look alike, but a close examination reveals key differences in one star from the next. Through years of hard work, astronomers like Angelo Secchi have explored these differences using systems of classification.

> "Science is the systematic classification of experience."
> —George Henry Lewis

In 1863 Secchi studied 4,000 different star patterns and concluded that every star in the sky could be categorized into one of five classes based on unique patterns. At the time, such a classification was revolutionary. It formed a new understanding of the universe.

Today, Secchi's system of classification is considered out of date, and a more detailed classification system has emerged, grouping stars into seven classes based on surface temperature, color, and size.

Branching Out

As the star example shows, classifications are not always permanent. But not all classifications are as complicated as the one described above, nor do they need to be held to strict scientific analysis. Take something as ordinary as barbeque sauce. It can be grouped by taste, ingredient, brand, and price. Classifying, sorting, and arranging can be applied to many subjects in all walks of life, from barbeque sauces to baby carriages.

Identify For each topic below, identify four or five categories, or subgroups. This is basic classification. (If one of these topics doesn't work for you, substitute another one.) Afterward share your work with your classmates.

movies	soft drinks	exercise

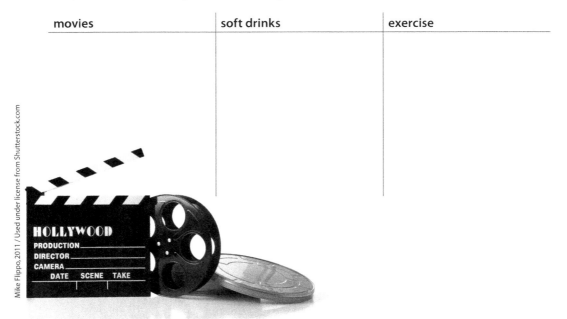

Mike Flippo, 2011 / Used under license from Shutterstock.com

Reading

Reading classification paragraphs helps you recognize the variety hidden in a complex topic.

LO2 Learning About Reading Strategies

Strategy 1: Analyzing the Categories

There are three basic questions to answer when reading a classification paragraph:

1. How does the writer break down the topic into categories?
2. How does the writer describe each category?
3. Are the categories equal?

The Process in Action

Here is an analysis of a paragraph about basic taste sensations.

1. How does the writer break down the topic into categories?

   Salty, sweet, sour, and bitter

2. How does the writer describe each category?

   A salty taste comes from substances that include sodium, such as potato chips. The sweet sensation comes from sugars, both processed and natural. Sour tastes come from acidic foods such as lemons, and bitter tastes come from alkaline foods such as coffee.

3. Are the categories equal?

   All of the categories seem related, and they are explained with the same type of details.

Strategy 2: Diagramming the Key Parts

Classification paragraphs generally follow a similar pattern. The first sentence or two introduces the topic and categories. Then each category is addressed separately, including supporting details, which may involve a definition, examples, or traits.

To help you visualize the categories and supporting details, you can use a line diagram.

Line Diagram

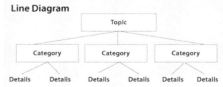

Practice Use these strategies for your next classification reading assignment. Afterward, discuss your work with a classmate.

LO3 Reading and Reacting to a Professional Paragraph

Read Read the following classification paragraph from *Psychology: A Journey*, a psychology college textbook written by Dennis Coon and John O. Mitterer. The paragraph classifies different types of parental discipline. Remember to use the reading process to help you complete your reading.

The Reading Process

Prereading Rereading

Reading Reflecting

About the Authors

Dennis Coon is an author, instructor, and doctor of psychology. He joined with John O. Mitterer, a doctor of cognitive psychology and an instructor at Brock University, in Ontario, Canada, to author *Psychology: A Journey*.

Effective Discipline

    Parents typically discipline children in one of three ways. Power *1* assertion refers to physical punishment or a show of force, such as taking away toys or privileges. As an alternative, some parents use withdrawal of love (withholding affection) by refusing to speak to a child, threatening to leave, rejecting the child, or otherwise acting as if the child is temporarily *5* unlovable. Management techniques combine praise, recognition, approval, rules, reasoning, and the like to encourage desirable behavior. Each of these approaches can control a child's behavior, but their side effects differ considerably.

"Effective Discipline" from COON/MITTERER. *Psychology: A Journey*, 4E. © 2011 Wadsworth, a part of Cengage Learning, Inc.

React Answer the following questions about the paragraph "Effective Discipline." Then discuss your responses with your classmates.

1. What is the main idea of this paragraph?

_____

2. What are the three main parts of this classification? Consider using a line diagram to identify them.

_____

3. How do the writers describe each category?

_____

4. What questions if any, do you still have about the topic?

_____

at Classification

Consider the Factors for Classifying

Identifying the factors for classifying will help you understand and evaluate classification paragraphs. The writer of the paragraph on page 121, for example, considers factors such as *color, ingredients,* and *taste* to break the topic of mustard into separate categories.

Here are three tips for identifying classification factors.

1. **Read the text multiple times.** After you read through the entire paragraph, carefully reread the body sentences, where the author most often describes the categories.

NOTE: In shorter pieces of writing, like paragraphs, a writer may use only one classification factor.

2. **Graph the main parts.** Use a line diagram to identify and display the main parts of the classification paragraph. This will help you identify the factor(s) behind the classification.

Line Diagram

3. **Look for a common factor(s).** Study the line diagram, especially the details for each category. Ask yourself what they have in common. The common factor in the paragraph on the previous page is the *actions* parents use to discipline their children.

SPECIAL NOTE: Discuss the paragraph with a classmate if you have trouble identifying the common factor or factors. (It may be that the writer didn't effectively think through his or her classification.)

Consider the Audience and Purpose

To judge the quality of a classification text, consider its audience and purpose. The audience for "Effective Discipline" is students because it comes from a college textbook. As such, its purpose is to inform. The audience for the paragraph about mustard on page 121 is much more general, and its purpose is to attract and inform readers interested in food-related topics. A strong classification paragraph should effectively inform its audience.

Vocabulary

audience
the intended readers of a written text

purpose
an author's reason for writing

LO4 Reading and Reacting to a Student Paragraph

Read   Read the following paragraph that classifies types of solar energy. Use the reading process to help you complete your reading.

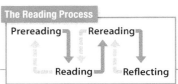

Plugging into Sunlight

With fossil fuels running out, people are discovering more and more   *1*
ways to use the free energy of the sun. The simplest form of solar energy
is solar lighting, which means designing buildings to take advantage of
natural light. A more advanced form is solar heating, or gathering the
sun's warmth and using it to heat a building. A third use of solar energy   *5*
is solar cooking. Box cookers are insulated boxes with clear tops, and
parabolic cookers use solar rays to boil water or cook food. A fourth use of
solar energy provides drinkable water to millions of people. Solar water
treatment devices can turn salt water into freshwater and can disinfect
water using the sun's rays. Finally, photovoltaic cells convert sunlight into   *10*
electrical energy, which can power household devices and even electrical
vehicles. Or course, the oldest type of solar power was not invented by
people but by plants. Photosynthesis turns sunlight, water, and minerals
into food for plants and the whole world!

React   Answer the questions below about the paragraph "Plugging into Sunlight." Then discuss your responses with your classmates.

1. What is the main idea of this paragraph?

   _____

2. How many categories are included in this classification?

   _____

3. Does the writer describe or explain each category? Give an example.

   _____

4. What is the intended purpose of this paragraph—to entertain, to inform, to persuade?

   _____

5. What questions, if any, do you still have about the topic?

   _____

Vocabulary

parabolic
curve-shaped

photovoltaic
capable of producing voltage

A CLOSER LOOK at Analyzing the Categories

As you evaluate the paragraph on the preceding page, pay special attention to the categories of solar energy. In effective classification writing, the categories, or subgroups, exhibit the following three qualities.

Categories should be . . .

- **exclusive,** meaning that one category does not overlap with other categories.
- **consistent,** meaning categories share the same classification factors.
- **equal,** meaning categories are described with a similar number of details.

Evaluate Analyze the categories by answering these three questions about them.

1. How does the writer break down the topic into categories?

   _____

   _____

2. How does the writer describe each category?

   _____

   _____

3. Are the categories equal? Explain.

   _____

   _____

Considering the Factors

As you analyze the categories in a classification, consider the common factor or factors used to make the categories.

Identify On your own or with a classmate, identify the common factor or factors used to create the classification on the previous page.

OLJ Studio, 2011 / Used under license from Shutterstock.com

LO5 Practicing Reading Skills

In a classification paragraph or essay, the author may provide examples of a category without specifically defining the category, or may provide a specific definition without examples. In either case, you must make inferences as you read.

Inferring Category Definitions

In the "Effective Discipline" paragraph, the authors sometimes provide examples of a category without a specific definition. As a reader, you must infer the definitions from the examples:

- **"Power assertion** refers to physical punishment or a show of force."
  (**Inferred definition:** Power assertion uses the parent's greater physical strength or authority to punish bad behavior.)
- **"Management techniques** combine praise, recognition, approval, rules . . ."
  (**Inferred definition:** Management techniques shape positive behaviors using positive reinforcement.)

Infer From each category and set of examples below, infer a specific category description.
1. Marine mammals include polar bears, walruses, sea lions, and sea otters.
2. Primates include lemurs, monkeys, baboons, great apes, and human beings.
3. Marsupial animals include kangaroos, opossums, koalas, and sugar gliders.

Inferring Examples

In the "Plugging into Sunlight" paragraph, the author sometimes provides definitions of categories without specific examples. As a reader, you must infer the examples:

- **"Solar lighting** . . . means designing buildings to take advantage of natural light."
  (**Inferred examples:** Windows, skylights, and open floor plans provide solar lighting.)
- **"Solar heating** . . . [is] gathering the sun's warmth and using it to heat a building.)
  (**Inferred examples:** Water-filled solar collectors connected to radiators would be an example of solar heating.)

Infer From each category and definition, infer examples that would fit in the category.
1. Reptiles are cold-blooded animals that lay eggs and have scaly skin.
2. Amphibians are cold-blooded animals that often change from water- to air-breathing forms.

Writing

Writing a classification paragraph is a manageable assignment if you choose a topic that can easily be broken down into categories. The instructions below will help you discover a good topic and lead you through the writing process.

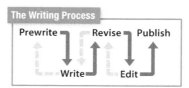

The Writing Process

Prewrite → Revise → Publish

Write → Edit

LO6 Planning a Classification Paragraph

You will explore the categories of a topic of your choice. To begin, choose four subject areas that interest you from the following list of the essentials of life.

Essentials of Life

food	intelligence	resources
clothing	personality	energy
shelter	senses	money
education	emotions	government
work	goals	laws
entertainment	health	rights
recreation	environment	science
religion	plants	measurement
family	animals	machines
friends	land	tools
community	literature	agriculture
communication	arts	business

1. **Subject area:** _____

2. **Subject area:** _____

3. **Subject area:** _____

4. **Subject area:** _____

ifong, 2011 / Used under license from Shutterstock.com

Select Review the subjects that you have listed above. Select one that could lead to classification topics. Then identify possible topics as is done below. Circle the topic that seems most promising.

Subject area: _government_

Topics: _types of political systems, types of U.S. political parties, types of monarchies, levels of state government_

Researching Your Topic

After you choose a topic, you may need to do some research to learn more about it before you identify your categories. (Three or five is a good number for a classification paragraph.) Internet sites, reference books, and textbooks are good places to start. Remember, the categories must be exclusive, consistent, and equal.

Identify Using a graphic organizer like the one below, list three to five categories for your topic. In the second column, describe each category. Make sure the description clarifies how the category is different from the rest.

INSIGHT

Remember that you will need an equal amount of detail to describe the categories.

Categories or types of _____	Description Details

Creating Your Topic Sentence

Your topic sentence should name your topic and introduce the categories you will describe in your paragraph. Use the following formula to create this sentence.

The specific topic	**+**	an introduction to the categories	**=**	an effective topic sentence.
sleeping disorders		four basic types of disorders		Experts identify four basic types of sleeping disorders.

Create Write a topic sentence for your paragraph using the formula above. If necessary, write two or three versions until your topic sentence says what you want it to say.

LO7 Writing the First Draft

After you are done planning, you are ready to write the first draft of your paragraph. Provided below is another sample classification paragraph.

Read Read the paragraph, noting how the writer classified the topic, mustard, into four distinct subgroups.

My Condiments to the Chef

Topic Sentence	When most Americans talk about mustard, they mean *1*
	a type of bright-yellow goo that the rest of the world hardly
Category 1	recognizes. Actually there are four basic types of mustard.
	Yellow mustard is the most common in America, made from
	finely ground mustard seeds, vinegar, and a bright yellow *5*
	coloring called turmeric. Yellow mustard is mild and is a
Category 2	common seasoning on hot dogs. For a spicier type of mustard,
	people enjoy brown mustard, which is made from coarse-
	ground mustard seeds and looks yellow and brown. For an
Category 3	even stronger flavor, mustard lovers turn to the famous *10*
	mustard called Dijon, named after the French city where it
	was first processed. Dijon mustard is finely ground and is
Category 4	usually mixed with wine instead of vinegar. Finally, there
	are many hybrid mustards categorized as specialty mustards,
Closing Sentence	including everything from honey to jalapeños. When it comes *15*
	to taste, there's a mustard for just about everybody.

Consider the Craft

1. What do you like best about this paragraph?

2. What are two of your favorite details?

3. What is the reason behind the arrangement of the categories?

Harris Shiffman, 2011 / Used under license from Shutterstock.com

The Working Parts of a Paragraph

A paragraph consists of three main parts, each of which has a special function. The information that follows explains each part.

Paragraph Outline

Topic Sentence: The topic sentence introduces the subject and refers to the types or categories.

Body Sentences: The body sentences name and describe each category, and, if possible, provide examples.

Closing Sentence: The closing sentence leaves the reader with an interesting final thought.

Drafting Tips

When you write a classification, your goal is to share information in a clear, organized manner. To that end, consider the following tips as you write your first draft.

- **To make your beginning clear,** make sure that your topic sentence identifies your topic and introduces your categories.
- **To help your readers follow your classification,** decide on an effective and consistent (similar) way to introduce each category. Also decide on a logical arrangement of the categories.
- **To make sure that your writing has balance,** provide an equal number of details for each category.
- **To emphasize your purpose,** use language that reflects your goal—to inform, to entertain, and so on.

INSIGHT

Remember that a paragraph is a limited unit of writing, so restrict yourself to just a few supporting details for each category. (If you have a lot to say about each category, perhaps you should develop a classification essay.)

Write Develop your first draft using the information on this page and your planning on LO5 and LO6 as a guide.

LO8 Revising the Writing

Start the revising process by reading your first draft two or three times to get a feel for your work so far. Then have one of your classmates read and react to your work using a response sheet as a guide.

Using Transitions

Transition words and phrases can help you identify each type or category and rank them, perhaps by age, importance, rarity, and so on.

One type	The simplest	The most common	The earliest
A second	A more complex	A less common	A later
A third	An advanced	A rare	A recent
The last	The most complex	A very rare	The newest

Revising in Action

Read aloud the unrevised and then revised version of the following excerpt. Note how the transition words identify and rank the categories.

The simplest form of solar energy is
. . . people are discovering more and more ways to use the free energy of the
, which
sun. Solar lighting means designing buildings to take advantage of natural
A more advanced form is
light. Solar heating is gathering the sun's warmth and using it to heat a *; or*
A third use of solar energy is
building. Solar cooking is a new reality for many. Box cookers are insulated

boxes with clear tops, and parabolic cookers use solar rays to boil water or cook

food. . . .

Revise   Improve your writing, using the following checklist and your classmate's comments on the response sheet. Continue working until you can check off each item in the list.

Ideas
☐ 1. Do I identify my subject?
☐ 2. Do I name and describe the types or categories?

Organization
☐ 3. Do I have an effective topic sentence, body sentences, and a closing sentence?
☐ 4. Do I use transition words and phrases to identify and rank the types?

Voice
☐ 5. Does my voice sound knowledgeable and interested?

LO9 Editing the Writing

Subjects and verbs must agree in number. These two pages cover basic subject-verb agreement and agreement with compound subjects.

Basic Subject-Verb Agreement

A singular subject takes a singular verb, and a plural subject takes a plural verb:

One percussion instrument is the drums.
    singular subject singular verb

Two percussion instruments are drums and cymbals
    plural subject   plural verb

In order to identify the actual subject, disregard any words that come between the subject and verb, such as words in a prepositional phrase:

One of the types of instruments is percussion.
singular subject   singular verb

(The words *types* and *instruments* are not subjects; both are objects of the prepositions.)

Agreement Practice Correct the following sentences so that the subjects and verbs agree. The first sentence has been done for you.

1. Percussion instruments ~~makes~~ make a noise by striking something.
2. Pianos, by that definition, is percussion instruments.
3. The hammers inside a piano strikes the strings to make a sound.
4. Of course, drums is also a type of percussion.
5. The drumsticks, made of hardwood, hits the skin of the drumhead to create the sound.
6. Another of the instrument types are winds.
7. This family of instruments include flutes, clarinets, and even brass.
8. Wind produce the sound in these instruments.

Apply Read your classification paragraph, making sure that your subjects and verbs agree.

Agreement with Compound Subjects

A compound subject is made of two or more subjects joined by *and* or *or*. When the subjects are joined by *and,* they are plural and require a plural verb:

A baritone and a trombone play the same range.

        plural subject   plural verb

When the subjects are joined by *or,* the verb must match the number of the last subject:

Either the woodwinds or the trumpet plays the main theme.

           singular subject singular verb

Either the trumpet or the woodwinds play the main theme.

          plural subject   plural verb

Agreement Practice   Correct the following sentences so that the subjects and verbs agree. The first sentence has been done for you.

1. Stringed instruments and their players fills out *(fill out)* the orchestra.

2. Violins and violas plays the higher notes.

3. A cello or bass handle the lower notes.

4. The horsehair bow and the string makes the sound.

5. Either music or screeches emerges depending on the player's talent.

6. A soloist or all the violins carries the melody.

7. The conductor or the concertmaster indicate when to bow.

8. The concertmaster and the strings sits closest to the audience.

Write   Write the end of each sentence, matching the verb to the compound subject.

1. The director and the orchestra _____

2. The orchestra or the director _____

Apply   Read your classification paragraph, making sure that your compound subjects agree with their verbs.

Marking a Paragraph

The model that follows has a number of errors.

Editing Practice   Correct the following paragraph, using the correction marks below. One correction has been done for you.

A Question of Taste

All the flavors that a person can taste ~~is~~ *are* made up of a few basic taste   *1*
sensations. In the Western world, people are used to thinking about four
tastes: salty, sweet, sour, and bitter The salty taste come from substances
that include sodium, such as snacks like potato chips or pretzels. The sweet
sensation comes from sugars, whether in processed foods like sweetened   *5*
cereals or naturally occurring in fruit or honey. Sour tastes come from
acidic foods (pH below 7) such as lemons and grapefruit, and bitter tastes
come from alkaline foods (pH above 7) such as coffee or dark chocolate. But
in the world Eastern, two other taste sensations are recognized. A savory
taste (umami) comes from amino acids, which are a basic part of meats   *10*
and proteins. And a spicy taste (piquancy) comes from substances like
the capsaicin in hot peppers. Given the savory and spicy nature of Indian,
Thai, chinese, and other Eastern foods, it's no wonder that these tastes are
recognized. With all the senses to consider chefs can make every dish a
unique work of art.   *15*

Correction Marks

⌐	delete	⌃	add comma	⌃ *word*	add word
d̲	capitalize	?	add question	⊙	add period
D̲	lowercase	⌃	mark	⌒	spelling
⌃	insert	⌄	insert an apostrophe	⌐⌐	switch

INSIGHT

In academic writing, the pronouns *I* and *you* have special rules for subject-verb agreement:

- *I* takes the verb *am* instead of *is*: I *am* (**not** I *is*).
- *I* also takes plural action verbs: I *sit* (**not** I *sits*).
- *You* always takes a plural verb: You *are*; you *sit* (**not** You *is*; you *sits*).

Correcting Your Paragraph

Now it's time to correct your own paragraph.

Apply   Create a clean copy of your revised paragraph and use the following checklist to check for errors. Continue working until you can check off each item in the list.

Words

- [ ] 1. Have I used specific nouns and verbs?
- [ ] 2. Have I used more action verbs than "be" verbs?

Sentences

- [ ] 3. Have I combined short choppy sentences?
- [ ] 4. Have I avoided shifts in sentences?
- [ ] 5. Have I avoided fragments and run-ons?

Conventions

- [ ] 6. Do I use correct verb forms (*he saw*, not *he seen*)?
- [ ] 7. Do my subjects and verbs agree (*she speaks*, not *she speak*)?
- [ ] 8. Have I used the right words (*their, there, they're*)?
- [ ] 9. Have I capitalized first words and proper nouns and adjectives?
- [ ] 10. Have I used commas after long introductory word groups?
- [ ] 11. Have I punctuated dialogue correctly?
- [ ] 12. Have I carefully checked my spelling?

Adding a Title

Make sure to add a title to your paragraph. Here are some simple strategies for coming up with a catchy one.

- Use a number:

  Four Types of Mustard

- Use an expression:

  A Question of Taste

- Think outside the box:

  Plugging into Sunlight

- Be clever:

  My Condiments to the Chef

Create   Prepare a clean final copy of your paragraph and proofread it.

"I find that different types of music are good for certain activities."
—Peter Steele

Review and Enrichment

You have been working with the classification paragraph. This section reviews and expands on that information by providing a classification essay to read and respond to. You will also be given a number of writing ideas to choose from and develop in a paragraph or an essay of your own. These activities will broaden your understanding of classification.

Prereading

One of the more famous classification systems is the Myers-Briggs Type Indicator, or as it is more commonly called, the Myers-Briggs test. This extensive questionnaire divides the topic "personality type" into 16 exclusive categories. This test was created during World War II as a means of placing women in specific wartime jobs based on personality type. Now, the Myers-Briggs test has become the most widely used tool for personality assessment. It is still used extensively for team building, marketing, and relationship counseling.

CONSIDER THE TRAITS

As you read the classification essay on the next page, focus first on the **ideas**—the topic that is being classified, the categories, and the details that support and explain each category. Then consider the **organization**—the way that the opening, middle, and closing parts are constructed. Also notice the authors' **voice**—their special way of speaking to the reader. And finally, ask yourself if these traits combine to produce a satisfying reading experience.

Explore   The Myers-Briggs test classifies people as either extroverted or introverted. Extroverts are outgoing, action-orientated people, while introverts are shy, thought-orientated people. Do you consider yourself an extrovert or an introvert? Write down your answer. Then ask a classmate how they perceive you—either as introverted or extroverted. Compare your answers.

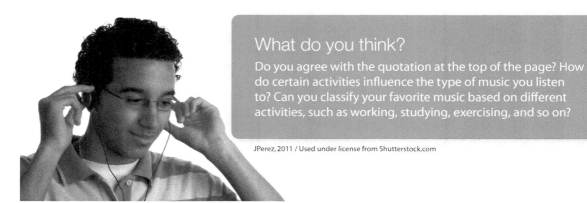

What do you think?

Do you agree with the quotation at the top of the page? How do certain activities influence the type of music you listen to? Can you classify your favorite music based on different activities, such as working, studying, exercising, and so on?

JPerez, 2011 / Used under license from Shutterstock.com

Reading and Reacting

Read This classification essay focuses on the four humors (liquids) that ruled western medical thought for over 2,000 years. Use the reading process to gain a full understanding of the reading.

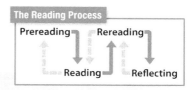

About the Author

Robert King is co-author of *Inquire: A Guide to 21st Century Learning* and two dozen novels.

The Humorous Humors

When we hear the word *humor*, we tend to think of a joke, but a person   *1*
in a *bad humor* is rarely suffering from a bad joke. The term *humor* used
in this way refers to its Greek origin, a word meaning "juice" or "sap." Way
back in 400 B.C., Hippocrates, the father of medicine, said that humans
were full of four basic types of sap—blood, yellow bile, black bile, and   *5*
phlegm. From that time until the mid-1800s, western medicine explained
and treated illness as an imbalance in these "humors."

The most recognizable humor is blood: "If you prick us do we not
bleed?" According to ancient doctors, this vital fluid came from the liver
and made a person red-cheeked and happy. For this reason, the word   *10*
sanguine meant both "bloody" and "happy." Blood was associated with
springtime, when young folks "got their blood up," becoming amorous and
foolhardy. In order to "bring down" all this hot, wet blood, doctors applied
cold, dry things. Given an extreme excess of blood, medieval physicians
solved the problem through bloodletting. As late as the American   *15*
Revolution, some army surgeons would let the blood from an ill soldier day
after day until the man recovered or died.

Another humor, yellow bile, did not apparently come from the liver
but from the gall bladder. This liquid somehow managed to be dry as well
as hot, making it associated with fire. As such, yellow bile produced a   *20*
fiery temper, with angry outbursts and roars of rage—making the person
choleric. Imbalances of this humor caused wars and riots—which spread
during the summer months until someone dowsed the sufferer with a
bucket of cold water. Excessive yellow bile could be drawn out as a vapor
through the application of large suction cups much like modern bathroom   *25*
plungers. The giant hickeys that remained, however, often made the
patient even angrier.

Black bile came from the spleen, which is why people often were
offended by someone's spleen (ill will). The Greek words for black bile,

melon chole, give us our modern word *melancholy*—which is depression. 30
Black bile was cold and dry, the opposite of blood, so it naturally led to
a condition opposite of happiness: moroseness. Autumn brought on the
imbalance of melancholy, with trees turning to bare sticks against a
sky that was losing birds and sun, both. Black bile was also associated
with earth, the dust to which we all return. Yes, sad stuff. Still, unlike 35
sanguine or choleric people—who were bled or dowsed back to health—the
melancholic improved through hot, wet things such as warm brandy and
steaming baths. Not surprisingly, many Romantic poets enjoyed being
melancholy.

The last humor revealed itself repeatedly in handkerchiefs throughout 40
time—the cold, wet stuff called phlegm. According to medieval doctors,
an excess of phlegm caused colds and made a person slow and dull—or
phlegmatic. Cold, wet winter was the season for this ailment. Associated
with water, phlegm forever dripped and ran. To get rid of excess phlegm,
people not only blew their noses but also used various medicines to purge 45
themselves. In some senses, the phlegmatic person had the least appeal of
any temperament type, being a slothful snuffler who seemed quite capable
of passing the imbalance to anyone within sneezing distance.

All these humors are somewhat humorous to modern day readers. Lest
we be too quick to judge our medical forebears, thought, let's remember 50
that the human body is a complex thing. The liver does seem to be the
source of a lot of blood, especially when you stab someone there. Consider,
too, that though people were fond of stabbing each other, they were
forbidden to take a look inside the dead man afterward—a hobby that da
Vinci later popularized. And let's not be too high and mighty about our 55
own medical knowledge. Most modern people don't even realize they have a
spleen let alone know what to do with it. Many modern people are on some
form of Prozac, though nobody knows why it works. Yes, we've come a long
way since the theory of the humors, but it is likely that in a hundred years,
our own medical knowledge will seem equally barbarous and humorous. 60

Vocabulary

humor
a juice or liquid; a mood or
temperament

phlegm
snot

sanguine
bloody or happy

amorous
in love (amore)

foolhardy
reckless, stupidly unafraid

bloodletting
the practice of draining
blood from a person to
improve health

choleric
furious, given to snapping
in anger

hickeys
a red welt caused by
suction against the skin

spleen
an organ beneath the
stomach, filters blood; ill will

moroseness
deep sadness

phlegmatic
sluggish and sleepy

forebears
those who went before

barbarous
uncivilized, savage

React Answer the following questions about the classification essay. Share your responses with your classmates.

1. What four categories does the author describe?

   _____

2. What details do you find most interesting, surprising, or disturbing?

   _____

3. What tone does the author use in describing these categories? What evidence from the text shows the author's tone?

   _____

4. Often the author introduces terms and defines them in context—*humor, sanguine, choleric*. Write two other unfamiliar terms that the author introduces and tell what context clues helped you understand them.

   _____

5. In the final paragraph, the author turns a critical eye on modern medicine. What two facts does he mention to show that we aren't as advanced as we might think? How does his final sentence connect to the real world?

   _____

6. How would you rate this classification essay and why?

   Weak ★ ★ ★ ★ ★ Strong

   _____

Drawing Inferences

An *inference* is a logical conclusion that you draw from evidence in the text. To practice drawing inferences, answer the following questions about the essay you just read. Afterward, share your responses with your classmates.

1. What inferences can you draw from the line "Not surprisingly, many Romantic poets enjoyed their melancholy"?

2. Read the following statement: "Consider, too, that though people were fond of stabbing each other, they were forbidden to take a look inside the dead man afterward—a hobby that da Vinci later popularized." Judging from this statement, infer the author's opinion about violence against living people and dissection of dead people.

Writing

Write a classification paragraph or classification essay following the guidelines on the next two pages. Check with your instructor about any specific requirements that she or he may have. And be sure to use the writing process to help you do your best work.

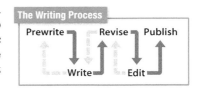

Prewriting

Choose one of the following or another appropriate writing idea for your classification writing.

Writing Ideas

1. Write about a topic that you identified in the planning activity on page 119.

2. Choose a topic based on one of your favorite interests (sports cars, clothing design, reality television, theater, and so on).

3. Write a classification based on your observations at a public place (park, library, bus stop, and so on).

4. Write a classification of attitudes toward politics, religion, or morality.

5. Write a classification about the wildlife or plant life in your neighborhood.

6. Write a classification of the ways to access news.

7. Write a classification based on one of the photographs in this book.

When planning . . .

Refer to LO5 and LO6 in this chapter to help you with your prewriting and planning. Also use the tips that follow.

- Choose a topic that you understand well or can easily learn about.
- If necessary, research your topic to find all the major categories or parts.
- Collect similar types of details for each category.
- Decide on a logical way to order your categories.
- Review the classification writing examples in this chapter to see how they are developed.

Writing and Revising

Use the tips that follow and the information in LO7 and LO8 to help you with your drafting and revising.

When writing . . .

- Include an opening, a middle, and a closing part in your classification writing. Each part has a specific role.
- Follow your planning notes, but also consider new ideas as they come to mind.
- Introduce each new category in the same basic way.
- Use transitions to shift from one category to the next.

When revising . . .

- Check that the order of your categories is logical and clear.
- Make sure the categories are exclusive, consistent, and equal.
- Decide if your classification will interest the reader. If not, improve your essay by adding new details, trying a different opening or closing strategy, and so on.
- Ask a trusted peer to react to your classification.

Editing

Refer to the checklist in LO9 when you are ready to edit your classification for style and correctness.

Carlos E. Santa Maria, 2011 / Used under license from Shutterstock.com

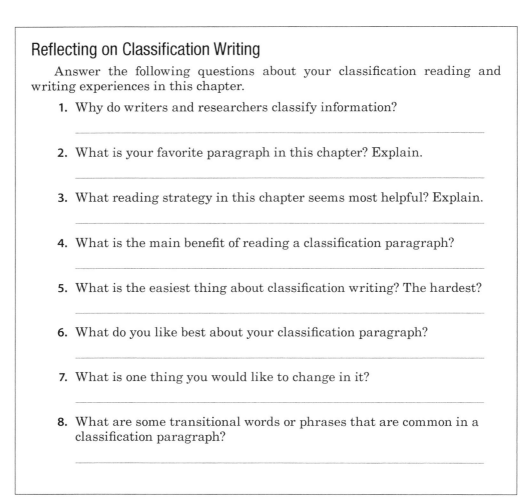

Reflecting on Classification Writing

Answer the following questions about your classification reading and writing experiences in this chapter.

1. Why do writers and researchers classify information?

2. What is your favorite paragraph in this chapter? Explain.

3. What reading strategy in this chapter seems most helpful? Explain.

4. What is the main benefit of reading a classification paragraph?

5. What is the easiest thing about classification writing? The hardest?

6. What do you like best about your classification paragraph?

7. What is one thing you would like to change in it?

8. What are some transitional words or phrases that are common in a classification paragraph?

Key Terms to Remember

When you read and write classification writing, it's important to understand the following terms.

- **Classification**—the act of arranging or organizing according to categories, or subgroups
- **Categories**—specifically defined divisions; general types or classes of ideas
- **Line diagram**—a graphic organizer that can be used to show main categories and supporting details
- **Classification factors**—the qualities the writer uses to divide a topic into categories

7

Cause-Effect

Flip a switch; a light comes on. The relationship is obvious.

Make a joke; a friend laughs. The reason may be less obvious. *Was it the joke itself or your delivery? Is your friend just being polite or reacting to your attempt at humor?*

These are simple examples of cause-effect relationships. More complex examples include the causes and effects of a disease, the causes and effects of interest rates on consumer spending, and the causes and effects of solar flares.

This chapter deals with the cause-effect form of thinking and writing. First, you will learn about the basics related to this form. Then you will read and react to both a professional and a student cause-effect paragraph before writing one of your own. The strategies you learn in this chapter will apply to cause-effect assignments in all of your classes.

Learning Outcomes

LO1 Understand cause-effect.

LO2 Learn about reading strategies.

LO3 Read and react to a professional paragraph.

LO4 Read and react to a student paragraph.

LO5 Practice reading skills.

LO6 Plan a cause-effect paragraph.

LO7 Write the first draft.

LO8 Revise the writing.

LO9 Edit the writing.

What do you think?

Explain what the quotation above means to you. Share your thoughts with a classmate.

Vladislav Gajic, 2011 / Used under license from Shutterstock.com

LO1 Understanding Cause-Effect

In a chemistry class, you learn that combining certain chemicals results in a particular reaction. "Results in" is another way of saying "causes an effect." A history text may explain the reasons behind a particular event, and the consequences of that event. "Reasons" is another way of saying "causes," and "consequences" another way of saying "effects."

> " . . . no thought or action is without its effects, present or ultimate, seen or unseen, felt or unfelt."
> —Norman Cousins

These two examples indicate how central cause-effect analysis is in your classes. The body of knowledge in all disciplines is expanded largely by seeking to discover how things work, and that means finding out what causes what. This knowledge is then passed along by explaining the cause-effect relationship related to new situations and circumstances. Understanding this relationship can be more beneficial than memorizing facts.

Much of your college reading will involve cause-effect analysis. Often, the word "cause" or "effect" (or a similar term) will be mentioned in the text itself. Even if these words aren't used, you can recognize a cause-effect explanation by its two-part structure. The explanation will either introduce various causes and then conclude with the main effect, or it will begin with a single cause and then explain its many effects. In a few cases, cause-effect writing may begin with multiple causes and then discuss their many effects. Keep this two-part structure in mind as you read the cause-effect paragraphs in this chapter.

INSIGHT

Finding cause-effect relationships is a way of analyzing a topic, as are classifying and comparing. Each type of analysis requires that you examine a topic closely, consider it deeply, and refine your understanding of it in the process.

Identify Name two or three recent news stories that explain a cause-effect relationship. Provide a one- or two-sentence summary of each example. Share your summaries with your classmates.

1. _____

   _____

2. _____

   _____

3. _____

   _____

Reading

Reading cause-effect paragraphs will introduce you to one of the more common tasks of college assignments—finding the reasons and results resting beneath the surface of complex topics.

LO2 Learning About Reading Strategies

These two strategies—studying the topic sentence and using a cause-effect organizer—will help you read cause-effect texts.

Strategy 1: Studying the Topic Sentence

By definition, a topic sentence introduces the reader to the topic of the paragraph and the key part of it that will be emphasized. So if you study the topic sentence in most cause-effect paragraphs, you should be able to learn a lot about the information that will follow. Here's an example:

Topic sentence: Though the fighting ceased in 1953, the effects of the Korean War are still felt today.

Discussion: The topic of the paragraph is the Korean War. As the topic sentence states, the paragraph will focus on the remaining effects of the war. The causes will not be a major emphasis.

Remember that some paragraphs will not begin with a clearly defined topic sentence. So this strategy won't work for all cause-effect paragraphs.

Strategy 2: Using a Cause-Effect Organizer

Part of understanding a cause-effect paragraph is keeping track of the important details. Completing a cause-effect organizer will help you do so.

Subject
Causes (Because of . . .)	Effects (. . . these conditions resulted.)
-	-
-	-
-	-

LO3 Reading and Reacting to a Professional Paragraph

Read This cause-effect paragraph comes from a science textbook called *Living in the Environment.* It explores the serious problem of the burning of tropical forests. Remember to use the reading process to help you gain a full understanding of the text.

The Reading Process

Prereading ⟶ Rereading

Reading ⟶ Reflecting

Burning Tropical Forests and Climate Change

The burning of tropical forests releases CO_2 into the atmosphere. Rising concentration of this gas can help warm the atmosphere, which is projected to change the global climate during this century. Scientists estimate that tropical forest fires account for at least 17 percent of all human-created greenhouse gas emissions, and that each year they emit twice as much CO_2 as all of the world's cars and trucks emit. The large-scale burning of the Amazon rain forest accounts for 75 percent of all Brazil's greenhouse gas emissions, making Brazil the world's fourth largest emitter of such gases, according to the National Inventory of Greenhouse Gases. And with these forests gone, even if savannah or second-growth forests replace them, far less CO_2 will be absorbed for photosynthesis, resulting in even more atmospheric warming.

1

5

10

"Burning Tropical Rainforests and Climate Change" from MILLER. *Living in the Environment,* 17E. © 2012 Brooks/Cole, a part of Cengage Learning, Inc.

React Answer the following questions about the paragraph. Then discuss your responses with your classmates.

1. What is the main idea of this paragraph?

   _____

2. Does the paragraph focus more attention on causes or effects? Consider using a cause-effect organizer to help you answer this question.

   _____

3. What are two things that you learned in this paragraph?

   _____

4. What questions do you still have about the topic?

   _____

A CLOSER LOOK   at Cause-Effect

Considering the Evidence

People used to think that ice floats because it's thin. After all, needles and razor blades float, and they're made of metal, which is heavier than water. Then someone demonstrated that when you push a needle, a razor blade, and a thin piece of ice to the bottom of a basin of water, the ice will return to the top while the other two remain at the bottom.

This demonstration shows how important it is to be sure about a cause-effect relationship. Just because something seems to cause something else, doesn't mean it actually does.

Evaluate   When studying the causes and effects in a paragraph, always judge the value of the evidence. It's important to know if the causes and effects seem reliable and reasonable.

Considering the Purpose

Sometimes writers use cause-effect reasoning to convince you to take an action. In that case, ask yourself the following questions.

1. What does the author hope to gain by convincing me of this cause-effect relationship?
2. What is the author's background related to the subject?
3. What other explanations might there be?
4. What evidence might be missing?

INSIGHT ───────────────────────────────

Never reject a point of view just because it doesn't match up to your own thinking. Remember, people used to quite reasonably believe that ice floats because it's thin. If they hadn't been prepared to entertain a better explanation, we might still be puzzled by ice *cubes,* which float despite being shaped like chunky rocks.

Review   Reread the paragraph on the previous page. Then discuss it with your classmates using the "purpose" questions above as a guide.

LO4 Reading and Reacting to a Student Paragraph

Read   Read the following cause-effect paragraph about the history of family structure in the United States. Remember to use the steps in the reading process to help you gain a full understanding of the text.

The Reading Process

Prereading ⟶ Rereading

⟶ Reading ⟶ Reflecting

The Changing Family

Throughout U.S. history, the way that people make a living has   *1*
effected the family unit. Early on, much of the country consisted of
family farms clustered around small towns and villages. The families
on these farms were often multigenerational, with parents, children,
and grandparents all living under the same roof. With the rise of   *5*
industrialism, however, family farms gave way to large agribusinesses,
and much of the rural population moved to cities to work in factories
and offices. The "nuclear family" was born, consisting of father, mother,
and two or three children. When the children of these families reached
working age, they moved out to start their own nuclear families. Today,   *10*
with industrialism on the decline and the Information Age redefining
work, the United States is experiencing another shift in the family. Many
adult children are remaining at home. In some cases, parents, children,
and grandparents are again living together. In others, single parents or
same-sex couples are raising children, often with the help of siblings or   *15*
friends. Even single people find themselves rooming together in larger
groups. With all these changes, the "alternative family" concept is quickly
becoming a norm.

React   Answer the following questions about the paragraph. Then discuss your answers with your classmates.

1. What is the main idea of this paragraph? _____

2. What causes and effects are included? Consider using a cause-effect organizer to help you answer this question. _____

3. What are two things that you learned in this paragraph?

_____

4. How would you rate this paragraph and why?

   Weak ★ ★ ★ ★ ★ Strong

_____

A CLOSER LOOK   at Considering the Evidence and Purpose

As you saw in LO3, cause-effect relationships are not always as simple as they might at first seem. It is important when reading to recognize the link between cause and effect and to make sure it is a reasonable one.

Identify Which of the following cause-effect patterns comes closest to the organization of the paragraph on the previous page?

1. Cause-Focused

| Topic Sentence |
| Causes |
| Effects |
| Closing Sentence |

2. Effect-Focused

| Topic Sentence |
| Causes |
| Effects |
| Closing Sentence |

3. Balanced

| Topic Sentence |
| Causes |
| Effects |
| Closing Sentence |

Consider How does the topic sentence help you learn from this paragraph?

_____

_____

What purpose might the writer have had for explaining this cause-effect relationship?

_____

_____

What other reasons could there be for changes in the family unit?

_____

_____

What else would you like to know about the subject?

_____

_____

Dasha Rusanenko, 2011 / Used under license from Shutterstock.com

LO5 Practicing Reading Skills

Often in a cause-effect paragraph, you run into unfamiliar terms and you have to make sure that the causes described are really causes. This page will help.

Vocabulary: Word Parts and New Sentences

As you read cause-effect paragraphs, you may run into unfamiliar terms. Word parts can help you understand these terms, and using these terms in new sentences can cement the definitions in your mind. The example below shows how word parts and new sentences can help define the "autonomic" nervous system.

auto (self)   +   **nomos (law)**   +   **ic (relating to)**
autonomic is "related to ruling itself"

The autonomic nervous system is the part of the brain that controls body functions such as breathing and heartbeat without requiring conscious effort.

Define Explore the word parts of the following examples by using the list of prefixes, suffixes, and roots in Appendix (as well as your dictionary). Then write a definition for each word and use the word in a sentence.

1. redefine   4. agribusiness
   _____   _____

2. emitter   5. concentration
   _____   _____

3. multigenerational   6. alternative
   _____   _____

Critical Thinking: Separating Causation and Correlation

You need to be able to tell the difference between correlation and causation. Correlation means that two things may occur together but have different causes. For example, you could say, "Every time my favorite show comes on, the tornado siren sounds." The favorite show doesn't set off the tornado siren. The favorite show airs Saturdays at noon, the same time when the city tests its tornado siren. The two are correlated, but there is no causation.

Check Indicate whether you think each situation represents correlation or causation. Explain your answers.
1. Whenever I brush my teeth, the meteorologist starts the weather report.
2. Whenever I forget to brush my teeth, my breath stinks.
3. I called my mother, and she started sneezing.
4. I showed my new cat to my mother, and she started sneezing.
5. Kennedy's secretary was Lincoln, and Lincoln's secretary was Kennedy.
6. Lee Harvey Oswald shot President Kennedy.
7. John Wilkes Booth shot President Lincoln.
8. John Wilkes Booth and Lee Harvey Oswald each had three names.

Writing

Beginning on this page, you will plan and write a cause-effect paragraph about a topic of your choice. Use the writing process to help you produce your best work.

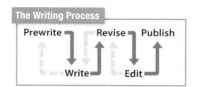

LO6 Planning a Cause-Effect Paragraph

To begin, you must choose a topic that both interests you and involves a cause-effect relationship.

Selecting a Topic

Think about the classes you are currently taking. What cause-effect ideas have you encountered in your studies? Also consider topics derived from the following categories.

- Family Life
- Politics
- Society

- Environment
- Entertainment
- Workplace

Select List four cause-effect topics that interest you. Then circle the one you would like to write about.

> 1. Benefits of vegetarianism
> 2. Why people save things
> 3. Results of the 2009 jet landing on the Hudson River
> 4. How superhero movies affect our culture

Researching the Causes and Effects

Once you have selected a topic, research the causes and effects involved and list them for further use.

Identify Use a cause-effect organizer to list possible causes and effects of your topic.

Subject	
Causes	Effects
-	-
-	-
-	-

Gathering and Evaluating Details

Effective cause-effect writing includes strong evidence. This means you must use trustworthy sources of information. Avoid sources that seems to approach your topic in a questionable way. Watch for sources that include the following types of information.

■ **Broad generalization:** A statement that is based on too little evidence or allows no exceptions

> Video games are the reason that today's youth have a shorter attention span.
> *(This claim ignores the possibility of other reasons.)*

■ **Straw man:** A claim that exaggerates or misinterprets an opponent's position

> If you cause deforestation, you hate the planet.

■ **False cause:** A claim that confuses sequence with causation (If A comes before B, A must have caused B.)

> Since that new skate park opened, vandalism among young people has increased.
> *(The two factors may have no real connection.)*

Creating Your Topic Sentence

Your topic sentence should name your topic and identify what you plan on emphasizing about it. Use the following formula.

The topic		the emphasis		an effective topic sentence.
U.S. Airways Flight 1549	**+**	struck a flock of geese, causing the plane to lose power in both its engines	**=**	In January 2009, U.S. Airways Flight 1549 struck a flock of geese, causing the plane to lose power in both its engines.

Create   Write your own topic sentence, following the example above.

The topic		the emphasis		an effective topic sentence.
	+		**=**	

LO7 Writing the First Draft

Your first draft is a first attempt to get your thoughts on paper in a reasonable order. It doesn't have to be perfect. You'll have time to polish it later.

Read Carefully read the following cause-effect paragraph about the emergency landing of Flight 1549.

Emergency Landing

Topic Sentence

In January 2009, U.S. Airways Flight 1549 struck a flock *1*
of geese, causing the plane to lose power in both its engines.
The situation forced pilot Chesley "Sully" Sullenberger to
perform an emergency landing on the Hudson River outside
of New York City. Not only did he land safely, but all 150   *5*
passengers survived without a single serious injury. The event
had many meaningful effects. Massive media coverage of the
landing made "Sully" a household name. Many hailed him as

Body Sentences

an American hero. Meanwhile the passengers on the flight,
though safe, suffered emotional trauma from the landing.   *10*
Many refuse to step back onto a plane. Maybe the greatest
effect, however, was the impact on the airline industry. The
emergency landing led to a greater awareness of the dangers
of bird populations near airways. Government agencies have
gone so far as to wipe out geese populations in the proximity   *15*
of airports. In the end, a tragic collision and remarkable

Closing Sentence

emergency landing may result in safer air travel for years to
come.

Consider the Craft

1. What do you like best about this paragraph?
2. What are two of your favorite details?
3. Does the paragraph focus more on causes or effects?
4. What is the value of this paragraph?

The Working Parts of a Paragraph

As you can see from the previous page, a paragraph has three main parts, each with its own specific purpose.

Paragraph Outline

Topic Sentence: A topic sentence introduces your reader to your topic and identifies the main point about it that you want to stress.

Body Sentences: The body sentences support the topic sentence, adding specific details to make the causes and effects clear to the reader.

Closing Sentence: A closing sentence (or two) often summarizes the topic or may offer an interesting final idea.

Tip

Transition words that show cause-effect relationships: accordingly / as a result / because / consequently / for this purpose / for this reason / hence / just as / since / so / such as / therefore / thus / to illustrate / whereas

---

Drafting Tips

When you write a cause-effect paragraph, try to be both clear and interesting. To accomplish this, consider the following strategies.

In the topic sentence . . .
- Introduce the topic in a dramatic way that captures your reader's interest.
- State the main cause-effect connection clearly.

In the middle . . .
- Make sure that your cause-effect details follow logically and make sense.
- Use chronological order if the events follow a clear time sequence.
- Use order of importance (either most to least important or least to most important) if time sequence doesn't apply.
- Include enough details to explain each cause or effect.

In the closing sentence . . .
- End by reflecting on the main cause-effect connection.
- Leave the reader with an interesting idea to think about.
- Consider suggesting possibilities for further study or investigation.

INSIGHT

Journalism, the sciences, and even the arts often use the cause-effect approach when exploring a topic. Mastering this form will serve you well in all your college classes.

Write Prepare your first draft using the information on this page and your planning in LO6 as a guide.

LO8 Revising the Writing

Start the revising process by reading your first draft two or three times to get a feel for your work so far. Then have one of your classmates read and react to your work using a response sheet as a guide.

Using an Academic Style

Cause-effect paragraphs often require an academic style. Consider the quick tips below as you revise your paragraph.

Quick Tips for Academic Style

- **Avoid personal pronouns.** Avoid using personal pronouns such as *I, we,* and *you* in your cause-effect paragraph.
- **Define technical terms.** If your readers are not experts on your topic, define the specialized vocabulary or technical words you use.
- **Beware of unnecessary intensifiers.** Words such as *really, totally,* and *completely* are usually associated with a personal style.

Revising in Action:

Read aloud the unrevised and then the revised version of the following excerpt. Note how the changes improved the excerpt's academic style.

> Maybe the greatest effect, however, was the impact on the airline industry.
> ~~I think the greatest effect was the impact on aviation.~~ The emergency
> landing led to a ~~completely and totally~~ greater awareness of the dangers of bird
> populations near ~~air hubs. You see~~ airways. government agencies have . . .

Revise   Use the following checklist and your classmate's comments on the response sheet to improve your writing. Continue working until you can check off each item in the list.

Revising Checklist

Ideas
- [ ] 1. Does the topic sentence clearly introduce the topic and focus (causes, effects, or both) of the paragraph?
- [ ] 2. Do the causes and effects seem important and reliable?
- [ ] 3. Are all the links between the causes and effects clear and logical?

Organization
- [ ] 4. Do I include a topic sentence, body sentences, and a closing sentence?
- [ ] 5. Have I used transitions to show cause-effect relationships?

Voice
- [ ] 6. Have I used an appropriate voice—serious and academic or relaxed and personal?

LO9 Editing the Writing

Pronouns and their antecedents, the words that are replaced by the pronouns, must agree in three ways: in number, in person, and in gender. This page covers basic pronoun antecedent agreement

Basic Pronoun-Antecedent Agreement

Number

Somebody needs to bring his or her laptop to the meeting.

(The singular pronouns *his* or *her* agree with the singular antecedent *somebody*.)

Person

If students want to do better research, they should talk to a librarian.

(The third-person pronoun *they* agrees with the antecedent *students*.)

Gender

Chris picked up his lawn mower from his parents' garage.

(The masculine pronoun *his* agrees with the antecedent *Chris*.)

Practice   Read the sentences below. Correct the pronouns so that they agree with their antecedents in number, person, and gender.

1. The musicians strummed his guitars.
2. After Shauna finished washing the dishes, it sparkled.
3. If the waitress wants a better tip, he should be more polite.
4. As the basketball players walked onto the court, he waved to the crowd.
5. Mrs. Jackson started their car.
6. Everyone can attend the extra study session if they need help.
7. Eric poured root beer in their favorite mug.

Apply   Read your cause-effect paragraph, watching for agreement issues with your pronouns and their antecedents. Correct any pronoun-antecedent agreement errors that you find.

Case of Pronouns

The case of a pronoun tells what role it can play in a sentence. There are three cases: *nominative, possessive,* and *objective.* Review the information below, which explains each case.

The nominative case is used for subjects and predicate nouns.
I, you, he, she, it, we, they

She walked to the bank. It was she who needed more money.

The possessive case shows possession or ownership.
my, mine, our, ours, his, her, hers, their, theirs, its, your, yours

The jacket is his. This jacket is mine. Your jacket is gone.

The objective case is used for direct or indirect objects and for objects of prepositions or infinitives.
me, us, you, him, her, it, them

Reid told her that going to the movie was fine with him.

Practice In each sentence below, select the correct pronoun in parentheses based on the case of the word.

1. Frank said that (he, him) needed someone to pick (his, him) up.
2. I looked over (their, them) expense report, and (they, them) went way over budget.
3. (She, her) worked on (she, her) new project.
4. The judge commended the competitor on (he, his) speed and agility.
5. (Their, them) lawn service is better than (our, ours) service.
6. It was (him, he) who spotted the bird.
7. The CEO increased (she, her) pay.
8. My brother and (I, me) attended the film festival.
9. (We, us) learned quickly how to recognize each other's voice.
10. On account of (I, me), my little brother does a lot of texting.

Apply Read your cause-effect paragraph, checking the pronouns you've used. Make sure each pronoun is in the correct case.

Marking a Paragraph

The model that follows has a number of errors.

Correct the following paragraph, using the marks below. One correction has been done for you.

Divided Along the 38th Parallel

Though the fighting ceased in 1953 the effects of the Korean War are   *1*

still felt today. The war began in 1950 when communist-occupied North

Korea. Waged war with south Korea. In a larger context, the war was

caused by the United States' desire to stop the spread of communism.

The effects of the conflict were considerable. Both sides suffered massive   *5*

casualties, and the Battle sparked the start of the cold war between the

United States and the Soviet Union. Today, Korea remain divided along

the 38th parallel. North Korea has a heavy military presence and has

suffered much poverty South Korea has thrived economically. Though the

countries have taken smalls steps toward political piece, the war has not   *10*

ended

Correction Marks

ℐ	delete	⅍	add comma	word ⋀	add word
d̲̲	capitalize	? ⋀	add question mark	⊙	add period
D̸	lowercase			◠	spelling
⋀	insert	⌄	insert an apostrophe	⊓	switch

INSIGHT

When checking for errors, it helps to use specific editing strategies. For example, to check for punctuation, you can circle all of the marks in your paper and check each one for correctness. To check for spelling, you should work from the bottom up in your writing. This strategy will help you focus on each word for spelling and usage.

Correcting Your Paragraph

Now it's time to correct your own paragraph.

Apply   Create a clean copy of your revised paragraph and use the following checklist to check for errors. Continue working until you can check off each item in the list.

Editing Checklist

Words

☐ 1. Have I used specific nouns and verbs?

☐ 2. Have I used more action verbs than "be" verbs?

Sentences

☐ 3. Have I varied the beginnings and lengths of sentences?

☐ 4. Have I combined short choppy sentences?

☐ 5. Have I avoided sentence errors such as fragments and comma splices?

Conventions

☐ 6. Do I use correct verb forms (*he saw*, not *he seen*)?

☐ 7. Do my subjects and verbs agree (*she speaks*, not *she speak*)?

☐ 8. Do my pronouns and antecedents agree?

☐ 9. Have I capitalized first words and proper nouns and adjectives?

☐ 10. Have I carefully checked my spelling?

Adding a Title

Make sure to add an effective title. Here are two strategies for creating one.

■ Grab the reader's attention:

Emergency Landing

■ Use an idea from the paragraph:

The Changing Family

> "Our thoughts, deeds, and words return to us sooner or later, with astounding accuracy."
> —Florence Shinn

Review and Enrichment

In the first part of this chapter, you have read cause-effect paragraphs and written one of your own. In this part, you will read and react to a professional cause-effect essay. After that, you will find a number of writing ideas to choose from for a cause-effect paragraph or essay. The reading and writing that you do in these pages will reinforce and enrich the work you have already completed.

Prereading

The actions of people provide a common starting point for cause-effect writing. Or stated in another way, cause-effect writing often examines what we do and why we do it. The professional essay starting on the next page explains the causes and effects of a certain method of studying.

CONSIDER THE TRAITS

As you read the cause-effect essay in this part, consider first the **ideas** it contains—the topic, focus, and causes and effects. Then pay attention to the **organization**—the way the opening, middle, and closing parts are put together. Also think about the authors' **voice**—the overall tone or personality of the writing. Finally, ask yourself if these traits combine to produce a strong essay.

Identify   List three or four actions you have observed, experienced, or read about that could provide topics for cause-effect essays or paragraphs. (One idea is provided for you.)

Seeing a young person helping an older person with a disability

_____

_____

_____

What do you think?

How would you explain the quotation above? And what does it have to do with causes and effects? Share your thoughts with your classmates.

Reading and Reacting

Read   Read the following cause-effect essay from *FOCUS on College and Career Success* by Constance Staley and Steve Staley. This essay explores a common but ineffective study strategy—cramming for tests. Use the reading process to help you gain a full understanding of the essay. And keep your class notebook handy for notes and personal thoughts at different points during your reading.

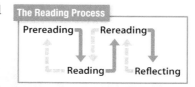

The Reading Process

Prereading   Rereading

Reading   Reflecting

About the Authors

Constance Staley is a professor at the University of Colorado, Colorado Springs. During her time in the classroom, she has worked with thousands of students, helping them prepare for and succeed in college. *FOCUS on College and Career Success* puts in one place all of the valuable advice that she has shared with students over the years.

Steve Staley is dean of academics and professor of management and humanities at Colorado Technical University. He has also taught at the Air Force Academy, the Naval War College, and the University of Colorado, and has been an Air Force instructor pilot and served as director of corporate communications and educational development in a high-tech firm.

Cramming: Does "All or Nothing" Really Work?

Imagine yourself as the actor in the following scenarios. Compare these situations to cramming for tests.   *1*

• You haven't called your significant other since last year. Suddenly you appear at her door with candy, flowers, concert tickets, and dinner reservations at the most exclusive restaurant in town. You   *5* can't understand why she isn't happier to see you.

• You don't feed your dog for several months. When you finally bring him a plate loaded with ten T-bone steaks to make up for your neglect, you notice he's up and died on you. Oops!

Of course, these situations are ridiculous, aren't they? How could   *10* anyone ever neglect such basic necessities of life? There's an important point to be made here. Many things in life require continuous tending. If you ignore them for a time, catching up is next to impossible. Your college courses should be added to the list.

Believe it or not, some students give themselves permission to follow *15* this all-or-nothing principle of cramming in their academic work. They sail along without investing much time or energy in their studies, and then they try to make up for lost time right before an exam by cramming. The word *cram* provokes a distinct visual image, and rightly so. Picture yourself packing for a vacation in a warm, sunny place and hardly being *20* able to close your suitcase because it's crammed full. You can't decide what to bring so you bring everything you can think of.

The same holds for cramming for a test. You try to stuff your brain full of information, including things you won't need. Since you haven't taken the time to keep up with learning as you go, you try to learn everything *25* at the last minute. Cramming is an attempt to overload information into your unreliable working memory. It's only available for a very short time. However, there are other reasons why cramming is a bad idea:

- Your anxiety level will rise quickly.

- Your sleep with suffer. *30*

- Your immune system may go haywire.

- You may oversleep and miss the exam altogether.

Despite the warnings here, most student cram at some time or other while taking college courses, and doing so may even give them a temporary high and make them feel like they're suffering for a cause. But generally, *35* slow and steady wins the race.

Vocabulary Practice

Explain or define the following words in the essay using your understanding of context clues and word parts as a guide. Also list the words and ideas in the text or any word parts that help you define each term.

- neglect
- tending
- investing
- overload

React   Answer the questions that follow about the essay on the previous pages. Then discuss your responses with your classmates.

1. What is the main idea of the essay?

    _____

2. What causes and effects are covered? Consider filling in a cause-effect organizer to help you answer the question.

Subject	
Causes	Effects
-	-
-	-
-	-

3. What are two things that you learned by reading this essay?

    _____

4. What questions, if any, do you still have about the topic?

    _____

5. How would you rate this essay and why?

    Weak ★ ★ ★ ★ ★ Strong

    _____

6. What was the authors' purpose for writing this essay?

    _____

Drawing Inferences

An *inference* is a logical conclusion you can make from context but that isn't specifically stated. However, a solid inference can result from a clear and careful understanding of a text. To practice drawing inferences, answer the following questions about the cause-effect selection on the previous pages. Then share your answers with your classmates.

1. What conclusions can you draw from this essay about mindset of many students in terms of studying and school work?

2. How would the authors recommend that you study? What line or lines in the essay suggest this?

Writing

Use the guidelines on the next two pages to write your own cause-effect paragraph or cause-effect essay. Check with your instructor about any specific requirements he or she may have for this writing. And be sure to use the writing process to help you do your best work.

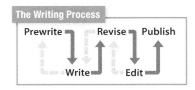

Prewriting

Choose one of the following or another appropriate idea for your cause-effect writing.

Writing Ideas

1. Write about one of the four cause-effect topics you identified in the planning activity in LO6.
2. Write about how a parent, teacher, or friend has affected your life.
3. Write about the causes and effects related to taking online classes.
4. Write about the effects of a movie or book on your life.
5. Write about the causes and effects of bottled water in our society.
6. Write about why people do or do not bother to vote.
7. Write about the widening gap between wealthy and poor Americans.
8. Write a cause-effect piece related to one of the photographs in this book.

When planning . . .

Refer to LO6 to help with your prewriting and planning. Also use the tips below.

- Choose a topic you care about. Writing about something you find interesting is always the best choice. Make sure it will interest your readers as well.
- Make certain your listed causes and effects are clearly related and will make sense to your readers.
- Research any fuzzy areas so all the cause-effect connections are plain.
- If necessary, change your thesis or your topic sentence to match what you learn from your research.

Writing and Revising

Use the tips that follow and the information in LO7 to help you with your drafting and revising.

When writing . . .

- Include an opening, a middle, and a closing part in your cause-effect piece. Each part has its own role to play.
- Try to follow one of the general cause-effect organizations shown on page 141.
- Write your first draft freely, using your notes as a guide, but allowing yourself to explore new connections and explanations as they come to mind.
- If questions arise as you are writing the draft, make a note to return to these parts later.

When revising . . .

- Let your first draft sit unread for a while. Then read it critically, with fresh eyes. Also, reading a printed copy can help you see it differently.
- Ask a classmate or another writer to review and critique your writing. Use a peer-review sheet to guide the critique.
- Make sure you have included enough details to explain the causes and effects.
- Consider the style of your writing. For most cause-effect writing, an academic style is appropriate.

Editing

Refer to the checklist earlier in this LO when you are ready to edit your cause-effect writing for style and correctness.

michaeljung, 2011 / Used under license from Shutterstock.com

Reflecting on Classification Writing

Answer the following questions about your cause-effect reading and writing experiences in this chapter.

1. Why is cause-effect such a common structure in textbooks?

   _____

2. What is the most important thing you learned about reading a cause-effect paragraph or essay?

   _____

3. What reading strategy in this chapter do you find most helpful? Explain.

   _____

4. What is your favorite cause-effect piece in this chapter? Why?

   _____

5. What do you like most about the cause-effect paragraph you wrote for this chapter? Why?

   _____

6. What is one thing you would like to change in your paragraph?

   _____

7. What is the hardest part about cause-effect writing?

   _____

Key Terms to Remember

Whenever you read and write cause-effect paragraphs and essays, it's important to understand the following terms.

- **Causes**—the reasons for an action or a condition
- **Effects**—the results of a cause or an action
- **Cause-effect organizer**—a graphic organizer used to list causes in one column and effects in another
- **Evidence**—the facts and details that support or explain the main points in writing

8

Comparison

> "Another possible source of guidance for teenagers is television, but television's message has always been that the need for truth, wisdom, and world peace pales by comparison with the need for a toothpaste that offers whiter teeth and fresher breath."
>
> —Dave Barry

Take a close look at the photograph below. It is full of contrasts. A tree is contrasted with a man-made power station. The dark green and brown foreground is contrasted with the light blue background. And even the vertical stature of the tree and power station contrasts with the horizontal field and sky.

But the photo also contains some interesting comparisons. The water vapor from the power plant looks similar to the clouds overhead. The green leaves of the tree match the green grass. And the vegetation and the power station are both involved with energy use and production.

A paragraph that examines similarities and differences is called a comparison-contrast paragraph. In this chapter, you will read and react to comparison-contrast paragraphs and learn how to write one of your own.

Learning Outcomes

LO1 Understand comparison-contrast.

LO2 Learn about reading strategies.

LO3 Read and react to a professional paragraph.

LO4 Read and react to a student paragraph.

LO5 Practice reading strategies.

LO6 Plan a comparison-contrast paragraph.

LO7 Write the first draft.

LO8 Revise the writing.

LO9 Edit the writing.

What do you think?

What contrast is illustrated in the quotation above? Hint: The word *pales* means "to lack, or to be short of."

Hervé Hughes/Hemis/Corbis

LO1 Understanding Comparison-Contrast

Creating a ranking requires you to make comparisons. A food critic ranking the "5 Best Pizzerias in Town" would need to compare different pizza places to come up with an appropriate list. This same type of thinking is required to evaluate a ranking. If you disagreed with the food critic's list, you would need to make your own comparison: *The crust at La Familia's Pizza sets it apart from Ann's Pizza.*

The effectiveness of a ranking depends on the points of comparison that are made. In the example above, crust is used to compare two different pizzerias. The sauce, the toppings, or the staff's attentiveness could also serve as valuable points of comparison. As you study a ranking, always ask yourself if it is the result of a meaningful comparison. Ask the same question as you read and respond to a comparison-contrast paragraph.

> "There are dark shadows on the earth, but its lights are stronger in the contrast."
> —Charles Dickens

Comparing vs. Contrasting

When you compare, you look for similarities between subjects. When you contrast, you look for differences. Some comparison-contrast paragraphs focus on the similarities, while others focus on the differences. Still others may present a balanced analysis—equal numbers of similarities and differences. It all depends on the information the writer has discovered—and the points of comparison she or he makes.

INSIGHT

Related types of analysis include cause-effect and classification. These two forms require you to carefully examine the subjects, just as making comparisons requires.

Identify   Write down a general field of study. Then write down jobs for people who graduate with that major. Finally, write two or three points of comparison for the jobs.

1. Field of study _____

2. Jobs in that field _____

   _____

3. Points of comparison _____

   _____

Reading

Comparison-contrast paragraphs involve two primary subjects, which must be evaluated equally. The strategies below will help you understand this type of paragraph.

LO2 Learning About Reading Strategies

Strategy 1: Recognizing Common Comparison-Contrast Patterns

Knowing the different patterns of organization used in comparison-contrast paragraphs will help you follow the main ideas in the text.

- **Point-by-point:** Some comparison-contrast writing is organized point by point. That is, each subject is addressed according to different points of comparison.
- **Subject-by-subject:** Other comparison-contrast writing discusses one subject in the first part and the other subject in the second part.
- **Similarities & differences:** Still other pieces address the similarities between the subjects in the first part and the differences in the second part.

INSIGHT
A writer may use a variation on one of the patterns, following it in general, but not exactly, from start to finish.

Point-by-Point

Topic Sentence

Point 1
Subject 1	Subject 2

| Point 2 |
| Subject 1 | Subject 2 |

| Point 3 |
| Subject 1 | Subject 2 |

| Closing Sentence |

Subject-by-Subject

Topic Sentence

| Subject 1 |

| Subject 2 |

| Closing Sentence |

Similarities & Differences

Topic Sentence

| Similarities |

| Differences |

| Closing Sentence |

Strategy 2: Recognizing Comparison-Contrast Transitions

As you read comparison-contrast paragraphs, watch for transitions or linking words that alert you to specific comparisons and contrasts.

Transitions that show comparisons

also	both	in the same way	much as	likewise
much like	one way	similarly	another way	as

Transitions that show contrasts

although	even though	by contrast	but	however
on the one hand	on the other hand	otherwise	though	

LO3 Reading and Reacting to a Professional Paragraph

Read   The following comparison-contrast paragraph comes from Gary Ferraro and Susan Andreatta's *Cultural Anthropology: An Applied Perspective,* a college textbook focusing on cultural anthropology. Remember to use the reading process to help you fully understand the text.

The Reading Process

Prereading → Rereading →

Reading → Reflecting

Cross-Cultural Miscues

Although both New Yorkers and Londoners speak English, there are   *1*
enough differences between American English and British English to
cause communication miscues. Speakers of English on opposite sides of the
Atlantic often use different words to refer to the same thing. To illustrate,
Londoners put their trash in a dustbin, not a garbage can; they take a   *5*
lift, not an elevator; and they live in flats, not apartments. To further
complicate matters, the same word used in England and the United States
can convey very different meanings. For example, in England the word
"homely" (as in the statement "I think your wife is very homely") means
warm and friendly, not plain . . . as in the United States; for the British,   *10*
the phrase "to table a motion" means to give an item a prominent place
on the agenda rather than to postpone taking action on an item, as in the
United States; and a rubber in British English is an eraser, not a condom.
These are just a few of the linguistic pitfalls that North Americans and
Brits may encounter when they attempt to communicate using their own   *15*
version of the "same" language.

"Cross-Cultural Miscues" from FERRARO/ANDREATTA. *Cultural Anthropology: An Applied Perspective,* 9E. © 2012 Wadsworth, a part of Cengage Learning, Inc.

React   Answer the following questions about the paragraph. Then discuss your responses with your classmates.

1. What is the main point of this comparison-contrast paragraph?

2. What pattern of organization do the authors use in the paragraph?

3. What transitions are used in the paragraph to help the reader follow the ideas? _____

4. How would you rate this comparison-contrast paragraph and why? _____
   Weak ★ ★ ★ ★ ★ Strong

5. What did you learn about American English and British English? _____

A CLOSER LOOK   at Comparison

Using Comparison-Contrast Graphic Organizers

Comparison-contrast paragraphs focus on details that show similarities and differences. For help identifying and organizing such details, consider using one of the graphic organizers below.

Comparison T-Chart

A T-chart helps you gather details about the two topics of comparison. On one side of the chart, write details relating to the first subject, and on the second side, write details relating to the second subject.

CONSIDER THE READING-WRITING CONNECTION

Graphic organizers like the ones below help you analyze the details in a comparison-contrast paragraph. They will also help you gather details for your own comparison-contrast paragraphs.

Subject A	Subject B
Details	Details

Venn Diagram

A Venn diagram is a useful graphic organizer for any type of comparison writing. It is especially helpful for complex comparisons that examine both similarities and differences.

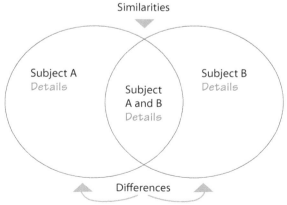

Similarities

Subject A
Details

Subject
A and B
Details

Subject B
Details

Differences

Graph   Use one of the graphic organizers from above to identify the details of the next comparison-contrast paragraph that you read.

LO4 Reading and Reacting to a Student Paragraph

Read Read the following student paragraph, which compares the writer's father with the writer. Remember to use the steps in the reading process.

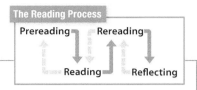

Old Versus New

People often say I look like a younger version of my father, but in most   *1*
ways, we are very different. Our appearance is similar in that I have Dad's
brown eyes and black hair. We even have similar smiles, according to my
mom. But no one would say we look the same in the clothes we wear. Dad
dresses old school in work pants and button-down shirts, always tucked in.   *5*
For me, it's jeans and a Padres jersey, never tucked in. Our different dress
shows our different personalities. Dad is quiet, shy, and hardworking,
while I am very friendly and sometimes a little crazy. Neither of us,
however, is interested in causing trouble. Most of our differences come
from our different backgrounds. Dad was born in Mexico in a small town   *10*
south of Monterrey. He moved to San Diego as a young man and has
worked very long hours as a cook ever since. It has taken him a long time
to feel comfortable in this country, while the United States is all I have
ever known. Dad's tough life has made him more careful and serious than
I am, but if he had lived my life, he would be much more like me.   *15*

React Answer the following questions about the paragraph. Then discuss your answers with your classmates.

1. What is the main point of this comparison-contrast paragraph?

   _____

2. What pattern of organization does the author use in the paragraph?

   _____

3. What key details (similarities and differences), does the author provide? Use a graphic organizer from the previous page to identify them.

   _____

4. How would you rate this comparison-contrast paragraph and why?

   Weak ★ ★ ★ ★ ★ Strong

   _____

A CLOSER LOOK   at Analyzing the Details

Considering Points of Comparison

Points of comparison are the factors the author uses to compare two subjects. The paragraph on the previous page considers three factors in comparing and contrasting: appearance, personality, and background.

Identify   Make a chart like the one below. Then fill it in with specific details about the writer and his father for each point of comparison

Point of comparison	Father	The Writer
Appearance (size, shape, hair color, clothing, etc.)		
Personality (attitude, outlook, feelings, actions, etc.)		
Background (place of birth, family, hometown, etc.)		

Identify   As you read other comparison-contrast paragraphs in this chapter, identify the points of comparison. By doing so, you can better analyze the quality of the paragraph. An effective comparison-contrast paragraph ...

- includes more than one point of comparison.
- provides details about both subjects for each point of comparison.

CONSIDER THE READING-WRITING CONNECTION

Points of comparison help readers analyze comparison-contrast paragraphs. They also help writers gather and organize their thoughts.

Shamleen, 2011 / Used under license from Shutterstock.com

LO5 Practicing Reading Skills

When you read, you encounter new words and old words used in new ways. This page will help you understand these words.

Vocabulary: Using a Dictionary

A dictionary helps you understand the exact definition (denotation) of a word as well as how to pronounce it. A dictionary can also provide other information. Let's look at an example dictionary definition:

> pronunciation   part of speech   origin
>
> word —**homely** \hom´-lē\ adj. [ME *hom,* fr. OE *haim* village, home + *ly* of, related to] 1. Plain or unattractive 2. Typical of a home 3. Comfortable and familiar 4. Natural and simple
>
> meanings (denotations)

Look Up Each term below comes from the model paragraphs in LO3 and LO4. Use a dictionary to find and write down the pronunciation, part of speech, and at least one meaning of each term below.

1. miscues _____
2. prominent _____
3. agenda _____
4. postpone _____

5. linguistic _____
6. pitfall _____
7. jersey _____
8. hardworking _____

Vocabulary: Understanding Connotation

Often, in addition to having a literal definition, a word will have a connotation. A connotation is the implied meaning or feeling of a word. In the paragraph "Old Versus New," the writer uses words with differing connotations to describe his father and himself.

Father (Connotations)	**Writer (Connotations)**
old school (traditional)	jeans (youthful)
work pants (practical)	Padres shirt (sports fan)
tucked in (proper)	untucked (relaxed)
small town (rural)	San Diego (urban)
long hours (hardworking)	friendly (popular)
tough life (determined)	"a little crazy" (risk-taking)

Identify For each word or phrase from "We Can Dance" in LO7, write a connotation.

1. basketball T-shirt _____
2. Obama country _____
3. sea of corn _____
4. hip-hop _____
5. techno _____
6. having a blast _____

Writing

Starting on this page, you will plan and write a comparison-contrast paragraph about two people. Follow the writing process to help you do your best work.

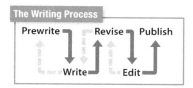

LO6 Planning a Comparison-Contrast Paragraph

These two pages will help you gather your thoughts about your topic before you actually begin writing.

Selecting a Topic

Choose two people that interest you for your paragraph. They could be people you know well or complete strangers; people who are dead or alive; famous people or unknowns. You can even include yourself in the comparison.

Select For each heading below, identify two people you would like to compare and contrast. Then select the two people you would most like to write about in your paragraph.

Family	1. _____	2. _____
Friends	1. _____	2. _____
Role Models	1. _____	2. _____
Famous People	1. _____	2. _____
Experts in Your Academic Major	1. _____	2. _____

Describing the People

Select Decide on three points of comparison to compare and contrast the two people. Consider the suggestions that follow.

- **Appearance:** Think of size, shape, hair color, eye color, skin color, gender, clothing, and so on.
- **Personality:** Think of attitude, outlook, feelings, actions, and so on.
- **Background:** Think of birthplace, schooling, hometown, family, and so on.
- **Interests:** Think of favorite activities, hobbies, friends, food, music, and so on.
- **Other**

Gathering Details

Below is an example of a Venn diagram that the author of the comparison-contrast paragraph on the next page used to note similarities and differences related to her three points of comparison.

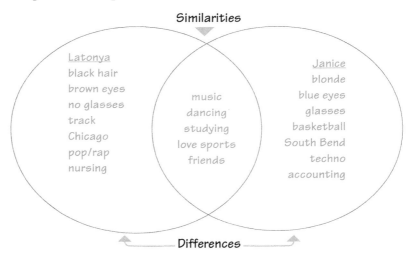

Similarities

Latonya
black hair
brown eyes
no glasses
track
Chicago
pop/rap
nursing

music
dancing
studying
love sports
friends

Janice
blonde
blue eyes
glasses
basketball
South Bend
techno
accounting

Differences

Gather   Complete a Venn diagram with details that show the similarities and differences between your two subjects. At the top of your graphic organizer, name each subject. Then list your details in the appropriate spaces.

Tip
At this point, you may want to consider a pattern of organization for the main ideas of your paragraph. Consider the three common comparison-contrast patterns in LO2.

Writing a Topic Sentence

After collecting details for your paragraph, you are ready to write a topic sentence. This sentence should name your subjects and identify an important comparison between them.

Topic		Key Point of Comparison		Topic Sentence
Author, her roommate	**+**	Our appearance makes us look like we have nothing in common	**=**	To look at my roommate and me, you'd think we have nothing in common.

Create   Develop a topic sentence for your comparison-contrast paragraph, using the formula shown above as a guide. If necessary, write two or three versions until your statement says what you want it to say.

LO7 Writing the First Draft

Writing a first draft is your first attempt to connect all the thoughts you have gathered about your topic. Don't try to make everything perfect. Instead, simply get all your ideas on paper.

Read Carefully read through the paragraph. Note how the writer organizes the main ideas using the point-by-point pattern.

We Can Dance

Topic Sentence

> To look at my roommate and me, you'd think we have   *1*
> nothing in common. First of all, we look like complete
> opposites. Janice is tall, with long blonde hair and blue eyes,
> while I'm short, with black curly hair and brown eyes. Janice
> loves wearing her basketball T-shirt from her Indiana State   *5*
> Championship team. I prefer dressing in my cross-country

Body Sentences

> gear. We're also from completely different places. I'm a city
> girl, born and raised on the south side of Chicago, right in the
> heart of Barack Obama country. Janice grew up on a farm
> in a sea of corn, near South Bend, Indiana. So why do Janice   *10*
> and I get along so well? Some might think it is our interest
> in sports, but that's only part of it. When we first moved in
> together, I turned on some hip-hop, and Janice started popping
> and locking. She was good! So I showed her some of my moves,
> and even tried the techno music she likes. Before you know it,   *15*

Closing Sentence

> we came to be the best of friends, going to parties and dances
> together and having a blast.

Consider the Craft

1. What do you like best about this paragraph?
2. What are your two favorite comparisons or contrasts?
3. Do you feel like the subjects make an interesting comparison?
4. How would you summarize the relationship between the two subjects?

The Working Parts of a Paragraph

A paragraph consists of three main parts, each of which has a special function. The information that follows explains each part.

Paragraph Outline

Topic Sentence: The topic sentence sets the stage for the paragraph. It should introduce both subjects and say something about the comparison.

Body Sentences: The body sentences share details about each subject for each point of comparison.

Closing Sentence: The closing sentence sums up the comparison by offering a final thought about the subjects.

Drafting Tips

When you write a comparison-contrast paragraph, you are showing how two subjects are alike or unalike. Consider the following techniques to give your reader a clear view of your subjects.

- **Use transitions that compare and contrast to connect ideas,** but be careful not to overuse them.

- **Address each subject with plenty of details,** making sure you use details that "show" rather than "tell."

- **At the same time, don't overuse details that make your paragraph too long.** Use only those that offer a key similarity or difference between the two subjects.

- **Provide comparisons,** but always back them up with sound logic.

Write Develop your first draft using the information on this page and your planning as a guide.

Christos Georghiou, 2011 / Used under license from Shutterstock.com

LO8 Revising the Writing

Start the revising process by reading your first draft two or three times to get a feel for your work so far. Then have one of your classmates read and react to your work using a response sheet as a guide.

Show, Don't Tell

Your paragraph will be stronger if you show similarities and differences, not just tell about them. Consider the examples that follow.

Showing vs. **Telling**

Showing	Telling
She's popping and locking.	She likes to dance.
She lives on a farm in a sea of corn.	She is a country girl.
She lives in her championship jersey.	She is an athlete.

Revising in Action:

Read aloud the unrevised and then the revised version of the following excerpt. Note the improvements made by showing instead of telling.

> . . . First of all, we look like complete opposites. Janice is ~~white and~~ tall, *with long blonde hair and blue eyes,*
> while I'm ~~black and~~ short, *with black curly hair and brown eyes.* ~~We like different sports.~~ Janice loves basketball,
> *wearing her basketball T-shirt from her Indiana State Championship team.*
> ~~and I like track.~~ We're also from completely different places. . . .
> *I prefer dressing in my cross-country gear and taking off down the road.*

Revise   Improve your writing, using the following checklist and your classmate's comments on the response sheet. Continue working until you can check off each item in the list.

Revising Checklist

Ideas

- ☐ **1.** Do I compare two interesting people?
- ☐ **2.** Do I use three points of comparison?
- ☐ **3.** Do I include details that show instead of tell?

Organization

- ☐ **4.** Do I have a topic sentence, body sentences, and a closing sentence?
- ☐ **5.** Have I used an appropriate organizational plan?
- ☐ **6.** Have I used transitions to connect my sentences?

Voice

- ☐ **7.** Do I sound knowledgeable and interested?

LO9 Editing the Writing

Commas tell the reader when to pause, making the writing easy to follow.

Commas After Introductory Words

Many sentences naturally start with the subject. Some sentences, however, start with an introductory phrase or clause. A comma is used to separate a long introductory word group from the rest of the sentence. When you read sentences like these out loud, you will naturally pause after the introductory words. That tells you that a comma is needed to separate these words from the rest of the sentence. See the examples that follow.

Introductory Word Groups:

After my third birthday, my brother was born. (prepositional phrase)

When he arrived on the scene, life changed for me. (dependent clause)

Punctuation Practice Read the sentences below, out loud. Listen for the natural pause after an introductory phrase or clause. Place a comma to set off the introductory words.

1. When my younger brother was born I was jealous.
2. Before he showed up I had Mom all to myself.
3. At the beginning of our relationship we didn't get along very well.
4. As the years passed my brother stopped being a pest and became a friend.
5. As a matter of fact we both came to love basketball.
6. Without my younger brother I wouldn't have anyone to push my basketball skills.
7. Taking that into account our long rivalry has helped us both.
8. Since our teenage years we've become best friends.
9. Although we still tease each other we're not being vicious.
10. When we bump fists I sometimes remember when we bumped heads.

Apply Read your comparison-contrast paragraph and look for sentences that begin with introductory phrases or clauses. If you do not find any, add an introductory phrase or clause to a few sentences to vary their beginnings. Does this help your writing read more smoothly? Remember to use a comma to separate a long introductory word group from the rest of the sentence.

Commas with Extra Information

Some sentences include phrases or clauses that add information in the middle or at the end of sentences. This information should be set off with commas. You can recognize this extra information because it can be removed without changing the basic meaning of the sentence. When you read the sentence out loud, there's a natural pause before and after the phrase or clause. This indicates where you are to place the commas.

Extra Information:

I have a tough time waking up, not surprisingly.

My mother, who works two jobs, makes me breakfast every morning.

Punctuation Practice In each sentence, use a comma or commas to separate extra information. Listen for the natural pause. Some sentences may not have extra information.

1. My mother works as a waitress which is a tough job.
2. She also works as a licensed practical nurse which is an even tougher job.
3. The nursing home the one on Main and 7th is strict.
4. A time card punched one second late is docked fifteen minutes an unfair policy.
5. A time card punched ten minutes early does not earn overtime.
6. The restaurant job pays minimum wage which is not much.
7. Tips from a good lunch not the busiest time can double Mom's pay.
8. What I've learned about determination real grit I learned from Mom.
9. She wants to help me qualify for a better job a selfless goal.
10. I want exactly the same thing no surprise there.

Apply Read your comparison paragraph and look for sentences that have extra information. If you haven't included any, add some extra information in a sentence or two. Do these additions make your writing more interesting? Remember to use commas to set off extra information in your sentences.

Marking a Paragraph

The model that follows has a number of errors.

Editing Practice Correct the following paragraph, using the correction marks below. One correction has been done for you.

Into the Spotlight

My wife and I love each other but it's hard to imagine how we could be *1*
more different. Lupe's a social butterfly. She been always meeting people
for coffee or talking to people on the phone. By contrast, I'm private. I
work at U.S. steel and come home. The only person I really want to be
with is Lupe, but she's always dragging me out to partys. Their is another *5*
big difference. Lupe who is a great singer and dancer loves theater. She's
been in a dozen plays. When it come to me the idea of being on stage is
terrifying. She convinced me once to be in a play I forgot my one line. so,
is there anything Lupe and I have in common? We love each other. Lupe
needs me to keep her grounded, and I need her to pry me out of the house. *10*
We've even figured out a way to work around the theater thing. Next
play she is in. I'll work set crew. That's how we get along so well. I work
backstage, setting props for her, and getting what she needs. Then she
walks into the spotlight and performs.

Correction Marks

⌐ delete	⅄ add comma	word ∧ add word
d̲ capitalize	? add question	⊙ add period
D̲ lowercase	∧ mark	spelling
∧ insert	ᵥ insert an apostrophe	switch

INSIGHT

As you've seen, commas are needed to set off extra information in a sentence.
Sometimes the extra information comes between the subject and the verb:

Lupe, who is a great singer and dancer, loves theater.

But when there is no extra information to set off, do not separate the subject and verb with a comma.

Incorrect: Lupe, loves theater.   **Correct:** Lupe loves theater.

Correcting Your Paragraph

Now it's time to correct your own paragraph.

Edit Prepare a clean copy of your revised writing and use the following checklist to look for errors. Continue working until you can check off each item in the list.

Editing Checklist

Words

☐   1. Have I used specific nouns and verbs?

☐   2. Have I used more action verbs than "be" verbs?

Sentences

☐   3. Have I varied the beginnings and lengths of sentences?

☐   4. Have I combined short choppy sentences?

☐   5. Have I avoided shifts in sentences?

☐   6. Have I avoided fragments and run-ons?

Conventions

☐   7. Do I use correct verb forms (*he saw,* not *he seen*)?

☐   8. Do my subjects and verbs agree (*she speaks,* not *she speak*)?

☐   9. Have I capitalized first words and proper nouns and adjectives?

☐ 10. Have I used commas after long introductory word groups?

☐ 11. Have I punctuated dialogue correctly?

☐ 12. Have I carefully checked my spelling?

Adding a Title

Make sure to add an attention-getting title. Here are three simple strategies for creating one.

- Use a phrase from the paragraph:

   Into the Spotlight

- Point to a similarity or difference:

   We Can Dance

- Use the word "versus":

   Old Versus New

Create Prepare a clean final copy of your paragraph and proofread it before sharing it.

> "There is no teaching to compare with example."
> —Sir Robert Baden-Powell

Review and Enrichment

You have been introduced to reading and writing comparison-contrast paragraphs. This section expands on that information by providing a comparison-contrast essay to read and respond to. You will also be given a number of writing ideas to choose from and develop. These activities will broaden your understanding of comparison.

Prereading

Many meaningful comparisons can be made about the places you have been, either in your hometown or on vacation. One neighborhood in your hometown may be very different from another. Or two places separated by an ocean may be more similar than you ever imagined.

CONSIDER THE TRAITS

As you read the essay that begins on the next page, focus first on the **ideas**. Then consider the **organization**—the comparison-contrast pattern used in the essay. Also note the author's **voice**—how he speaks to the reader. Finally, ask yourself if these traits combine to produce a satisfying reading experience.

Identify Think of two places you know a lot about. Then answer the following questions about both places. Share your thoughts with a classmate.

1. Write three adjectives to describe each place.

  Place 1: _____

  Place 2: _____

2. What is the main feature of each place?

  Place 1: _____

  Place 2: _____

3. What feeling do you get in each place?

  Place 1: _____

  Place 2: _____

What do you think?

Explain what you think Sir Robert Baden-Powell means in the quotation at the top of the page. Do you agree with him? Share your thoughts with your classmates.

Reading and Reacting

Read The following comparison-contrast essay takes a look at critical and creative thinking. The essay focuses on these subjects but also compares them to two types of breathing.

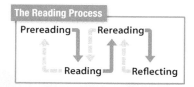

About the Author

Robert King is coauthor of *Inquire: A Guide to 21st Century Learning* as well as two dozen published novels.

Thinking Like Breathing

Which is more important for today's students, critical thinking or   *1*
creative thinking? It's a trick question. I may as well ask which is more
important, breathing out or breathing in? "Whichever one I need to do
right now" is one good answer to this last question. Another is "Neither is
more important since I need both to stay alive." It's the same with critical   *5*
and creative thinking.

The Thought Exchange

Creative and critical thinking are two halves of a cycle: inspiration and
expiration.

Creative thinking draws in possibilities. It is an expansive process,   *10*
filling you with new ideas from the outside. Creativity reaches beyond
what is known and into the unknown . . . to discover something new.
Creativity is not necessarily discerning. You don't separate nitrogen from
oxygen before you breathe it in. Your chest simply expands, and in it
comes. Creative thinking floods you with new possibilities.   *15*

Critical thinking, on the other hand, sorts through the possibilities to
do something practical. Critical thinking analyzes, applies, and evaluates.
It categorizes, compares, contrasts, and traces causes and effects. It's
like separating oxygen from the air to enrich your cells, or extracting the
carbon dioxide from your blood to get rid of the waste. Critical thinking   *20*

takes what creative thinking has amassed and sorts it, keeping the best
and discarding the worst.

Thinking as Respiration

All sorts of activities require this exchange between critical and
creative thinking. For example, think of the process of solving a problem.   *25*
You start by analyzing the problem (critical), and then you brainstorm
solutions (creative). Next you evaluate the solutions and choose the best
one (critical). At that point, you have to create your solution (creative).
Once it is done, you need to test it and evaluate it (critical). Finally, you
can make improvements to your solution and put it into practice (creative).   *30*

You'll find you use a similar process when you write an essay, create
a college schedule, and even plan a party. Most activities require an
interchange between critical and creative thinking, and you switch back
and forth as easily as breathing.

Vocabulary

critical thinking
close, careful thinking that
analyzes a topic, seeking
realities

creative thinking
open-minded exploration
of a topic, seeking
possibilities

inspiration
breathing in; also,
something that provides
an idea

expiration
breathing out

nitrogen
gas that makes up most of
our environment

oxygen
gas needed to support
animal life

carbon dioxide
gas waste product of animal
respiration

respiration
the act of breathing

Casper Simon, 2011 / Used under license from Shutterstock.com

React   Answer the following questions about "Thinking Like Breathing." Then share your responses with your classmates.

1. What are the two main subjects of this essay?

_____

_____

2. Does this essay focus on the similarities or differences of the two subjects? Explain.

_____

_____

3. What details are provided about the two subjects? Use a T-chart or a Venn diagram to identify them.

_____

_____

4. How does the use of headings help you understand the essay's organization?

_____

_____

5. How would you rate this essay and why?

   Weak ★ ★ ★ ★ ★ Strong

_____

_____

6. What did you learn about the two subjects?

_____

_____

Vocabulary Practice

Explain or define the following words in the essay by using context clues and your understanding of word parts. Also list the clues or word parts that help you define the terms.

- expansive (line 10)
- discerning (line 13)
- extracting (line 19)
- amassed (line 21)

Writing

Write a comparison-contrast paragraph or essay following the guidelines on the next two pages. Check with your instructor about any specific requirements that he or she may have.

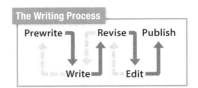

Prewriting

Choose one of the following writing ideas for your comparison-contrast writing or find an appropriate topic of your own.

Writing Ideas

1. Write about the pair of places you chose to compare in the activity on Prereading.

2. Write a review comparing two of your favorite restaurants.

3. Write about the music of two bands or artists from a similar genre.

4. Write a comparison of two historical figures.

5. Write a comparison of two of your professors' teaching styles.

Leah-Anne Thompson, 2011 / Used under license from Shutterstock.com

---

When planning . . .

Refer to LO6 to help you with your prewriting and planning. Also use the tips that follow.

- Choose subjects that are specific enough for a paragraph or an essay and that you know a lot about or can research effectively.
- Choose appropriate points of comparison and a pattern of organization.
- Collect plenty of details relating to those points of comparison. Use a graphic organizer to collect and organize the details.
- Review the examples of comparison-contrast writing in this chapter to see how they are developed.

Writing and Revising

Refer to LO7 to help you write and revise your first draft. Also use the tips that follow.

When writing . . .

- Include opening, middle, and closing parts in your writing. Each part has a specific role.
- Follow the pattern of organization and points of comparison you chose during your planning, but be open to making changes in organization or content if the writing is not logically coming together.
- Use transitional words to help the reader follow your ideas.

When revising . . .

- Ask yourself if your paragraph or essay contains any dead spots that either need more details or should be cut back.
- Decide if any parts are confusing or cause you to stumble. Rewrite these parts as needed.
- Determine if you have organized your details in the best way.
- Have at least one trusted peer react to your writing.

Editing

Refer to the checklist in LO9 when you are ready to edit your comparison-contrast writing for style and correctness.

Reflecting on Comparison-Contrast Writing

Answer the following questions about your reading and writing experiences in this chapter.

1. What makes a comparison-contrast paragraph enjoyable to read?

   _____

2. What is your favorite paragraph in this chapter?

   _____

3. Which reading strategy in this chapter seems the most helpful? Explain.

   _____

4. What is the most important thing you have learned about reading comparison-contrast paragraphs?

   _____

5. What do you like most about the first comparison-contrast paragraph that you wrote in this chapter? Explain.

   _____

6. What is one thing that you would like to change in your paragraph?

   _____

7. What is the most important thing that you have learned about comparison-contrast writing?

   _____

8. What is the hardest thing about this type of writing? The easiest?

   _____

Key Terms to Remember

When you read and write comparison-contrast paragraphs and essays, it's important to understand the following terms.

- **Comparing**—showing how two or more subjects are similar
- **Contrasting**—showing how two or more subjects are different
- **Points of comparison**—the special elements or features used to make a comparison (size, strength, appearance, and so on)
- **Patterns of organization for comparison-contrast writing**—point-by-point, subject-by-subject, or similarities and differences.

9

"Use soft words and hard arguments."
—English Proverb

Argumentation

Have you ever wondered why political candidates participate in debates? It's no accident. Argumentation plays a central role in any civilization. Given our variety of personalities, backgrounds, values, and assumptions, the only way of coming to a consensus is to discuss our opinions. That discussion requires the ability to argue in its original sense: to clearly state a position, to back it up with reasonable support, and to address any arguments against it.

Of course, argumentation plays its daily role outside of politics, as well. Every day in school, at work, and at home, we present our opinions and the reasons to support them. In this chapter, you will learn to refine your own ability to present arguments.

Learning Outcomes

LO1 Understand argumentation.
LO2 Learn about reading strategies.
LO3 Read and react to a professional paragraph.
LO4 Read and react to a student paragraph.
LO5 Practice reading skills.
LO6 Plan an argumentation paragraph.
LO7 Write the first draft.
LO8 Revise the writing.
LO9 Edit the writing.

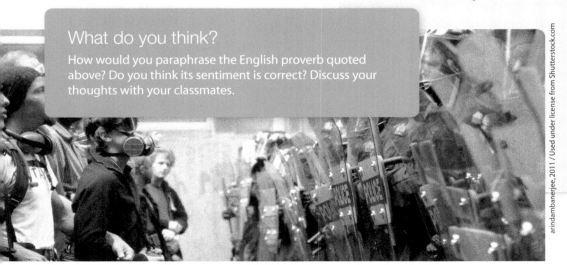

What do you think?

How would you paraphrase the English proverb quoted above? Do you think its sentiment is correct? Discuss your thoughts with your classmates.

arindambanerjee, 2011 / Used under license from Shutterstock.com

LO1 Understanding Argumentation

As the quotation below shows, the word "argument" is commonly misused. It doesn't mean to bicker, squabble, or fight. Those things happen when people don't engage in honest debate.

To argue means to present and support a disputable position. It assumes first considering all sides of a situation and then coming to an opinion. This is why Andre Maurois says, "The difficult part in an argument is not to defend one's opinion, but rather to know it."

Once you've done your research, you will be prepared to argue a position convincingly. It's simply a matter of organizing and presenting the support that led you to your conclusion. As Dale Carnegie puts it, "The best argument is that which seems merely an explanation."

> "People generally quarrel because they cannot argue."
> —Gilbert K. Chesterton

Argumentation Versus Persuasion

The main purpose of persuasion is to be convincing. A campaigning politician trying to gain votes through persuasion will very likely appeal more to the voters' personal interests—"Follow me. I can fix the economy!"—than to logic and reason. A thorough, logical argument may be persuasive, but that is not its main purpose. Its real intent is to prove the strength of a certain line of thinking.

Identify Brainstorm a list of debatable topics you would like to know more about. (Avoid topics on which you already have a firm opinion, unless you are honestly prepared to have that opinion challenged.) Compare your list with those of your classmates, and chose an interesting topic to explore in a paragraph of argumentation.

INSIGHT
In order to be convincing, you must be aware of opposing viewpoints on your topic and either counter them directly or present a weight of evidence that overshadows them. Notice how the examples in this chapter address counterarguments.

Reading

Reading argument paragraphs requires a close examination of the main claim and supporting details. This section provides valuable reading practice.

LO2 Learning About Reading Strategies

In an argument, the author takes a position, supports it with evidence, and addresses counterclaims. The reader considers the evidence presented and decides whether to accept the author's position.

Strategy 1: Considering the Author's Background

Before you read, consider the author's background with the topic. This can help you understand the writer's authority or possible bias. (Often, you can find details about the author in the writing or a short biography that accompanies it. Sometimes you may have to do a Web search or other research to learn more.) Fill in a chart like the following one.

Topic	
Author:	
Author's Position	
Author's Background	

Strategy 2: Considering the Reader's Background

Also review your own background and assumptions about a topic before reading. That way, you'll be best prepared to reflect sincerely on the author's argument. To the chart above, add the following:

My Position:	
My Background:	

LO3 Reading and Reacting to a Professional Essay

Read   In this argumentation paragraph, the author discusses benefits of "wind farming." Use the reading process to get the most from the paragraph, along with the reading strategies on the previous page.

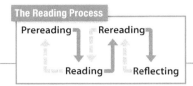

Support Wind Farm Energy

To counteract its dependence on fossil fuels, the United States must   *1*
invest in wind farms for its energy needs. A wind farm is made up of a
group of large wind turbines, which convert wind into electric energy.
The benefits of wind farms are numerous. First, wind is a free and
renewable source of energy. In comparison, fossil fuels like oil and coal   *5*
are limited in supply and cost money to extract from the earth. Secondly,
wind farms are a clean energy source. Unlike power plants, which emit
dangerous pollutants, wind farms release no pollution into the air or
water, meaning less smog, less acid rain, and fewer green house emissions.
And then there's this: the National Wind Resource Center reports that   *10*
running a single wind turbine has the potential to displace 2,000 tons of
carbon dioxide, or the equivalent of one square mile of forest trees ("The
Opportunity"). But despite being the fastest growing energy source in
the U.S., wind energy accounts for only one percent of power supplied in
the country ("Renewable"). If the United States wants to limit carbon   *15*
emissions and lessen its dependence on fossil fuels, it must act now and
invest more money in wind farms. The answer is in the air.

Works Cited

"The Opportunity." *Windcenter.com.* NWRC, n.d. Web. 31 Jan. 2012.
"Renewable Energy Sources in the United States." *nationalatlas.gov.* National Atlas of
the United States, 26 Jan. 2011. Web. 31 Jan. 2012.

React   Answer the following questions. Then discuss your responses with your classmates.

1. What is the paragraph's main idea? _____

2. What main claims does the author offer to support this idea? _____

3. How are alternatives (counterclaims) addressed? _____

4. How would you rate this paragraph? **Weak ★ ★ ★ ★ ★ Strong** Why?

_____

A CLOSER LOOK   at Argumentation

When reading argumentation, it is important to keep an open mind but watch for bias. To do so, consider the writer's treatment of claims and counter claims.

Identifying Claims

You can use a graphic like the one below to help identify the claims in an argument. List each claim separately, and then write any supporting details below it.

Position: _____

Claim 1: _____

Supporting Evidence: _____

_____

Claim 2: _____

Supporting Evidence: _____

_____

Considering Counterclaims

Also consider any counterclaims addressed in the writing. List each separately, with reasons given to dismiss them.

Counterclaim 1: _____

Dismissing Arguments: _____

_____

Counterclaim 2: _____

Dismissing Arguments: _____

_____

Identify   Use graphics like the ones above to list claims, evidence, counterclaims, and dismissing arguments for the paragraph on the previous page.

LO4 Reading and Reacting to a Student Paragraph

Read Read the following argument paragraph about text messaging while driving. Remember to use the steps in the reading process.

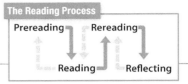

The Reading Process

Prereading → Rereading →

Reading → Reflecting

Text Messaging and Driving Don't Mix

Text messaging while driving should be banned in all states because the practice is making U.S. roadways dangerous. Car crashes rank among the leading causes of death in the United States, but many blame the frequency of drinking and driving and ignore the dangers of texting and driving. Studies by the National Highway Traffic Safety Administration show that text messaging while driving is about six times more likely to result in an accident than drunk driving (Pennsylvania Truck Accident Lawyers). And according to the Human Factors and Ergonomics Society, mobile devices contribute to 2,600 deaths and 330,000 injuries per year ("The Use of Cell Phones"). The major danger associated with texting is the distraction it causes to the driver. A driver whose eyes are concentrating on a phone instead of the road is more likely to get in an accident. Some critics say teenage drivers are the problem, but 20 percent of adults in a recent AAA study admitted to regularly sending text messages while driving ("Text Messaging"). At least 34 states and the District of Columbia understand the aforementioned dangers and have passed bans on texting while driving ("Cell Phone"). Let's make all of our roads a safer place; the time has come to make text messaging while driving illegal in every state.

Works Cited

"Cell Phone and Texting Laws." *GHSA.org.* Governors Highway Safety Association, Sept. 2011. Web. 31 Jan. 2012.

"Text Messaging and Cell Phone Use While Driving." *AAAFoundation.org.* AAA, 12 Oct. 2009. PDF file.

"The Use of Cell Phones While Driving." *USLegal.com.* US Legal, Inc., 2010. Web. 31 Jan. 2012.

Pennsylvania Truck Accident Lawyers. "Teens, Texting and Driving." *Findlaw.com.* Findlaw, 1 Oct. 2009. Web. 31 Jan. 2012.

React Answer the following questions. Then discuss your responses with your classmates.

1. What is the main idea in this paragraph? What claims does the writer make to support this idea? _____

2. What counterclaims does he address? _____

3. How effective is this paragraph? **Weak** ★ ★ ★ ★ ★ **Strong** Why? _____

A CLOSER LOOK at Considering Counterclaims

A good argument does not ignore opposing viewpoints. Instead, it acknowledges them and explains why they don't destroy the argument. When reading, notice how well the author does or does not address your ideas to the contrary. When writing, the better you predict your own reader's possible objections to your argument, the better you can address them, thereby making your argument stronger.

Identify On your own paper, make a chart like the one below. List two counterclaims addressed in the paragraph on the previous page. Then explain how the writer responds to those counterclaims. Finally, list any other objections readers might have, and provide an idea of how you might address them.

Position:

Counterclaim 1:	Response:
Counterclaim 2:	Response:
Reader Objection:	Your Response:

INSIGHT

Not all possible objections need be addressed in argument writing. By countering the most important ones and providing plenty of support for your own position, you may outweigh minor objections without actually stating them. For example, the writer of the paragraph on the previous page doesn't address the possible objection, "Sometimes a text message is important," because his statistics ("six times more likely to result in an accident than drunk driving" and "2,600 deaths per year") already overshadow that counterclaim.

Marquis, 2011 / Used under license from Shutterstock.com

LO5 Practicing Reading Skills

As you read an argument, watch for the difference between facts and opinions. This page will help you understand the difference.

Critical Thinking: Separating Facts and Opinions

A fact is a statement that can be directly proven to be true. An opinion is a personal belief that is disputable because it cannot be directly proven. Opinions often present the meaning of facts, give suggestions for policies, or predict what might happen in the future. Note how a fact (shown below in the center) can spawn opposite opinions.

Opinions	Facts	Opinions
We need to build many more wind farms.	Wind energy currently accounts for only 1 percent of power supplied in the country.	Wind energy will never be able to replace fossil fuels.
Wind farms should be built in forests to double the carbon savings.	A single wind turbine can displace 2,000 tons of carbon dioxide, the same amount as 1 square mile of forest.	Trees should never be felled to make room for wind farms.

Identify Tell whether each piece of text below is an opinion or a fact.

1. Text messaging while driving should be banned. _____

2. Mobile devices contribute to 2,600 deaths per year. _____

3. Thirty-four states have banned texting while driving. _____

4. Teenagers are the problem. _____

5. Twenty percent of adults admit to texting while driving. _____

6. The time has come to outlaw texting while driving. _____

Write For each fact listed below, write two opposite opinions.

Opinions	Facts	Opinions
	Wind turbines can produce electrical energy only when the wind is blowing.	
	The four most productive wind turbines operate in Denmark, while the tallest wind turbine at 205 meters is in Germany.	

Writing

In your own argument paragraph, you will develop a claim about a debatable topic. Be sure to write about a topic that you truly care about. Use the writing process to help you do your best work.

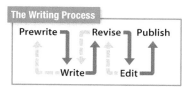

LO6 Prewriting: Planning

Your prewriting begins by selecting a topic that interests you, developing a position about it, and refining that position.

Selecting a Topic

Will began his topic search by browsing newspapers, magazines, and the Internet for current issues that people have strong feelings about. When a friend of his almost ran off the road because of texting, Will had found his topic.

Select List three or four debatable issues you could write about in an argument paragraph. Choose your favorite topic.

_____   _____

_____   _____

Stating a Position

Once you decide on a topic, you need to state a preliminary position about it. In one sentence, write a defensible position statement using the formula below.

Topic		Position		Position Statement
Text messaging while driving	**+** _would, should, must, ought to, needs_	**+** be banned in all states	**=**	Text messaging while driving should be banned in all states.

Create Write a position statement by providing the topic, selecting a verb, and indicating your position.

Topic: _____ **+** | _would, should, must, ought to, needs_ | **+**

Position: _____ **=**

Position Statement: _____

Refining Your Position

With your initial position written, use the following strategies to develop and refine your opinion on the issue:

- **Research** all possible positions on the issue. Who supports each position and why? Who opposes your position and why?
- **Gather** solid evidence regarding your issue. Does the most compelling evidence support or oppose your position?
- **Refine** your position. At this point, you may have new convictions about your position, or you may have changed your mind about it. Before you are ready to write, clarify your position statement.

Gathering Details

When you take a stand on an issue, you must gather convincing support to defend your position. The writer of the paragraph in LO4 gathered four different types of details to support his position: facts, statistics, testimonials, and predictions.

Support Chart

Fact	At least 34 states and the District of Columbia have passed laws against text messaging while driving.
Statistic	According to the U.S. Department of Transportation, mobile devices contribute to 2,600 deaths per year.
Testimony	In the words of U.S. Secretary of Transportation Ray LaHood, "This is an important safety step, and we will be taking more to eliminate the threat of distracted driving."
Prediction	Roads will be safer if texting while driving is banned in all states.

Gather   Create a support chart below with the research you have gathered about your issue. Try to include at least one fact, statistic, piece of testimony, and prediction. If you have not found supporting details for each category, consider doing additional research.

Vocabulary

facts
details that offer statements or claims of verified information

statistics
details that offer concrete numbers about a topic

testimonials
details that offer insight from an authority on the topic

predictions
details that offer insights into possible outcomes or consequences by forecasting what might happen under certain conditions

LO7 Writing the First Draft

Let your first draft be an experiment to get your thoughts and research down on paper. Don't worry about trying to get everything perfect.

Read   Read and consider the following argument for a mandatory public service program.

Citizen Service

Topic Sentence

Our country and our youth would benefit from a one- or   *1*
two-year period of national service after high school. Democracy
has a long history of service by private citizens. Think of
the citizen soldiers of Ancient Greece or the Minutemen of
colonial America. Consider today's National Guard members,   *5*
Reservists, and Peace Corps volunteers. Ask most people who
have served, and they will tell you the experience helped them
grow up and discover their potential. It also made them more

Body Sentences

conscious of their responsibility to their nation. Of course,
some may object that mandatory service would violate our   *10*
liberties. However, we already require public education from
kindergarten through high school. Adding another year or two
shouldn't matter, especially since people would have a choice
of how they wished to serve. The military's various branches
would offer possibilities, as would the Peace Corps, Americorps,   *15*
and other civilian volunteer organizations. In these various
services, people would learn life and career skills, and under
a bill currently going through Congress, they could also earn
grants for college ("Mandatory"). A nation is only as good as its

Closing Sentence

people. Adding a year or two of public service to our educational   *20*
track would benefit us all.

Works Cited

"Mandatory Public Service." *FactCheck.org.* U. of Penn., 21 Apr. 2009.
    Web. 31 Jan. 2012.

Consider the Craft

1. How effectively does the paragraph make its claim?
2. How effectively does it address counterclaims?
3. What do you like most about this paragraph?
4. What improvements might you suggest?

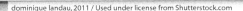
dominique landau, 2011 / Used under license from Shutterstock.com

The Working Parts of a Paragraph

As the previous page shows, a paragraph has three main parts, each with its own purpose.

Paragraph Outline

Topic Sentence: The topic sentence states your position.

Body Sentences: The body sentences support the position using logical reasoning and reliable details. These sentences also address counterclaims.

Closing Sentence: A closing sentence (or two) reinforces your argument and (if appropriate) encourages your reader to adopt it.

Drafting Tips

When writing an argument paragraph, appeal to the reader with logical reasoning and compelling evidence.

TRAITS

Transition words that show importance: first of all / to begin / secondly / another reason / the best reason / also / in addition / more importantly / most importantly / finally

In the opening...

- Lead up to your claim, if necessary, by providing reasonable background.
- Make your claim firmly but respectfully.

In the middle...

- Give the reader plenty of solid reasons to adopt your point of view.
- Use valid research to back up your position.
- Address any counterclaims politely, providing a convincing argument against them.

In the closing...

- Restate your position in light of the reasons you have provided.
- If appropriate, give your reader a call to action.

Write Prepare the first draft of your argument paragraph using the information on this page and the planning in LO6 as a guide.

LO8 Revising the Writing

Start the revising process by reading your first draft two or three times to get a feel for your work so far. Then have one of your classmates read and react to your work using a response sheet as a guide.

Five Common Logical Fallacies

A logical fallacy is a false assertion that weakens an argument. Below are five common logical fallacies that should be removed from your writing.

- A **bare assertion** denies that an issue is debatable, claiming, "That's just how it is."
  > Withdrawal of troops is our only option for peace.
  > *(The claim discourages discussion of other ways to promote peace.)*
- A **threat** is a simple way to sabotage an argument, claiming, "If you don't agree with me, you'll regret it."
  > If you don't accept alternative fuel sources, get ready to move back to the Stone Age.
- A **slippery slope** fallacy argues that a single step will start an unstoppable chain of events.
  > If we build a skate park, vandalism is going to run rampant in our city.
- An **unreliable testimonial** is a statement made by a biased or unqualified source. A testimonial only has force if it is made by an authority.
  > As TV's Dr. Daniels, I recommend Xanax for all my patients.
- A **half-truth** contains part of but not the whole truth.
  > Three out of five doctors recommend ibuprofen, according to a recent study.
  > *(This may be true in this one study but not universally.)*

Revise Improve your writing using the following checklist and your partner's comments on the response sheet. Continue until you can check off each item.

Revising Checklist

Ideas
- ☐ **1.** Does my topic sentence identify an issue and my position?
- ☐ **2.** Do I include a variety of supporting details?
- ☐ **3.** Do I avoid errors in logic?

Organization
- ☐ **4.** Do I have a topic sentence, body sentences, and a closing sentence?
- ☐ **5.** Have I used transitions to connect my ideas?

Voice
- ☐ **6.** Do I sound knowledgeable and passionate about the issue?

LO9 Editing: Mechanics

"Mechanics" refers to the standards of presenting written language; capitalization and number use are two of the mechanics issues writers encounter.

Capitalization Errors

Capitalizing proper nouns and proper adjectives (adjectives derived from proper nouns) is a basic rule of capitalization. There are times, however, when certain words are capitalized in one instance but not in another. The quick guide below refers to a number of these special cases.

Capitalize	Do Not Capitalize
American	un-American
January, May	winter, spring
The South is quite conservative	Turn south at the stop sign.
Duluth City College	a Duluth college
Chancellor John Bohm	John Bohm, our chancellor
President Obama	the president of the United States
Earth (planet name)	the earth
Internet	electronic communications network

Proofreading Practice In each sentence below, indicate which words should be capitalized, using the correction mark (≡).

INSIGHT

Different languages use capitalization differently. Even different Englishes (U.S. and British, for example) treat capitals differently.

1. with november around the corner, it's only so long until winter engulfs minnesota.
2. Flag burning is the definition of an un-american activity.
3. I caught up with chancellor Greg Williams of the university of pittsburgh.
4. I used the internet to find out that Missouri is nicknamed the show-me state.
5. My favorite french restaurant rests in a quiet neighborhood off college avenue.
6. The west coast is known for its laid-back lifestyle.
7. Does the winter sports season begin before or after december?
8. The president of the united states lives in the white house.

Apply As you edit your paragraph, be careful to discern common nouns from proper nouns. Remember: Do not capitalize common nouns and titles that appear near, but are not part of, a proper noun.

Using Numbers

When a paragraph includes numbers or statistics, you will have to know whether to write them as words or as numerals. Below are three basic rules to follow.

Numerals or Words

Numbers from one to one hundred are usually written as words; numbers 101 and greater are usually written as numerals.

two   seven   twenty-five   103   1,489

Numerals Only

Use numerals for the following forms: decimals, percentages, pages, chapters, addresses, dates, telephone numbers, identification numbers, and statistics.

13.1   20 percent   Highway 41   chapter 6
February 12, 2010   (273) 289-2288   2.4 feet

Words Only

Use words to express numbers that begin a sentence.

Thirteen players suffered from food poisoning.

Proofreading Practice In each sentence below, cross out any incorrect numbers and write the correct form above.

1. My 2 cousins, Braden and Candace, live 4 miles apart on Highway Eleven.

2. 300 raffle tickets were bought at the gates.

3. The results showed twenty-five percent of participants were born before January first, 1985.

4. Please review chapter seventeen for the test on Monday.

5. The coastal reef is two point eight knots away.

6. 15 of us are hoping to complete the three point one-mile race.

Apply Read your argument paragraph, paying special attention to sentences that include numbers and statistics. Present numbers in the correct way: either as numerals or as words.

Marking a Paragraph

Before you finish editing your revised paragraph, you can practice by editing the following model.

Editing Practice Correct the following paragraph, using the marks below. One correction has been done for you.

A Super Blow to Roscoe

For the good of the local economy, the Roscoe City Council must vote   *1*
down a proposal to build a SuperMart store on Highway Thirty-One.
The discount chain may slash prices, it will slash local businesses in the
process. a University of Iowa study showed a group of small towns lost up
to 47 percent of they're retail trade after ten years of a SuperMart moving   *5*
in nearby. Grocery stores and retail businesses were hit the hardest. If a
SuperMart comes to Roscoe local grocers like Troyer's will have to lower
wages or risk clozing. A 2007 study showed how a SuperMart caused
a one point five percent reduction in earnings for local grocery stores.
Proponents of a SuperMart expansion says the store will bring new jobs,   *10*
more sales taxes, and great bargains. But all SuperMart will accomplish
is reallocating where existing income is spent. The Roscoe City Council
should look for alternatives to jump-start the community's economy vote no
for SuperMart.

Correction Marks

ℰ delete	⅄ add comma	ᴡᴏʳᵈ∧ add word
d̲̲ capitalize	? add question	⊙ add period
D̲ lowercase	∧ mark	⬭ spelling
∧ insert	ⱽ insert an apostrophe	⊓ switch

Correcting Your Paragraph

Now it's time to correct your own paragraph.

Apply   Create a clean copy of your paragraph and use the following checklist to check for errors. When you can answer *yes* to a question, check it off. Continue working until all items are checked.

Editing Checklist

Words

☐   1. Have I used specific nouns and verbs?
☐   2. Have I used more action verbs than "be" verbs?

Sentences

☐   3. Have I varied the beginnings and lengths of sentences?
☐   4. Have I combined short choppy sentences?
☐   5. Have I avoided shifts in sentences?
☐   6. Have I avoided fragments and run-ons?

Conventions

☐   7. Do I use correct verb forms (*he saw*, not *he seen*)?
☐   8. Do my subjects and verbs agree (*she speaks*, not *she speak*)?
☐   9. Have I used the right words (*their, there, they're*)?
☐ 10. Have I capitalized first words and proper nouns and adjectives?
☐ 11. Have I used commas after long introductory word groups?
☐ 12. Have I carefully checked my spelling?

Adding a Title

Make sure to add an attention-getting title. Here are three simple strategies for creating one.

- Create a slogan:

  Support Wind Farm Energy

- Sum up your argument:

  Texting and Driving Don't Mix

- Use a play on words:

  A Super Blow to Roscoe

Create   Prepare a clean final copy of your paragraph and proofread it.

> "When I'm getting ready to reason with a man, I spend one-third of my time thinking about myself and what I am going to say—and two-thirds thinking about him and what he is going to say."
>
> — Abraham Lincoln

Review and Enrichment

On the next seven pages you will be asked to read and respond to a professional argument essay about how personal lawsuits are brought against corporations. You will also encounter several ideas for writing your own argument.

Prereading

Social issues can be complicated. Each of us comes to a social topic with our own assumptions based on our backgrounds, our needs, and our desires. Somehow we all have to come to a consensus about what is best, meshing the rights of the individual with the workings of a civilization.

CONSIDER THE TRAITS

As you read the argumentation essay that follows, pay attention to the **ideas** first—the claims and counterclaims, and how they are either supported or answered. Then note the essay's **organization**—the way in which the opening introduces the topic, the body expands upon it, and the closing revisits it.

Argumentation plays a central role in that process. It allows us each to present and support our positions, so that they can all be weighed against one another to come up with the best solutions for our common challenges.

Identify   Think of a local issue that matters a lot to you: a shortage of student parking space; a need for more bike paths; class scheduling conflicts; gender, age, or ethnicity issues in employment; and so on. Freewrite for 5 to 10 minutes about why that issue is important to you.

_____

_____

_____

What do you think?

What does the Abraham Lincoln quotation above tell you about presenting an effective argument? With your classmates, discuss your reaction to this quotation.

Reading and Reacting

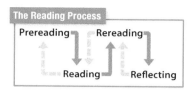

Read Read the following argumentative essay about "frivolous lawsuits." Notice the variety of details used to illustrate the topic's impact upon and importance to our society.

About the Author

Laraine Flemming is a textbook writer with 20 years' experience teaching, from elementary to college level, but her first teaching position was in a psychiatric hospital in Vinita, Oklahoma. It was there that she became utterly convinced of the transformative power of reading, which led her eventually to publish reading texts of her own. Flemming has a Ph.D. from State University of New York in Buffalo.

What Exactly Is a Frivolous Lawsuit?

The lawsuit of seventy-nine-year-old Stella Liebeck, launched against   1
McDonald's in 1994 after spilling hot coffee on herself as she went through
the drive-through lane, immediately became the stuff of comedy. A *Seinfeld*
episode even used it, making one of the characters sue for damages after he
spilled coffee on himself. But the general attitude toward the suit, on television   5
and off, was summed up in the response of another *Seinfeld* character, Elaine,
who expressed puzzlement at the very idea of a lawsuit involving hot coffee
being spilled and McDonald's being somehow liable, "Who ever heard of this
anyway? Suing a company because their coffee is too hot? Coffee is supposed to
be hot." In other words, the suit was a ridiculous joke.   10
    What got left out of all the jokes, though, were the actual details of the
case. Liebeck suffered third-degree burns. Third-degree burns are the most
serious kind, especially for a woman of her age. Plus, there had been at least
700 previous cases of people being scalded by McDonald's coffee before Liebeck
went to court. McDonald's had settled other claims but did not want to give   15
Liebeck the $20,000 compensation she had requested. So she sued and the
case went to court.
    What Liebeck's lawyers proved was that McDonald's was making its
coffee 30 to 50 degrees hotter than other restaurants. In fact, the Shriner
Burn Institute had already warned McDonald's not to serve coffee above 130   20
degrees. Yet the liquid that burned Liebeck was the usual temperature for
McDonald's brew—about 190 degrees. As a result of Liebeck's suit, McDonald's
coffee is now sold at the same temperature as most other restaurants.
    Yes, there probably are trivial lawsuits filed on a regular basis. But
Liebeck's wasn't one of them. It's actually ironic that the "hot coffee" lawsuit,   25
as it's come to be called, is often cited as an illustration of why the country
desperately needs tort reform. Yet a closer examination of this issue suggests
that citizens might want to think twice before joining in the chorus of calls to
enact tort reform.
    Tort reform legislation, in place or pending, differs from state to state.   30
Thus one of the questions involved in the debate is how tort reform should go
forward. Should it be on a state or federal level?

In general, though, the tort reform movement focuses on three goals: (1) the need to limit the circumstances under which injured people may file a lawsuit after being injured by a product or procedure, (2) the goal of making it more difficult for people injured by a product or procedure to obtain a trial by jury, and (3) the desire to place limits on the amount of money injured parties may be awarded.   35

In the eyes of some, like political activist and organizer Jon Greenbaum, the idea that the country is desperately in need of tort reform is a myth. From his perspective, the right to sue corporations or companies if their products were defective or their procedures badly managed or fraudulent was a consumer victory won in the 1950s. In his eyes, now is not the time to abandon that right. He thinks implementing tort reform would be a step backward for consumers, not a step forward: "It will limit our ability to hold corporations accountable for their misdeeds. Corporate America has succeeded to a great extent by buying up our legislators and capturing regulatory bodies. We must not let them wrest control of the judicial system as well."   40   45

That, however, would not be the position of Court Koenning, the president of Citizens Against Lawsuit Abuse of Houston. For him, lawsuits demanding compensation for injury due to defective products or procedures reveal a growing canker on American society—the abdication of personal responsibility. As he writes, "The somebody's gotta pay attitude is pervasive and that does not bode well for future generations. We need to reacquaint ourselves with personal responsibility and stop playing the blame game. We need to realize that every dilemma or personal disappointment is not fodder for a lawsuit and does not warrant a treasure trove of cash."   50   55

These are all stirring sentiments. But they need to be viewed in the light of what consumers "playing the blame game" in court have actually tried to accomplish. In Los Angeles, California, consumers have gone to court to stop health insurers from canceling policies of people newly diagnosed with a serious illness. The insurance cancellations, usually based on technicalities, seem to target people who will require long-term and expensive care, for which the insurance companies would have to pay if the policies weren't cancelled.   60

In Harrisburg, Pennsylvania, consumers turned to the courts to take action against "mortgage rescue" companies who, for a fee, claimed they could help those falling behind on their payments. But after the fee was paid, no help was forthcoming. In Hartford, Connecticut, consumers also went to court against a pharmaceutical company that was blocking generic alternatives to the high-priced drugs on which the company's profits were based.   65   70

This is not to say that all personal injury complaints taken to court are worthy of respect. Did anyone really want to see the woman who sued a cosmetics company for changing the shade of her hair become a millionaire? But many of the personal injury lawsuits brought by consumers do real good, helping not just the litigant but the public in general. We might want to consider that fact next time we hear or read another argument in favor of tort reform because what we might be reforming is our own right to seek justice by legal means.   75

Sources: Court Koenning, "Starbucks 'Hot Tea' Lawsuit Highlights a Void in Personal Responsibility," www.setexasrecord.com; Jon Greenbaum, "McDonald's Hot Coffee Lawsuit and Beyond: The Tort Reform Myth Machine," CommonDreams.org   80

React   Answer the following questions about the argumentative essay. Share your responses with your classmates.

1. What is Flemming's position (main claim) in the essay?

   _____

2. How might her personal or professional background have influenced this position?

   _____

3. What was your own opinion about the topic before reading the essay?

   _____

4. How might your own background have influenced your opinion?

   _____

5. What claims and counterclaims does the author include in the essay? (List at least three.)

   _____

   _____

   _____

6. How are her claims supported? How are counterclaims answered?

   _____

7. How would you rate this argument and why?

   Weak ★ ★ ★ ★ ★ Strong

   _____

8. What did you learn from the argument that you hadn't known before?

   _____

Writing

Follow the guidelines on the next two pages to write your own paragraph or essay of argumentation. Check with your instructor about any specific requirements that he or she may have.

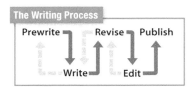

Prewriting

Choose one of the following ideas for your argumentative writing. Or decide upon another idea of your own.

Writing Ideas

1. Choose one of the debatable topics you brainstormed in LO1, or one of the local issues you identified in LO6.

2. Think about a problem you would like to see fixed. Use an argumentation essay to suggest a solution.

3. Choose a cause that you believe needs to be championed. Use an argumentation essay to explain what is threatening it and why it must succeed.

4. Challenge yourself by arguing the other side. Select a current topic of debate and argue against your own opinion on it, in favor of an opposing viewpoint.

5. Think about an important person in your life. What one opinion does that person hold strongest? Write an argumentation essay either supporting or challenging that opinion. (Consider sharing your essay with the person after it is finished.)

When planning . . .

Refer to LO6 to help with your prewriting and planning. Also use the tips below.

- State your main idea clearly, so that you can remain focused during writing.
- Consider your reader. What opinion will that person likely have about the subject? What questions or objections might your reader have?
- Consider your purpose. If your reader's opinion matches your own, your purpose will be to further the reader's understanding of the topic and any counterarguments. If your reader's opinion is contrary to yours, your purpose will be to soothe any objections and provide convincing support for yours.
- Consider your voice. For a paragraph or an essay of argument, your voice should usually be respectful but confident.

Writing and Revising

Refer to LO7 to help you write and review your first draft. Also use the tips below to help with your drafting and revising.

When writing . . .

- Include an opening, a middle, and a closing in your argument. Each part has a specific role to play.
- Follow your planning notes, but remain free to expand upon new ideas.
- If you encounter a claim or counterclaim that you have not researched, note it in your text and keep on writing. Research that claim or counterclaim after finishing your first draft rather than getting sidetracked during writing.
- Try to keep your intended audience in mind. Picture someone in particular and keep your voice appropriately confident and respectful.

When revising . . .

- Be prepared to reorganize your ideas for better impact. Often a new arrangement will suggest itself as you reread your first draft.
- Make sure your writing doesn't antagonize the reader by taking on a negative or condescending tone.
- Also make sure your writing sounds confident, not apologetic.
- Watch for spots where your argument seems "thin." If a point needs more support, find it. If an important counterclaim has not been mentioned, address it.
- Ask a classmate or another writer to review and critique your writing. Use a peer-review sheet to guide the critique.

Editing

Refer to the checklist in LO9 when you are ready to edit your argument for style and correctness.

Monkey Business Images, 2011 / Used under license from Shutterstock.com

Reflecting on Argument Writing

Answer the following questions about your argumentation reading and writing experience in this chapter.

1. Why is argumentation so important?

   _____

2. What is your favorite sample argument in this chapter? Why?

   _____

3. What reading strategy in this chapter do you find most helpful? Explain.

   _____

4. What is the most important thing you learned about reading a paragraph or an essay of argumentation?

   _____

5. What do you like most about the paragraph of argumentation you wrote for this chapter? Why?

   _____

6. What is one thing you would like to change in your paragraph?

   _____

7. What is the most important thing you have learned about writing paragraphs and essays of argumentation?

   _____

Key Terms to Remember

Whenever you read and write argumentation, it's important to understand the following terms.

- **Claims**—reasons in support of the main topic. Without claims to support it, an argument is merely an unfounded opinion.
- **Counterclaims**—reasons against the main topic. When addressed respectfully and confidently, counterclaims can actually strengthen an argument by showing that you have carefully thought over the entire subject.
- **Logical fallacies**—false assertions. These actually weaken an argument by making it seem less than carefully considered.

10

> "If you can't explain it simply, you don't understand it well enough."
> —Albert Einstein

Summarizing

Longer forms of academic reading and writing, like essays, are often packed with important information. For a reader, memorizing all the key details in longer texts can be a tall order. Summarizing the writing is a more effective way to learn the information. Summarization is the process of identifying and explaining the key ideas of a reading in your own words.

Writing a summary is one of the best ways of becoming actively involved in your reading. Summarizing a text also helps you to evaluate how much you know about the material and to remember what you read. If you have trouble explaining any ideas, then you know you need to reread the passage.

In this chapter, you will read and summarize a number of academic passages. You will also learn strategies for identifying key ideas and explaining them in your own words.

Learning Outcomes

LO1 Understand summarizing.
LO2 Learn about reading strategies.
LO3 Read and react to a summary.
LO4 Write a summary.
LO5 Practice additional summary writing.

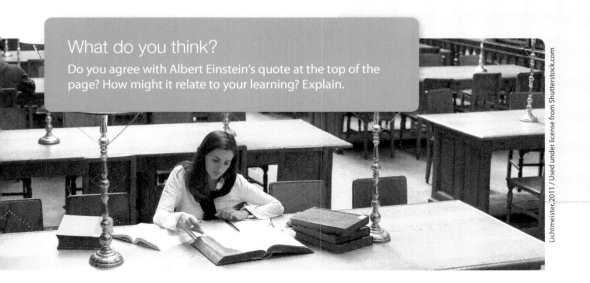

What do you think?

Do you agree with Albert Einstein's quote at the top of the page? How might it relate to your learning? Explain.

LO1 Understanding Summarizing

In some ways you practice summarizing every day in conversations with your friends, family members, and co-workers. For example, when someone asks you what you did over the weekend, you wouldn't tell every detail about it. Instead you would summarize or highlight the most important points in your own words.

> "The simpler you say it, the more eloquent it is."
> —August Wilson

When you write a summary, you should use your own words, except for any specific, essential words for ideas from the text. The key is to share only the main ideas of the text, rather than every last detail. Your goal is to provide a glimpse of the whole text, not a detailed look at the parts.

Summary Versus Paraphrase

A paraphrase, also written in your own words, does not reduce a text to its basic meaning. Rather, it explains the full meaning of a challenging reading. Because a paraphrase often includes explanations or interpretations, it can actually be longer than the original. A summary, by contrast, provides a brief explanation of the main ideas in the text and should be about one-third the length of the original.

INSIGHT

A typical one- or two-page essay can be summarized in one well-formed paragraph. The first sentence in a summary is the topic sentence. The sentences that follow must support the topic sentence.

Identify Telling friends about a movie is one example of informal summarizing. List three or four other examples of summaries that commonly occur in your conversations.

1. _Recapping a television episode for a friend is one example of informal summarizing_

2. _____

3. _____

4. _____

Reading

Summarizing is an important learning tool in all of your class work, especially for report and research assignments. But to summarize a text, you need to understand it in its original form. The strategies below will help.

LO2 Learning About Reading Strategies

Strategy 1: Using a Table Diagram

Part of the challenge when reading a text is keeping track of the main idea and key supporting points. A graphic organizer called a table diagram works well for this purpose. Identify the thesis, or main idea, of the reading on the table top and list the key supporting points underneath. Then refer to this information as you write a summary of the text.

Table Diagram

Thesis or main idea

supporting points	supporting points	supporting points	supporting points

ajt, 2011 / Used under license from Shutterstock.com

Strategy 2: Understanding the Structure of Writing

Most informational texts are shaped in the following way: The first part introduces the topic and states the thesis or main idea. The middle paragraphs support and develop the thesis. The closing part usually reviews what has been said and may offer an additional idea or two. Keeping this structure in mind should help you find the key information in a text.

Beginning

Middle

Ending

LO3 Reading and Reacting to a Summary

In order to read and react to a summary, you must first read and react to the text that is being summarized. What follows is an academic text followed by a model summary of the text.

Read Read the following passage from the article entitled, "How Our Skins Got Their Color," by Marvin Harris. Use the reading process to help you fully understand the text.

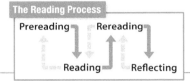

The Reading Process

Prereading ⟶ Rereading
Reading ⟶ Reflecting

How Our Skins Got Their Color

Human skin owes its color to the presence of particles known as melanin. The primary function of melanin is to protect the upper levels of the skin from being damaged by the sun's ultraviolet rays. This radiation poses a critical problem for our kind because we lack the dense coat of hair that acts as a sunscreen for most mammals. . . . Hairlessness exposes us to two kinds of radiation hazards: ordinary sunburn, with its blisters, rashes, and risk of infection; and skin cancers, including malignant melanoma, one of the deadliest diseases known. Melanin is the body's first line of defense against these afflictions. The more melanin particles, the darker the skin, and the lower the risk of sunburn and all forms of skin cancer. This explains why the highest rates for skin cancer are found in sun-drenched lands such as Australia, where light-skinned people of European descent spend a good part of their lives outdoors wearing scanty attire. Very dark-skinned people such as heavily pigmented Africans of Zaire seldom get skin cancer, but when they do, they get it on depigmented parts of their bodies—palms and lips.

If exposure to solar radiation had nothing but harmful effects, natural selection would have favored inky black as the color for all human populations. But the sun's rays do not present an unmitigated threat. As it falls on the skin, sunshine converts a fatty substance in the epidermis into vitamin D. The blood carries vitamin D from the skin to the intestines, where it plays a vital role in the absorption of calcium. In turn, calcium is vital for strong bones. Without it, people fall victim to the crippling diseases rickets and osteomalacia. In women, calcium deficiencies can result in a deformed birth canal, which makes childbirth lethal for both mother and fetus.

Vitamin D can be obtained from a few foods, primarily the oils and livers of marine fish. But inland populations must rely on the sun's rays and their own skins for this crucial substance. The particular color of a

1

5

10

15

20

25

human population's skin, therefore, represents in large degree a trade-off   *30*
between the hazards of too much versus too little solar radiation: acute
sunburn and skin cancer on the one hand, and rickets and osteomalacia on
the other. It is this trade-off that largely accounts for the preponderance
of brown people in the world and for the general tendency for skin color to
be darkest among equatorial populations and lightest among populations   *35*
dwelling at higher latitudes.

Marvin Harris, "How Our Skins Got Their Color," Our Kind: Who We Are, Where We Came From, and Where We Are Going, Harper Collins, 1989.

Vocabulary

dense	**epidermis**	**preponderance**
thick	uppermost layer of skin	majority
pigmented	**rickets**	**equatorial populations**
colored by pigment	softening of bones in the	people who live close to the
unmitigated	young	earth's equator
not made less severe	**osteomalacia**	
	softening of bones in adults	

React   Answer the questions below about the essay on the previous page. Then discuss your responses with your classmates.

1. What is the thesis or main idea of the text? _____

2. What key points are explained in the middle paragraph? _____

3. What example does the author use in the third paragraph to explain the relationship between the benefits and hazards of sunlight to the skin? _____

4. How would you rate this passage and why?

   Weak ★ ★ ★ ★ ★ Strong _____

Drawing Inferences

An *inference* is a logical conclusion that you can make about something that is not actually said or stated in a text. A worthy inference does, however, result from a clear and careful understanding of what *is* said. To practice drawing inferences, answer the following questions about the text on the previous page. Afterward, share your responses with your classmates.

1. Reread the first two sentences of the last paragraph. What inference related to vitamin D and diet can you make about populations who live near marine life?

2. Using the information from the passage, what can you infer about your own skin color?

Read   Carefully read the following summary of the text about skin and sunlight. Notice that it is not more than one-third the length of the original text.

Summary of the Text

In the passage from "How Our Skins Got Their Color," Marvin Harris explores the impact of sunlight on skin health and skin color. There are two main dangers caused by overexposure to the sun. They are sunburn and skin cancer. The presence of melanin particles protects skin from these dangers. Melanin also influences skin color—the more melanin particles present, the darker the skin. But while too much sunlight can cause health problems, so too can lack of sunlight, since sunlight provides the body with vitamin D. Lack of vitamin D can cause a person's bones to soften. The author concludes that this balancing act between too much and too little sun exposure is why a large percentage of the world's population has brown skin.

React   Answer the following questions about the summary. Then share your responses with your classmates.

1. What information is provided in the topic sentence of the summary?

2. What information is provided in the body or middle sentences? Name three ideas.

3. What information is provided in the closing sentence?

4. Does the writer of the summary use his own words for the most part? Why do you think this is important?

5. Does the summary help you understand the original passage? Explain.

INSIGHT

When you are writing a summary for a report or research paper, note the source of the text (title of the text, author, page number, and so on). This will make it easier for you to acknowledge or cite the source in your actual report.

LO4　Writing a Summary

In this part of the chapter, you will write a summary of your own following the guidelines presented in this section.

Read　To get started, read and react to the article below by Constance Staley and Steve Staley. Use the reading process to help you gain a complete understanding of the text.

About the Authors

Constance Staley is an author and educator. She is an expert in helping students prepare for and succeed in college. *FOCUS on College and Career Success* puts in one place all of the valuable advice she has shared with students over the years.

Steve Staley is dean of academics and professor of management and humanities at Colorado Technical University. He has also taught at the Air Force Academy, the Naval War College, and the University of Colorado.

Get Physically Energized

To make sure you're physically energized, try these suggestions.　*1*

1. **Snap to your body's rhythm.** Have you noticed times of the day when it's easier to concentrate than others? Perhaps you regularly crash in the middle of the afternoon, for example, so you go for a chocolate fix, or a coffee pick-me-up. Everyone has a biological clock. Paying attention　*5* to your body's natural rhythms is important. Plan to do activities that require you to be alert during your natural productivity peaks. That's better than plodding although a tough assignment when the energy just isn't there. Use low energy times to take care of mindless chores that require little to no brainpower.　*10*

2. **Up and at 'em.** What about 8:00 a.m. classes? Don't use your body's natural rhythms as an excuse to sleep through class! ("I'm just not a morning person . . .") If you're truly not a morning person, don't sign up for early morning classes. If you are coming off working a night shift, you may need some rest first. Sleeping through your obligations won't　*15* do much for your success—and you'll be playing a continual game of catch-up, which takes even more time. Some experts advise that you start your day as early as possible. Marking six items off your to-do list before lunch can give you a real high.

3. **Sleep at night, study during the day.** Burning the midnight oil and　*20* pulling all-nighters aren't the best ideas, either. It only takes one all-nighter to help you realize that a lack of sleep translates into a drop in performance. Without proper sleep, your ability to understand and remember course material is impaired. Research shows that the

average adult requires seven to eight hours of sleep each night. If   *25*
you can't get that much for whatever reason, take a short afternoon
nap. Did you know that the Three Mile Island nuclear meltdown in
Pennsylvania in 1979 and the Chernobyl disaster in the Ukraine in
1986 took place at 4 a.m. and 1:23 a.m., respectively? Experts believe
it's no coincidence that both these events took place when workers   *30*
would normally be sleeping.

4. **"Burn the premium fuel."** You've heard it before: Food is the fuel that
makes us run. The better the fuel, the smoother we run. It's that
simple. . . . When the demands on your energy are high, such as exam
week, use premium fuel. If you don't believe it, think about how many   *35*
people you know get sick during times of high stress. Watch how
many of your classmates are hacking and coughing their way through
exams—or in bed missing them altogether.

"Get Physically Energized" from STALEY/STALEY. *FOCUS on College and Career Success*, 1E. ©
2012 Wadsworth, a part of Cengage Learning, Inc.

React   Answer the following questions about the reading. Your responses to these
questions will help you write your summary.

1. What is the thesis or main idea of the text? _____

2. What key points in the middle paragraphs explain or develop the thesis?
   Consider listing them on a table diagram. _____

Thesis or main idea			
supporting points	supporting points	supporting points	supporting points

3. How does the structure of the text help you identify the key points? _____

4. How would you rate this essay and why?
   Weak ★ ★ ★ ★ ★ Strong _____

Vocabulary Practice

Explain or define the following words in the text by using context clues and your
understanding of word parts. List the word or word parts that help you define each term.

- plodding (line 8)
- obligations (line 15)
- impaired (line 24)
- premium (line 32)

Writing Guidelines

The following guidelines will help you write a paragraph summary of an essay or extended passage.

Planning Your Summary

Most of your prewriting and planning will occur when you read and react to the text. During your planning . . .

- Name the thesis or main idea of the text.
- Identify the key points that support the thesis.

INSIGHT

In academic texts, each middle paragraph often addresses one key supporting point. This point is usually stated in the topic sentence.

Writing the First Draft

Remember that you are writing a paragraph, starting with a topic sentence and following with supporting ideas. As you write your first draft . . .

- Use your own words as much as possible.
- Start with a topic sentence, naming the title, author, and topic of the text.
- Continue with the key points that explain the thesis. (Avoid specific details.)
- Arrange your ideas in the most logical order.
- Add a closing sentence, if one seems necessary.

Revising the Writing

Remember that your summary should address just the essential information from the original text. As you review your first draft . . .

- Determine if it identifies the main idea of the text.
- Decide if you've limited yourself to key supporting information.
- See if your summary reads smoothly and logically.
- Determine if you've used your own words, except for key ideas. (See the next page.)

Editing the Writing

Be sure that your summary is clear and accurate if you are turning it in for evaluation. As you edit your revised summary . . .

- Check that you've used complete sentences.
- Check for spelling, capitalization, and punctuation errors. Pay special attention to titles and quoted material. (See the next page.)
- Check for proper usage and grammar.

Write Write a paragraph summary of the text in LO4 using the information above as a guide. Be prepared to refer to the original text many times as you develop your writing.

A CLOSER LOOK at Revising and Editing

Revising

The information that follows will help you check your summary for (1) recognizing the source and (2) identifying exact ideas from the text.

Recognizing the Source   Follow your instructor's guidelines for identifying the source of your summary (if you are turning it in for evaluation). The following example shows you how to identify the title and author in the topic sentence of your summary.

- In this passage from "Religious Faith Versus Spirituality," author Neil Bissoondath explores spirituality. . . .

Identifying Exact Ideas from the Text   In your summary, you may find it necessary to include a few exact ideas or specialized words from the original text. When this type of information is taken directly from the text, enclose it within quotation marks.

- **Exact idea:** The author describes himself as "soaring with a lightness I'd never known before" after the ceremony.
- **Specialized word:** One teacher recognized as a master teacher serves as a "standard-bearer" for all great teachers.

Editing

This information will help you correctly capitalize and punctuate titles and quoted materials.

Capitalizing Titles   Capitalize the first and last words in a title and all important words in between. Do not capitalize words such as *a, for, by, in, and,* and *the* if they occur within the title.

- **Title:** Chinese Space, American Space *(All the words are important so they are all capitalized.)*
- **Title:** Catcher in the Rye *("In" and "the" occur within the title so they are lowercased.)*

Punctuating Titles   Use quotation marks to set off the titles of chapters, essays, articles, and so on. Italicize or underline the titles of books, magazines, newspapers, Web sites, and so on.

- **Title of an Essay:** "Chinese Space, American Space"
- **Title of a Book:** *Catcher in the Rye*

Placement of Other Punctuation Place commas and periods inside quotation marks. Place question marks or exclamation marks inside the quotation marks when they punctuate the quotation and outside when they punctuate the sentence.

- **Placement of a Comma:** In this passage from "Religious Faith Versus Spirituality," author Neil Bissoondath explores spirituality. *(Commas and periods are always placed inside the quotation marks.)*

- **Placement of a Question Mark:** The essay "Yes, Accidents Happen. But Why?" analyzes the causes of accidents. *(The question mark punctuates the quotation, so it is placed inside the quotation marks.)*

- Have you read "Spanglish Spoken Here"? *(The question mark punctuates the entire sentence, so it is placed outside the quotation marks.)*

Check Be sure to use the information on these two pages to help you revise and edit your summary, correctly capitalizing and punctuating titles and quoted material.

Supri Suharjoto, 2011 / Used under license from Shutterstock.com

LO5 Practicing Additional Summary Writing

This section includes two texts that you can use for additional summary-writing practice. Always read and react to the text before writing your summary

First Text

Read Read the following passage from *Living in the Environment* by G. Tyler Miller and Scott Spoolman. The writing discusses a common misconception about sharks and explains why they are important to the environment.

About the Authors

G. Tyler Miller and Scott Spoolman are textbook writers, specializing in environmental science.

Why Should We Protect Sharks?

More than 400 known species of sharks inhabit the world's oceans.   *1*
They vary widely in size and behavior, from the goldfish-sized dwarf dog shark to the whale shark, which can grow to a length of 18 meters (60 feet) and weigh as much as two full-grown African elephants. . . .

Sharks have been around for more than 400 million years. As keystone   *5*
species, some shark species play crucial roles in helping to keep their ecosystems functioning. Feeding at or near the tops of food webs, they remove injured and sick animals from the ocean. Without this service provided by sharks, the oceans would be teeming with dead and dying fish and marine mammals.   *10*

In addition to playing their important ecological roles, sharks could help to save human lives. If we learn why they almost never get cancer, we could possibly use this information to fight cancer in our own species. Scientists are also studying their highly effective immune systems, which allow wounds in sharks to heal without becoming infected.   *15*

Many people argue that we should protect sharks simply because they, like any other species, have a right to exist. But another reason for the importance of sustaining this threatened portion of the earth's biodiversity is that some sharks are keystone species, which means that we and other species need them.

"Why Should We Protect Sharks?" from MILLER. *Living in the Environment,* 17E. © 2012 Brooks/ Cole, a part of Cengage Learning, Inc.

Vocabulary

species
kinds

ecosystems
a community of organisms
and the environment they
life in

crucial
very important

biodiversity
the number of plants and
animals living in the same
place

React   Answer the questions below about the text on the previous page. Then discuss your responses with your classmates.

1. What is the thesis or main idea of the text? _____

2. What key points in the middle paragraphs explain or develop the thesis? Consider listing them on a table diagram. _____

Thesis or main idea			
supporting points	supporting points	supporting points	supporting points

3. How would you rate this text and why?

   Weak ★ ★ ★ ★ ★ Strong _____

4. What did you learn abut the topic? Name at least two things. _____

Drawing Inferences

An *inference* is a logical conclusion that you can make about something that is not actually said or stated in a text. A worthy inference does, however, result from a clear and careful understanding of what *is* said. To practice drawing inferences, answer the following questions about the reading on the previous page. Afterward, share your responses with your classmates.

1. What conclusions can you draw about the authors' personal feelings toward sharks?

2. What conclusions can you draw about sharks from the title of the article?

Write   Write a summary of this text using your responses above and the information in LO4 as a basic guide.

Second Text

Read   Read the following passage from *Sociology: Your Compass for a New World,* a sociology text by Robert J. Brym and John Lie. In the passage, the authors discuss the idea that all people are connected by six degrees of separation, using actor Kevin Bacon as the prime example.

About the Authors

Robert J. Brym is a professor of sociology at the University of Toronto. He has won numerous awards for his teaching and scholarly work.

John Lie is a professor of social theory and political economy at the University of California, Berkley.

Six Degrees of Kevin Bacon

The *Internet Movie Database* (2003) contains information on the half million actors who have ever performed in a commercially released movie. While this number is large, you might be surprised to learn that, socially, they form a small world. We can demonstrate this fact by first selecting an actor who is not an especially big star—someone like Kevin Bacon. We can then use the *Internet Movie Database* to find out which other actors have ever been in a movie with him (University of Virginia, 2003). Acting in a movie with *another* actor constitutes a link. Actors two links away from Bacon have never been in a movie with him but have been in a movie with another actor who has been in a movie with him. Remarkably more than 85 percent of the half million actors in the database have one, two, or three links to Bacon. We conclude that although film acting stretches back more than a century and has involved people in many countries, the half million people who have ever acted in films form a pretty small world.

What is true for the world of film actors turns out to be true for the rest of us, too. Jeffrey Travers and Stanley Milgram (1969) conducted a famous study in which they asked 300 randomly selected people to mail a document to a complete stranger. However, the people could not mail the document directly to them. They had to mail it to a person they knew on a first-name basis, who, in turn, could send it only to a person he or she knew on a first name basis, and so forth. Travers and Milgram defined this passing of a letter from one person to another as a link, or a "degree of separation." Remarkably, it took only six links on average for the document to reach the stranger. The idea soon became widespread that there are no more than six degrees of separation between any two people in the United States.

1

5

10

15

20

25

Vocabulary

constitutes	remarkably	widespread
forms	worthy of attention	found by a large spread of people

React   Answer the questions below about the text on the previous page. Then discuss your responses with your classmates.

1. What is the thesis or main idea of the text?

_____

2. What key points explain or develop the thesis? Consider using a table diagram to list these points.

Thesis or main idea

supporting points	supporting points	supporting points	supporting points

3. How would you rate this text and why?

   Weak ★ ★ ★ ★ ★ Strong _____

4. What did you learn about the topic? Name at least two things.

_____

Drawing Inferences

An *inference* is a logical conclusion that you can make about something that is not actually said or stated in a text. A worthy inference does, however, result from a clear and careful understanding of what *is* said. To practice drawing inferences, answer the following questions about the text on the previous page. Afterward, share your responses with your classmates.

1. What conclusion do the writers make about people in the film industry? How does it relate to the United States as a whole?

2. Why might it be difficult to complete the study in the second paragraph?

Write   Write a summary of this text using your responses above and the information in LO4 as a basic guide.

Reflecting on Summary Writing

Answer the following questions about your summary-writing experiences in this chapter.

1. Why is summary writing valuable?

   _____

2. How is careful reading connected to effective summary writing?

   _____

3. What are three important things to remember when writing a summary?

   _____

4. Which of the reading strategies is most helpful when it comes to aiding your summary writing? Explain.

   _____

5. What do you like most about the summary you wrote in this chapter? Explain.

   _____

6. What one thing would you like to change in your summary?

   _____

7. When will you use summary writing in the future?

   _____

Key Terms to Remember

When you write summaries, it's important to understand the following terms.

- **Summary**—the core of a text presented in a condensed form
- **Paraphrase**—a form of summary writing with explanations and interpretations; may be as long or longer than the source text
- **Table diagram**—a graphic organizer for identifying the thesis and key supporting points in a text

11

> "I won't say ours was a tough school, but we had our own coroner. We used to write essays like: What I'm going to be if I grow up."
> —Lenny Bruce

Reading and Writing Essays

As you have seen in previous chapters, a paragraph can be a self-contained unit with an opening, a middle, and a closing. The opening introduces your topic; the middle provides support; the closing gives a last thought about the topic.

Often a topic is simply too big to cover in a single paragraph. That is when an essay becomes necessary.

Like a standalone paragraph, an essay has an opening, a middle, and a closing. However, the opening of an essay is a full paragraph itself. The middle of an essay consists of one or more paragraphs of support. And the closing is also a separate paragraph. Sometimes, in a longer essay, the opening or closing may use more than one paragraph.

In this chapter, you will be introduced to the workings of an essay of definition. You will read and react to a professional essay and then write an essay of your own. Along the way, you will learn how paragraphs in an essay are similar to and different from the paragraphs you have previously read and written.

Learning Outcomes

LO1 Understand essays of definition.

LO2 Learn about reading strategies.

LO3 Read and react to a professional essay.

LO4 Plan an essay.

LO5 Write the first draft.

LO6 Revise the writing.

LO7 Edit the writing.

What do you think?

The quotation above pokes fun at a common experience of writing essays in school. What is the most memorable essay you wrote before college? Discuss with your classmates what makes it memorable.

Omer N Raja, 2011 / Used under license from Shutterstock.com

LO1 Understanding Essays of Definition

As the earlier chapter on definition explains, definition writing is often done to convey information. Much of the writing in your various textbooks is intended to define terms, for instance. A definition essay may instead explore an idea. Much of the writing in academic journals is this sort of exploration. Lastly, an essay of definition can simply be an explanation of what something means to the writer: kindness, art, the power of music, and so on.

Often, writing an essay of definition requires research. The writer must understand the term well enough to write an effective opening paragraph and thesis statement. Then the writer must supply effective support in the body paragraphs, each with its own topic sentence and supporting details. Finally, the closing paragraph should present a new insight into the term defined, based upon the details in the body.

> "In high school, I won a prize for an essay on tuberculosis. When I got through writing the essay, I was sure I had the disease."
> —Constance Baker Motley

INSIGHT

Sometimes a definition can open our eyes to a topic we had not noticed before. In *The Non-Designer's Design Book,* graphic designer Robin Williams describes reading about Joshua trees while visiting her parents. After that reading, she finally noticed the Joshua tree standing in their front yard, and in every yard in the neighborhood. Have you had an experience similar to Williams' or Motley's? Discuss it with your classmates.

Marie Lumiere, 2011 / Used under license from Shutterstock.com

Identify Identify at least one possible topic for definition in each of the following categories. (One example is provided.) Then discuss your responses with your classmates.

Arts and Crafts: _____

History: _____

Journalism: _____

Nutrition: _____

Reading

An essay of definition can broaden your knowledge of the world by introducing you to an unfamiliar topic.

LO2 Learning About Reading Strategies

The following strategies will help you to quickly grasp the information in an essay of definition.

Strategy 1: Outlining the Essay

To understand the overall structure of an essay, make an outline like the one below.

- **Start with the essay's thesis statement.** This is often the final sentence of the opening paragraph.
- **Then find the topic sentence in each body paragraph.** This is often (but not always) the first sentence of the paragraph.
- **Find the closing thought.** This restatement of the thesis may be located near the beginning of the closing paragraph or at its end.

Thesis Statement: _____
      Topic Sentence A. _____
      Topic Sentence B. _____
      Topic Sentence C. _____
      Topic Sentence D. _____
      Topic Sentence E. _____
Closing Thought: _____

Strategy 2: Summarizing the Essay

Once you have outlined the specifics of the essay, write a one-paragraph summary of it in your own words. Rewrite the idea of thesis statement as your topic sentence. Then rewrite the idea of each topic sentence from the essay, making them the supporting points of your paragraph. Finally, conclude by rewriting the closing thought.

Topic Sentence: _____
Support: _____
_____
_____
_____
Conclusion: _____

LO3 Reading and Reacting to a Professional Essay

Read   Use the reading process as you go through this definition of life stages, from the book *Diversified Health Occupations*.

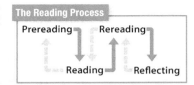

The Reading Process

Prereading   Rereading

Reading   Reflecting

About the Authors

Louise Simmers is a retired medical educator with a BS in nursing from the University of Maryland and a M.Ed from Kent State University. She has worked as a medical-surgical, coronary-intensive care, and public health nurse and has won two Ohio state awards for outstanding health-occupational teaching.

Karen Simmers-Nartker has a BS in nursing from Kent State and special certifications from the Emergency Nurses Association and the American Heart Association. She is the charge nurse for an intensive-care unit. Sharon Simmers-Kobelak has a Bachelor of Business Administration degree from Miami University, Ohio. She works in the educational publishing industry.

Life Stages

Even though individuals differ greatly, each person passes through certain stages of growth and development from birth to death. These stages are frequently called life stages. A common method of classifying life stages is as follows:

- Infancy: birth to 1 year
- Early childhood: 1-6 years
- Late childhood: 6-12 years
- Adolescence: 12-18 years
- Early adulthood: 40-65 years
- Late adulthood: 65 years and older

As individuals pass through these life stages, four main types of growth and development occur: physical, mental or cognitive, emotional, and social. Physical refers to body growth and includes height and weight changes, muscle and nerve development, and changes in body organs. Mental or cognitive refers to intellectual development and includes learning how to solve problems, make judgments, and deal with situations. Emotional refers to feelings and includes dealings with love, hate, joy, fear, excitement, and other similar feelings. Social refers to interactions and relationships with other people.

Each stage of growth and development has its own characteristics and has specific developmental tasks that an individual must master. These tasks progress from the simple to the more complex. For example,

1

5

10

15

20

an individual first learns to sit, then crawl, then stand, then walk, and then, finally, run. Each stage establishes the foundation for the next stage. In this way, growth and development proceeds in an orderly pattern. It is important to remember, however, that the rate of progress varies among individuals. Some children master speech early, others master it later. Similarly, an individual may experience a sudden growth spurt and then maintain the same height for a period of time. 25

Erik Erikson, a psychoanalyst, has identified eight states of psychosocial development. His eight stages of development, the basic conflict or need that must be resolved at each stage, and ways to resolve the conflict are shown in [the] table [below]. Erikson believes that if an individual is not able to resolve a conflict at the appropriate stage, the individual will struggle with the same conflict later in life. For example, if a toddler is not allowed to learn and become independent by mastering basic tasks, the toddler may develop a sense of doubt in his or her abilities. This sense of doubt will interfere with later attempts at mastering independence. 30 35

Health care providers must understand that each life stage creates certain needs in individuals. Likewise, other factors can affect life stages and needs. An individual's sex, race, heredity (factors inherited from parents, such as hair color and body structure), culture, life experiences, and health status can influence needs. Injury or illness usually has a negative effect and can change needs or impair development. 40 45

Erikson's Eight Stages of Psychosocial Development*		
Stage of Development	*Basic Conflict*	*Major Life Event*
Infancy: Birth to 1 Year; Oral-Sensory	Trust vs. Mistrust	Feeding
Toddler: 1-3 Years; Muscular-Anal	Autonomy vs. Shame/Doubt	Toilet Training
Preschool: 3-6 Years; Locomotor	Initiative vs. Guilt	Independence
School-Age: 6-12 Years; Latency	Industry vs. Inferiority	School
Adolescence: 12-18 Years	Identity vs. Role Confusion	Peer
Young Adulthood: 19-40 Years	Intimacy vs. Isolation	Love Relationships
Middle Adulthood: 40-65 Years	Generativity vs. Stagnation	Parenting
Older Adulthood: 66 Years to Death	Ego Identity vs. Despair	Reflection on and Acceptance of Life

*Table adapted from *Diversified Health Occupations,* minus the "Ways to Resolve Conflict" column.

"Life Stages" from SIMMERS. *Diversified Health Occupations,* 7E. © 2009 Delmar Learning, a part of Cengage Learning, Inc. Reproduced by permission. www.cengage.com/permissions

arbit, 2011 / Used under license from Shutterstock.com

Vocabulary

adolescence
a period of development between childhood and adulthood

cognitive
having to do with thought

intellectual
involving thinking

psychoanalyst
a therapist who deals with the mind

psychosocial
relating to both mental and social topics

impair
weaken or harm

React   Answer the following questions to help your understanding of the essay, "Life Stages." Then discuss your answers with your classmates.

Outlining to Understand

1. What is the thesis statement of this essay?

   _____

   _____

2. What is the topic sentence of each body paragraph?

   a. _____

   _____

   b. _____

   _____

   c. _____

   _____

3. What is the topic sentence of the closing paragraph?

   _____

   _____

Summarizing to Understand

In your own words, write a one-paragraph summary of the essay, using the outline above as a guide. Compare your summary with those of your classmates.

Topic Sentence: _____

Support: _____

_____

_____

_____

_____

Conclusion: _____

Writing

Starting on this page, you will plan and write an essay of definition about a topic you are studying. Be sure to use the writing process to do your best work.

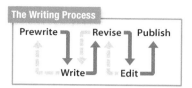

LO4 Planning an Essay of Definition

While an essay of definition can change its readers, it can also change its writer. Writing an essay of definition is a chance to explore a topic more fully than you have before. As a result, your understanding of the topic will deepen. At the same time, your writing skills will improve.

Selecting a Topic

Below are listed four topics Azzie listed as possible topics for definition, using the **categories from LO1. She decided to write about marriage.**

- Arts: _Self-expression_
- Journalism: _Slanted language_
- History: (Marriage)
- Nutrition: _Vegetarianism_

Select In LO1 you listed a topic for each of the categories, Arts, Journalism, History, and Nutrition. Choose one of the topics you listed and use it for your own essay of definition.

"The point of the essay is to change things."
—Edward Tufte

hektor2, 2011 / Used under license from Shutterstock.com

Using Resources to Gather Details

There are many resources you can use to begin developing your essay of definition. Here are a few of the most helpful.

- **Dictionary:** Often, your term will have a specific definition in a dictionary. **This can be a good starting place for understanding the term.** Just make sure to use the correct definition—many words have several possible meanings.
- **Thesaurus:** A thesaurus lists synonyms—words with similar meanings. It also lists antonyms—words with opposite meanings. A synonym or an antonym may be useful in your opening statement.
- **Negative definition:** Sometimes explaining what a term is not can help to reveal what it is.
- **Examples:** Specific examples or instances can help your reader to understand your definition.
- **Function or purpose:** Explaining what something does can help to define that thing.
- **Description:** If what you are defining can be divided into parts, a description of those parts can help make it clear.

The writer of the essay on the next page started a sheet to gather details about marriage from various resources.

Dictionary:	"1 a (1) : the state of being united to a person of the opposite sex as husband or wife in a consensual and contractual relationship recognized by law" *Merriam-Webster's Dictionary*
Thesaurus:	"wedding, matrimony, nuptials." Microsoft Word
Negative definition:	In my opinion, marriage is not just a contract between people. Nor is it always feelings of love.
Examples:	My parents have been married for 35 years. I still see them talking and laughing a lot. Sometimes they also argue.
Function/purpose:	A way of protecting children while they grow. (But what about after children are grown and gone?)
Description:	Joy and passion come and go. So do pain and disappointment. A good marriage seems to be about care and respect beneath it all.

Collect Use a table like the one above to gather your own details about your topic.

LO6 Writing the First Draft

When writing your first draft, don't worry about making everything perfect. Just get your thoughts down on paper.

Read Carefully read and consider the following definition essay about marriage.

Let's Talk Marriage

The thesis statement introduces the topic.

Weddings are great, but marriages can be tough. Many marriages end early, and divorces can be ugly. We might wonder why anyone bothers to get married in the first place. Still, something about marriage keeps people coming back for more. *1*

The author builds upon a dictionary definition.

Historically, marriage has been a public contract between two people, promising to support each other until death. In many cultures, it has also been a contract between two families, each giving something to help launch the new couple. Biologically, marriage has also provided a safe haven for children to grow to adulthood. *5* *10*

Negative definitions put the topic in a new perspective.

However, nowadays that contract and safe haven seem to matter less. Our society has less of a stigma about divorce than in previous decades. Many people argue that it is better for children to grow up with separated parents than with parents who argue all the time. The topic of "being in love" seems to be most important. People say, "I love you. Let's get married," then, "I don't love you anymore. Let's get divorced." That seems a pretty narrow definition of love. *15*

Examples are used to round out the definition.

My parents have been married for 35 years, and I think they know true love. Sometimes they argue. I've seen my mom cry over some of their fights. I've seen my dad cry, too. Often their fights have been over how to raise their children. I've also seen my parents support each other through tough times, like when my dad had to have back surgery, or when my mom lost her favorite job. The most important thing is, I see how much they like to spend time together, even just sitting and talking. I see how they still make each other laugh. *20* *25*

The author uses further examples to discuss one aspect of the definition.

As for raising children, I'm starting to think that never ends. My brothers and I are all out of the house, but our mom and dad still help out when we need something. Also, when I think about it, I can remember hearing my mom or dad on the phone asking their own parents for advice. *30*

The closing paragraph gives a final thought about the topic.

All things considered, successful marriages seem to be **about respect and care. Joys come and goes. Passion comes and goes. Pain comes and goes. Disappointments come and go.** Good marriages show a type of love that outlasts them all. *35*

Michiel de Wit, 2011 / Used under license from Shutterstock.com

The Working Parts of an Essay

As you saw from the outline and paragraph format in LO2, a paragraph and an essay have certain things in common. Both have an opening, a middle, and an ending, and each of those parts plays its own role. Compare the two graphics below.

Parts of a Paragraph	Parts of an Essay
Thesis Statement	Opening paragraph (leads to thesis statement)
Detail Sentence	Supporting paragraph
Detail Sentence	Supporting paragraph
Detail Sentence	Supporting paragraph
Detail Sentence	Supporting paragraph
Closing Statement	Ending paragraph (leads to closing sentence)

Noting Differences

While the two structures bear similarities, note these important differences.

Paragraph	Essay
The parts of a paragraph are sentences.	Each part of an essay is a full paragraph
A standalone paragraph opens with a thesis statement and ends with a closing statement.	The first paragraph usually builds toward the thesis statement.
	Middle paragraphs usually open with a topic sentence.
	The final paragraph builds toward a strong closing sentence.
Sentences are arranged in a spatial, chronological (time), or logical order.	Paragraphs use transitions to lead from one to the next.

Write Develop your first draft using the information on this page, plus your planning as a guide.

LO7 Revising: Improving the Writing

Ernest Hemingway said, "I rewrote the ending of *Farewell to Arms,* the last page of it, 39 times before I was satisfied." Most of us don't make that many revisions, but the fact is, professional writers revise. They know that adding, cutting, rearranging, and rewording are what make writing come to life.

To do your best revision, let your first draft sit for a few days if possible, so that you can view it with fresh eyes. Then read it a number of times looking for strong and weak parts. Be sure to read it aloud at least once. Then have at least one classmate or other peer read and react to your work. Use the response sheet below to guide that conversation.

INSIGHT

Write clear comments and notes in the margins and between the lines of your writing to guide your revision. Make these marks as soon as they occur to you, so that you won't forget.

Peer Review Sheet

Essay title: _____

Writer: _____

Reviewer: _____

1. Which part seems best: Introductory paragraph, a middle paragraph, or closing paragraph? Why?

   _____

   _____

2. Which part needs some work? Why?

   _____

   _____

3. Does the essay adequately define the term? Explain why or why not.

   _____

   _____

4. Does the essay make you think? Explain your thoughts after reading it.

   _____

   _____

Using Transitions Between Paragraphs

Sometimes a thought is enough to lead a reader from one paragraph to the next. Consider the relationship between the final sentence of this paragraph and the first sentence of the next one:

> . . . That seems a pretty narrow definition of love.
> My parents have been married for 35 years, and I think they know true love.

Often, however, a transition word or phrase is needed to signal the relationship of one paragraph to the next. In this sentence, "However, nowadays that contract and safe haven seem to matter less," the writer uses the word *however* to contrast the thoughts of two paragraphs.

INSIGHT
Transition words can also lead from sentence to sentence within a paragraph.

Transition Words

- **Words used to show location:**

above	away from	beyond	into	over
across	behind	by	near	throughout
against	below	down	off	to the right
along	beneath	in back of	on top of	under
among	beside	in front of	onto	
around	between	inside	outside	

- **Words used to show time:**

about	before	later	soon	until
after	during	meanwhile	then	when
afterward	finally	next	third	yesterday
as soon as	first	next week	today	
at	immediately	second	tomorrow	

- **Words used to compare things (show similarities):**

also	in the same way	likewise
as	like	similarly

- **Words used to contrast things (show differences):**

although	even though	on the other hand	still
but	however	otherwise	yet

- **Words used to emphasize a point:**

again	for this reason	particularly	to repeat
even	in fact	to emphasize	truly

- **Words used to conclude or summarize:**

all in all	finally	in summary	therefore
as a result	in conclusion	last	to sum up

- **Words used to add information:**

additionally	and	equally important	in addition
again	another	finally	likewise
along with	as well	for example	next
also	besides	for instance	second

- **Words used to clarify:**

for instance	in other words	put another way	that is

Revise   Review your first draft and have someone else read it as well. (See the peer review sheet in LO7.) Then use the following checklist to guide your revision. Keep revising until you can check off each item in the list.

Ideas

☐   1. Does my essay define an interesting topic?

☐   2. Do I use various types of sources to make my definition?

☐   3. Do I thoroughly explore the idea?

Organization

☐   4. Does my opening paragraph clearly identify the topic?

☐   5. Do my middle paragraphs all reveal something interesting about the topic?

☐   6. Does my closing paragraph lead to a strong closing statement?

Voice

☐   7. Does my writing voice show my interest in the topic?

☐   8. Does my voice engage the reader?

LO8 Editing: Checking for Correctness

Edit   Create a clean copy of your paragraph and use the following checklist to check it for words, sentences, and conventions.

Words

☐   1. Have I used specific nouns and verbs?

☐   2. Have I used more action verbs than "be" verbs?

Sentences

☐   3. Have I varied the beginnings and lengths of sentences?

☐   4. Have I combined short choppy sentences?

☐   5. Have I avoided shifts in sentences?

☐   6. Have I avoided fragments and run-ons?

Conventions

☐   7. Do I use correct verb forms (*he saw*, not *he seen*)?

☐   8. Do my subjects and verbs agree (*she speaks*, not *she speak*)?

☐   9. Have I used the right words (*their, there, they're*)?

☐ 10. Have I capitalized first words and proper nouns and adjectives?

☐ 11. Have I used commas after long introductory word groups?

☐ 12. Have I carefully checked my spelling?

> "People are pretty much alike. It's only that our differences are more susceptible to definition than our similarities."
> —Linda Ellerbee

Review and Writing Enrichment

On the next six pages, you will find a professional essay of definition to read and respond to, followed by several ideas for writing your own definitions. Completing these activities will deepen your understanding of writing essays, particularly essays of definition.

Reading

It is human nature to classify things. We lump one group of creatures together as "fish," another group as "birds." Then we offer definitions to make our classifications clear. Often, we have to further those definitions to account for special cases—like penguins and ostriches.

Much of your education is spent learning definitions, evaluating them, and **offering definitions of your own. Defining helps us to understand.**

Identify Consider two courses you are currently taking in school. List one topic in each that you would like to understand more fully. Share your thoughts with your classmates.

Course: _____

    Topic: _____

Course: _____

    Topic: _____

What do you think?

Do you agree with Linda Ellerbee that "people are pretty much alike"? What do you think she means by the sentence after that? Do you agree with her conclusion? Share your thoughts with your classmates.

Reading and Reacting

Read This section from *An Invitation to Health: Choosing to Change, Brief Edition*, defines the word "forgive" and explains the health benefits of practicing forgiveness. Use the reading process to get the most out of this brief essay.

The Reading Process

Prereading ⟶ Rereading ⟶ Reading ⟶ Reflecting

About the Author

Dianne Hales is a nationally known freelance journalist, author of more than a dozen books, and recipient of more than a dozen writing awards.

"Forgiving"

While "I forgive you" may be three of the most difficult words to say, they are also three of the most powerful—and the most beneficial for the body as well as the soul. Being angry, harboring resentments, or reliving hurts over and over again is bad for your health in general and your heart in particular. The word forgive comes from the Greek word for "letting go," and that's what happens when you forgive: You let go of all the anger and pain that have been demanding your time and wasting your energy.   *1*   *5*

To some people, forgiveness seems a sign of weakness or submission. People may feel more in control, more powerful, when they're filled with anger, but forgiving instills a much greater sense of power. Forgiving a friend or family member may be more difficult than forgiving a stranger because the hurt occurs in a context in which people deliberately make themselves vulnerable (Fincham).   *10*

When you forgive, you reclaim your power to choose. It doesn't matter whether someone deserves to be forgiven; you deserve to be free. However, forgiveness isn't easy. It's not a one-time thing but a process that takes a lot of time and work involving both the conscious and unconscious mind (Karremans). Most people pass through several stages in their journey to forgiveness. The initial response may involve anger, sadness, shame, or other negative feelings. Later there's a reevaluation of what happened, then reframing to try to make sense of it or to take mitigating circumstances into account. This may lead to a reduction in negative feelings, especially if the initial hurt turns out to be accidental rather than intentional.   *15*   *20*

Works Cited

Fincham, Frank. "Forgiveness: Integral to a Science of Close Relationships?" *Prosocial Motives, Emotions, and Behavior: The Better Angels of our Nature.* Mario Mikulincer and Phillip R. Shaver (Eds.), Washington, DC: American Psychological Association, 2010, pp. 347-365.

Karremans, J. C., et al. "The Malleability of Forgiveness." *Prosocial Motives, Emotions, and Behavior: The Better Angels of our Nature.* Mario Mikulincer and Phillip R. Shaver (Eds.), Washington, DC: American Psychological Association, 2010, pp. 285-301.

React   Answer the following questions about Dianne Hales' essay of definition. Share your responses with your classmates.

1. What term is defined by the essay?

   _____

2. What is the thesis of the essay? Write it in your own words.

   _____

3. What origin of "forgive" does the author give?

   _____

4. What negative definition or definitions does the author give?

   _____

5. According to the author, what is the function, or purpose of forgiving?

   _____

6. How would you rate this essay and why?

   Weak ★ ★ ★ ★ ★ **Strong**

   _____

7. What did you learn from this essay?

   _____

Drawing Inferences

An *inference* is a logical conclusion you can make about something not actually stated in a text, but which is based upon clues in the text. To practice drawing inferences, respond to the following questions about the essay on the previous page. Then share your answers with your classmates.

1. **What is meant in line 10: "but forgiving instills a much greater sense of power"?**

2. How do "anger, sadness, shame, or other negative feelings" relate to forgiveness? Provide an example of each.

Writing

Write an essay of definition following the guidelines on the next two pages. Check with your instructor for any specific requirements she or he may have.

Prewriting

Choose one of the following writing ideas for your essay of definition. Or come up with one of your own.

Writing Ideas

1. Write about one of the topics you identified in the prereading activity in LO1.

2. Write to define an emotion.

3. Write to define an abstract noun such as friendship, enemy, charity, nature, or the like.

4. Write to define a topic you wish everyone found exciting. Use your definition to explain what makes that topic so fascinating to you.

5. Choose a word from a dictionary and write a definition essay about it, expanding it with synonyms and antonyms, negative definitions, real-life examples, explanations of function or purpose, and descriptions of parts.

When planning . . .

Refer to LO4 to help guide your prewriting and planning. Also use the tips below.

- Choose a term to define that will support an essay. Your topic should be broad enough to allow for some exploration and discussion.

- Choose a topic that you feel a strong interest in. Writing about a subject you care about is always easiest and leads to best results.

- Gather plenty of details about your topic so that you will have enough material to draw from when writing.

- Arrange those details in an order that seems sensible to you. (You can always adjust that order when writing or revising.)

Writing and Revising

Refer to LO6 to help as you write your first draft and revise it. Also use the following tips to help with the process.

When writing . . .

- Include an opening paragraph that draws the reader in and leads to your thesis statement.
- Include several middle paragraphs, each exploring one main idea about your topic.
- Include a closing paragraph that rewords your thesis and leads to a strong closing sentence.
- Use transitions to lead from one paragraph to the next.
- Follow your planning notes, but also feel free to explore new ideas that come to mind as you write.
- Use many types of details to help define your chosen subject.

When revising . . .

- Let your essay sit for a few days if possible, then reread it aloud.
- Ask if your definition will interest and engage a reader. If it doesn't, determine what changes need to be made.
- Ask if your middle paragraphs are in the best order. If they aren't, rearrange them to make the best sense and to lead the reader from one idea to the next.
- Ask if any areas need transitions to help carry the reader along. Insert any needed transitions.
- Have at least one trusted peer read your essay. Ask for an honest reaction.

Editing

Refer to the checklist in LO8 when editing your essay of definition for style and correctness.

Reflecting on Argument Writing

Answer the following questions about your reading and writing experiences in this chapter.

1. What do you find enjoyable about reading essays of definition?

   _____

2. What is your favorite essay in this chapter? Explain.

   _____

3. Which reading strategy in this chapter do you find most helpful? Explain.

   _____

4. What is the most important thing you have learned about reading an essay of definition?

   _____

5. What do you like most about the essay of definition you wrote in this chapter? Explain.

   _____

6. What is one thing you would like to change about that essay?

   _____

7. What is the most important thing you have learned about writing an essay of definition?

   _____

Key Terms to Remember

When you read and write definition essays, it's important to understand the following terms.

- **Transition**—a connecting word, phrase, or thought that leads from one paragraph to another, or from one sentence to another within a paragraph
- **Synonyms**—words that are similar in meaning
- **Antonyms**—words that are opposite in meaning
- **Negative definition**—an explanation of what something is not, which by contrast helps to reveal what it is

Part III:

Sentence Workshops

12

"We cannot always build the future for our youth,
but we can build our youth for the future."
—Franklin Delano Roosevelt

Sentence Basics

As you know, sentences are built from some very simple parts—nouns, verbs, and modifiers. Every sentence has, at its base, the pairing of a noun and a verb, or a few of them. The other words in the sentence merely modify the noun and verb.

These are sentence basics—the building blocks of thought. With these blocks, you can build tiny towers or magnificent mansions. It all comes down to understanding how to put the pieces together and deciding what you want to create. This chapter can help.

Learning Outcomes

LO1 Understand subjects and predicates.

LO2 Work with special subjects.

LO3 Work with special predicates.

LO4 Understand adjectives.

LO5 Understand adverbs.

LO6 Use prepositional phrases.

LO7 Use clauses.

LO8 Apply sentence basics in a real-world context.

What do you think?

How do we "build our youth for the future," as Roosevelt suggests in the quotation above? What part do language and writing play in building our youth?

Losevsky Pavel, 2011 / Used under license from Shutterstock.com

LO1 Subjects and Verbs (Predicates)

The subject of a sentence tells what the sentence is about. The verb (predicate) of a sentence tells what the subject does or is.

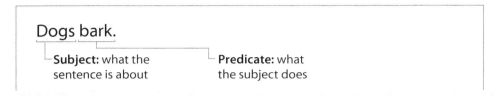

Simple Subject and Simple Predicate

The simple subject is the subject without any modifiers, and the simple predicate is the verb and any helping verbs without modifiers or objects.

The black and white <u>Schnauzer</u> <u>barked</u> all day long.
                    simple subject simple predicate

Complete Subject and Complete Predicate

The complete subject is the subject with modifiers, and the complete predicate is the predicate with modifiers and objects.

<u>The black and white Schnauzer</u> <u>barked all day long</u>.
       complete subject   complete predicate

Implied Subject

In commands, the subject *you* is implied. Commands are the only type of sentence in English that can have an implied subject.

<u>(You)</u>   <u>Stop barking!</u>
implied subject   complete predicate

Inverted Order

Most often in English, the subject comes before the predicate. However, in questions and sentences that begin with *here* or *there*, the subject comes after the predicate.

          subject   subject
Why <u>are you</u> so loud?   Here <u>is a</u> biscuit.
   predicate   predicate

Creating Subjects and Verbs (Predicates)

Identify/Write   For each sentence below, identify the simple subject (SS) and simple predicate (SP). Then write a similar sentence of your own and identify the simple subject and simple predicate in the same way.

1. For thousands of years, humans bred dogs.

   _____

2. All dog breeds descended from wolf ancestors.

   _____

3. At the end of the Ice Age, humans lived nomadically with their dogs.

   _____

4. Ever since that time, dogs enjoyed going for walks.

   _____

Identify/Write   For each sentence below, identify the complete subject (CS) and complete predicate (CP). Then write a similar sentence of your own and identify the complete subject and complete predicate in the same way.

1. An Irish wolfhound stands as tall as a small pony.

   _____

2. Wolfhounds were bred to hunt their ancestors.

   _____

3. Wolfhounds also were used for hunting boar.

   _____

4. Why are boars extinct in Ireland?

   _____

5. There were too many wolfhounds.

   _____

Vocabulary

simple subject
the subject without any modifiers

simple predicate
the verb and any helping verbs without modifiers or objects

complete subject
the subject with modifiers

complete predicate
the predicate with modifiers and objects

implied subject
the word *you* implied in command sentences

LO2 Special Types of Subjects

As you work with subjects, watch for these special types.

Compound Subjects

A **compound subject** is two or more subjects connected by *and* or *or*.

My <u>sister and I</u> swim well. <u>Terri, Josh, and I</u> love to dive.
compound subject   compound subject

"To" Words (Infinitives) as Subjects

An **infinitive** can function as a subject. An infinitive is a verbal form that begins with *to* and may be followed by objects or modifiers.

<u>To become a park ranger</u> is my dream.
      infinitive subject

"Ing" Words (Gerunds) as Subjects

A **gerund** can function as a subject. A gerund is a verb form that ends in *ing* and may be followed by objects or modifiers.

<u>Hiking</u> builds strong calves.   <u>Hiking the Appalachian trail</u> is amazing.
gerund subject   gerund subject

Noun Clause as Subject

A **noun clause** can function as a subject. The clause itself has a subject and a verb but cannot stand alone as a sentence. Noun clauses are introduced by words like *what, that, when, why, how, whatever,* or *whichever.*

<u>Whoever hikes the trail</u> should bring replacement boots.
   noun clause subject

<u>Whatever you need</u> must be carried on your back.
   noun clause subject

CONSIDER THE TRAITS

Note that each of these special subjects still functions as a noun or a group of nouns. A sentence is still, at root, the connection between a noun and a verb.

Say It

Pair up with a partner and read each sentence aloud. Take turns identifying the type of subject—compound subject, infinitive subject, gerund subject, or noun-clause subject. Discuss your answers.

1. You and I should go hiking sometime.

2. To reach the peak of Mount Rainier would be amazing.

3. Whoever wants to go should train with mountaineering.

4. Hiking the Rockies at altitude is challenging.

Creating Special Subjects

Identify/Write   For each sentence below, identify the complete subject as a compound subject (CS), infinitive (I), gerund (G), or noun clause (NC). Then write a similar sentence of your own and identify the complete subject in the same way.

1. Planning for success is the key to success. _____

2. To complete the course in two years is my main goal. _____

3. The fan and the air conditioner are running. _____

4. Working through our differences won't be easy. _____

5. A donut, a cup of coffee, and good conversation make my morning. _____

6. Lifting the ban on street parking will help the neighborhood. _____

7. To live life to its fullest is not as easy as it sounds. _____

8. Whoever finds the money will keep it. _____

9. Are Hannah, Michelle, and Sharissa going? _____

10. Whenever he arrives is the starting time. _____

Olena Simko, 2011 / Used under license from Shutterstock.com

Vocabulary

compound subject
two or more subjects connected by *and* or *or*

infinitive
a verb form that begins with *to* and can be used as a noun (or as an adjective or adverb)

gerund
a verb form that ends in *ing* and is used as a noun

noun clause
a group of words beginning with words like *that, what, whoever,* and so on; containing a subject and a verb but unable to function as a sentence

LO3 Special Verbs (Predicates)

As you work with predicates, watch for these special types.

Compound Predicates

A **compound predicate** consists of two or more predicates joined by *and* or *or*.

I <u>watched and laughed</u>. My cat <u>stalked, pounced, and tumbled</u>.
    compound predicate   compound predicate

Predicates with Direct Objects

A **direct object** follows a transitive verb and tells what or who receives the action of the verb.

I pointed the <u>laser</u>. My cat saw the <u>spot</u>. He batted <u>it</u> and nipped the <u>ground</u>.
      direct object   direct object   direct objects

Predicates with Indirect Objects

An **indirect object** comes between a transitive verb and a direct object and tells to whom or for whom an action was done.

I gave <u>him</u> a rest. My cat shot <u>me</u> a puzzled look.
   indirect object   indirect object

Passive Predicates

When a predicate is **passive**, the subject of the sentence is being acted upon rather than acting. Often, the actor is the object of the preposition in a phrase that starts with *by*. To make the sentence **active**, rewrite it, turning the object of the preposition into the subject.

Passive

My <u>cat</u> <u>was exhausted</u> by the <u>game</u>.
subject   passive verb   object of the preposition

Active

The <u>game</u> <u>exhausted</u> <u>my cat</u>.
subject   active verb   direct object

Say It

Pair up with a partner and read each sentence aloud. Take turns identifying the sentence as active or passive. If the sentence is passive, speak the active version out loud.

1. My cat was mesmerized by the laser.

2. The light danced in his paws.

3. The laser glowed red on the wall.

4. The light was chased all down the hallway by my cat.

Creating Special Predicates

Identify/Write For each sentence below, write and label any compound predicate (CP), direct object (DO), and indirect object (IO). Then write a similar sentence of your own and identify the compound predicate and direct or indirect object in the same way.

1. Our pet rabbits hopped and thumped. _____

2. The lop-ear leaped the gate. _____

3. I gave her a carrot. _____

4. She crouched and nibbled. _____

5. The lionhead sniffed and bounded. _____

6. I gave him some dried banana. _____

7. Those rabbits give me hours of entertainment. _____

Identify/Write For each passive sentence below, write and label the simple subject (SS), the simple predicate (SP), and the object of the preposition *by* (O). Then rewrite each sentence, making it active. (See "Passive Predicates" on the previous page.)

1. The rabbits are fed by my sister. _____

2. Their cages are cleaned by her as well. _____

3. She is seen by them as their food goddess. _____

Vocabulary

compound predicate
two or more predicates joined by *and* or *or*

direct object
a word that follows a transitive verb and tells what or who receives the action of the verb

indirect object
a word that comes between a transitive verb and a direct object and tells to whom or for whom an action was done

passive
the voice created when a subject is being acted upon

active
the voice created when a subject is acting

LO4 Adjectives

To modify a noun, use an adjective or a phrase or clause acting as an adjective.

Adjectives

Adjectives answer these basic questions: *which, what kind of, how many, how much.*

To modify the noun **athletes,** ask . . .

Which athletes?   ⟶   college athletes

What kind of athletes?   ⟶   female athletes

How many athletes?   ⟶   ten athletes

ten female college athletes

Adjective Phrases and Clauses

Phrases and clauses can also act as adjectives to modify nouns.

To modify the noun **athletes,** ask . . .

Which athletes?   ⟶   athletes who are taking at least 12 credit hours

What kind of athletes?   ⟶   athletes with a 3.0 average

The administration will approve loans for athletes with a 3.0 average who are taking at least 12 credit hours.

INSIGHT

It's less important to know the name of a phrase or clause than to know how it functions. If a group of words answers one of the adjective questions, the words are probably functioning as an adjective.

Pete Saloutos, 2011 / Used under license from Shutterstock.com

Say It

Pair up with a classmate to find adjectives—words, phrases, or clauses—that modify the nouns below. Take turns asking the questions while the other person answers.

1. **Sports**
   Which sports?
   What kind of sports?
   How many sports?

2. **Classes**
   Which classes?
   What kind of classes?
   How many classes?

Using Adjectives

Answer/Write For each noun, answer the questions using adjectives—words, phrases, or clauses. Then write a sentence using two or more of your answers.

1. **Tournaments**

   Which tournaments?_____

   What kind of tournaments? _____

   How many tournaments? _____

   Sentence: _____

   _____

2. **Opponents**

   Which opponents? _____

   What kind of opponents? _____

   How many opponents? _____

   Sentence: _____

   _____

3. **Victories**

   Which victories? _____

   What kind of victories?_____

   How many victories?_____

   Sentence: _____

   _____

LO5 Adverbs

To modify a verb, use an adverb or a phrase or clause acting as an adverb.

Adverbs

Adverbs answer these basic questions: *how, when, where, why, how long,* and *how often.*

To modify the verb **dance,** ask . . .

How did they dance? ⟶	danced vigorously
When did they dance? ⟶	danced yesterday
Where did they dance? ⟶	danced there
How often did they dance? ⟶	danced often

Yesterday, **the bride and groom** often vigorously **danced,** there in the middle of the floor.

Adverb Phrases and Clauses

Phrases and clauses can also act as adverbs to modify verbs.

To modify the verb **dance,** ask . . .

How did they dance? ⟶	danced grinning and laughing
When did they dance? ⟶	danced from the first song
Where did they dance? ⟶	danced all around the room
Why did they dance? ⟶	danced to celebrate their wedding
How long did they dance? ⟶	danced until the last song

Grinning and laughing, **the bride and groom danced** all around the room from the first song until the last song to celebrate their wedding.

CONSIDER SPEAKING AND LISTENING

Read the last sentence aloud. Though it may look imposing on the page, it sounds natural, probably because adverbs and adjectives are a common part of our speech. Experiment with these modifiers in your writing as well.

Using Adverbs

Answer/Write   For each verb, answer the questions using adverbs—words, phrases, or clauses. Then write a sentence using three or more of your answers.

1. **Ran**

   How did they run? _____

   When did they run? _____

   Where did they run? _____

   Why did they run? _____

   How long did they run? _____

   How often did they run? _____

   Sentence: _____

   _____

2. **Jumped**

   How did they jump? _____

   When did they jump? _____

   Where did they jump? _____

   Why did they jump? _____

   How long did they jump? _____

   How often did they jump? _____

   Sentence: _____

   _____

LO6 Prepositional Phrases

One of the simplest and most versatile types of phrases in English is the prepositional phrase. A prepositional phrase can function as an adjective or an adverb.

Building Prepositional Phrases

A prepositional phrase is a preposition followed by an object (a noun or pronoun) and any modifiers.

Preposition	+	Object	=	Prepositional Phrase
at		noon		at noon
in		an hour		in an hour
beside		the green clock		beside the green clock
in front of		my aunt's vinyl purse		in front of my aunt's vinyl purse

As you can see, a propositional phrase can be just two words long, or many words long. As you can also see, some prepositions are themselves made up of more than one word. Here is a list of common prepositions.

Prepositions

aboard	back of	except for	near to	round
about	because of	excepting	notwithstanding	save
above	before	for	of	since
according to	behind	from	off	subsequent to
across	below	from among	on	through
across from	beneath	from between	on account of	throughout
after	beside	from under	on behalf of	'til
against	besides	in	onto	to
along	between	in addition to	on top of	together with
alongside	beyond	in behalf of	opposite	toward
alongside of	but	in front of	out	under
along with	by	in place of	out of	underneath
amid	by means of	in regard to	outside	until
among	concerning	inside	outside of	unto
apart from	considering	inside of	over	up
around	despite	in spite of	over to	upon
as far as	down	instead of	owing to	up to
aside from	down from	into	past	with
at	during	like	prior to	within
away from	except	near	regarding	without

INSIGHT

A preposition is pre-positioned before the other words it introduces to form a phrase. Other languages have post-positional words that follow their objects.

Using Prepositional Phrases

Create For each item below, create a prepositional phrase by writing a preposition and an object (and any modifiers). Then write a sentence using the prepositional phrase.

1. | Preposition | + | Object (and any modifiers) |

Sentence: _____

2. | Preposition | + | Object (and any modifiers) |

Sentence: _____

3. | Preposition | + | Object (and any modifiers) |

Sentence: _____

4. | Preposition | + | Object (and any modifiers) |

Sentence: _____

5. | Preposition | + | Object (and any modifiers) |

Sentence: _____

Vocabulary

prepositional phrase
a group of words beginning with a preposition and including an object (noun or pronoun) and any modifiers

LO7 Clauses

A clause is a group of words with a subject and a predicate. If a clause can stand on its own as a sentence, it is an independent clause, but if it cannot, it is a dependent clause.

Independent Clause

An independent clause has a subject and a predicate and expresses a complete thought. It is the same as a simple sentence.

Clouds piled up in the stormy sky.

Dependent Clause

A dependent clause has a subject and a predicate but does not express a complete thought. Instead, it is used as an adverb clause, an adjective clause, or a noun clause.

An adverb clause begins with a subordinating conjunction (see below) and functions as an adverb, so it must be connected to an independent clause to be complete.

CONSIDER SPEAKING AND LISTENING

In each example below, read the dependent clause out loud. (The dependent clause is in red.) Can you hear how each dependent clause sounds incomplete? Read it to another person, and the listener will probably say, "What about it?" These clauses depend on a complete thought to make sense.

after	as long as	given that	since	unless	where
although	because	if	so that	until	whereas
as	before	in order that	that	when	while
as if	even though	provided that	though	whenever	

Even though the forecast said clear skies, the storms rolled in.

An adjective clause begins with a relative pronoun *(which, that, who)* and functions as an adjective, so it must be connected to an independent clause to be complete.

I don't like a meteorologist who often gets the forecast wrong.

A noun clause begins with words like those below and functions as a noun. It is used as a subject or an object in a sentence.

how	what	whoever	whomever
that	whatever	whom	why

I wish he had known what the weather would be.

Using Clauses

Identify/Write   For each sentence below, write and label any adverb clauses (ADVC), adjective clauses (ADJC), or noun clauses (NC). Then write a similar sentence of your own and identify the clauses.

1. I wonder why weather is so unpredictable.

2. Storms still surprise meteorologists who have years of experience.

3. Many different factors determine what will happen in the sky.

4. Until we can track all factors, we can't predict perfectly.

5. Whoever gives a forecast is making a guess.

6. Since weather is so uncertain, predictions have percentages.

7. A 50 percent chance of rain means that there is a 50 percent chance of fair weather.

8. When air crosses a large lake, it picks up moisture.

9. Because of lake-effect rain, Valparaiso is called "Vapor Rain Snow."

10. Buffalo gets whatever moisture Lake Erie dishes up.

Vocabulary

independent clause
a group of words with a subject and predicate that expresses a complete thought

dependent clause
a group of words with a subject and predicate that does not express a complete thought

adverb clause
a dependent clause beginning with a subordinating conjunction and functioning as an adverb

adjective clause
a dependent clause beginning with a relative pronoun and functioning as an adjective

noun clause
a dependent clause beginning with a subordinating word and functioning as a noun

LO8 Real-World Application

Identify In the e-mail below, write and identify simple subjects (SS), simple predicates (SP), and dependent clauses (DC).

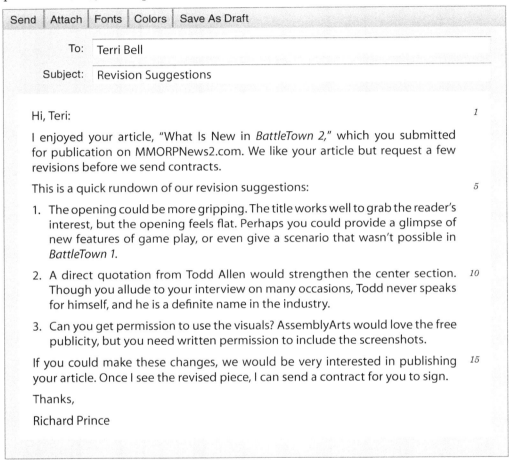

Send | Attach | Fonts | Colors | Save As Draft

To: Terri Bell

Subject: Revision Suggestions

Hi, Teri: *1*

I enjoyed your article, "What Is New in *BattleTown 2*," which you submitted for publication on MMORPNews2.com. We like your article but request a few revisions before we send contracts.

This is a quick rundown of our revision suggestions: *5*

1. The opening could be more gripping. The title works well to grab the reader's interest, but the opening feels flat. Perhaps you could provide a glimpse of new features of game play, or even give a scenario that wasn't possible in *BattleTown 1*.

2. A direct quotation from Todd Allen would strengthen the center section.   *10* Though you allude to your interview on many occasions, Todd never speaks for himself, and he is a definite name in the industry.

3. Can you get permission to use the visuals? AssemblyArts would love the free publicity, but you need written permission to include the screenshots.

If you could make these changes, we would be very interested in publishing   *15* your article. Once I see the revised piece, I can send a contract for you to sign.

Thanks,

Richard Prince

Expand Answer the adjective and adverb questions below. Then expand the sentence using some of the words, phrases, and clauses you have created.

The agent called.

Which agent? _____

What kind of agent? _____

Called *when?* _____

Called *how?* _____

Sentence: _____

13

"A complex system that works is invariably found to have evolved from a simple system that works."
—John Gaule

Simple, Compound, and Complex Sentences

Most leaves have a central stem with veins extending from it. Sometime this structure forms a simple oval, but at other times, two or more ovals connect to form a compound leaf. And the shape of some leaves is complex, as if a number of leaves were fused together.

Sentences are similar. All have a noun and a verb, but some stop at this simple structure. In other cases, two or more sentences combine to make a compound sentence. And when a sentence has one or more dependent clauses fused to it, it becomes complex.

This chapter shows how to create simple, compound, and complex sentences. As with leaves, variety makes sentences beautiful.

Learning Outcomes

LO1 Create simple sentences.

LO2 Create simple sentences with compound subjects.

LO3 Create simple sentences with compound verbs (predicates).

LO4 Create compound sentences.

LO5 Create complex sentences.

LO6 Create complex sentences with relative clauses.

LO7 Apply simple, compound, and complex sentences in a real-world document.

What do you think?

Which type of leaf is most beautiful—a simple, compound, or complex leaf? Why?

raresirimie, 2011 / Used under license from Shutterstock.com

LO1 Simple Sentences

A **simple sentence** consists of a subject and a verb. The subject is a noun or pronoun that names what the sentence is about. The verb tells what the subject does or is.

Rachel sang.
subject verb

Modifiers

Other words can be added to modify the subject. Words that modify the subject answer the adjective questions: *which, what kind of, how many, how much.*

My new roommate Rachel sang. *(Which Rachel do you mean?)*

Other words can also modify the verb. These words and phrases answer the adverb questions: *how, when, where, why, to what degree,* and *how often.*

Rachel sang in the shower at the top of her lungs.
          (Where and how did Rachel sing?)

Direct and Indirect Objects

The verb might also be followed by a noun or pronoun that receives the action of the verb. Such a word is called the **direct object**, and it answers the question *what* or *whom?*

Rachel sang "I Need a Hero." *(What did Rachel sing?)*

Another noun or pronoun could come between the verb and the direct object, telling *to whom* or *for whom* an action is done. Such a word is the **indirect object**.

I gave her a picture of Chuck Norris.
          (I gave a picture of Chuck Norris to whom?)

Vocabulary

simple sentence
a subject and a verb that together form a complete thought

direct object
a noun or pronoun that follows a verb and receives its action

indirect object
a noun or pronoun that comes between a verb and a direct object, telling *to whom* or *for whom* an action is done

Say It

Team up with a partner and follow these steps: One of you speaks the sentence aloud, and the other asks the question in italics. Then the first person says the sentence again, inserting an answer.

1. We sang songs. *(Where did you sing songs?)*
2. The song was our favorite. *(Which song was your favorite?)*
3. Rachel sang. *(What did Rachel sing?)*
4. I sang a song. *(To whom did you sing a song?)*

INSIGHT

In item 1, you are adding modifiers to the verb and in item 2, you are adding modifiers to the subject. In item 3, you are adding a direct object, and in item 4, you are adding an indirect object.

Creating Simple Sentences

Create Provide a noun for a subject and a verb for a predicate. Then write a sentence with the noun and verb, adding details that answer the questions asked.

1.
Subject	Verb

Which? _____

2.
Subject	Verb

What kind of? _____

3.
Subject	Verb

When? _____

4.
Subject	Verb

Where? _____

5.
Subject	Verb

How? _____

LO2 Simple Sentences with Compound Subjects

A simple sentence can have a compound subject (two or more subjects).

A Simple Sentence with Two Subjects

To write a simple sentence with two subjects, join them using *and* or *or*.

One Subject: Lee worked on the Rube Goldberg machine.
Two Subjects: Lee and Jerome will add the lever arm that tips the bucket.
Lee or Jerome will add the lever arm that tips the bucket.

One Subject: Ms. Claymore will help them attach the flywheel.
Two Subjects: Ms. Claymore and her aide will help them attach the flywheel.
Either Ms. Claymore or her aide will help them attach the flywheel.

A Simple Sentence with Three or More Subjects

To write a simple sentence with three or more subjects, create a series. List each subject, placing a comma after all but the last, and place an *and* or *or* before the last.

Three Subjects: Jerome, Lee, and Sandra are finishing the machine soon.
Five Subjects: Jerome, Lee, Sandra, Ms. Claymore, and her aide will enter the machine in a contest.

NOTE: When a compound subject is joined by *and,* the subject is plural and requires a plural verb. When a compound subject is joined by *or,* the verb should match the last subject.

Ms. Claymore and her aide need to submit the entry form.

Ms. Claymore or her aide needs to submit the entry form.

CONSIDER THE TRAITS

A compound subject does not make the sentence compound. As long as both (or all) of the subjects connect to the same verb or verbs, the sentence is still considered simple.

Say It

Speak each of the following sentences out loud.
1. Jerome *loves* the Rube Goldberg project.
2. Jerome *and* Sandra *love* the Rube Goldberg project.
3. Jerome *or* Sandra *works* on it every day after school.
4. Jerome, Sandra, *and* Lee *have* contributed most.
5. Jerome, Sandra, *or* Lee *has* contributed most.

Using Compound Subjects

Create Write subjects for each of the boxes provided. Then write a sentence that includes the subjects as a compound subject using *and* or *or*.

1. | Subject | Subject |

2. | Subject | Subject |

3. | Subject | Subject | Subject |

4. | Subject | Subject | Subject |

5. | Subject | Subject | Subject | Subject |

6. | Subject | Subject | Subject | Subject |

Vocabulary

compound subject
two or more subjects in a simple sentence

LO3 Simple Sentences with Compound Verbs

A simple sentence can also have two or more verbs (predicates). Remember that the predicate tells what the subject is doing or being, so as long as both predicates connect to the same subject, the sentence is still a simple sentence.

A Simple Sentence with Two Verbs

To create a compound predicate with two parts, join two verbs using *and* or *or.*

> **One Verb:** The band rocked.
>
> **Two Verbs:** The band rocked and danced.

Remember that the predicate includes not just the verbs, but also words that modify or complete the verbs.

> **One Predicate:** The band played their hit single.
>
> **Two Predicates:** The band played their hit single and covered other songs.

A Simple Sentence with Three or More Verbs

To create a compound predicate with three or more parts, list the verbs in a series, with a comma after each except the last, and the word *and* or *or* before the last.

> **Three Verbs:** The singer crooned, wailed, and roared.
>
> **Five Verbs:** The fans clapped, screamed, danced, cheered, and swayed.

If each verb also includes modifiers or completing words (direct and indirect objects), place the commas after each complete predicate.

The crowd members got to their feet, waved their hands back and forth, and sang along with the band.

CONSIDER THE TRAITS

A compound verb does not make the sentence compound. As long as both (or all) of the verbs connect to the same subject or subjects, the sentence is still considered simple.

Using Compound Predicates

Create For each subject below, create predicates. Then write a simple sentence that joins the compound predicates with *and* or *or*.

1. The reporters

> Predicate

> Predicate

2. The police

> Predicate

> Predicate

3. The manager

> Predicate

> Predicate

4. The bouncer

> Predicate

> Predicate

> Predicate

Vocabulary

compound predicate
two or more predicates in a
simple sentence

LO4 Compound Sentences

A compound sentence is made out of simple sentences joined by a coordinating conjunction: *and, but, or, nor, for, so,* or *yet.*

Compound of Two Sentences

Most compound sentences connect two simple sentences, which are also called independent clauses. Connect the sentences by placing a comma after the first sentence and using a coordinating conjunction after the comma.

Two Sentences: We ordered pizza. I got just one piece.

Compound Sentence: We ordered pizza, but I got just one piece.

Compound of Three or More Sentences

Sometimes, you might want to join three or more short sentences in a compound sentence.

Three Sentences: Tim likes cheese. Jan likes veggie. I like pepperoni.

Compound Sentence: Tim likes cheese, Jan likes veggie, and I like pepperoni.

You can also join the sentences using semicolons. Authors sometimes use this approach to describe a long, involved process or a flurry of activity.

Tim ate the cheese pizza; Jan ate the veggie pizza; Ray showed up and ate the pepperoni pizza; I got back in time for the last slice.

NOTE: Remember that a compound sentence is made of two or more complete sentences. Each part needs to have its own subject and verb.

CONSIDER THE TRAITS

The word *and* indicates that the second clause provides additional information. The words *but, or, nor,* and *yet* create a contrast. The words *for* and *so* indicate that one clause is the cause of the other.

Creating Compound Sentences

Write   Write a simple sentence for each prompt; then combine them as a compound sentence.

1. What pizza do you like? _____

   What pizza does a friend like? _____

   Compound Sentence: _____

   _____

2. Where do you go for pizza? _____

   What other place do people go? _____

   Compound Sentence: _____

   _____

3. Who likes thin crust pizza? _____

   Who likes pan pizza? _____

   Who likes stuffed pizza? _____

   Compound Sentence: _____

   _____

4. What is the weirdest pizza? _____

   What is the grossest pizza? _____

   What is the stinkiest pizza? _____

   Compound Sentence: _____

   _____

5. When do you eat pizza? _____

   When do your friends eat pizza? _____

   When does your family eat pizza? _____

   Compound Sentence: _____

   _____

Vocabulary

compound sentence
two or more simple sentences
joined with a coordinating
conjunction

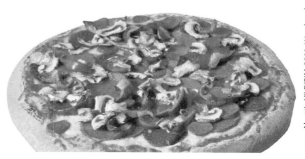

Alaettin YILDIRIM, 2011 / Used under license from Shutterstock.com

LO5 Complex Sentences

A complex sentence shows a special relationship between two ideas. Instead of connecting two sentences as equal ideas (as in a compound sentence), a complex sentence shows that one idea depends on the other.

Using a Subordinating Conjunction

You can create a complex sentence by placing a subordinating conjunction before the sentence that is less important. Here are common subordinating conjunctions:

after	before	so that	when
although	even though	that	where
as	if	though	whereas
as if	in order that	till	while
as long as	provided that	'til	
because	since	until	

CONSIDER SPEAKING AND LISTENING

Read the example complex and compound-complex sentences aloud. Despite their daunting names, these sentences aren't that complicated. You use them all the time in speech. Experiment with them in your writing.

The subordinating conjunction shows that this sentence depends on the other sentence and can't stand without it.

Two Sentences: We played strong offense. We won the football game.

Complex Sentence: Because we played strong offense, we won the football game.

We won the football game because we played strong offense.

NOTE: The subordinating conjunction goes at the beginning of the less important clause, but the two clauses could go in either order. When the dependent clause comes second, it usually isn't set off with a comma.

Compound-Complex

You can create a compound-complex sentence by placing a subordinating conjunction before a simple sentence and connecting it to a compound sentence.

Simple Sentence: I threw two touchdowns.

Compound Sentence: Jake kicked the extra points, and the other team couldn't catch up.

Compound-Complex: After I threw two touchdowns, Jake kicked the extra points, and the other team couldn't catch up.

Creating Complex Sentences

Write   Write a simple sentence for each prompt. Then select a subordinating conjunction from the facing page, place it at the beginning of one sentence, and combine the two sentences into a single complex sentence.

1. What did you play? _____

   Did you win or lose? _____

   Complex sentence: _____

   _____

2. Who did you play? _____

   Why did you play the opponent? _____

   Complex sentence: _____

   _____

3. Who won the game? _____

   Why did that side win? _____

   Complex sentence: _____

   _____

4. Where did you play? _____

   Where else could you have played? _____

   Complex sentence: _____

   _____

5. What surprised you? _____

   Why did it surprise you? _____

   Complex sentence: _____

   _____

6. How long did you play? _____

   When did you stop? _____

   Complex sentence: _____

   _____

Vocabulary

complex sentence
a sentence with one independent clause and one or more dependent clauses

compound-complex sentence
a sentence with two or more independent clauses and one or more dependent clauses

LO6 Complex Sentences with Relative Clauses

In a complex sentence, one idea depends on the other. You've seen how a dependent clause can start with a subordinating conjunction. Another type of dependent clause starts with a relative pronoun.

Relative Clauses

A relative clause is a group of words that begins with a relative pronoun *(that, which, who, whom)* and includes a verb and any words that modify or complete it:

Relative Clauses:	that leads into the garden
	which usually leans against the shed
	who planted the scallions
	whom I asked to help me weed

Each relative clause above has a subject and a verb, but none of the clauses is a complete sentence. All need to be connected to a complete sentence.

Complex Sentences:	I followed the path that leads into the garden.
	I looked for the shovel, which usually leans against the shed.
	We have many onions thanks to a friend who planted the scallions.
	I worked with Tina, whom I asked to help me weed.

That and *Which*

The pronoun *that* signals that the information after it is necessary to the sentence. The pronoun *which* signals that the information is not necessary, so the clause is set off with a comma.

That:	The scallions that we planted this spring taste strongest. (*That* defines the scallions.)
Which:	I love scallions, which I eat raw or fried. (*Which* does not define the scallions but just adds more information about them.)

Who and *Whom*

The pronoun *who* is the subject of the relative clause that it introduces. The pronoun *whom* is a direct object of a clause it introduces.

Who:	I helped the woman who harvested scallions. (*Who* is the subject.)
Whom:	I thanked the woman whom I helped. (*Whom* is the direct object.)

Using Relative Clauses

Create For each item, write a relative clause beginning with the pronoun provided. Then write a complex sentence that includes the relative clause. In case you need a topic idea, think of a party you have attended or one that you would like to attend.

1. Relative clause: _that_____

   Complex sentence: _____

   _____

2. Relative clause: _who_____

   Complex sentence: _____

   _____

3. Relative clause: _which_____

   Complex sentence: _____

   _____

4. Relative clause: _whom_____

   Complex sentence: _____

   _____

5. Relative clause: _that_____

   Complex sentence: _____

   _____

6. Relative clause: _which_____

   Complex sentence: _____

   _____

INSIGHT

In some languages, if the relative pronoun is the object of the clause it introduces, another pronoun is inserted in the clause: *I liked the gift that my boss gave it to me.* In English, no additional pronoun is inserted: *I liked the gift that my boss gave to me.*

Vocabulary

relative clause
a group of words that begins with a relative pronoun and includes a verb but cannot stand alone as a sentence

relative pronoun
a word *(that, which, who, whom)* that relates a relative clause with another word in the sentence

LO7 Real-World Application

Rewrite   Read the following message about a meeting. Note how every sentence is a simple sentence. Rewrite the message, combining sentences into some compound or complex sentences and improving the flow.

Dear Mr. Lindau:

You asked about the Monday production meeting. I will summarize it. The production staff met with the editors. The writers explained their new project. It focuses on twenty-first-century skills. The writers presented two chapters. They will become a prototype.

The new project needs to be visual. It should appeal to students and teachers. The design needs to make text accessible. The writing has an open quality. It still feels academic. The book should be available for sale in the fall. A teacher's edition will follow.

The designers are beginning work on a prototype. The writers continue to create chapters.

Dear Mr. Lindau:

_____

_____

_____

_____

_____

_____

_____

_____

_____

_____

_____

CONSIDER THE WORKPLACE

Using a variety of sentences in workplace writing will help ideas flow and will present a polished image.

14

"My idea of an agreeable person is a person who agrees with me."

—Benjamin Disraeli

Agreement

When two people agree, they can work together. They have the same goals and outlook, and they can become a team.

Subjects and verbs are much the same. If the subject is plural, the verb needs to be as well, or they can't work together. Pronouns also need to agree with their antecedents in terms of number. Without agreement, these words fight each other, and instead of conveying ideas, they disrupt communication.

This chapter focuses on the agreement between subjects and verbs and between pronouns and antecedents. It also tackles other pronoun problems. After you work through the exercises here, you'll find it easy to write agreeable sentences.

Learning Outcomes

LO1 Make subjects and verbs agree.

LO2 Make two subjects agree with verbs.

LO3 Practice agreement with *I* and *you*.

LO4 Practice agreement with indefinite pronouns.

LO5 Practice pronoun-antecedent agreement.

LO6 Correct other pronoun problems.

LO7 Check agreement in a real-world context.

What do you think?

What makes a person agreeable? What makes subjects and verbs agreeable?

LO1 Subject-Verb Agreement

A verb must agree in number with the subject of the sentence. If the subject is singular, the verb must be singular. If the subject is plural, the verb must be plural.

singular subject + singular verb = agreement

The truck needs a tune-up.

plural subject + plural verb = agreement

The trucks need tune-ups.

NOTE: Plural subjects often end in *s,* but plural verbs usually do not. Also note that only present tense verbs and certain *be* verbs have separate singular and plural forms.

Present:	singular	plural	**Past:**	singular	plural
	walks	walk		walked	walked
	sees	see		saw	saw
	eats	eat		ate	ate
	is/am	are		was	were

To make most verbs singular, add just an *s.*

run—runs   write—writes   stay—stays

The verbs *do* and *go* are made singular by adding an *es.*

do—does   go—goes

When a verb ends in *ch, sh, x,* or *z,* make it singular by adding *es.*

latch—latches   wish—wishes   fix—fixes   buzz—buzzes

When a verb ends in a consonant followed by *a y,* change the *y* to *i* and add *es.*

try—tries   fly—flies   cry—cries   quantify—quantifies

INSIGHT

The "Say It" activity on the next page will help you become familiar with the subject-verb agreement patterns in English. Practice it aloud, and for added practice, write the sentences as well.

Say It

Read the following sentences aloud, emphasizing the words in italics.
1. The bird *sings*. The birds *sing*. The phone *rings*. The phones *ring*.
2. The person *is*. The people *are*. The child *is*. The children *are*.
3. He *works*. They *work*. She *learns*. They *learn*.
4. The woman *does*. The women *do*. The man *goes*. The men *go*.
5. She *wishes*. They *wish*. He *boxes*. They *box*.

Correcting Basic Subject-Verb Agreement

Write For each sentence below, write the correct form of the verb in parentheses.
1. A philosophy major _____ about thinking. (know)
2. A philosopher _____ to find philosophical work. (try)
3. An employer rarely _____ to hire philosophers. (wish)
4. But such students _____ able to think (is).
5. My roommate _____ philosophy. (study)
6. He also _____ to study the want ads for jobs. (need)
7. He _____ employers need thinkers. (say)
8. That idea _____ sense. (make)
9. But that idea doesn't _____ people hire him. (make)
10. At his job, he _____ lawn mowers very philosophically. (fix)

Correct Correct any agreement errors you find by writing the line number and the verb you would change. Cross it out and write the correct present tense verb.

The philosopher Plato say the material world aren't the real world. *1*
He say we sees shadows on a cave wall. Plato believe in eternal forms of
perfection. Every real table in the world are patterned after the perfect
form of a table. In that way, people too is patterned after the perfect form
of people. Though Plato live more than three hundred years before Jesus, *5*
many Christian thinkers likes his concept of eternal forms. The idea fit
well with the ideas of a soul and a creator. Many modern thinkers, though,
has the opposite idea. They says that only physical things is real. Plato, of
course, disagree.

Write For each plural verb below, write one sentence using the verb in its singular form.
1. fly _____
2. do _____
3. fish _____
4. wax _____

Vocabulary

agree in number
match, as when a subject and verb are both singular, or when they are both plural

LO2 Agreement with Two Subjects

Sentences with **compound subjects** have special rules to make sure that they agree.

When a sentence has two or more subjects joined by *and*, the verb should be plural.

plural subject + **plural verb** = **agreement**

Jumbo and Dumbo march.

When a sentence has two or more subjects joined by *or, nor,* or *but also,* the verb should agree with the last subject.

singular subject + **singular verb** = **agreement**

 or

Either Jumbo or Dumbo trumpets.

Not only Jumbo but also Dumbo trumpets.

Say It

Read the following sentences aloud, emphasizing the words in *italics*.

1. Jumbo *and* Dumbo *perform*. Jumbo *or* Dumbo *performs*.
2. The man *and* woman *dance*. The man *or* woman *dances*.
3. The Democrat *and* the Republican *agree*. The Democrat *or* the Republican *agrees*.
4. Not only Dave *but also* Tim *writes*.
5. The dog, cat, *and* guinea pig *greet* me. The dog, cat, *or* guinea pig *greets* me.

Fixing Agreement with Two Subjects

Write For each sentence below, write the correct form of the verb in parentheses.

1. The acrobat and clown _____ the crowd. (entertain)

2. The acrobat or clown _____ a pie in the face. (get)

3. A trapeze artist and a tightrope walker _____ an ovation. (receive)

4. Not only the acrobat but also the clown _____ highly paid. (are)

5. Neither the lion tamer nor the sword swallower _____ insurance. (have)

6. The human cannonball or the lion tamer _____ the scariest job. (have)

7. Either Todd or Lewis _____ to join the circus. (plan)

8. Thrills and hard work _____ Todd or Lewis. (await)

9. Not only Todd but also Lewis _____ a daredevil. (are)

10. The clowns or the ringmaster _____ each act. (introduce)

Correct Correct any agreement errors you find by writing the line number and incorrect verb, crossing it out, and writing the correct present tense verb.

> Childhood dreams and fantasies rarely comes true. A firefighter   *1*
> or police officer are what many children dream of being. Imagine a
> world filled with firefighters and police! Neither the accountant nor the
> landscaper figure big in childhood plans. A princess or a wizard are also
> a popular choice for kids. Job openings and pay for both careers is pretty   *5*
> slim. Even the job of astronaut or explorer have become scarce. The trials
> of joblessness and the responsibilities of adulthood conspires to convince
> people to seek other careers. Childhood stars sometimes get "real" jobs, too.
> Johnny Whitaker and Wil Wheaton works with computers. They traded
> childhood dreams for adult ones.   *10*

Write Write a sentence with a compound subject joined by *and*. Write a sentence with a compound subject joined by *or*. Check subject-verb agreement.

_____

Vocabulary

compound subject
two or more subjects that share the same verb or verbs

LO3 Agreement with *I* and *You*

The pronouns *I* and *you* usually take plural verbs, even though they are singular.

plural verb

Correct: I go to Great America and ride roller coasters. You do too.

singular verb

Incorrect: I goes to Great America and rides roller coasters. You does too.

NOTE: The pronoun *I* takes the singular verbs *am* and *was*. **Do not** use *I* with *be* or *is*.

Correct: I am excited. I was nervous. I am eager to ride the roller coaster.

Incorrect: I are exited. I were nervous. I is eager to ride the roller coaster.

Quick Guide

Using *am, is, are, was,* and *were*

	Singular	Plural
Present Tense	I *am* you *are* he *is* she *is* it *is*	we *are* you *are* they *are*
Past Tense	I *was* you *were* he *was* she *was* it *was*	we *were* you *were* they *were*

INSIGHT

The word *am* exists for one reason only, to go along with the word *I*. There is no other subject for the verb *am*. In academic or formal writing, *I* should never be used with *be* or *is*. Think of René Descartes saying, "I think, therefore I am."

Say It

Read the following word groups aloud, emphasizing the words in *italics*.
1. I *laugh* / You *laugh* / She *laughs* / They *laugh*
2. I *work* / You *work* / He *works* / They *work*
3. I *do* / You *do* / He *does* / They *do*
4. I *am* / You *are* / She *is* / They *are*
5. I *was* / You *were* / He *was* / They *were*

Correcting Agreement with *I* and *You*

Write   For each blank below, write the correct forms of the verb in parentheses. (Do not change the tense.)

1. I _____ louder than he _____ . (laugh)

2. You _____ as well as she _____ . (climb)

3. We _____ together, or you _____ alone. (work)

4. Stan _____ silverware while I _____ pans. (wash)

5. I _____ often, but he _____ rarely. (help)

6. The group _____ on Sunday, but I _____ later. (watch)

7. I _____ first, and she _____ after. (eat)

8. You _____ tired, and I _____ too. (is)

9. Last year, I _____ short, but you _____ tall. (was)

10. You _____ helpful; I hope I _____ also. (is)

Correct   Correct any agreement errors you find by writing the line number and incorrect verb. Cross it out and write the correct verb.

> I is starting a class in astronomy, and I wonders if I can borrow your   *1*
> telescope. You rarely uses it anymore, and I needs it to be able to look at
> the moons of Jupiter. My professor says that even a moderate-size telescope
> will show the moons. She have instructions for finding Jupiter. I knows
> how to use the telescope, but if you is afraid I would break it, you could set   *5*
> it up for me.
> Another idea would be for us to stargaze together. I has a place away
> from city lights, and I has lawn chairs and blankets we could use. If you
> agrees to come along and set up the telescope, I agrees to bring snacks for
> us.   *10*
> What do you think? I hopes I'm not asking too much and that you isn't
> mad about the request. I just is excited to see Jupiter's moons, and I thinks
> you might like to see them, too.

Write   Write two sentences using "I" as the subject. Then write two more using "you" as the subject. Check your subject-verb agreement.

_____

_____

LO4 Agreement with Singular Indefinite Pronouns

An **indefinite pronoun** is intentionally vague. Instead of referring to a specific person, place, or thing, it refers to something general or unknown.

Singular Indefinite Pronouns

Singular indefinite pronouns take singular verbs:

Singular
someone
somebody
something
anyone
anybody
anything
no one
nobody
nothing
everyone
everybody
everything
one
each
either
neither

Someone cooks every night.

No one gets out of kitchen duty.

Everyone benefits from the chore schedule.

Note that indefinite pronouns that end in *one, body,* or *thing* are singular, just as these words themselves are singular. Just as you would write, "That thing is missing," so you would write "Something is missing." The words *one, each, either,* and *neither* can be tricky because they are often followed by a prepositional phrase that contains a plural noun. The verb should still be singular.

One of my friends is a great cook.

Each of us wants to cook as well as he does.

Remember that a compound subject joined with *and* needs a plural verb, and a compound subject joined with *or* needs a verb that matches the last subject.

Anything and everything taste terrific in his meals.

No one or nothing keeps him from making a wonderful meal.

Say It

Read the following word groups aloud, emphasizing the words in *italics*.

1. No one *is* / Nobody *has* / Nothing *does*

2. Everyone *is* / Everybody *has* / Everything *does*

3. One of my friends *is* / Each of my friends *has* / Either of my friends *does*

Correcting Indefinite Pronoun Agreement I

Write For each sentence below, write the correct form of the verb in parentheses. (Do not change the tense.)

1. Everyone _____ an application. (complete)

2. Somebody _____ to get the job. (have)

3. Each of the jobs _____ available. (are)

4. Neither of the applicants _____ qualified. (are)

5. Either of the prospects _____ to be trained. (hope)

6. Nobody _____ to go home empty-handed. (want)

7. Everybody _____ bills to pay. (have)

8. Someone or something _____ to give. (have)

9. Either of the positions _____ well. (pay)

10. One of my friends _____ for word on the job. (wait)

Write Write sentences using each indefinite pronoun as a subject. Choose present tense verbs and check subject-verb agreement.

1. Someone _____

   _____

2. Nothing _____

   _____

3. Neither _____

   _____

4. Everyone _____

   _____

5. Each _____

   _____

6. Anybody _____

   _____

Vocabulary

indefinite pronoun
a special type of pronoun that does not refer to a specific person or thing

Agreement with Other Indefinite Pronouns

Other indefinite pronouns are always plural, or have a singular or plural form, depending on how they are used.

Plural Indefinite Pronouns

Plural indefinite pronouns take plural verbs:

Many of us follow classical music.

Several are big fans.

Plural

both
few
many
several

Singular or Plural Indefinite Pronouns

Some indefinite pronouns or quantity words are singular or plural. If the object of the preposition in the phrase following the pronoun is singular, the pronoun takes a singular verb; if the object is plural, the pronoun takes a plural verb.

Most of the song thrills us.

Most of the songs thrill us.

Singular or Plural

all
any
half
part
most
none
some

Notice the shift in meaning, depending on the prepositional phrase. "Most of the song" means that one song is mostly thrilling. "Most of the songs" means that all but a few of many songs are thrilling. Here's another startling difference.

Half of the concert features Tchaikovsky.

Half of the concerts feature Tchaikovsky.

In the first example, half of one concert features the Russian master. In the second example, half of many concerts feature Tchaikovsky's music. What a difference one *s* can make!

Say It

Read the following word groups aloud, emphasizing the words in *italics*.
1. Both *are* / Few *have* / Many *do* / Several *were*
2. All of the piece *is* / Any of the pieces *are* / Half of the piece *does*
3. Part of the song *is* / Most of the songs *are* /
   None of the instruments *are* / Part of the instrument *is*

Correcting Indefinite Pronoun Agreement II

Write   For each blank below, write the correct form of the verb in parentheses. (Do not change the tense.)

1. Several _____ attending, but all of us _____ listening. (are)

2. All of the songs _____ dramatic, but all of the drama _____ intentional. (is)

3. Everyone _____ Tchaikovsky, but few _____ only him. (likes)

4. One of my friends _____ to classical radio; several _____ to MP3's. (listen)

5. Half of the album _____ symphonies, and half of the symphonies _____ brass fanfares. (feature)

6. Most of us _____ about music, and some of us _____ music, too. (read)

7. Of the music fans, several _____ hard-core, but none of them _____ a composer. (is)

8. One of my friends _____ trombone, and some of my friends _____ piano. (play)

9. Few _____ played in an orchestra, but one of us _____ played in a band. (has)

CONSIDER SPEAKING AND LISTENING
After completing the sentences in the first exercise, say them aloud, emphasizing the underlined verbs.

Write   Write sentences using each indefinite pronoun as a subject. Choose present tense verbs and check subject-verb agreement.

1. Part _____

2. Most _____

3. Few _____

4. Several _____

5. Both _____

6. All _____

LO5 Pronoun-Antecedent Agreement

A pronoun must agree in **person**, **number**, and **gender** with its **antecedent**. (The antecedent is the word the pronoun replaces.)

The woman brought her briefcase but forgot her computer.

antecedent + **pronoun** = **agreement**
(third person   (third person
singular   singular
feminine)   feminine)

Quick Guide

	Singular	Plural
First Person:	I, me (my, mine)	we, us (our, ours)
Second Person:	you (your, yours)	you (your, yours)
Third Person: masculine feminine neuter	he, him (his) she, her (her, hers) it (its)	they, them (their, theirs) they, them (their, theirs) they, them (their, theirs)

Two or More Antecedents

When two or more antecedents are joined by *and,* the pronoun should be plural.

Kali and Teri filled their baskets with eggs.

When two or more singular antecedents are joined by *or, nor,* or *but also,* the pronoun or pronouns should be singular.

Kali or Teri filled her basket with eggs.

Not only Kali but also Teri filled her basket with eggs.

NOTE: Avoid sexism when choosing pronouns that agree in number.

Sexist: Each child should bring his basket.
Correct: Each child should bring her or his basket.
Correct: Children should bring their baskets.

Correcting Pronoun-Antecedent Agreement

Write   For each blank below, write the pronoun that agrees with the underlined word or words.

1. <u>Ted</u> has written a patriotic poem and _____ will read _____ poem at the Fourth of July festival.

2. <u>Shandra</u> and <u>Shelli</u> will bring _____ lawn chairs to the fireworks display.

3. Either <u>John</u> or <u>Grace</u> will play _____ or _____ favorite marches over the sound system.

4. Not only <u>John</u> but also <u>Dave</u> plays trombone and will bring _____ instrument to play with the band.

5. Each <u>person</u> should bring _____ or _____ own flag.

6. <u>Mayor Jenny White</u> or <u>Congressperson Mark Russell</u> will give the invocation, and then _____ or _____ will introduce the main speaker.

7. <u>Rick</u> and <u>Linda</u> will sing _____ rendition of the national anthem.

8. <u>Acrobats</u> will stroll through the park on _____ ten-foot-tall stilts.

9. Each <u>acrobat</u> will have to keep _____ or _____ balance on uneven ground among running children.

10. <u>Ducks</u> and <u>ducklings</u> in the lake will have to make _____ way to quieter waters when the fireworks begin.

Revise   Rewrite each of the following sentences to avoid sexism.

1. Every acrobat should check his equipment.

   _____

2. Each acrobat must keep her balance.

   _____

3. One of the acrobats left his stilts at the park.

   _____

Vocabulary

person
the person speaking (first person—*I, we*), the person being spoken to (second person—*you*), or the person being spoken about (third person—*he, she, it, they*)

number
singular or plural
gender
masculine, feminine, neuter, or indefinite

antecedent
the noun (or pronoun) that a pronoun refers to or replaces

LO6 Other Pronoun Problems

Missing Antecedent

If no clear antecedent is provided, the reader doesn't know what or whom the pronoun refers to.

Confusing: In Illinois, they claim Lincoln as their own.
(Who does "they" refer to?)

Clear: In Illinois, the citizens claim Lincoln as their own.

Vague Pronoun

If the pronoun could refer to two or more words, the passage is ambiguous.

Indefinite: Sheila told her daughter to use her new tennis racket.
(To whom does the pronoun "her" refer, Sheila or her daughter?)

Clumsy: Sheila told her daughter to use Sheila's new tennis racket.

Clear: Sheila lent her new tennis racket to her daughter.

Double Subject

If a pronoun is used right after the subject, an error called a double subject occurs.

Incorrect: Your father, he is good at poker.

Correct: Your father is good at poker

Incorrect Case

Personal pronouns can function as subjects, objects, or possessives. If the wrong case is used, an error occurs.

Incorrect: Them are funny videos.

Correct: They are funny videos.

The list on the right tells you which pronouns to use in each case.

INSIGHT

Use *my* before the thing possessed and use *mine* afterward: *my cat,* but *that cat is mine.* Do the same with *our/ours, your/yours,* and *her/hers.*

Subject	Object	Possessive
I	me	my, mine
we	us	our, ours
you	you	your, yours
he	him	his
she	her	her, hers
it	it	its
they	them	their, theirs

Correcting Other Pronoun Problems

Write For each blank below, write the correct pronoun from the choices in parentheses.

1. _____ need to help_____ with the taxes.

   (I, me, my, mine)   (you, your, yours)

2. _____ should help_____ and see what_____ needs.

   (you, your, yours)   (she, her, hers)   (she, her, hers)

3. _____ can show _____ that account of _____ .

   (he, him, his)   (I, me, my, mine)   (you, your, yours)

4. _____ gave_____ permission for_____ to see.

   (you, your, yours)   (you, your, yours)   (I, me, my, mine)

5. _____ asked_____ accountant to help _____ .

   (we, us, our, ours)   (we, us, our, ours)   (we, us, our, ours)

Revise Rewrite each sentence below, correcting the pronoun problems.

1. Bob and Josh took his assignment to class.

   _____

2. Lupita needed to visit with Kelly, but she had no time.

   _____

3. Before climbing in, it broke.

   _____

4. They say that a cure for cancer is coming.

   _____

5. Trina and Lois, they bought frozen custard.

   _____

6. Carl asked Tim to cook his lunch.

   _____

Vocabulary

ambiguous
unclear, confusing

M. Unal Ozmen, 2011 / Used under license from Shutterstock.com

LO7 Real-World Application

Correct In the letter below, correct the agreement errors. Write the line number and any word you would change. Then show the change. Use the correction marks at the bottom of the page.

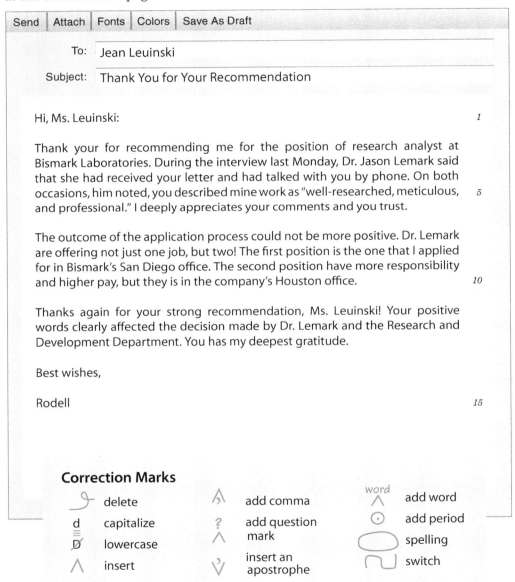

| Send | Attach | Fonts | Colors | Save As Draft |

To: Jean Leuinski

Subject: Thank You for Your Recommendation

Hi, Ms. Leuinski: 1

Thank your for recommending me for the position of research analyst at Bismark Laboratories. During the interview last Monday, Dr. Jason Lemark said that she had received your letter and had talked with you by phone. On both occasions, him noted, you described mine work as "well-researched, meticulous,   5 and professional." I deeply appreciates your comments and you trust.

The outcome of the application process could not be more positive. Dr. Lemark are offering not just one job, but two! The first position is the one that I applied for in Bismark's San Diego office. The second position have more responsibility and higher pay, but they is in the company's Houston office.   10

Thanks again for your strong recommendation, Ms. Leuinski! Your positive words clearly affected the decision made by Dr. Lemark and the Research and Development Department. You has my deepest gratitude.

Best wishes,

Rodell   15

Correction Marks

ℐ	delete	/ˌ\	add comma	word ∧	add word
d (cap)	capitalize	?	add question mark	⊙	add period
D (lc)	lowercase	⌄	insert an apostrophe	⌒	spelling
∧	insert			⌒⌐	switch

15

"I say that what we really need is a car that can be shot when it breaks down.'"

—Russell Baker

Sentence Problems

Cars are great when they go, but when a car breaks down, it is a huge headache. There's going to be a look under the hood, a bit of scrabbling beneath the thing, maybe a push, maybe a jack, and probably a tow truck and a big bill.

Sentences also are great until they break down. But you don't have to be a skilled mechanic to fix sentences. This chapter outlines a few common sentence problems and shows how to fix them. You'll be on your way in no time!

Learning Outcomes

LO1 Correct common fragments.

LO2 Correct tricky fragments.

LO3 Correct comma splices.

LO4 Correct run-on sentences.

LO5 Correct rambling sentences.

LO6 Correct misplaced and dangling modifiers.

LO7 Correct shifts in sentence construction.

LO8 Check for fragments in a real-world context.

LO9 Correct comma splices and run-ons in a real-world context.

LO10 Correct sentence problems in a real-world context.

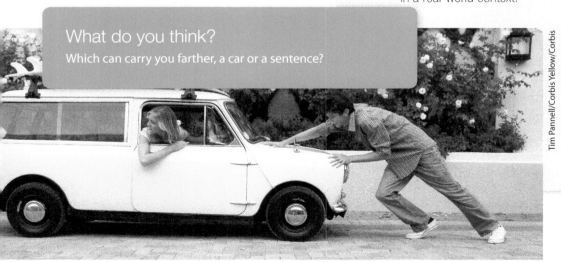

What do you think?
Which can carry you farther, a car or a sentence?

Tim Pannell/Corbis Yellow/Corbis

LO1 Common Fragments

In spoken communication and informal writing, sentence fragments are occasionally used and understood. In formal writing, fragments should be avoided.

Missing Parts

A sentence requires a subject and a predicate. If one or the other or both are missing, the sentence is a fragment. Such fragments can be fixed by supplying the missing part.

Fragment:	Went to the concert.
Fragment + Subject:	We went to the concert.
Fragment:	Everyone from Westville Community College.
Fragment + Predicate:	Everyone from Westville Community College may participate.
Fragment:	For the sake of student safety.
Fragment + Subject and Predicate:	The president set up a curfew for the sake of student safety.

Incomplete Thoughts

A sentence also must express a complete thought. Some fragments have a subject and a verb but do not express a complete thought. These fragments can be corrected by providing words that complete the thought.

Fragment:	The concert will include.
Completing Thought:	The concert will include an amazing light show.
Fragment:	If we arrive in time.
Completing Thought:	If we arrive in time, we'll get front-row seats.
Fragment:	That opened the concert.
Completing Thought:	I liked the band that opened the concert.

Say It

Read these fragments aloud. Then read each one again, but this time supply the necessary words to form a complete thought.

1. The student union building.
2. Where you can buy used books.
3. Walked to class every morning.
4. When the instructor is sick.
5. The cop was.

Correct Add words to correct each fragment below. Write the complete sentence on the lines provided.

1. Went to the office.

_____

2. The photographer, standing at the door.

_____

3. Will debate the pros and cons of tanning.

_____

4. Native Americans.

_____

5. Is one of the benefits of art class.

_____

Correct The following paragraph contains numerous fragments. Either add what is missing or combine fragments with other sentences to make them complete. Use the correction marks shown below.

> Some people are good at memorizing facts. They piece things together.   *1*
>
> Like the inside of a jigsaw puzzle. Slowly build a big picture. Others are
>
> better at grasping overall shapes. Then filling in the middle with facts.
>
> Either way, have to finish the puzzle.

Correction Marks

℗ delete	⅄ add comma	word ∧ add word
d capitalize	? add question	⊙ add period
D̶ lowercase	∧ mark	spelling
∧ insert	⌄ insert an apostrophe	switch

Correct On your own paper or orally, correct the following fragments by supplying the missing parts. Use your imagination.

1. In the newspaper.
2. We bought.
3. The purpose of sociology class.
4. Somewhere above the clouds tonight.
5. Was the reason.

Vocabulary

fragment
a group of words that is missing a subject or a predicate (or both) or that does not express a complete thought

LO2 Tricky Fragments

Some fragments are more difficult to find and correct. They creep into our writing because they are often part of the way we communicate in our speaking.

Absolute Phrases

An **absolute phrase** looks like a sentence that is missing its helping verb. An absolute phrase can be made into a sentence by adding the helping verb or by connecting the phrase to a complete sentence.

Absolute Phrase (Fragment):	Our legs trembling from the hike.
Absolute Phrase + Helping Verb:	Our legs were trembling from the hike.
Absolute Phrase + Complete Sentence:	We collapsed on the couch, our legs trembling from the hike.

Informal Fragments

Fragments that are commonly used in speech should be eliminated from formal writing. Avoid the following types of fragments unless you are writing dialogue.

Interjections:	Hey! Yeah!	**Questions:**	How come? Why not? What?
Exclamations:	What a nuisance! How fun!		
Greetings:	Hi, everybody. Good afternoon.	**Answers:**	About three or four. As soon as possible.

NOTE: Sentences that begin with *here* or *there* have a **delayed subject**, which appears after the verb. Other sentences (commands) have an **implied subject** (*you*). Such sentences are not fragments.

Delayed Subject:	Here are some crazy fans wearing wild hats.
Implied Subject:	Tackle him! Bring him down!

Say It

Read these fragments aloud. Then add words to form a complete thought.

1. Are three types of laptop computers.
2. Our instructor explaining the assignment.
3. About three in the morning.
4. Is my favorite Web site.
5. My friend working at a half-priced disk shop.

Complete Rewrite each tricky fragment below, making it a sentence.

1. Our boisterous behavior announcing our approach.

_____

2. A tidy hedge surrounding the trimmed lawn.

_____

3. The owner's gaze tracking us from the front porch.

_____

4. His dogs barking loudly from the backyard.

_____

5. Our welcome feeling less likely with each step.

_____

Delete The following paragraph contains a number of informal fragments. Identify and delete each one. Reread the paragraph and listen for the difference.

> Wow! It's amazing what archaeologists can discover from bones. *1*
> Did you know that Cro-Magnon (our ancestors) and Neanderthal tribes
> sometimes lived side by side? Sure did! In other places, when climate
> change drove our ancestors south, Neanderthals took their place.
> Neanderthals were tough and had stronger arms and hands than Cro- *5*
> Magnons had. Neanderthal brains were bigger, too. What? So why aren't
> there any Neanderthals around now? Huh? Well, although Neanderthal
> tribes used spears and stone tools, our ancestors were much better
> toolmakers. Yeah! Also, Neanderthals mainly ate big animals, while Cro-
> Magnon ate anything from fish to pigs to roots and berries. So in the long *10*
> run, Cro-Magnon hominids prospered while Neanderthal tribes dwindled
> away.

Vocabulary

absolute phrase
a group of words with a
noun and a participle (a word
ending in *ing* or *ed*) and the
words that modify them

delayed subject
a subject that appears after
the verb, as in a sentence that
begins with *here* or *there* or a
sentence that asks a question

implied subject
the word *you,* assumed to
begin command sentences

LO3 Comma Splices

Comma splices occur when two sentences are connected with only a comma. A comma splice can be fixed by adding a coordinating conjunction (*and, but, or, nor, for, so,* or *yet*) or a subordinating conjunction (*while, after, when,* and so on). The two sentences could also be joined by a semicolon (;) or separated by a period.

Comma Splice: The Eiffel Tower was a main attraction at the Paris Exposition, the Ferris wheel was its equivalent at the Chicago Exposition.

Corrected by adding a coordinating conjunction:	The Eiffel Tower was a main attraction at the Paris Exposition, and the Ferris wheel was its equivalent at the Chicago Exposition.
Corrected by adding a subordinating conjunction:	While the Eiffel Tower was a main attraction at the Paris Exposition, the Ferris wheel was its equivalent at the Chicago Exposition.
Corrected by replacing the comma with a semicolon:	The Eiffel Tower was a main attraction at the Paris Exposition; the Ferris wheel was its equivalent at the Chicago Exposition.

INSIGHT

A comma is not strong enough to join sentences without a conjunction. A semicolon can join two closely related sentences. A period or question mark can separate two sentences.

Comma Splice: An engineer named George Washington Gale Ferris planned the first Ferris wheel, many people thought he was crazy.

Corrected by adding a coordinating conjunction:	An engineer named George Washington Gale Ferris planned the first Ferris wheel, but many people thought he was crazy.
Corrected by adding a subordinating conjunction:	When an engineer named George Washington Gale Ferris planned the first Ferris wheel, many people thought he was crazy.
Corrected by replacing the comma with a period:	An engineer named George Washington Gale Ferris planned the first Ferris wheel. Many people thought he was crazy.

Correcting Comma Splices

Practice A Correct the following comma splices by adding a coordinating conjunction (*and, but, yet, or, nor, for, so*), adding a subordinating conjunction (*when, while, because,* and so on), or replacing the comma with a semicolon or period. Use the approach that makes the sentence read most smoothly.

1. We set out for a morning hike, it was raining.
2. The weather cleared by the afternoon, we hit the trail.
3. Both Jill and I were expecting wonderful scenery, we were not disappointed.
4. The view of the valley was spectacular, it was like a portrait.
5. We snacked on granola bars and apples, we enjoyed the view.
6. Then we strapped on our backpacks, the final leg of the hike awaited us.
7. The trail became rockier, we had to watch our step.
8. We reached the end of our hike, the sun was setting.
9. We're on the lookout for a new trail, it will be tough to beat this one.
10. We're done with our physical activities, it is time to watch a movie.

Practice B Correct any comma splices in the following e-mail message.

Send	Attach	Fonts	Colors	Save As Draft

To: HR Staff

Subject: Agenda for Conference

HR Staff:

At 8:15 a.m. on Friday, we will meet in Conference Room B, breakfast will be provided.

We will discuss our strategy for the show, we will then set up our materials at show table 15. The busiest crowd flow is expected from 10 a.m. to 11 a.m., the second busiest should be from 1 p.m. to 3 p.m.

Please bring plenty of energy and enthusiasm to the show, be ready to discuss the strengths of our products.

Thanks,

Phil Dawson

Vocabulary

comma splice
a sentence error that occurs when two sentences are connected with only a comma

LO4 Run-On Sentences

A run-on sentence occurs when two sentences are joined without punctuation or a connecting word. A run-on can be corrected by adding a comma and a conjunction or by inserting a semicolon or period between the two sentences.

Run-On: Horace Wilson taught in Tokyo in 1872 he introduced the Japanese to baseball.

Corrected by adding a comma and coordinating conjunction:	Horace Wilson taught in Tokyo in 1872, and he introduced the Japanese to baseball.
Corrected by adding a subordinating conjunction and a comma:	While Horace Wilson taught in Tokyo in 1872, he introduced the Japanese to baseball.
Corrected by inserting a semicolon:	Horace Wilson taught in Tokyo in 1872; he introduced the Japanese to baseball.

CONSIDER THE TRAITS

Here's an additional way to correct a run-on sentence: Turn one of the sentences into a phrase or series of phrases; then combine it with the other sentence.

The first team in Japan was formed in 1878 without a thought about how popular the sport would become.

Run-On: The first team in Japan was formed in 1878 no one knew how popular the sport would become.

Corrected by adding a comma and a coordinating conjunction:	The first team in Japan was formed in 1878, yet no one knew how popular the sport would become.
Corrected by adding a subordinating conjunction and a comma:	When the first team in Japan was formed in 1878, no one knew how popular the sport would become.
Corrected by inserting a period:	The first team in Japan was formed in 1878. No one knew how popular the sport would become.

Correcting Run-On Sentences

Correct   Correct the following run-on sentences. Use the approach that makes the sentence read most smoothly.

1. In 1767 English scientist Joseph Priestley discovered a way to infuse water with carbon dioxide this invention led to carbonated water.

2. Carbonated water is one of the main components of soft drinks it gives soft drinks the fizz and bubbles we enjoy.

3. The first soft drinks in America were dispensed out of soda fountains they were most often found at drug stores and ice-cream parlors.

4. Interestingly, soda was sold at drug stores it promised healing properties.

5. Most of the formulas for American soft drinks were invented by pharmacists the idea was to create nonalcoholic alternatives to traditional medicines.

6. The first carbonated drink bottles could not keep bubbles from escaping it was more popular to buy a soda from a soda fountain.

7. A successful method of keeping bubbles in a bottle was not invented until 1892 it was called a crowned bottle cap.

8. The first diet soda to be sold was known as "No-Cal Beverage" in 1959 the first diet cola hit the stores.

Rewrite   Rewrite the following paragraph, correcting any run-on sentences that you find.

> Arbor Day is an undervalued holiday in America. On this holiday, *1*
> people are encouraged to plant trees it is celebrated on the fourth Friday
> of April. It was created by J. Sterling Morton he was President Grover
> Cleveland's Secretary of Agriculture. The holiday is now observed in a
> number of other countries. *5*

Vocabulary

run-on sentence
a sentence error that occurs when two sentences are joined without punctuation *or* a connecting word

LO5 Rambling Sentences

A rambling sentence occurs when a long series of separate ideas are connected by one *and, but,* or *so* after another. The result is an unfocused sentence that goes on and on. To correct a rambling sentence, break it into smaller units, adding and cutting words as needed.

Rambling: When we signed up for the two-on-two tournament, I had no thoughts about winning, but then my brother started talking about spending his prize money and he asked me how I would spend my share so we were counting on winning when we really had little chance and as it turned out, we lost in the second round.

Corrected: When we signed up for the two-on-two tournament, I had no thoughts about winning. Then my brother started talking about spending the prize money. He even asked me how I would spend my share. Soon, we were counting on winning when we really had little chance. As it turned out, we lost in the second round.

Say It

Read the following rambling sentences aloud. Afterward, circle all of the connecting words (*and, but, so*), and be prepared to suggest different ways to break each rambling idea into more manageable units.

1. I enjoyed touring the hospital and I would enjoy joining the nursing staff and I believe that my prior work experience will be an asset but I also know that I have a lot more to learn.

2. The electronics store claims to offer "one-stop shopping" and they can take care of all of a customer's computer needs and they have a fully trained staff to answer questions and solve problems so there is really no need to go anywhere else.

Losevsky Pavel, 2011 / Used under license from Shutterstock.com

Correcting Rambling Sentences

Correct Correct the following rambling sentences by dividing them into separate sentences. Afterward, share your corrections with a classmate.

1. The dancer entered gracefully onto the stage and she twirled around twice and then tiptoed to the front of the stage and the crowd applauded.

2. I went to the movies last night and when I got to the theater, I had to wait in a super-slow line and when I finally got to the front, the show I wanted to see was sold out.

3. I like to listen to music everywhere but I especially like to rock out in my car so I scream and dance and I don't care if anyone sees me through the windows.

EDHAR, 2011 / Used under license from Shutterstock.com

CONSIDER EXTENDING

Share your corrections with a classmate. Did you change each rambling sentence in the same way?

Answer Answer the following questions about rambling sentences.

1. How can you recognize a rambling sentence?

2. Why is a rambling sentence a problem?

3. How can you correct one?

Vocabulary

rambling sentence
a sentence error that occurs when a long series of separate ideas are connected by one *and, but,* or *so* after another

LO6 Misplaced / Dangling Modifiers

Dangling Modifiers

A modifier is a word, phrase, or clause that functions as an adjective or adverb. When the modifier does not clearly modify another word in the sentence, it is called a **dangling modifier**. This error can be corrected by inserting the missing word and/or rewriting the sentence.

Dangling Modifier: After strapping the toy cowboy to his back, my cat stalked sullenly around the house.
(The cat could strap the toy cowboy to his own back?)

Corrected: After I strapped the toy cowboy to his back, my cat stalked sullenly around the house.

Dangling Modifier: Trying to get the cowboy off, the bowl got knocked off the shelf. *(The bowl was trying to get the cowboy off?)*

Corrected: Trying to get the cowboy off, the cat knocked the bowl off the shelf.

Misplaced Modifiers

When a modifier is placed beside a word that it does not modify, the modifier is misplaced and often results in an amusing or **illogical** statement. A **misplaced modifier** can be corrected by moving it next to the word that it modifies.

Misplaced Modifier: My cat was diagnosed by the vet with fleas.
(The vet has fleas?)

Corrected: The vet diagnosed my cat with fleas.

Misplaced Modifier: The vet gave a pill to my cat tasting like fish.
(The cat tastes like fish?)

Corrected: The vet gave my cat a pill tasting like fish.

INSIGHT ————————————————————————————————

Avoid placing any adverb modifiers between a verb and its direct object.
Misplaced: I will throw quickly the ball.
Corrected: I will quickly throw the ball.
Also, do not separate two-word verbs with an adverb modifier.
Misplaced: Please take immediately out the trash.
Corrected: Please immediately take out the trash.

Say It

Read the following sentences aloud, noting the dangling or misplaced modifier in each one. Then tell a classmate how you would correct each error.
1. After tearing up the couch, I decided to get my cat a scratching post.
2. I have worked to teach my cat to beg for three weeks.

Correcting Dangling and Misplaced Modifiers

Rewrite Rewrite each of the sentences below, correcting the misplaced and dangling modifiers.
1. I bought a hound dog for my brother named Rover. _____
2. The doctor diagnosed me and referred me to a specialist with scoliosis. _____
3. The man was reported murdered by the coroner. _____
4. Please present the recommendation that is attached to Mrs. Burble. _____
5. Jack drove me to our home in a Chevy. _____
6. I couldn't believe my brother would hire a disco DJ who hates disco. _____
7. We saw a fox and a vixen on the way to the psychiatrist. _____
8. I gave the secretary my phone number that works in reception. _____
9. I found a pair of underwear in the drawer that doesn't belong to me. _____
10. We offer jackets for trendy teens with gold piping. _____

Correct For each sentence, correct the placement of the adverb.
1. Give quickly the report to your boss. _____
2. We will provide immediately an explanation. _____
3. Fill completely out the test sheet. _____

INSIGHT

When a modifier comes at the beginning of the sentence or the end of the sentence, make sure it modifies the word or phrase closest to it. Ask yourself, "Who or what is being described?"

Vocabulary

dangling modifier
a modifying word, phrase, or clause that appears to modify the wrong word or a word that isn't in the sentence

illogical
without logic; senseless, false, or untrue

misplaced modifier
a modifying word, phrase, or

clause that has been placed incorrectly in a sentence, often creating an amusing or illogical idea

LO7 Shifts in Sentences

Shift in Person

A **shift in person** is an error that occurs when first, second, and/or third person are improperly mixed in a sentence.

> **Shift in person:**   If you exercise and eat right, an individual can lose weight. (The sentence improperly shifts from second person—*you*— to third person—*individual*.)
>
> **Corrected:**   If you exercise and eat right, you can lose weight.

Shift in Tense

A **shift in tense** is an error that occurs when more than one verb tense is improperly used in a sentence.

> **Shift in tense:**   He tried every other option before he agrees to do it my way. (The sentence improperly shifts from past tense— *tried*—to present tense—*agrees*.)
>
> **Corrected:**   He tried every other option before he agreed to do it my way.

Shift in Voice

A **shift in voice** is an error that occurs when active voice and passive voice are mixed in a sentence.

> **Shift in voice:**   When she fixes the radiator, other repairs may be suggested. (The sentence improperly shifts from active voice—*fixes*— to passive voice—*may be suggested*.)
>
> **Corrected:**   When she fixes the radiator, she may suggest other repairs.

Say It

Read the following sentences aloud, paying careful attention to the improper shift each contains. Then tell a classmate how you would correct each error.

1. David exercises daily and ate well.
2. Marianne goes running each morning and new friends might be met.
3. After you choose an exercise routine, a person should stick to it.
4. Lamar swam every morning and does ten laps.
5. The personal trainer made a schedule for me, and a diet was suggested by her.

Correcting Improper Shifts in Sentences

Rewrite Rewrite each sentence below, correcting any improper shifts in construction.

1. You should be ready for each class in a person's schedule. _____

2. I work for my brother most days and classes are attended by me at night. _____

3. When you give me a review, can he also give me a raise? _____

4. As we walked to school, last night's football game was discussed by us. _____

5. I hoped to catch the bus until I see it leave. _____

Correct Correct the improper shifts in person, tense, or voice in the following paragraph. Use the correction marks below when you make your changes.

> Some people are early adopters, which means technology is adopted   *1*
> by them when it is new. Other people are technophobes because you are
> afraid of technology, period. I am not an early adopter or a technophobe,
> but a person has to see the value in technology before I use it. Technology
> has to be cheap, intuitive, reliable, and truly helpful before you start using   *5*
> it. I let others work out the bugs and pay the high prices before a piece
> of technology is adopted by me. But when I decide it is time to get a new
> gadget or program, you buy it and use it until it is worn out. Then I look
> for something else that is even cheaper and more intuitive, reliable, and
> helpful, which is then bought by me.   *10*

Correction Marks

⅋	delete	⅄	add comma	word ∧	add word
d̲	capitalize	? ∧	add question mark	⊙	add period
D̶	lowercase			⌣	spelling
∧	insert	⌄	insert an apostrophe	⌓	switch

Vocabulary

person
first person (*I* or *we*—the person speaking), second person (*you*—the person spoken to), or third person (*he, she, it,* or *they*—the person or thing spoken about)

voice of verb
whether the subject is doing the action of the verb (active voice) or is being acted upon (passive voice)

shift in person
an error that occurs when first, second, and third person are improperly mixed in a sentence

shift in tense
an error that occurs when more than one verb tense is improperly used in a sentence

shift in voice
an error that occurs when active voice and passive voice are mixed in a sentence

LO8 Real-World Application

Correct   Correct any sentence fragments in the following business memo. Use the correction marks below.

Slovik Manufacturing   *1*

Date: August 8, 2011

To: Jerome James, Personnel Director

From: Ike Harris, Graphic Arts Director

Subject: Promotion of Mona Veal from Intern to Full-Time Graphic Artist   *5*

For the past five months, Mona Veal as an intern in our Marketing Department. I recommend that she be offered a position as a full-time designer. Are the two main reasons behind this recommendation.

1. Mona has shown the traits that Slovik Manufacturing values in a graphic designer. Creative, dependable, and easy to work with.   *10*

2. Presently, we have two full-time graphic designers and one intern. While this group has worked well. The full-time designers have averaged 3.5 hours of overtime per week. Given this fact. Our new contract with Lee-Stamp Industries will require more help, including at least one additional designer.   *15*

If you approve this recommendation. Please initial below and return this memo.

Yes, I approve the recommendation to offer Mona Veal a full-time position.

_ _ _ _ _ _ _

Attachment: Evaluation report of Mona Veal   *20*

cc: Elizabeth Zoe
    Mark Moon

Correction Marks

⌢	delete	⩓	add comma	*word* ∧	add word
d̲̲	capitalize	?	add question mark	⊙	add period
D̲	lowercase	∧			spelling
∧	insert	⌄	insert an apostrophe		switch

LO9 Real-World Application

Correct Correct any comma splices or run-on sentences in the following e-mail message. Use the correction marks on the previous page.

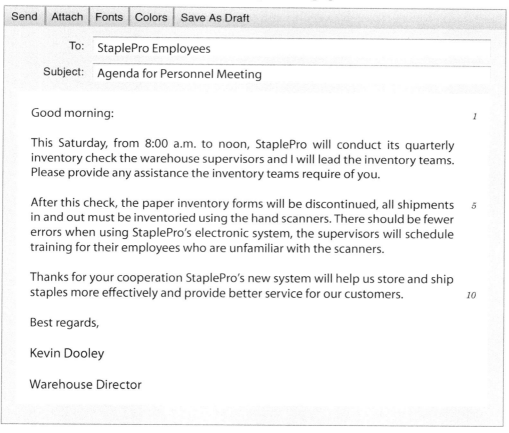

| Send | Attach | Fonts | Colors | Save As Draft |

To: StaplePro Employees

Subject: Agenda for Personnel Meeting

Good morning: *1*

This Saturday, from 8:00 a.m. to noon, StaplePro will conduct its quarterly inventory check the warehouse supervisors and I will lead the inventory teams. Please provide any assistance the inventory teams require of you.

After this check, the paper inventory forms will be discontinued, all shipments   *5*
in and out must be inventoried using the hand scanners. There should be fewer errors when using StaplePro's electronic system, the supervisors will schedule training for their employees who are unfamiliar with the scanners.

Thanks for your cooperation StaplePro's new system will help us store and ship staples more effectively and provide better service for our customers.   *10*

Best regards,

Kevin Dooley

Warehouse Director

Reflect Reflect on what you have learned about comma splices and run-on sentences by answering the following questions.

1. What is the difference between a comma splice and a run-on sentence?

_____

2. How can you correct comma splices and run-on sentences? (Name at least three ways.)

_____

3. What are three common coordinating conjunctions that you can use to connect two sentences?

_____

LO10 Real-World Application

Correct Correct any dangling modifiers, misplaced modifiers, or shifts in construction in the following message. Use the correction marks below.

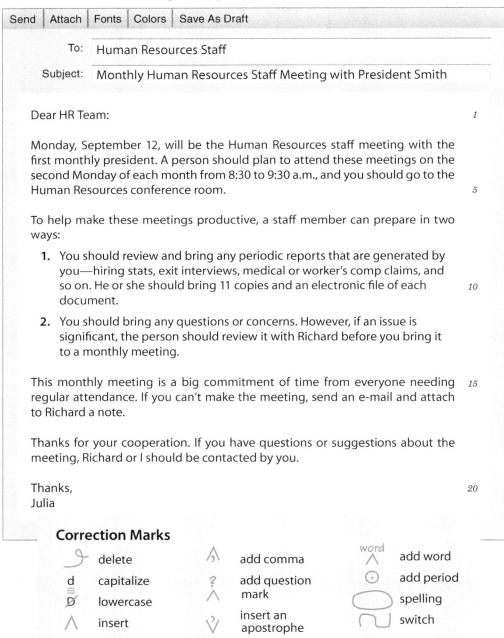

| Send | Attach | Fonts | Colors | Save As Draft |

To: Human Resources Staff

Subject: Monthly Human Resources Staff Meeting with President Smith

Dear HR Team: *1*

Monday, September 12, will be the Human Resources staff meeting with the first monthly president. A person should plan to attend these meetings on the second Monday of each month from 8:30 to 9:30 a.m., and you should go to the Human Resources conference room.   *5*

To help make these meetings productive, a staff member can prepare in two ways:

1. You should review and bring any periodic reports that are generated by you—hiring stats, exit interviews, medical or worker's comp claims, and so on. He or she should bring 11 copies and an electronic file of each   *10* document.

2. You should bring any questions or concerns. However, if an issue is significant, the person should review it with Richard before you bring it to a monthly meeting.

This monthly meeting is a big commitment of time from everyone needing   *15* regular attendance. If you can't make the meeting, send an e-mail and attach to Richard a note.

Thanks for your cooperation. If you have questions or suggestions about the meeting, Richard or I should be contacted by you.

Thanks,   *20*
Julia

Correction Marks

ℐ delete	⁁ add comma	*word* ⁁ add word
d capitalize	? add question mark	⊙ add period
ᴅ̶ lowercase	⌄ insert an apostrophe	⌒ spelling
⋀ insert		⌐⌐ switch

Rewrite The sentences that follow come from church bulletins and are amusing due to misplaced or dangling modifiers or other sentence problems. Rewrite each sentence to remove these problems.

1. Remember in prayer the many who are sick of our church and community.

   _____

2. For those of you who have children and don't know it, we have a nursery downstairs.

   _____

3. The ladies of the church have cast off clothing of every kind. They can be seen in the church basement Saturday.

   _____

4. The third verse of "Blessed Assurance" will be sung without musical accomplishment.

   _____

Write Write the first draft of a personal narrative (true story) in which you share a time when you misplaced or lost something important to you or to someone else. Here are some tips for adding interest to your story:

- Start right in the middle of the action.
- Build suspense to keep the reader's interest.
- Use dialogue.
- Use sensory details (what you heard, saw, felt, and so on).

Afterward, exchange your writing with a classmate. Read each other's narrative first for enjoyment and a second time to check it for the sentence errors discussed in this chapter.

CONSIDER THE WORKPLACE

Journalists and publishers need to be especially careful to avoid mistakes in their writing. But errors in writing reflect badly on all professionals.

Part IV:

Word Workshops

16

"If you want to make an apple pie from scratch, you must first create the universe."

—Carl Sagan

Noun

Astrophysicists tell us that the universe is made up of two things—matter and energy. Matter is the stuff, and energy is the movement or heat of the stuff.

Grammarians tell us that thoughts are made up of two things—nouns and verbs. Nouns name the stuff, and verbs capture the energy. In that way, the sentence reflects the universe itself. You can't express a complete thought unless you are talking about matter and energy. Each sentence, then, is the basic particle of thought.

This chapter focuses on nouns, which describe not just things you can see—such as people, places, or objects—but also things you can't see—such as love, justice, and democracy. The exercises in this chapter will help you sort out the stuff of thinking.

Learning Outcomes

LO1 Understand classes of nouns.

LO2 Use singular and plural nouns.

LO3 Form tricky plurals.

LO4 Use count and noncount nouns.

LO5 Use articles.

LO6 Use other noun markers.

LO7 Use nouns correctly in a real-world context.

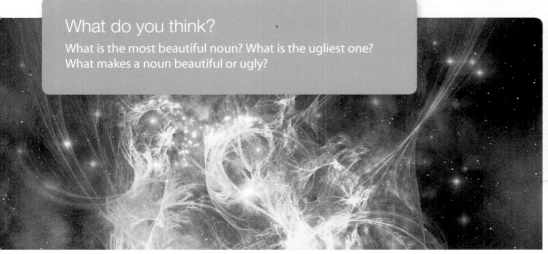

What do you think?

What is the most beautiful noun? What is the ugliest one? What makes a noun beautiful or ugly?

LO1 Classes of Nouns

All nouns are either *common* or *proper*. They can also be *individual* or *collective, concrete* or *abstract*.

Common or Proper Nouns

Common nouns name a general person, place, thing, or idea. They are not capitalized as names. Proper nouns name a specific person, place, thing, or idea, and they are capitalized as names.

	Common Nouns	**Proper Nouns**
Person:	politician	Barack Obama
Place:	park	Yellowstone
Thing:	marker	Sharpie
Idea:	religion	Hinduism

Individual or Collective Nouns

Most nouns are individual: They refer to one person or thing. Other nouns are collective, referring most commonly to a group of people or animals.

	Individual Nouns	**Collective Nouns**
Person:	secretary	staff
	catcher	team
	student	class
	daughter	family
Animal:	lamb	herd
	locust	swarm
	wolf	pack
	kitten	litter
	goose	gaggle

Concrete or Abstract

If a noun refers to something that can be seen, heard, smelled, tasted, or touched, it is a concrete noun. If a noun refers to something that can't be sensed, it is an abstract noun. Abstract nouns name ideas, conditions, or feelings.

Concrete Nouns	**Abstract Nouns**
judge	impartiality
brain	mind
heart	courage
train	transportation

Using Different Classes of Nouns

Identify In each sentence below, identify the underlined nouns as common (C) or proper (P).

1. <u>William Faulkner</u> wrote about the <u>death</u> of the <u>Old South.</u>
2. His novel *The Unvanquished* tells about the <u>aftermath</u> of the <u>Civil War.</u>
3. He chronicles the <u>end</u> of <u>slavery</u> but also of the genteel class in the <u>South.</u>
4. His novel *Absalom, Absalom!* describes the <u>creation</u> and end of a <u>plantation.</u>

Identify In each sentence below, identify the underlined nouns as individual (I) or collective (CL).

1. <u>Quentin Compson</u> appears often in the collected <u>works</u> of Faulkner.
2. The Compson <u>family</u> is the <u>centerpiece</u> of Yoknapatawpha County.
3. The novel *The Sound and the Fury* tells of the plight of the <u>Compsons.</u>
4. <u>Benjamin Compson</u> watches a <u>group</u> golf in what was once their farm field.

Identify In each sentence below, identify the underlined nouns as concrete (CT) or abstract (A).

1. The <u>Compsons</u> become a <u>symbol</u> of the decline of the South.
2. <u>Faulkner</u> depicts the family with <u>compassion</u> and <u>humor.</u>
3. Other <u>novels</u> tell of other denizens of Faulkner's <u>imagination.</u>
4. Faulkner won the <u>Pulitzer Prize</u> for his <u>novel</u> *A Fable,* set outside the county.

Vocabulary

common noun
noun referring to a general person, place, thing, or idea; not capitalized as a name

proper noun
noun referring to a specific person, place, thing, or idea; capitalized as a name

individual noun
noun referring to one person or thing

collective noun
noun referring to a group of people or animals

concrete noun
noun referring to something that can be sensed

abstract noun
noun referring to an idea, a condition, or a feeling— something that cannot be sensed

LO2 Singular or Plural

The **number** of a noun indicates whether it is singular or plural. A **singular** noun refers to one person, place, thing, or idea. A **plural** noun refers to more than one person, place, thing, or idea. For most words, the plural is formed by adding *s*. For nouns ending in *ch, s, sh, x,* or *z,* add an *es*.

	Most Nouns Add *s*		**Nouns Ending in *ch, s, sh, x,* or *z* Add *es***	
	Singular	Plural	Singular	Plural
Person:	sister	sisters	coach	coaches
Place:	park	parks	church	churches
Thing:	spoon	spoons	kiss	kisses
Idea:	solution	solutions	wish	wishes

Same in Both Forms or Usually Plural

Some nouns are the same in both forms, and others are usually plural.

Same in Both Forms		**Usually Plural**	
Singular	Plural	Plural	
deer	deer	clothes	series
fish	fish	glasses	shears
moose	moose	pants	shorts
salmon	salmon	proceeds	species
sheep	sheep	savings	tongs
swine	swine	scissors	trousers

Irregular Plurals

Irregular plurals are formed by changing the words themselves. That is because the plural form comes from Old English or Latin.

From Old English		**From Latin**	
Singular	Plural	Singular	Plural
child	children	alumnus	alumni
foot	feet	axis	axes
goose	geese	crisis	crises
man	men	datum	data
mouse	mice	millennium	millennia
person	people	medium	media
tooth	teeth	nucleus	nuclei
woman	women	phenomenon	phenomena

Using Singular and Plural Nouns

Identify For each word, fill in the blank with either the singular or plural form, whichever is missing. If the word usually uses the plural form or is the same in both forms, write an X.

1. crisis _____
2. _____ species
3. child _____
4. automobile _____
5. _____ shears
6. _____ teeth
7. _____ clothes
8. deer _____
9. swine _____
10. phenomenon _____
11. _____ girls
12. _____ millennia
13. man _____
14. fish _____
15. _____ pants
16. _____ moose
17. axis _____
18. boy _____
19. _____ mice
20. goose _____
21. _____ data
22. alumnus _____
23. _____ savings
24. tree _____
25. _____ women

Vocabulary

number
whether a word is singular or plural

singular
referring to one thing

plural
referring to more than one thing

irregular plural
a plural noun formed by changing the word rather than by adding *s*

LO3 Tricky Plurals

Some plural nouns are more challenging to form. Words ending in *y, f,* or *fe* and certain compound nouns require special consideration.

Nouns Ending in *y*

If a common noun ends in *y* after a consonant, change the *y* to *i* and add *es*. If the noun ends in *y* after a vowel, leave the *y* and add *s*.

y After a Consonant		*y* After a Vowel	
Singular	**Plural**	**Singular**	**Plural**
fly	flies	bay	bays
lady	ladies	key	keys
penny	pennies	toy	toys
story	stories	tray	trays

Nouns Ending in *f* or *fe*

If a common noun ends in *f* or *fe,* change the *f* or *fe* to a *v* and add *es*—unless the *f* sound remains in the plural form. Then just add an *s*.

v Sound in Plural		*f* Sound in Plural	
Singular	**Plural**	**Singular**	**Plural**
calf	calves	belief	beliefs
life	lives	chef	chefs
self	selves	proof	proofs
shelf	shelves	safe	safes

Compound Nouns

A compound noun is made up of two or more words that function together as a single noun. Whether the compound is hyphenated or not, make it plural by placing the *s* or *es* on the most important word in the compound.

Important Word First		Important Word Last	
Singular	**Plural**	**Singular**	**Plural**
editor in chief	editors in chief	bird-watcher	bird-watchers
mother-in-law	mothers-in-law	human being	human beings
professor emeritus	professors emeritus	test tube	test tubes
secretary of state	secretaries of state	well-wisher	well-wishers

Forming Tricky Plurals

Form Plurals For each word below, create the correct plural form.

1. day _____
2. shelf _____
3. middle school _____
4. pony _____
5. bay _____
6. life _____
7. chief _____
8. loaf _____
9. tray _____
10. compact car _____

11. mother-in-law _____
12. ray _____
13. lady _____
14. carafe _____
15. stepsister _____
16. poof _____
17. nose tackle _____
18. party _____
19. son-in-law _____
20. baby _____

Form Plurals In the sentences below, correct the plural errors by writing the correct forms.

1. If I give you two pennys for your thoughts, will you give me two cents' worths?
2. Have you read *The Secret Lifes of Cheves*?
3. The professor emerituses are working on two mathematical prooves.
4. I won't question your believes or insult your wells-wisher.
5. The ladys tried to quiet their screaming babys.
6. Time is sure fun when you're having flys.
7. The compacts car are equipped with remote-access keis.
8. I like chicken pattys but don't like salmons patty.
9. I read about dwarves and elfs.
10. Stack those books on the shelfs above the saves.

Vocabulary

compound noun
noun made up of two or more words

LO4 Count and Noncount Nouns

Some nouns name things that can be counted, and other nouns name things that cannot. Different rules apply to each type.

Count Nouns

Count nouns name things that can be counted—*pens, people, votes, cats,* and so forth. They can be singular or plural, and they can be preceded by numbers or articles (*a, an,* or *the*).

Singular	Plural
apple	apples
iguana	iguanas
thought	thoughts
room	rooms

INSIGHT

Many native English speakers aren't even aware of count and noncount nouns, though they use them correctly out of habit. Listen for their use of count and noncount nouns.

Noncount Nouns

Noncount nouns name things that cannot be counted. They are used in singular form, and they can be preceded by *the,* but rarely by *a* or *an.*

This semester, I'm taking **mathematics** and **biology** as well as **Spanish**.

Substances	Foods	Activities	Science	Languages	Abstractions
wood	water	reading	oxygen	Spanish	experience
cloth	milk	boating	weather	English	harm
ice	wine	smoking	heat	Mandarin	publicity
plastic	sugar	dancing	sunshine	Farsi	advice
wool	rice	swimming	electricity	Greek	happiness
steel	meat	soccer	lightning	Latin	health
aluminum	cheese	hockey	biology	French	joy
metal	flour	photography	history	Japanese	love
leather	pasta	writing	mathematics	Afrikaans	anger
porcelain	gravy	homework	economics	German	fame

Two-Way Nouns

Two-way nouns can function as count or noncount nouns, depending on their context.

Please set a **glass** in front of each place mat. (count noun)

The display case was made of tempered **glass**. (noncount noun)

Using Count and Noncount Nouns

Sort Read the list of nouns below and sort the words into columns of count and noncount nouns.

window	aluminum	holiday	health	rain
English	shoe	tricycle	poetry	ice
bowling	plum	Japanese	lawyer	teaspoon

Using Count and Noncount Nouns

Correct Read the following paragraph and correct the noun errors. Write the line number and any words you would change, and then show the change. The first line has been corrected for you.

Our kitchen redesign involved tearing out the plastics that covered   *1*
the counter and removing the flashings around the edges. We installed
new aluminums to replace the old metals. Also, the cupboard doors, which
used to be made of woods, were replaced by doors made of glasses. We have
a new jar for holding flours and a new refrigerator with a special place   *5*
for milks and a dispenser for waters. Everything is illuminated by new
lightings, and a larger window lets more sunlights in.

Correction Marks

✐ delete	⅄ add comma	word ∧ add word
d̲̳ capitalize	? add question mark	⊙ add period
D̲ lowercase	∧	⬭ spelling
∧ insert	ᵛ, insert an apostrophe	⎘ switch

LO5 Articles

Articles help you to know if a noun refers to a specific thing or to a general thing. There are two basic types of articles—definite and indefinite.

Definite Article

The definite article is the word *the*. It signals that the noun refers to one specific person, place, thing, or idea.

Look at the rainbow.
(Look at a specific rainbow.)

NOTE: *The* can be used with most nouns, but usually not with proper nouns.

Incorrect: The Joe looked at the rainbow.
Correct: Joe looked at the rainbow.

INSIGHT

If your heritage language does not use articles, pay close attention to the way native English speakers use *the* when referring to a specific thing. Note, however, that *the* is not usually used with proper nouns naming people or animals.

Indefinite Articles

The indefinite articles are the words *a* and *an*. They signal that the noun refers to a general person, place, thing, or idea. The word *a* is used before nouns that begin with consonant sounds, and the word *an* is used before nouns that begin with vowel sounds.

I enjoy seeing a rainbow.
(I enjoy seeing any rainbow.)

NOTE: Don't use *a* or *an* with noncount nouns or plural count nouns.

Incorrect: I love a sunshine.
Correct: I love the sunshine.

NOTE: If a word begins with an *h* that is pronounced, use *a*. If the *h* is silent, use *an*.

Incorrect: I stared for a hour.
Correct: I stared for an hour.

Using Articles

Identify Add the appropriate indefinite article (*a* or *an*) to each of the words below. The first one has been done for you.

1. ___an___ orchard
2. _____ petunia
3. _____ hose
4. _____ honor
5. _____ avocado

6. _____ evening
7. _____ house
8. _____ hour
9. _____ shark
10. _____ eye

11. _____ error
12. _____ opportunity
13. ___ honest mistake
14. _____ emblem
15. _____ handkerchief

Correct Write the line number and either delete or replace any articles that are incorrectly used. The first sentence has been done for you.

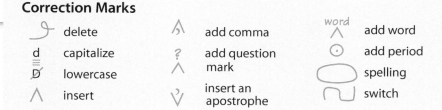

Climate scientists see a shift in *a* weather. With a increase in the   *1*
levels of carbon dioxide, the atmosphere traps a heat of the sun. More
heat in an air means more heat in the oceans. If a ocean gets warmer,
the storms it creates are more intense. An hurricane could develop to
an higher category, with stronger winds and a increase in a lightning. A   *5*
Earth is already an storm world, but with a rise in global temperatures,
a weather could become more extreme.

Correction Marks

9 delete

d capitalize
D̶ lowercase

∧ insert

⅄ add comma

? add question
∧ mark

∨ insert an apostrophe

word
∧ add word

⊙ add period

spelling

switch

Vocabulary

article
the most common type of noun marker (*a*, *an*, or *the*)

definite article
the word *the*, used to mark a noun that refers to a specific person, place, or thing

indefinite article
the words *a* or *an*, used to mark a noun that refers to a general person, place, or thing

LO6 Other Noun Markers

Possessive Adjective

A **possessive adjective** is the possessive form of a noun or pronoun. Possessive adjectives can be formed by adding *'s* to singular nouns and *'* to plural nouns.

Paul's car is in the shop, but **Taylor's** is fixed.

Florida's coast is beautiful.

The **Kings'** porch has screens.

That is **my** pen. This pen is **mine.**

It's **your** choice. The choice is **yours.**

Possessive Pronouns

	Singular		Plural	
	Before	After	Before	After
First Person	my	mine	our	ours
Second Person	your	yours	your	yours
Third Person	his	his	their	theirs
	her	hers	their	theirs
	its	its	their	theirs

Indefinite Adjectives

An **indefinite adjective** signals that the noun it marks refers to a general person, place, thing, or idea. Some indefinite adjectives mark count nouns and others mark noncount nouns.

Each person brought food. **Much** food was set out.

With Count Nouns			With Noncount Nouns	With Count or Noncount		
each	either	every	much	all	any	more
few	many	neither		most	some	
several						

Demonstrative Adjectives

A **demonstrative adjective** marks a specific noun. The words *this* and *that* (singular) or *these* and *those* (plural) demonstrate exactly which one is meant.

These pickles are from **that** jar.   **This** taste comes from **those** spices.

Quantifiers

A **quantifier** tells *how many* or *how much* there is of something.

With Count Nouns		With Noncount Nouns		With Count or Noncount		
each	a couple of	a bag of	a little	no	a lot of	most
several	every	a bowl of	much	not any	lots of	all
a number of	many	a piece of	a great deal of	some	plenty of	
both	a few					
nine						

Using Noun Markers

Identify Write the appropriate noun marker in parentheses for each sentence.

1. I brought one of (*my, mine*) favorite recipes, and you brought one of (*your, yours*).
2. Is this (*her, hers*) recipe, or is it (*their, theirs*)?
3. How (*many, much*) sugar should I add to the batter?
4. I can't believe the recipe does not use (*any, each*) flour.
5. Next, we should make (*this, these*) casserole.
6. Your face tells me you don't like (*that, those*) idea.
7. After making the dough, we had (*several, a little*) butter left over.
8. We liked (*a number of, much*) the recipes.
9. The best pie of all was (*her, hers*).
10. Let's make sure everyone has a copy in (*their, theirs*) recipe files.

Correct Write the line number and show the changes you would make to correct any incorrectly used noun markers. The first one has been done for you.

> An omelet can contain as few or as ~~much~~ *many* ingredients as you wish.   *1*
> Of course, a good omelet starts with three or four eggs. Blend the eggs in
> yours biggest bowl and add a couple of milk. Next, you can include much
> vegetables. Try fresh ingredients from yours garden. Add a cup of chopped
> scallions, fresh tomatoes, or green peppers. And a number of spinach can   *5*
> give the omelet a savory flavor. You can also add several meat. Mix in a
> couple of bacon or many ham. Or you might include several sausage. Fry
> the omelet, fold it, sprinkle it with a couple of cheese, and enjoy!

Correction Marks

Ꝺ	delete	⩘	add comma	*word* ∧	add word
d̲	capitalize	?	add question mark	⊙	add period
D̸	lowercase	∧		⌇	spelling
∧	insert	⩔	insert an apostrophe	⌐⌐	switch

Vocabulary

possessive adjective
the possessive form of a noun or pronoun, showing ownership of another noun

indefinite adjective
an indefinite pronoun (*many, much, some*) used

as an adjective to mark a nonspecific noun

demonstrative adjective
a demonstrative pronoun (*this, that, these, those*) used as an adjective to mark a specific noun

quantifier
a modifier that tells *how many* or *how much*

LO7 Real-World Application

Correct In the e-mail that follows, correct any errors with nouns, articles, or other noun markers. Use the correction marks below.

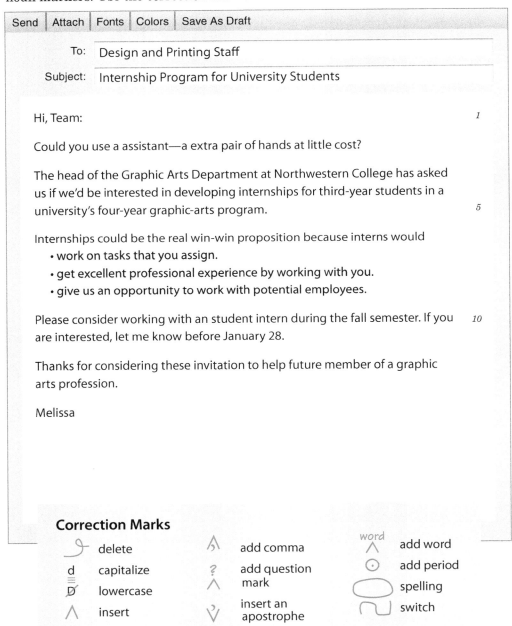

| Send | Attach | Fonts | Colors | Save As Draft |

To: Design and Printing Staff

Subject: Internship Program for University Students

Hi, Team: 1

Could you use a assistant—a extra pair of hands at little cost?

The head of the Graphic Arts Department at Northwestern College has asked us if we'd be interested in developing internships for third-year students in a university's four-year graphic-arts program.   5

Internships could be the real win-win proposition because interns would
• work on tasks that you assign.
• get excellent professional experience by working with you.
• give us an opportunity to work with potential employees.

Please consider working with an student intern during the fall semester. If you   10
are interested, let me know before January 28.

Thanks for considering these invitation to help future member of a graphic arts profession.

Melissa

Correction Marks

♪ delete	⌃ add comma	word ⌃ add word
d̲ capitalize	? add question	⊙ add period
D̶ lowercase	⌃ mark	⌒ spelling
⌃ insert	⌄ insert an apostrophe	⌐ switch

17

"Clothes make the man. Naked people have little or no influence on society."

—Mark Twain

Pronoun

An old saying goes that clothes make the man. Well, not quite. Just because a suit is standing on a mannequin in the window doesn't mean that a living, breathing, and thinking person is in the room. The clothes are just temporary stand-ins.

Pronouns, similarly, are stand-ins for nouns. They aren't nouns, but they suggest nouns or refer back to them. That's why it's especially important for the pronoun to clearly connect to whatever it is replacing.

This chapter will help you make sure your pronoun stand-ins work well.

Learning Outcomes

LO1 Understand personal pronouns.

LO2 Create pronoun-antecedent agreement.

LO3 Correct other pronoun problems.

LO4 Create agreement with indefinite pronouns.

LO5 Use relative pronouns.

LO6 Use other pronouns.

LO7 Use pronouns correctly in a real-world context.

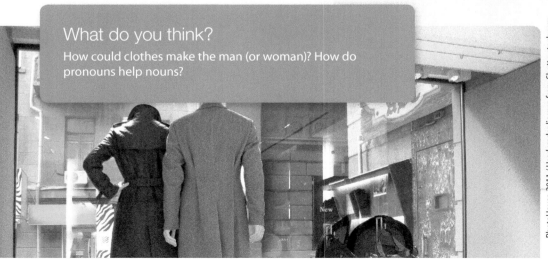

What do you think?

How could clothes make the man (or woman)? How do pronouns help nouns?

PhotoHouse, 2011 / Used under license from Shutterstock.com

LO1 Personal Pronouns

A pronoun is a word that takes the place of a noun or another pronoun. The most common type of pronoun is the personal pronoun. Personal pronouns indicate whether the person is speaking, is being spoken to, or is being spoken about.

Person	Singular			Plural		
	Nom.	Obj.	Poss.	Nom.	Obj.	Poss.
First (speaking)	I	me	my/mine	we	us	our/ours
Second (spoken to)	you	you	your/yours	you	you	your/yours
Third (spoken about) masculine	he	him	his	they	them	their/theirs
feminine	she	her	her/hers	they	them	their/theirs
neuter	it	it	its	they	them	their/theirs

Nom.=nominative case / **Obj.**=objective case / **Poss.**=possessive case

Case of Pronouns

The case of a personal pronoun indicates how it can be used.

- Nominative pronouns are used as the subjects of sentences or as subject complements (following the linking verbs *am, is, are, was, were, be, being,* or *been*).

  He applied for the job, but the person hired was she.

- Objective pronouns are used as direct objects, indirect objects, or objects of prepositions.

  The police officer warned us about them.

- Possessive pronouns show ownership and function as adjectives.

  Her lawn looks much greener than mine.

Gender

Pronouns can be masculine, feminine, or neuter.

He showed her how to fix it.

Say It

Read the following aloud.
1. *I* am / *You* are / *He* is / *She* is / *It* is / *We* are / *They* are
2. Show *me* / Show *you* / Show *him* / Show *her* / Show *them* / Show *us*
3. *My* car / *Your* car / *His* car / *Her* car / *Their* car
4. The car is *mine*. / The car is *yours*. / The car is *his*. / The car is *hers*. / The car is *theirs*.

Using Personal Pronouns

Select For each sentence below, select the correct personal pronoun in parentheses.
1. *(I, me, my)* love to hang out at the corner coffee shop.
2. *(I, Me, My)* friends and I gather there on Saturday morning.
3. One friend, Zach, is making a film, and *(he, him, his)* asked me to be in it.
4. We read over the lines, and other patrons listened to *(we, us, our)*.

Correct In the following paragraph, correct the pronouns. Write the line number and any incorrect pronoun. Cross it out and write a correction beside it.

> Zach, Rachel, and me went to the coffee shop on Saturday afternoon, *1*
> when them is usually closed. The owners agreed to let we film there. Zach
> rearranged the tables a little to make room for the camera, and him and
> me set up the equipment. The camera rolled, and Rachel and me started
> into our lines. A couple of times, we had to stop because the owners were *5*
> laughing so much them couldn't hold a straight face. Rachel and me had a
> hard time being straight when it came to ours kissing scene. It went well,
> and her and me got through it in one take.

Vocabulary

pronoun
a word that takes the place of a noun or other pronoun

personal pronoun
a pronoun that indicates whether the person is speaking, is spoken to, or is spoken about

case
whether a pronoun is used as a subject, an object, or a possessive

nominative
used as a subject or subject complement

objective
used as a direct object, an indirect object, or an object of

a preposition

possessive
used to show ownership

masculine
male

feminine
female

neuter
neither male nor female

LO2 Pronoun-Antecedent Agreement

The **antecedent** is the word that a pronoun refers to or replaces. A pronoun must have the same person, number, and gender as the antecedent, which is called **pronoun-antecedent agreement**.

> **third-person**   **third-person**   **third-person**
> **singular feminine**   **singular feminine**   **singular feminine**
>
> Colleen thought she would need a lift, but her car started.

Agreement in Person

A pronoun needs to match its antecedent in **person** (first, second, or third).

> **third person**   **second person**
>
> **Incorrect:** If people keep going, you can usually reach the goal.
> **Correct:** If you keep going, you can usually reach the goal.
> **Correct:** If people keep going, they can usually reach the goal.

Agreement in Number

A pronoun needs to match its antecedent in **number** (singular or plural).

> **singular**   **plural**
>
> **Incorrect:** Each lifeguard must buy their own uniform.
> **Correct:** Lifeguards must buy their own uniforms.
> **Correct:** Each lifeguard must buy her or his own uniform.

Agreement in Gender

A pronoun needs to match its antecedent in **gender** (masculine, feminine, or neuter).

> **feminine**   **masculine**
>
> **Incorrect:** Mrs. Miller will present his speech.
> **Correct:** Mrs. Miller will present her speech.

Say It

Speak the following words aloud.
1. First person: *I, me, my, mine; we, us, our, ours*
2. Second person: *you, your, yours*
3. Third person feminine: *she, her, hers; they, them, their, theirs*
4. Third person masculine: *he, him, his; they, them, their, theirs*
5. Third person neuter: *it, its; they, them, their, theirs*

Correcting Agreement Errors

Correct Person   Rewrite each sentence to correct the person error.

1. When you go to the multiplex, a person has a lot of movies to choose from.
2. Each of us has to buy their own ticket and snacks.
3. If the viewer arrives early enough, you can see a triple feature.
4. One can be overwhelmed by how many movies you can see.

Correct Number   Rewrite each sentence to correct the number error.

5. Each moviegoer chooses what movies they want to see.
6. A snack-counter attendant serves treats, and they also clean up messes.
7. Movie critics give his opinion about different films.
8. A critic shouldn't give away the ending because they would ruin the movie.

Correct Gender   Rewrite each sentence to correct the gender error.

9. A critic shouldn't give away the ending because he would ruin the movie.
10. When Roger Ebert critiques a film, she's right most of the time.
11. Anita accidentally left his purse at the theater.
12. The multiplex sits on a hilltop, and she looks like a palace.

Vocabulary

antecedent
the word that a pronoun refers to or replaces

pronoun-antecedent agreement
matching a pronoun to its antecedent in terms of person, number, and gender

person
whether the pronoun is speaking, being spoken to, or being spoken about

number
whether the pronoun is singular or plural

gender
whether the pronoun is masculine, feminine, or neuter

LO3 Other Pronoun Problems

Pronouns are very useful parts of speech, but if they are mishandled, they can cause problems.

Vague Pronoun

Do not use a pronoun that could refer to more than one antecedent.

> **Unclear:** Raul played baseball with his friend and his brother.
> **Clear:** Raul played baseball with his friend and his friend's brother.

Missing Antecedent

Avoid using *it* or *they* without clear antecedents.

> **Unclear:** They say humans share 97 percent of DNA with chimps.
> **Clear:** Scientists say humans share 97 percent of DNA with chimps.
>
> **Unclear:** It says in the *Times* that the Democrats back the bill.
> **Clear:** The *Times* says that the Democrats back the bill.

Double Subjects

Do not place a pronoun right after the subject. Doing so creates an error called a **double subject**, which is not a standard construction.

> **Nonstandard:** Rudy and Charlie, they went fishing.
> **Standard:** Rudy and Charlie went fishing.

Usage Errors *(They're, You're, It's)*

Do not confuse possessive pronouns (*your, their, its*) with contractions (*you're, they're, it's*). Remember that contractions use apostrophes in place of missing letters.

> **Incorrect:** Keep you're car in it's own lane.
> **Correct:** Keep your car in its own lane.

CONSIDER SPEAKING AND LISTENING

The pronoun problems on this page may not cause confusion in spoken English. In written English, these problems can derail meaning. Correct them in your writing.

Correcting Other Pronoun Problems

Rewrite Rewrite each sentence to correct the pronoun-reference problems.

1. Sarah asked her sister and her friend to help her move.
2. It said on the news that the accident will cost billions to fix.
3. They say that dark energy takes up 75 percent of the universe.
4. Dan wants his father and his friend to help.
5. They have found a way to make deep-water drilling safer.
6. It says on the parking ticket that I have to pay $50.

Correct In the following paragraph, correct the pronoun errors. Write the line number and any words you would change. Then show how you would change them.

> For 28 years, it reported in the *Weekly World News* all kinds of   *1*
> outlandish stories. Often the paper reported about Elvis or the Loch Ness
> monster being spotted and his impromptu concerts for die-hard fans. A
> bat-human hybrid named Bat Boy and an alien named P'lod appeared
> repeatedly in the tabloid, and he even supposedly had an affair with   *5*
> Hillary Clinton. Since this was during the Monica Lewinski scandal,
> maybe she was getting back at him. The writers and editors of the *Weekly*
> *World News,* they rarely publicly acknowledged that their stories were
> jokes, but said that he or she had to "suspend disbelief for the sake of
> enjoyment."   *10*

Correction Marks

ﻭ delete	⋏ add comma	word ⋀ add word
d̲ capitalize	? add question	⊙ add period
D̶ lowercase	⋀ mark	⟨⟩ spelling
⋀ insert	⌄ insert an apostrophe	⌒ switch

Vocabulary

vague pronoun
using a pronoun that could refer to more than one antecedent

missing antecedent
using a pronoun that has no clear antecedent

double subject
error created by following a subject with a pronoun

usage error
using the wrong word (e.g., *they're* instead of *their*)

LO4 Indefinite Pronouns

An **indefinite pronoun** does not have an antecedent, and it does not refer to a specific person, place, thing, or idea. These pronouns pose unique issues with subject-verb and pronoun-antecedent agreement.

Singular Indefinite Pronouns

Some indefinite pronouns are singular. When they are used as subjects, they require a singular verb. As antecedents, they must be matched to singular pronouns.

each	anyone	anybody	anything
either	someone	somebody	something
neither	everyone	everybody	everything
another	no one	nobody	nothing
one			

> Nobody is expecting to see Bigfoot on our camping trip.
>
> Someone used his or her own money to buy a Bigfoot detector at a novelty shop.

Plural Indefinite Pronouns

Some indefinite pronouns are plural. As subjects, they require a plural verb, and as antecedents, they require a plural pronoun.

both	few	several	many

> A few of the campers hear thumps in the night.
>
> Several of my friends swear they can see eyes glowing eight feet off the ground.

Singular or Plural Indefinite Pronouns

Some indefinite pronouns can be singular or plural, depending on the object of the preposition in the phrase that follows them.

all	any	most	none	some

> Most of us are too frightened to sleep.
>
> Most of the night is over already anyway.

Correcting Agreement

Correct Rewrite each sentence to correct the agreement errors. (Hint: The sentences are about a group of female campers.)

1. Everyone needs to set up their own tent.

_____

2. No one are getting out of work.

_____

3. Anyone who wants to be dry should make sure they have a rain fly.

_____

4. Nothing are more miserable than a wet sleeping bag.

_____

5. Few is wanting to end up drenched.

_____

6. Several wants to go hiking to look for Bigfoot.

_____

7. Many has doubts that he exists.

_____

8. A few says they might have dated him in high school.

_____

9. A Bigfoot hunter should make sure they have a camera along.

_____

10. Most of the hunters is also going to carry a big stick.

_____

11. Most of the afternoon are available for different activities.

_____

12. None of the girls is planning to hike after dark.

_____

13. None of the food are to be left out to attract animals or Bigfoot.

_____

Vocabulary

indefinite pronoun
a pronoun that does not refer to a specific person, place, thing, or idea

LO5 Relative Pronouns

A relative pronoun introduces a dependent clause and relates it to the rest of the sentence.

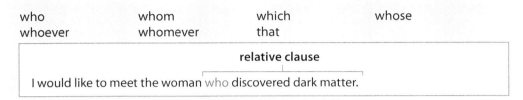

who   whom   which   whose
whoever   whomever   that

> relative clause
> I would like to meet the woman who discovered dark matter.

Who/Whoever and Whom/Whomever

Who, whoever, whom, and whomever refer to people. Who or whoever functions as the subject of the relative clause, while whom or whomever functions as the object of the clause.

> I am amazed by a person who could imagine matter that can't be seen.
> The woman whom I met was named Vera Rubin.
>   relative clause   relative clause

NOTE: In the second relative clause, whom introduces the clause even though it is the direct object, not the subject (I met whom).

That and Which

That and which usually refer to things. When that introduces the clause, the clause **is not** set off with commas. When which introduces the clause, the clause **is** set off with commas.

> I saw a documentary that explained about dark matter and dark energy.
> The show is Into the Wormhole, which is on the Science Channel.
>   relative clause   relative clause

Whose

Whose shows ownership or connection.

> relative clause
> Morgan Freeman, whose voice is soothing, hosts the show.

NOTE: Do not confuse whose with the contraction who's (who is).

Using Relative Pronouns

Select For each sentence, select the correct relative pronoun.

1. Vera Rubin, *(who, whom)* first discovered dark matter, wasn't seeking fame.
2. In the 1960s, she avoided black holes, *(that, which)* were a hot topic.
3. Instead, Rubin focused on the rotation of spiral galaxies, *(that, which)* few other people studied.
4. She expected stars *(that, which)* were on the outside of galaxies would move faster than stars *(that, which)* were near the center.
5. Instead, Rubin discovered the same speed for stars *(that, which)* were in different parts of the galaxy.
6. The only way for the galaxy to move that way would be if it had ten times the mass *(that, which)* was visible.
7. Rubin, *(who, whom, whose)* had never courted fame, became a very controversial figure when she presented her findings about dark matter.
8. Other astrophysicists *(who, whom)* disbelieved her did similar observations and calculations and confirmed her findings.
9. Rubin, *(who, whom, whose)* theory once was radical, became one of the great contributors to modern science.
10. *(Whoever, Whomever)* wrestles with the idea of dark matter should remember that over fifty years ago, one woman was the first to wrestle with the idea.

Write Write a relative clause for each of these relative pronouns:

1. who 3. whom 5. which
2. whoever 4. whomever 6. that

Write a sentence including one of your clauses.

Vocabulary

relative pronoun
a pronoun that begins a relative clause, connecting it to a sentence

relative clause
a type of dependent clause that begins with a relative pronoun that is either the subject or the direct object of the clause

LO6 Other Pronoun Types

Other types of pronouns have specific uses in your writing: asking questions, pointing to specific things, reflecting back on a noun (or pronoun), or intensifying a noun (or pronoun).

Interrogative Pronoun

An **interrogative pronoun** asks a question—*who, whose, whom, which, what.*

> What should we call our band? Who will be in it?

Demonstrative Pronoun

A **demonstrative pronoun** points to a specific thing—*this, that, these, those.*

> That is a great name! This will look terrific on a cover!

Reflexive Pronoun

A **reflexive pronoun** reflects back to the subject of a sentence or clause—*myself, ourselves, yourself, yourselves, himself, herself, itself, themselves.*

> I credit myself for the name. You can credit yourself for the logo.

Intensive Pronoun

An **intensive pronoun** emphasizes the noun or pronoun it refers to—*myself, ourselves, yourself, yourselves, himself, herself, itself, themselves.*

> You yourself love the name Psycho Drummer. I myself couldn't be happier.

Reciprocal Pronoun

A **reciprocal pronoun** refers to two things in an equal way—*each other, one another.*

> We shouldn't fight with each other. We should support one another.

Say It

Speak the following words aloud.
1. Interrogative: *Who* is? / *Whose* is? / *Which* is? / *What* is? / *Whom* do you see?
2. Demonstrative: *This* is / *That* is / *These* are / *Those* are
3. Reflexive: I helped *myself.* / You helped *yourself.* / They helped *themselves.*
4. Intensive: I *myself* / You *yourself* / She *herself* / He *himself* / They *themselves*
5. Reciprocal: We helped *each other.* / We helped *one another.*

Using Other Types of Pronouns

Identify Indicate the type of each underlined pronoun: *interrogative, demonstrative, reflexive, intensive,* or *reciprocal.*

1. <u>That</u> is why this band needs a road crew. _____

2. <u>What</u> are we supposed to do without power cords? _____

3. I <u>myself</u> would not mind playing unplugged. _____

4. You need to remind <u>yourself</u> that we don't have acoustic guitars. _____

5. <u>That</u> is the whole problem. _____

6. The guitars <u>themselves</u> prevent us from playing unplugged. _____

7. <u>Who</u> could hear an unplugged electric guitar? _____

8. <u>What</u> person will stand a foot away to listen? _____

9. <u>This</u> is ridiculous. _____

10. <u>That</u> won't work as a power cord. _____

11. I <u>myself</u> am about to quit this band. _____

12. We should be ashamed of <u>ourselves</u>. _____

13. We shouldn't blame <u>each other</u>. _____

14. As a band, we should help <u>one another</u> get through this. _____

15. Let's buy <u>ourselves</u> another set of cords. _____

Write Create a sentence using *myself* as a reflexive pronoun, and a second using *myself* as an intensive pronoun.

1. _____

2. _____

LO7 Real-World Application

Correct Correct any pronoun errors in the letter that follows. Write the line number and any words you would change. Cross out the word and show the change you would make.

X Psycho Drummer
12185 W. 22nd Avenue, Elkhorn, WI 53100 Ph: 262.555.7188

1   July 30, 2011

Ms. Marcia Schwamps, Manager
Piedog Studios
350 South Jackson Street
5   Elkhorn, WI 53100

Dear Ms. Schwamps:

One of your recording technicians says that you are looking for session musicians whom could play instruments for other artists. My band-mate Jerome and me would like to offer ours services.

10   Jerome and me are the power duo whom are called Psycho Drummer, a name that refers to Jerome hisself. He is a master percussionist, and him has trained hisself in many styles from heavy metal to rock, pop, jazz, blues, and even classical.

I am the guitarist in Psycho Drummer. I play electric and acoustic 15 (six- and 12-string) guitars as well as electric bass, and I too have trained me in they.

Attached, you will find ours résumés, a list of recent gigs us have played, and a review of we from the *Walworth County Week*.

20   Please consider Jerome and I for work as session musicians at Piedog Studios. We look forward to hearing from yous and would very much appreciate an interview/audition.

Sincerely,

25   *Terrance "Tear-It-Up" Clark*

Terrance "Tear-It-Up" Clark
Guitarist
Enclosures 3

Correction Marks

⌐ʃ	delete
d̲	capitalize
Ɖ	lowercase
∧	insert
∧ʓ	add comma
?	add question mark
word ∧	add word
⊙	add period
⌒	spelling
⌣	switch

18

Verb

You've probably heard that a shark has to keep swimming or it suffocates. That's not entirely true. Yes, sharks breathe by moving water across their gills, but they can also lie on the bottom and push water through their gills or let currents do the work. Still, most sharks stay on the move, and when a shark is still, it has to work harder to breathe.

Verbs are much the same way. They like to stay on the move. Most verbs are action words, describing what is happening. Some verbs describe states of being—much like sharks sitting on the bottom, breathing. Either way, though, the verb gives life to the sentence, and often it is a word with big teeth. This chapter gives a view into the compelling world of verbs.

Learning Outcomes

LO1 Understand and use verb classes.

LO2 Work with number and person.

LO3 Work with voice.

LO4 Form present and future tenses.

LO5 Form past tense.

LO6 Form progressive tense.

LO7 Form perfect tense.

LO8 Understand verbals.

LO9 Use verbals as objects.

LO10 Apply learning to real-world examples.

What do you think?

Do you prefer *doing* or *being*? Why?

ArchMan, 2011 / Used under license from Shutterstock.com

LO1   Verb Classes

Verbs show action or states of being. Different classes of verbs do these jobs.

Action Verbs

Verbs that show action are called action verbs. Some action verbs are transitive, which means that they transfer action to a direct object.

Trina hurled the softball.
(The verb *hurled* transfers action to the direct object *softball*.)

Others are intransitive: They don't transfer action to a direct object.

Trina pitches.
(The verb *pitches* does not transfer action to a direct object.)

Linking Verbs

Verbs that link the subject to a noun, a pronoun, or an adjective are linking verbs. Predicates with linking verbs express a state of being.

Trina is a pitcher.
(The linking verb *is* connects *Trina* to the noun *pitcher*.)

She seems unbeatable.
(The linking verb *seems* connects *She* to the adjective *unbeatable*.)

Linking Verbs

is	am	are	was	were	be	being	been	become
grow	feel	seem	look	smell	taste	sound	appear	remain

NOTE: The bottom-row words are linking verbs if they don't show action.

INSIGHT

If you are mathematically minded, think of a linking verb as an equal sign. It indicates that the subject equals (or is similar to) what is in the predicate.

Helping Verbs

A verb that works with an action or linking verb is a **helping** (or auxiliary) verb. A helping verb helps the main verb form tense, mood, and voice.

Trina has pitched two shut-out games, and today she may be pitching her third. (The helping verb *has* works with the main verb *pitched*; the helping verbs *may be* work with *pitching*. Both form special tenses.)

NOTE: Helping verbs work with verbs ending in *ing* or in past tense form.

Helping Verbs

am	been	could	does	have	might	should	will
are	being	did	had	is	must	was	would
be	can	do	has	may	shall	were	

Using Verb Classes

Identify/Write   For each sentence below, identify the underlined verbs as transitive action verbs (T), intransitive action verbs (I), linking verbs (L), or helping verbs (H). Then write your own sentence using the same class of verb.

1. I <u>love</u> fast-pitch softball, but I rarely <u>pitch</u>. _____

2. I <u>play</u> first base; it <u>is</u> a pressure-filled position. _____

3. Runners <u>charge</u> first base, and I <u>tag</u> them out. _____

4. Double-plays <u>require</u> on-target throws, clean catches, and timing. _____

5. If a runner <u>steals</u>, the pitcher and second baseperson <u>work</u> with me. _____

6. We <u>catch</u> the runner in a "pickle" and <u>tag</u> her out. _____

7. Softball <u>is</u> exciting, and I <u>will</u> play all summer. _____

8. I <u>look</u> worn out after a game, but I <u>feel</u> completely exhilarated. _____

Vocabulary

action verb
word that expresses action

transitive verb
action verb that transfers action to a direct object

intransitive verb
action verb that does not transfer action to a direct object

linking verb
verb that connects the subject with a noun, a pronoun, or an adjective in the predicate

helping (auxiliary) verb
verb that works with a main verb to form some tenses, mood, and voice

LO2 Number and Person of Verb

Verbs reflect number (singular or plural) and person (first person, second person, or third person).

Number

The number of the verb indicates whether the subject is singular or plural. Note that most present tense singular verbs end in *s,* while most present tense plural verbs do not.

Singular: A civil war re-enactment involves infantry, cavalry, and artillery units.
Plural: Civil war re-enactors stage amazing battle scenes from the war.

Person

The person of the verb indicates whether the subject is speaking, being spoken to, or being spoken about.

	Singular	**Plural**
First Person:	(I) am	(we) are
Second Person:	(you) are	(you) are
Third Person:	(she) is	(they) are

Note that the pronoun *I* takes a special form of the *be* verb—*am.*

Correct: I am eager to see the cannons fire.
Incorrect: I is eager to see the cannons fire.

The pronoun *I* also is paired with plural present tense verbs.

Correct: I hope to see a bayonet charge.
Incorrect: I hopes to see a bayonet charge.

In a similar way, the singular pronoun *you* takes the plural form of the *be* verb—*are, were.*

Correct: You are in for a treat when the battle begins.
Incorrect: You is in for a treat when the battle begins.

Correct: You were surprised at how steady the horses were in combat.
Incorrect: You was surprised at how steady the horses were in combat.

Using Number and Person

Provide For each sentence below, provide the correct person and number of the present tense *be* verb *(is, am, are)*.

1. We _____ at the Civil War encampment.
2. It _____ a gathering of Union and Confederate regiments.
3. You _____ in a uniform of Union blue.
4. I _____ in the gray of the Confederacy.
5. A light artillery brigade _____ a group of mobile cannon.
6. A cavalry regiment _____ a group of mounted soldiers.
7. The camp doctors _____ equipped to do amputations.
8. The medicine they use _____ sometimes worse than the disease.
9. I _____ amazed by all of the tent encampments.
10. You _____ interested in becoming a re-enactor.

Rewrite Rewrite each sentence below to fix the errors in the number and person of the verb.

1. I jumps the first time a cannon goes off.

   _____

2. The guns blows huge white smoke rings whirling into the air.

   _____

3. The cavalry regiments charges together and battles with sabers.

   _____

4. In the fray, one cavalry officer fall from his horse.

   _____

5. The infantry soldiers lines up in two rows and sends out volleys of bullets.

   _____

6. After the battle, President Lincoln deliver a solemn address.

   _____

Vocabulary

number
singular or plural

person
whether the subject is
speaking *(I, we)*, is being
spoken to *(you)*, or is being
spoken about *(he, she, it, they)*

LO3 Voice of the Verb

The **voice** of the verb indicates whether the subject is acting or being acted upon.

Voice

An **active voice** means that the subject is acting. A **passive voice** means that the subject is acted on.

Active: The cast sang the song "Our State Fair."
Passive: The song "Our State Fair" was sung by the cast.

	Active Voice		**Passive Voice**	
	Singular	Plural	Singular	Plural
Present Tense	I see you see he/she/it sees	we see you see they see	I am seen you are seen he/she/it is seen	we are seen you are seen they are seen
Past Tense	I saw you saw he saw	we saw you saw they saw	I was seen you were seen it was seen	we were seen you were seen they were seen
Future Tense	I will see you will see he will see	we will see you will see they will see	I will be seen you will be seen it will be seen	we will be seen you will be seen they will be seen
Present Perfect Tense	I have seen you have seen he has seen	we have seen you have seen they have seen	I have been seen you have been seen it has been seen	we have been seen you have been seen they have been seen
Past Perfect Tense	I had seen you had seen he had seen	we had seen you had seen they had seen	I had been seen you had been seen it had been seen	we had been seen you had been seen they had been seen
Future Perfect Tense	I will have seen you will have seen he will have seen	we will have seen you will have seen they will have seen	I will have been seen you will have been seen it will have been seen	we will have been seen you will have been seen they will have been seen

Active voice is preferred for most writing because it is direct and energetic.

Active: The crowd gave the cast a standing ovation.
Passive: The cast was given a standing ovation by the crowd.

Passive voice is preferred when the focus is on the receiver of the action or when the subject is unknown.

Passive: A donation was left at the ticket office.
Active: Someone left a donation at the ticket office.

Using Voice of a Verb

Rewrite   Read each passive sentence below and rewrite it to be active. Think about what is performing the action and make that the subject. The first one is done for you.

1. *State Fair* was put on by the community theater group.
   The community theater group put on State Fair.

2. The Frake family was featured in the musical. _____

3. Many songs were sung and danced by the cast. _____

4. Pickles and mincemeat were rated by judges at the fair. _____

5. Mrs. Frake's mincemeat was spiked with too much brandy.
   _____

6. The judges of the contest were overcome by the strength of the mincemeat.
   _____

7. Two couples were shown falling in love at the fair. _____

8. The singers were assisted by a stalwart piano player in the orchestra pit.
   _____

9. The first act was climaxed by the song "It's a Grand Night for Singing."
   _____

10. The cast was applauded gratefully by the crowd. _____

Write   Using the chart on the facing page, write a sentence for each situation below.

1. (A present tense singular active sentence)
   _____

2. (A past tense plural passive sentence)
   _____

CONSIDER WORKPLACE

In workplace writing, use active voice for most messages. Use passive voice to deliver bad news.

Vocabulary

voice
active or passive

active voice
voice created when the subject is performing the action of the verb

passive voice
voice created when the subject is receiving the action of the verb

LO4 Present and Future Tense Verbs

Basic verb tenses tell whether action happens in the past, in the present, or in the future.

Present Tense

Present tense verbs indicate that action is happening right now.

Master musicians and new professionals gather at the Marlboro Music Festival.

Present tense verbs also can indicate that action happens routinely or continually.

Every summer, they spend seven weeks together learning music.

Present Tense in Academic Writing

Use present tense verbs to describe current conditions.

Pianist Richard Goode plays beside talented young artists.

Use present tense verbs also to discuss the ideas in literature or to use historical quotations in a modern context. This use is called the "historical present," which allows writers to continue speaking.

The audiences at Marlboro rave about the quality of the music, or as the *New York Times* says, "No matter what is played . . . the performances at Marlboro are usually extraordinary."

NOTE: It is important to write a paragraph or an essay in one tense. Avoid shifting needlessly from tense to tense as you write.

Future Tense

Future tense verbs indicate that action will happen later on.

Marlboro Music will launch the careers of many more young stars.

Using Present and Future Verb Tenses

Write For each sentence below, supply the present tense form of the verb indicated in parentheses.

1. Young musicians _____ to Marlboro Music by special invitation. (came)

2. Seasoned professionals _____ them like colleagues, not students. (treated)

3. Musicians _____ side by side for weeks before performing. (worked)

4. The town of Marlboro, New Hampshire, _____ only 987 citizens. (had)

5. Many times that number _____ to the concerts each summer. (came)

Change Replace the verbs in the following paragraph, making them all present tense. Write the line number and the present tense verb.

>   A sixteen-year-old cellist named Yo Yo Ma arrived at Marlboro   *1*
> Music. He couldn't believe his fortune to be surrounded by such great
> musicians. He began to play and soon fell in love with music. A festival
> administrator named Jill Hornor also caught his eye, and he fell in love
> with her as well. They were married.   *5*

Write Write a sentence of your own, using each word below in the form indicated in parentheses.

1. thought (present) _____

2. lived (future) _____

3. hoped (present) _____

4. cooperated (future) _____

Vocabulary

present tense
verb tense indicating that action is happening now

future tense
verb tense indicating that action will happen later

LO5 Past Tense Verbs

Past tense verbs indicate that action happened in the past.

When referring to his campaign in Asia Minor, Julius Caesar reported, "I came. I saw. I conquered."

Forming Past Tense

Most verbs form their past tense by adding *ed*. If the word ends in a silent *e*, drop the *e* before adding *ed*.

help ⟶ helped   love ⟶ loved
look ⟶ looked   hope ⟶ hoped

If the word ends in a consonant before a single vowel and the last syllable is stressed, double the final consonant before adding *ed*.

stop ⟶ stopped   occur ⟶ occurred
plan ⟶ planned   refer ⟶ referred

If the word ends in a *y* preceded by a consonant, change the *y* to *i* before adding *ed*.

study ⟶ studied   hurry ⟶ hurried
worry ⟶ worried   carry ⟶ carried

Irregular Verbs

Some of the most commonly used verbs form past tense by changing the verb itself. See the chart below:

Pres.	Past	Pres.	Past	Pres.	Past	Pres.	Past	Pres.	Past	Pres.	Past
am	was, were	dig	dug	fly	flew	hide	hid	see	saw	stand	stood
become	became	do	did	forget	forgot	keep	kept	shake	shook	steal	stole
begin	began	draw	drew	freeze	froze	know	knew	shine	shone	swim	swam
blow	blew	drink	drank	get	got	lead	led	show	showed	swing	swung
break	broke	drive	drove	give	gave	pay	paid	shrink	shrank	take	took
bring	brought	eat	ate	go	went	prove	proved	sing	sang	teach	taught
buy	bought	fall	fell	grow	grew	ride	rode	sink	sank	tear	tore
catch	caught	feel	felt	hang	hung	ring	rang	sit	sat	throw	threw
choose	chose	fight	fought	have	had	rise	rose	sleep	slept	wear	wore
come	came	find	found	hear	heard	run	ran	speak	spoke	write	wrote

Using Past Tense Verbs

Write For each verb, write the correct past tense form.

1. swing _____
2. think _____
3. slip _____
4. reply _____
5. teach _____
6. cry _____
7. sing _____
8. give _____
9. cap _____
10. fly _____

11. type _____
12. cope _____
13. shop _____
14. grip _____
15. gripe _____
16. pour _____
17. soap _____
18. trick _____
19. try _____
20. tip _____

Edit Make changes to the following paragraph, converting it from present tense to past tense. Write the line number and any word you would change. Cross it out and write the change.

> When I am fresh out of college, I get my first job as an assistant *1*
> editor at a sports publisher. At this company, acquisitions editors follow
> trends, talk with authors, and work with them to create a manuscript.
> Developmental editors then work with the manuscript to develop it into
> a worthwhile book. Assistant editors help with all stages of production. *5*
> They edit manuscripts and typemark them. Then they check the galleys—
> or long sheets of printout film that paste-up artists cut and wax to create
> pages. Those are the days of manual layout. Assistant editors have to
> check the paste-up pages for dropped copy. They also proofread and enter
> changes, and check bluelines. Publishing is completely different now, but *10*
> back then, I get my first experience in real-world work. I am glad just to
> have an office of my own.

Correction Marks

⌇ delete	⋏ add comma	word ∧ add word
d̲ capitalize	⸮ add question mark	⊙ add period
⌀ lowercase	⋀	⌒ spelling
∧ insert	⌄ insert an apostrophe	⌢ switch

Vocabulary

past tense
verb tense indicating that action happened previously

LO6 Progressive Tense Verbs

The basic tenses of past, present, and future tell when action takes place. The progressive tense or aspect tells that action is ongoing.

Progressive Tense

Progressive tense indicates that action is ongoing. Progressive tense is formed by using a helping verb along with the *ing* form of the main verb.

Work habits were changing rapidly.

There are past, present, and future progressive tenses. Each uses a helping verb in the appropriate tense.

For thousands of years, most humans were working in agriculture.

Currently in the West, most humans are working in nonagricultural jobs.

In the future, people will be making their living in unimaginable ways.

Forming Progressive Tense

Past:	was/were	+	main verb	+	ing
Present:	am/is/are	+	main verb	+	ing
Future:	will be	+	main verb	+	ing

INSIGHT

Avoid using progressive tense with the following:

- Verbs that express thoughts, attitudes, and desires: *know, understand, want, prefer*
- Verbs that describe appearances: *seem, resemble*
- Verbs that indicate possession: *belong, have, own, possess*
- Verbs that signify inclusion: *contain, hold*

   Correct: I **know** your name.
   Incorrect: I **am knowing** your name.

Using Progressive Tense

Form   Rewrite each sentence three times, changing the tenses as requested in parentheses.

Humans require food, but agribusiness makes food production very efficient.

1. (present progressive) _____

_____

2. (past progressive) _____

_____

3. (future progressive) _____

_____

People provide a product or service, and others pay for it.

4. (present progressive) _____

_____

5. (past progressive) _____

_____

6. (future progressive) _____

_____

The products and services in greatest demand produce the most wealth.

7. (present progressive) _____

_____

8. (past progressive) _____

_____

9. (future progressive) _____

_____

Vocabulary

progressive tense
verb tense that expresses
ongoing action

LO7   Perfect Tense Verbs

The perfect tense tells that action is not ongoing, but is finished, whether in the past, present, or future.

Perfect Tense

Perfect tense indicates that action is completed. Perfect tense is formed by using a helping verb along with the past tense form of the main verb.

Each year of my career, I have learned something new.

There are past, present, and future perfect tenses. These tenses are formed by using helping verbs in past, present, and future tenses.

In my first year, I had learned to get along in a corporate structure.

This year, I have learned new technology skills.

By this time next year, I will have learned how to be an effective salesperson.

Forming Perfect Tense

Past:	had	+	past tense main verb
Present:	has/have	+	past tense main verb
Future:	will have	+	past tense main verb

Perfect Tense with Irregular Verbs

To form perfect tense with irregular verbs, use the past participle form instead of the past tense form. Here are the past participles of common irregular verbs.

Pres.	Past Part.	Pres.	Past Part.	Pres.	Past Part.	Pres.	Past Part.	Pres.	Past Part.	Pres.	Past Part.
am, be	been	dig	dug	fly	flown	hide	hidden	see	seen	stand	stood
become	become	do	done	forget	forgotten	keep	kept	shake	shaken	steal	stolen
begin	begun	draw	drawn	freeze	frozen	know	known	shine	shone	swim	swum
blow	blown	drink	drunk	get	gotten	lead	led	show	shown	swing	swung
break	broken	drive	driven	give	given	pay	paid	shrink	shrunk	take	taken
bring	brought	eat	eaten	go	gone	prove	proven	sing	sung	teach	taught
buy	bought	fall	fallen	grow	grown	ride	ridden	sink	sunk	tear	torn
catch	caught	feel	felt	hang	hung	ring	rung	sit	sat	throw	thrown
choose	chosen	fight	fought	have	had	rise	risen	sleep	slept	wear	worn
come	come	find	found	hear	heard	run	run	speak	spoken	write	written

Using Perfect Tense

Form Rewrite each sentence three times, changing the tenses as requested in parentheses.

I work hard and listen carefully.

1. (past perfect) _____

_____

2. (present perfect) _____

_____

3. (future perfect) _____

_____

I gain my position by being helpful, and I keep it the same way.

4. (past perfect) _____

_____

5. (present perfect) _____

_____

6. (future perfect) _____

_____

My colleagues depend on me, and I deliver what they need.

7. (past perfect) _____

_____

8. (present perfect) _____

_____

9. (future perfect) _____

_____

Vocabulary

perfect tense
verb tense that expresses completed action

LO8 Verbals

A **verbal** is formed from a verb but functions as a noun, an adjective, or an adverb. Each type of verbal—gerund, participle, and infinitive—can appear alone or can begin a **verbal phrase**.

Gerund

A **gerund** is formed from a verb ending in *ing,* and it functions as a noun.

Kayaking is a fun type of exercise. (subject)
I love kayaking. (direct object)

A **gerund phrase** begins with a gerund and includes any objects and modifiers.

Running rapids in a kayak is exhilarating. (subject)
I enjoy paddling a kayak through white water. (direct object)

Participle

A **participle** is formed from a verb ending in *ing* or *ed,* and it functions as an adjective.

Exhilarated, I ran my first rapids at age 15. (*exhilarated* modifies *I*)
That was an exhilarating ride! (*exhilarating* modifies *ride)*

A **participial phrase** begins with a participle and includes any objects and modifiers.

Shocking my parents, I said I wanted to go again.

Infinitive

An **infinitive** is formed from *to* and a present tense verb, and it functions as a noun, an adjective, or an adverb.

To kayak is to live. (noun)
I will schedule more time to kayak. (adjective)
You need courage and a little craziness to kayak. (adverb)

An **infinitive phrase** begins with an infinitive and includes any objects or modifiers.

I want to kayak the Colorado River through the Grand Canyon.

Using Verbals

`Identify` Identify each underlined verbal by selecting the correct choice in parentheses (gerund, participle, infinitive).

1. <u>Rock climbing</u> is an extreme sport. (gerund, participle, infinitive)
2. I'd like <u>to climb</u> El Capitan one day. (gerund, participle, infinitive).
3. <u>Rappelling down a cliff in Arizona</u>, I almost slipped. (gerund, participle, infinitive).
4. <u>Catching myself</u>, I checked my lines and carabiners. (gerund, participle, infinitive).
5. <u>To fall while climbing</u> could be fatal. (gerund, participle, infinitive).
6. I keep my equipment in top shape <u>to avoid a mishap</u>. (gerund, participle, infinitive).

`Form` Complete each sentence below by supplying the type of verbal requested in parentheses.

1. My favorite exercise is _____. (gerund)
2. _____ would get me into shape. (gerund)
3. _____ , I could stay in shape (participle)
4. Perhaps I will also try _____ . (gerund)
5. When exercising, remember _____ . (infinitive)
6. _____ , I'll lose weight. (participle)

`Write` For each verbal phrase below, write a sentence that correctly uses it.

1. to work out _____
2. choosing a type of exercise _____
3. excited by the idea _____

Vocabulary

verbal
gerund, participle, or infinitive; a construction formed from a verb but functioning as a noun, an adjective, or an adverb

verbal phrase
phrase beginning with a gerund, a participle, or an infinitive

gerund
verbal ending in *ing* and functioning as a noun

gerund phrase
phrase beginning with a gerund and including objects and modifiers

participle
verbal ending in *ing* or *ed* and functioning as an adjective

participial phrase
phrase beginning with a participle and including objects and modifiers

infinitive
verbal beginning with *to* and functioning as a noun, an adjective, or an adverb

infinitive phrase
phrase beginning with an infinitive and including objects and modifiers

LO9 Verbals as Objects

Though both infinitives and gerunds can function as nouns, they can't be used interchangeably as direct objects. Some verbs take infinitives and not gerunds. Other verbs take only gerunds and not infinitives.

Gerunds as Objects

Verbs that express facts are followed by gerunds.

admit	deny	enjoy	miss	recommend
avoid	discuss	finish	quit	regret
consider	dislike	imagine	recall	

I miss walking along the beach.
not I miss to walk along the beach.

I regret cutting our vacation short.
not I regret to cut our vacation short.

Infinitives as Objects

Verbs that express intentions, hopes, and desires are followed by infinitives.

agree	demand	hope	prepare	volunteer
appear	deserve	intend	promise	want
attempt	endeavor	need	refuse	wish
consent	fail	offer	seem	
decide	hesitate	plan	tend	

We should plan to go back to the ocean.
not We should plan going back to the ocean.

We will endeavor to save money for the trip.
not We will endeavor saving money for the trip.

Gerunds or Infinitives as Objects

Some verbs can be followed by either a gerund or an infinitive.

begin	hate	love	remember	stop
continue	like	prefer	start	try

I love walking by the ocean.
or I love to walk by the ocean.

Using Verbals as Objects

Select For each sentence below, select the appropriate verbal in parentheses.

1. I imagine (walking, to walk) along the Pacific Coast.
2. We want (seeing, to see) whales or dolphins when we are there.
3. I hope (getting, to get) some beautiful shots of the ocean.
4. We should avoid (getting, to get) sunburned when we are on the beach.
5. I enjoy (getting, to get) sand between my toes.
6. Maybe a surfer will offer (showing, to show) me how to surf.
7. We deserve (going, to go) on vacation more often.
8. Later, we will regret not (taking, to take) the time for ourselves.
9. I have never regretted (taking, to take) a vacation.
10. I wish (having, to have) a vacation right now.

Write For each verb below, write your own sentence using the verb and following it with a gerund or an infinitive, as appropriate.

1. quit

    _____

2. recall

    _____

3. tend

    _____

4. volunteer

    _____

5. discuss

    _____

6. decide

    _____

Vocabulary

gerund
verbal ending in *ing* and functioning as a noun

infinitive
verbal beginning with *to* and functioning as a noun, an adjective, or an adverb

LO10 Real-World Application

Revise Rewrite the following paragraph, changing passive verbs to active verbs.

> Bedford's school music program should be supported by Grohling Music Suppliers. Our instrument rentals and our sheet-music services have been used extensively by the school system. In these tough economic times, the school should be assisted by us.
>
> _____
>
> _____
>
> _____

Revise In the following paragraph, change future perfect verbs into past perfect verbs. Write the line number and the words you would change. Then show the change.

> We will have provided reduced-cost sheet music to the school system   _1_
>
> and will have added used and refurbished instrument rentals. In   _2_
>
> addition, we will have provided best-customer discounts to schools that   _3_
>
> will have rented and bought in volume.   _4_

Revise In the following paragraph, correct misused verbals. Write the line number and the words you would change. Then show the change.

> I hope exploring these possibilities with you. We could recommend to   _1_
>
> make some of these changes the first year. I admit to have a soft spot for   _2_
>
> student performers. I recall to get my first flute as a student and to begin   _3_
>
> with music then.   _4_

19

"Where lipstick is concerned, the important thing is not color, but to accept God's final word on where your lips end."

—Jerry Seinfeld

Adjective and Adverb

The purpose of makeup is to accentuate the beauty that is already in your face. The focus should be on you, not on the mascara, lipstick, foundation, or blush you use.

In the same way, the real beauty of a sentence lies in the nouns and verbs. Adjectives and adverbs can modify those nouns and verbs, bringing out their true beauty, but these modifiers should not overwhelm the sentence. Use them sparingly to make your meaning clear, not to distract with flash. This chapter will show you how to get the most out of those few adjectives and adverbs.

Learning Outcomes

LO1 Understand adjective basics.

LO2 Put adjectives in order.

LO3 Use adjectivals.

LO4 Understand adverb basics.

LO5 Place adverbs well.

LO6 Use adverbials.

LO7 Apply adjectives and adverbs in real-world contexts.

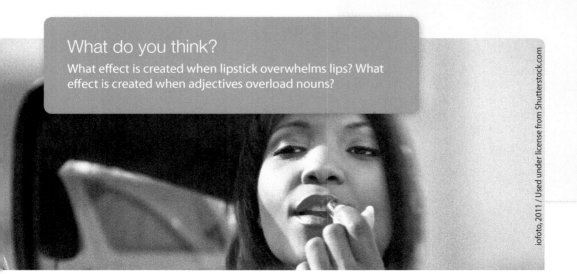

What do you think?

What effect is created when lipstick overwhelms lips? What effect is created when adjectives overload nouns?

iofoto, 2011 / Used under license from Shutterstock.com

LO1 Adjective Basics

An adjective is a word that modifies a noun or pronoun. Even articles such as *a, an,* and *the* are adjectives, because they indicate whether you mean a general or specific thing. Adjectives answer these basic questions: *which, what kind of, how many/how much.*

Adjectives often appear before the word they modify.

I saw a beautiful gray tabby cat.

A predicate adjective appears after the noun it modifies and is linked to the word by a linking verb.

The cat was beautiful and gray.

Proper adjectives come from proper nouns and are capitalized.

I also saw a Persian cat.

Forms of Adjectives

Adjectives come in three forms: positive, comparative, and superlative.

- Positive adjectives describe one thing without making any comparisons.

  Fred is a graceful cat.

- Comparative adjectives compare the thing to something else.

  Fred is more graceful than our dog, Barney.

- Superlative adjectives compare the thing to two or more other things.

  He is the most graceful cat you will ever see.

NOTE: For one- and two-syllable words, create the comparative form by adding *er,* and create the superlative form by added *est.* For words of three syllables or more, use *more* (or *less*) for comparatives and *most* (or *least*) for superlatives. Also note that *good* and *bad* have special superlative forms:

Positive		Comparative		Superlative	
good	happy	better	happier	best	happiest
bad	wonderful	worse	more wonderful	worst	most wonderful
big		bigger		biggest	

Using the Forms of Adjectives

Identify/Write For each sentence below, identify the underlined adjectives as positive (P), comparative (C), or superlative (S). Then write a new sentence about a different topic, but use the same adjectives.

1. The shelter had a <u>Siamese</u> cat with <u>crossed</u> eyes and <u>black</u> feet. _____

2. She was <u>more inquisitive</u> than the other cats. _____

3. Her eyes were the <u>bluest</u> I had ever seen on a cat. _____

4. Her <u>surprising</u> meow was <u>loud</u> and <u>insistent</u>. _____

5. But her name—Monkey—was the <u>most surprising</u> fact of all. _____

Correct Read the paragraph below and correct adjective errors. Write the line number and the word you would change. Then show the change. The first one is done for you.

Some people say dogs are ~~more~~ tamer than cats, but cats have a more   *1*
great place in some people's hearts. Cats were probably first attracted
to human civilizations during the most early days of the agricultural
revolution. The sudden surplus of grains attracted many mice, which in
turn attracted cats. Cats that were the most best mousers were welcomed   *5*
by humans. In time, more cute and more cuddly cats became pets. But
cats have never given up their wildness. Even now, a barn cat that is not
used to human touch can be feraler than a dog.

Correction Marks

⌐	delete	⋀	add comma	⋀ (word)	add word
d	capitalize	?	add question	⊙	add period
Ð	lowercase	⋀	mark	⌒	spelling
⋀	insert	⌄	insert an apostrophe	⌒	switch

Vocabulary

adjective
word that modifies a noun or pronoun

articles
the adjectives *a, an,* and *the*

predicate adjective
adjective that appears after a linking verb and describes the subject

positive adjective
word that modifies a noun or pronoun without comparing it

comparative adjective
word that modifies a noun or pronoun by comparing it to something else

superlative adjective
word that modifies a noun or pronoun by comparing it to two or more things

LO2 Adjective Order

Adjectives aren't all created equally. Native English speakers use a specific order when putting multiple adjectives before a noun, and all speakers of English can benefit from understanding this order.

Begin with . . .

1. articles	a, an, the
demonstrative adjectives	that, this, these, those
possessives	my, our, her, their, Kayla's

Then position adjectives that tell . . .

2. time	first, second, next, last
3. how many	three, few, some, many
4. value	important, prized, fine
5. size	giant, puny, hulking
6. shape	spiky, blocky, square
7. condition	clean, tattered, repaired
8. age	old, new, classic
9. color	blue, scarlet, salmon
10. nationality	French, Chinese, Cuban
11. religion	Baptist, Buddhist, Hindu
12. material	cloth, stone, wood, bronze

Finally place . . .

13. nouns used as adjectives	baby [seat], shoe [lace]

Example:

that ruined ancient stone temple
(**1** + **7** + **8** + **12** + **noun**)

John Copland, 2011 / Used under license from Shutterstock.com

NOTE: Avoid using too many adjectives before a noun. An article and one or two adjectives are usually enough. More adjectives may overload the noun.

Too many: their first few expensive delicious French bread appetizers

Effective: their first French bread appetizers

Placing Adjectives in Order

Order Rearrange each set of adjectives and articles so that they are in the correct order. The first one has been done for you.

1. blue   square   that

                   that square blue _____ button

2. my   Scottish   rugged

_____ kilt

3. plastic   brand-new   few

_____ beads

4. worthless   a   brass

_____ tack

5. classic   many   Kenyan

_____ masks

6. aluminum   soda   Ted's

_____ can

7. key   Catholic   my

_____ chain

8. dilapidated   this   old

_____ shack

9. wool   her   woven

_____ cardigan

10. identical   seven   music

_____ stands

11. young   the   bright

_____ faces

12. last   real   our

_____ option

LO3 Adjective Questions and Adjectivals

Adjectives answer four basic questions: *which, what kind of, how many/how much.*

Guy

Which?	that guy
What kind of?	cool tattooed guy
How many/how much?	one guy

that one cool tattooed guy

Adjectivals

A single word that answers one of these questions is called an adjective. If a phrase or clause answers one of these questions, it is an adjectival phrase or clause.

Guy

Which?	guy leaning on the Mustang
What kind of?	guy who exudes attitude

Look at that guy, who exudes attitude, leaning on the Mustang.

The following types of phrases and clauses can be adjectivals:

Prepositional phrase:	with his arms crossed
Participial phrase:	staring at something
Adjective clause:	who doesn't even own the Mustang

INSIGHT

Instead of trying to memorize the names of different types of phrases and clauses, just remember the adjective questions. Turn them into a cheer—*which, what kind of, how many/ how much.*

Say It

Partner with a classmate. One of you should say the noun, and the other should ask the adjective questions. Then the first person should answer each question with adjectives or adjectivals.

1. **convertibles**
   Which convertibles?
   What kind of convertibles?
   How many convertibles?

2. **detergent**
   Which detergent?
   What kind of detergent?
   How much detergent?

Using Adjectives and Adjectivals

Answer/Write   For each word, answer the adjective questions using adjectives and adjectivals. Then write a sentence using two or more of your answers.

1. **Dogs**

   Which dogs? _____

   What kind of dogs? _____

   How many dogs? _____

   Sentence: _____

   _____

2. **Sports**

   Which sports? _____

   What kind of sports? _____

   How many sports? _____

   Sentence: _____

   _____

3. **Proposals**

   Which proposals? _____

   What kind of proposals? _____

   How many proposals? _____

   Sentence: _____

   _____

Vocabulary

adjectival
phrase or clause that answers one of the adjective questions and modifies a noun or pronoun

prepositional phrase
phrase that starts with a preposition and includes an object and modifiers

participial phrase
phrase beginning with a participle (*ing* or *ed* form of verb) plus objects and modifiers; used as an adjective

adjective clause
clause beginning with a relative pronoun and including a verb, but not able to stand alone; functioning as an adjective

LO4 Adverb Basics

An **adverb** modifies a verb, a **verbal**, an adjective, an adverb, or a whole sentence. An adverb answers six basic questions: *how, when, where, why, to what degree, how often*.

Sheri leaped fearlessly.
(*Fearlessly* modifies the verb *leaped*.)

Sheri leaped quite readily.
(*Quite* modifies *readily*, which modifies *leaped*.)

Obviously, she wants to fly.
(*Obviously* modifies the whole sentence.)

NOTE: Most adverbs end in *ly*. Some can be written with or without the *ly*, but when in doubt, use the *ly* form.

loud ——► loudly   tight ——► tightly   deep ——► deeply

Forms of Adverbs

Adverbs have three forms: positive, comparative, and superlative.

■ **Positive adverbs** describe without comparing.

Sheri leaped high and fearlessly.

■ **Comparative adverbs** (*-er, more,* or *less*) describe by comparing with one other action.

She leaped higher and more fearlessly than I did.

■ **Superlative adverbs** (*-est, most,* or *least*) describe by comparing with more than one action.

She leaped highest and most fearlessly of any of us.

NOTE: Some adjectives change form to create comparative or superlative forms.

well ——► better ——► best   badly ——► worse ——► worst

Using the Forms of Adverbs

Provide For each sentence below, provide the correct form of the adverb in parentheses—positive, comparative, or superlative.

1. My friend likes to eat _____ (quickly).

2. She eats _____ (quickly) than I do.

3. She eats _____ (quickly) of anyone I know.

4. My brother eats _____ . (reluctantly)

5. He eats _____ (reluctantly) than a spoiled child.

6. He eats _____ (reluctantly) of anyone on Earth.

7. I eat _____ . (slowly)

8. I eat _____ (slowly) than I used to.

9. I eat _____ (slowly) of anytime in my life.

10. I suppose the three of us eat pretty _____ (badly).

Choose For each sentence, write the correct word in parentheses. If the word modifies a noun or pronoun, choose the adjective form (*good, bad*). If the word modifies a verb, a verbal, an adjective, or an adverb, choose the adverb form (*well, badly.*)

1. My brother went to a (good, well) play.

2. He said the actors did (good, well), and that the plot was (good, well).

3. He even got a (good, well) deal on tickets for (good, well) seats.

4. He wanted (bad, badly) to see this play.

5. The problem was that one patron behaved (bad, badly).

6. He had a (bad, badly) attitude and once even booed.

7. My brother told him to stop, but the guy took it (bad, badly).

8. The ushers did (good, well) when they removed the guy.

9. The audience even gave them a (good, well) ovation.

10. My brother says the overall evening went (good, well).

Vocabulary

adverb
word that modifies a verb, a verbal, an adjective, an adverb, or a whole sentence

verbal
word formed from a verb but functioning as a noun, an adjective, or an adverb

positive adverb
adverb that modifies without comparing

comparative adverb
adverb that modifies by comparing with one other thing

superlative adverb
adverb that modifies by comparing to two or more things

LO5 Placement of Adverbs

Adverbs should be placed in different places in sentences, depending on their use.

How Adverbs

Adverbs that tell *how* can appear anywhere except between a verb and a direct object.

Steadily we hiked the trail.
We steadily hiked the trail.

We hiked the trail steadily.
not We hiked steadily the trail.

When Adverbs

Adverbs that tell *when* should go at the beginning or end of the sentence.

We hiked to base camp yesterday. Today we'll reach the peak.

Where Adverbs

Adverbs that tell *where* should follow the verb they modify, but should not come between the verb and the direct object. (NOTE: Prepositional phrases often function as *where* adverbs.)

The trail wound uphill and passed through rockslide debris.
We avoided falling rocks throughout our journey.
not We avoided throughout our journey falling rocks.

To What Degree Adverbs

Adverbs that tell *to what degree* go right before the adverb they modify.

I learned very definitely the value of good hiking boots.

How Often Adverbs

Adverbs that tell *how often* should go right before an action verb, even if the verb has a helping verb.

I often remember that wonderful hike.   I will never forget the sights I saw.

Placing Adverbs Well

Place   For each sentence below, insert the adverb (in parentheses) in the most appropriate position. Write the word before the adverb, the adverb, and the word that follows it. The first one has been done for you.

1. In order to scare off bears, we *occasionally* made noise. (occasionally)

2. Bears avoid contact with human beings. (usually)

3. A bear surprised or cornered by people will turn to attack. (often)

4. A mother bear with cubs is likely to attack. (very)

5. If a bear approaches, playing dead may work. (sometimes)

6. Climbing a tree is not the best idea. (usually)

7. Black bears climb trees. (often)

8. Grizzly bears just knock the tree down. (usually)

9. Another defense is to open your coat to look large. (especially)

10. At the same time, try to make a loud noise. (very)

Revise   In the paragraph below, move adverbs into their correct positions. Write the line number, the word before the adverb, the adverb, and the word after it.

Spotting wildlife is one often of the highlights of a hiking trip. Deer   1
appear in fields occasionally, and lucky hikers might glimpse a bear
sometimes in the distance. Porcupines, raccoons, and other creatures
amble out of the woods curiously. Not usually hikers will see mountain
lions because the cats are ambush predators. Mountain lions attack groups   5
of people rarely and usually avoid human contact. Do keep children from
behind straggling.

LO6 Adverbials

Adverbs answer six basic questions: *how, when, where, why, to what degree,* and *how often.*

Today, **the children** repeatedly and very excitedly **splashed** barefoot outside.

NOTE: Avoid this sort of adverb overload in your sentences.

Children splashed.

How?	splashed barefoot
When?	splashed today
Where?	splashed outside
Why?	splashed excitedly
To what degree?	splashed very excitedly
How often?	splashed repeatedly

© Don Smith, / Getty Images

Adverbials

Often, the adverb questions are answered by adverbial phrases and clauses, which answer the same six questions.

Children splashed.

How?	splashed jumping up and down
When?	splashed during the downpour
Where?	splashed in the puddles in the driveway
Why?	splashed for the joy of being wet
To what degree?	splashed until they were drenched
How often?	splashed throughout the storm

During the downpour **and** throughout the storm, **the children splashed,** jumping up and down in the puddles in the driveway for the joy of being wet **and** until they were drenched.

NOTE: Again, avoid this sort of adverbial overload in your sentences.

The following types of phrases and clauses can be adverbials:

Prepositional phrase:	in the puddles in the driveway
Participial phrase:	jumping up and down
Dependent clause:	until they were drenched

Using Adverbials

Answer/Write   For each sentence, answer the adverb questions using adverbs and adverbials. Then write a sentence using three or more of your answers.

1. **They danced.** _____

   How did they dance? _____

   When did they dance? _____

   Where did they dance? _____

   Why did they dance? _____

   To what degree did they dance? _____

   How often did they dance? _____

   Sentence: _____

   _____

2. **They sang.**

   How did they sing? _____

   When did they sing? _____

   Where did they sing? _____

   Why did they sing? _____

   To what degree did they sing? _____

   How often did they sing? _____

   Sentence: _____

   _____

INSIGHT

The adverb questions can be memorized by turning them into a cheer: *how, when, where, why, to what degree, how often!*

Vocabulary

adverbial
phrase or clause that answers one of the adverb questions

LO7 Real-World Application

Correct   In the following document, correct the use of adjectives and adverbs. Write the line number and the words you would change. Then show the change.

Clowning Around

1328 West Mound Road
Waukesha, Wi 53100
262-555-8180

1   January 6, 2012

Mrs. Judy Bednar
38115 North Bayfield Drive
Waukesha, WI 53100

5   Dear Ms. Bednar:

It's time for a party birthday! You've thought of everything—balloons, decorations, cake . . . But what about awesomely entertainment? How many kids are coming, and how much time do you have to keep them entertained?

10   Fear not. At Clowning Around, we specialize in making every birthday the funnest and memorablest it can be. For young kids, we offer balloon colorful animals, magic amazing tricks, and backyard goofy games. For older kids, we have water wild games and magic street illusions. And for kids of all ages, we have the most funny

15   clowns, the most bravest superheroes, and the most amazingest impressionists.

That's right. You can throw a terrific party for your loved one worrying without about the entertainment— and paying without a lot either. See the enclosed

20   brochure for our services and rates. Then give us a call at Clowning Around, and we'll make your party next an event to remember.

Let's talk soon!

Dave Jenkins

25   Dave Jenkins
CEO, Clowning Around

Enclosure: Brochure

Correction Marks

ℐ	delete
d̲̲	capitalize
D̸	lowercase
∧	insert
⌃	add comma
? ∧	add question mark
word ∧	add word
⊙	add period
⌒	spelling
⌒	switch

20

> "A family is a unit composed not only of children but of men, women, an occasional animal, and the common cold."
>
> —Ogden Nash

Conjunction and Preposition

A family is a network of relationships. Some people have an equal relationship, like wives and husbands or brothers and sisters. Some people have unequal relationships, like mothers and daughters or fathers and sons. And the very young or very old are often considered dependent on those in their middle age.

Ideas also have relationships, and conjunctions and prepositions show those relationships. When two ideas are equal, a coordinating conjunction connects them. When two ideas are not equal, a subordinating conjunction makes one idea depend on the other. And prepositions create special relationships between nouns and other words.

Conjunctions and prepositions help you connect ideas and build whole families of thought.

Learning Outcomes

LO1 Use coordinating and correlative conjunctions.

LO2 Use subordinating conjunctions.

LO3 Understand common prepositions.

LO4 Use *by, at, on,* and *in.*

LO5 Use conjunctions and prepositions in real-world documents.

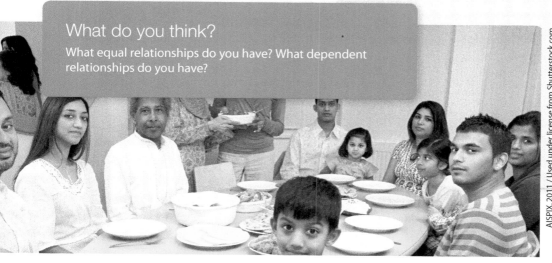

What do you think?

What equal relationships do you have? What dependent relationships do you have?

AISPIX, 2011 / Used under license from Shutterstock.com

LO1   Coordinating and Correlative Conjunctions

A conjunction is a word or word group that joins parts of a sentence—words, phrases, or clauses.

Coordinating Conjunctions

A coordinating conjunction joins grammatically equal parts—a word to a word, a phrase to a phrase, or a clause to a clause. (A clause is basically a sentence.)

Coordinating Conjunctions

and   but   or   nor   for   so   yet

Equal importance: A coordinating conjunction shows that the two things joined are of equal importance.

> Rachel and Lydia enjoy arts and crafts.
> (*And* joins words in an equal way.)

> They have knitted sweaters and pieced quilts.
> (*And* joins the phrases *knitted sweaters* and *pieced quilts*.)

> I tried to knit a sweater, but the thing unraveled.
> (*But* joins the two clauses, with a comma after the first.)

Items in a series: A coordinating conjunction can also join more than two equal things in a series.

> Rachel, Lydia, and I will take a class on making mosaics.
> (*And* joins *Rachel, Lydia,* and *I*. A comma follows each word except the last.)

> We will take the class, design a mosaic, and complete it together.
> (*And* joins three parts of a compound verb.)

Correlative Conjunctions

Correlative conjunctions consist of a coordinating conjunction paired with another word. They also join equal grammatical parts: word to word, phrase to phrase, or clause to clause.

Correlative Conjunctions

either/or   neither/nor   whether/or   both/and   not only/but also

Stressing equality: Correlative conjunctions stress the equality of parts.

> Not only Rachel but also Lydia has made beautiful quilts.
> (*Not only/but also* stresses the equality of *Rachel* and *Lydia*.)

Using Coordinating and Correlative Conjunctions

`Correct` For each sentence below, write the best coordinating conjunction in parentheses.

1. I would like to learn knitting (but, for, or) crocheting.
2. Lydia, Rachel, (and, nor, yet) I enjoy making cloth with our hands.
3. We have different talents, (or, so, yet) we teach each other what we know.
4. Lydia is best at knitting, (nor, but, for) I am best at tatting.
5. Rachel is our weaver, (but, yet, so) she is the loom master.
6. Each week, Lydia, Rachel, (and, but, or) I meet to share our works.
7. We want to broaden our skills, (and, or, yet) it's hard to learn something new.
8. I like needlepoint, Rachel likes quilting, (and, nor, so) Lydia likes construction.
9. Come join us one day, (and, for, so) we love to teach beginners.
10. We'll show you our work, (but, nor, for) you'll decide what you want to learn.

`Write` Create sentences of your own, using a coordinating conjunction (*and, but, or, nor, for, so, yet*) as requested.

1. joining two words: _____
2. joining two phrases: _____
3. creating a series: _____
4. joining two clauses (place a comma after the first clause, before the conjunction): _____

`Write` Create a sentence using a pair of correlative conjunctions:

_____

CONSIDER THE TRAITS

When two ideas correlate, they work together. They co-relate. Thinking in this way can help you remember the term *correlative conjunctions*.

Vocabulary

conjunction
word or word group that joins parts of a sentence

coordinating conjunction
conjunction that joins grammatically equal components

correlative conjunction
pair of conjunctions that stress the equality of the parts that are joined

LO2 Subordinating Conjunctions

A subordinating conjunction is a word or word group that connects two clauses of different importance. (A clause is basically a sentence.)

Subordinating Conjunctions

after	as long as	if	so that	till	whenever
although	because	in order that	than	unless	where
as	before	provided that	that	until	whereas
as if	even though	since	though	when	while

Subordinate clause: The subordinating conjunction comes at the beginning of the less-important clause, making it subordinate (it can't stand on its own). The subordinate clause can come before or after the more important clause (the independent clause).

Summer is too hot to cook inside. I often barbecue.
(two clauses)

Because summer is too hot to cook inside, I often barbecue.
(*Because* introduces the subordinate clause, which is followed by a comma.)

I often barbecue because summer is too hot to cook inside.
(If the subordinate clause comes second, a comma usually isn't needed.)

Special relationship: A subordinating conjunction shows a special relationship between ideas. Here are the relationships that subordinating conjunctions show:

Time	after, as, before, since, till, until, when, whenever, while
Cause	as, as long as, because, before, if, in order that, provided that, since, so that, that, till, until, when, whenever
Contrast	although, as if, even though, though, unless, whereas

Whenever the temperature climbs, I cook on the grill.
(time)

I grill because I don't want to heat up the house.
(cause)

Even though it is hot outside, I feel cool in the shade as I cook.
(contrast)

Using Subordinating Conjunctions

Write   For the blank in each sentence, provide an appropriate subordinating conjunction. Then write what type of relationship it shows.

1. _____ I marinated the chicken, I put it on the grill.
   (time, cause, contrast)

2. Grilling bratwurst is tough _____ the
   grease causes big flames.   (time, cause, contrast)

3. _____ of trichinosis, pork should not be pink inside.
   (time, cause, contrast)

4. I like grilling chicken _____ my favorite food is steak.
   (time, cause, contrast)

5. I grill my steak rare_____ the FDA recommends well-done.
   (time, cause, contrast)

6. Some people use barbecue sauce _____
   I prefer marinades.   (time, cause, contrast)

7. I use a gas grill _____ it is fast and
   convenient.   (time, cause, contrast)

8. Purists use only charcoal _____ it creates a nice flavor.
   (time, cause, contrast)

9. _____ I was in Texas, I had great brisket.
   (time, cause, contrast)

10. _____ brisket can be tough, this was tender.
    (time, cause, contrast)

Write   Create three of your own sentences, one for each type of relationship.

1. time: _____

2. cause: _____

3. contrast: _____

Vocabulary

subordinating conjunction
word or word group that
connects clauses of different
importance

subordinate clause
word group that begins with
a subordinating conjunction
and has a subject and verb
but can't stand alone as a
sentence

independent clause
group of words with a subject
and verb and that expresses
a complete thought; it can
stand alone as a sentence

LO3 Common Prepositions

A **preposition** is a word or word group that shows a relationship between a noun or pronoun and another word. Here are common prepositions:

Prepositions

aboard	back of	except for	near to	round
about	because of	excepting	notwithstanding	save
above	before	for	of	since
according to	behind	from	off	subsequent to
across	below	from among	on	through
across from	beneath	from between	on account of	throughout
after	beside	from under	on behalf of	'til
against	besides	in	onto	to
along	between	in addition to	on top of	together with
alongside	beyond	in behalf of	opposite	toward
alongside of	but	in front of	out	under
along with	by	in place of	out of	underneath
amid	by means of	in regard to	outside	until
among	concerning	inside	outside of	unto
apart from	considering	inside of	over	up
around	despite	in spite of	over to	upon
as far as	down	instead of	owing to	up to
aside from	down from	into	past	with
at	during	like	prior to	within
away from	except	near	regarding	without

Prepositional Phrases

A **prepositional phrase** starts with a preposition and includes an object of the preposition (a noun or pronoun) and any modifiers. A prepositional phrase functions as an adjective or adverb.

The Basset hound flopped on his side on the rug.
(*On his side* and *on the rug* modify the verb *flopped*.)

He slept on the rug in the middle of the hallway.
(*On the rug* modifies *slept; in the middle* modifies *rug;* and *of the hallway* modifies *middle.*)

CONSIDER THE TRAITS

A prepositional phrase can help break up a string of adjectives. Instead of writing "the old, blue-awninged store," you can write "the old store with the blue awning."

Using Common Prepositions

Create For each sentence, fill in the blanks with prepositional phrases. Create them from the prepositions on the facing page and nouns or pronouns of your own choosing. Be creative!

1. Yesterday, I ran _____ .

2. Another runner _____ waved at me.

3. I was so distracted, I ran _____ .

4. The other runner then ran _____ .

5. We both had looks of surprise _____ .

6. I leaped _____ .

7. The other runner jogged _____ .

8. Then we both were _____ .

9. The incident _____ was a lesson.

10. The lesson was not to run _____ .

Model Read each sentence below and write another sentence modeled on it. Note how the writer uses prepositional phrases to create specific effects.

1. The coupe shot between the semis, around the limousine, down the tunnel, and up into bright sunlight.

    _____

2. I will look for you, but I also look to you.

    _____

3. Before the freedom of the road and the fun of the trip, I have finals.

    _____

4. Walk through the hallway, down the stairs, through the door, and into the pantry.

    _____

Vocabulary

preposition
word or word group that creates a relationship between a noun or pronoun and another word

prepositional phrase
phrase that starts with a preposition, includes an object of the preposition (noun or pronoun) and any modifiers; and functions as an adjective or adverb

LO4 *By, At, On,* and *In*

Prepositions often show the physical position of things—above, below, beside, around, and so on. Four specific prepositions show position but also get a lot of other use in English.

Uses for *By, At, On,* and *In*

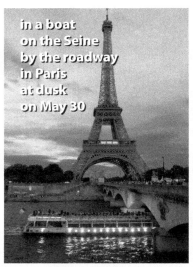

in a boat
on the Seine
by the roadway
in Paris
at dusk
on May 30

Rostislav Glinsky, 2011 / Used under license from Shutterstock.com

By means "beside" or "up to a certain place or time."

by the creek, by the garage

by noon, by August 16

At refers to a specific place or time.

at the edge, at the coffee shop

at 6:45 p.m., at midnight

On refers to a surface, a day or date, or an electronic medium.

on the table, on the T-shirt

on July 22, on Wednesday

on the computer, on the DVD

In refers to an enclosed space; a geographical location; an hour, a month, or a year; or a print medium.

in the hall, in the bathroom

in Madison, in France

in a minute, in December, in 2014

in the magazine, in the book

INSIGHT ————————————————————————————————————

Native English speakers follow these rules without thinking about them. Listen to the way native speakers use *by, at, on,* and *in,* and practice their use until it seems second nature.

Say It

Team up with a partner. Have the first person read one of the words below, and have the second person use it in a prepositional phrase beginning with *by, at, on,* or *in.* The first person should check if the form is correct. (Some have more than one correct answer.) Then you should switch roles.

1. the den
2. June 23
3. 9:33 p.m.
4. the MP3 player
5. the corner
6. Pittsburgh
7. the counter
8. the diner
9. sunset
10. the newspaper

Using *By, At, On,* and *In*

Provide   For each sentence, write the correct preposition in parentheses.

1. The guests arrived (by, on, in) 7:30 p.m., so we could eat (at, on, in) 8:00 p.m.
2. Put your suitcase (by, at, on, in) the trunk or (by, at, on) the rooftop luggage rack.
3. I looked for the new album (by, at, on, in) a music store, but could find it only (by, at, on, in) the Internet.
4. We waited (by, at, on, in) the lobby for a half hour, but Jerry didn't show up or even call (by, at, on, in) his cell phone.
5. Three people standing (by, at, in) the corner saw a traffic accident (by, at, on) the intersection of 45th and Monroe.
6. (By, At, On, In) April 1 of 2012, many pranksters may post apocalypse hoaxes (by, at, on, in) the Internet.
7. Let's meet (by, at, on) the convenience store (at, on, in) 7:00 p.m.
8. Place your order form (by, at, on, in) the postage-paid envelope, write your return address (by, at, on, in) the envelope, and post it.
9. A cat lay (by, at, on) the windowsill and looked me (by, at, on, in) the eye.
10. (At, On, In) noon of January 7, the school's pipes (at, on, in) the basement froze and caused flooding.

Write   Write a sentence that uses all four of these prepositions in phrases: *by, at, on, in.*

LO5 Real-World Application

Revise   Read the following e-mail, noting how choppy it sounds because all of the sentences are short. Rewrite the e-mail. Connect some of the sentences using a coordinating conjunction and a comma, and connect others using a subordinating conjunction. You can also change other words as needed. Reread the e-mail to make sure it sounds smooth.

Subordinating Conjunctions

after	as long as	if	so that	till	whenever
although	because	in order that	than	unless	where
as	before	provided that	that	until	whereas
as if	even though	since	though	when	while

Coordinating Conjunctions

and	but	or	nor
for	so	yet	

Send	Attach	Fonts	Colors	Save As Draft

To: dkraitsman@delafordandco.com

Subject: Completed Photo Log

Attach: Photolog.doc

Dear Deirdra: *1*

Attached, please find the photo log. The log shows all photos on the Web site. Some photos are from Getty Images. Others are from Shutterstock. A few are from Corbis. All photos have been downloaded. The downloads have the right resolution.   *5*

I hope you are pleased with the log. It includes permissions details. It also shows the resolution. I included a description of each photo.

I am available for more work. I could compile another photo log. I could also do the permissions work on these photos. I do writing and editing as well.

Thank you for this project. I look forward to hearing from you.   *10*

Thanks,

Roger Haverson

Photo Editor

Correct Read the following party invitation, noting the incorrect use of the prepositions *by, at, on,* and *in.* Correct the errors by deleting the prepositions and replacing them.

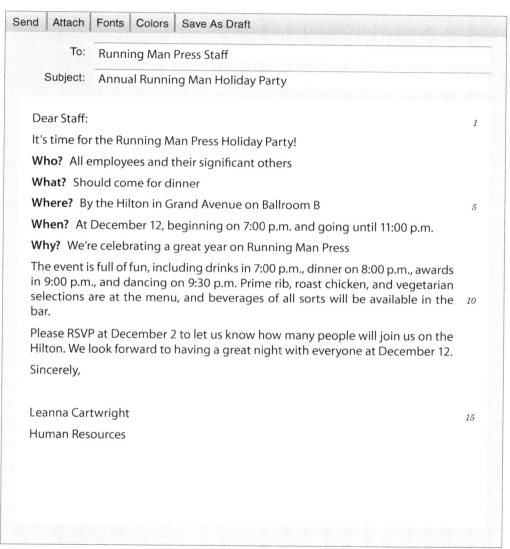

| Send | Attach | Fonts | Colors | Save As Draft |

To: Running Man Press Staff

Subject: Annual Running Man Holiday Party

Dear Staff: *1*

It's time for the Running Man Press Holiday Party!

Who? All employees and their significant others

What? Should come for dinner

Where? By the Hilton in Grand Avenue on Ballroom B   *5*

When? At December 12, beginning on 7:00 p.m. and going until 11:00 p.m.

Why? We're celebrating a great year on Running Man Press

The event is full of fun, including drinks in 7:00 p.m., dinner on 8:00 p.m., awards in 9:00 p.m., and dancing on 9:30 p.m. Prime rib, roast chicken, and vegetarian selections are at the menu, and beverages of all sorts will be available in the   *10* bar.

Please RSVP at December 2 to let us know how many people will join us on the Hilton. We look forward to having a great night with everyone at December 12.

Sincerely,

Leanna Cartwright   *15*

Human Resources

CONSIDER THE WORKPLACE

Correct use of *by, at, on,* and *in* will mark you as a writer comfortable with English.

Part V:

Punctuation and Mechanics Workshops

21

> "Words, once they are printed,
> have a life of their own."
> —Carol Burnett

Capitalization

By now you know writing requires correct capitalization. You know that every first word in a sentence should be capitalized and so should all proper nouns and proper adjectives. But what are the special uses of capitalization? And why are some nouns capitalized in one instance but not another?

This chapter will guide you in the conventional use of capital letters in writing. Throughout the section, examples demonstrate correct capitalization and serve as a handy reference during editing and proofreading.

Learning Outcomes

LO1 Understand basic capitalization rules.

LO2 Understand advanced capitalization rules.

LO3 Understand capitalization of titles, organizations, abbreviations, and letters.

LO4 Understand capitalization of names, courses, and Web terms.

LO5 Apply capitalization in real-world documents.

What do you think?

What does a word that is capitalized reveal to you? What does incorrect capitalization reveal about a writer?

Dariusz Sas, 2011 / Used under license from Shutterstock.com

LO1 Basic Capitalization

All first words, proper nouns, and proper adjectives must be capitalized. The following guidelines and examples will help explain these rules.

Proper Nouns and Adjectives

Capitalize all proper nouns and all proper adjectives (adjectives derived from proper nouns). The chart below provides a quick overview of capitalization.

Quick Guide: Capitalization at a Glance

Days of the week	Saturday, Sunday, Tuesday
Months	March, August, December
Holidays, holy days	Christmas, Hanukah, Presidents' Day
Periods, events in history	the Renaissance, Middle Ages
Special events	Tate Memorial Dedication Ceremony
Political parties	Republican Party, Green Party
Official documents	Bill of Rights
Trade names	Frisbee disc, Heinz ketchup
Formal epithets	Alexander the Great
Official titles	Vice-President Al Gore, Senator Davis
Official state nicknames	the Garden State, the Beaver State
Planets, heavenly bodies	Earth, Mars, the Milky Way
Continents	Asia, Australia, Europe
Countries	France, Brazil, Japan, Pakistan
States, provinces	Montana, Nebraska, Alberta, Ontario
Cities, towns, villages	Portland, Brookfield, Broad Ripple
Streets, roads, highways	Rodeo Drive, Route 66, Interstate 55
Sections of the United States and the world	the West Coast, the Middle East
Landforms	Appalachian Mountains, Kalahari Desert
Bodies of water	Lake Erie, Tiber River, Atlantic Ocean
Public areas	Central Park, Rocky Mountain National Park

First Words

Capitalize the first word in every sentence and the first word in a direct quotation that is a full sentence.

Preparing for the final exam will help you get a good grade.

Shawna asked, "**D**oes anyone want to study with me at the coffee house?"

Correcting Capitalization

Practice A   In each sentence below, capitalize the appropriate words.

1. Singer jack johnson finds musical inspiration in his hometown of oahu, hawaii.

2. Hawaii is the only state made up entirely of islands and is located in the pacific ocean.

3. Known as the aloha state, it's home to the hawaii volcanoes national park.

4. Another national park, the U.S.S. *arizona* memorial, is dedicated to the navy members who were lost during the attack on pearl harbor.

5. On december, 7, 1941, the United States naval base at pearl harbor, Hawaii, was attacked by japan.

6. The attack triggered the united states' entry in world war II.

7. President franklin d. roosevelt declared December 7 as "a day that will live in infamy."

8. Hawaii's beautiful beaches and tropical temperatures attract tourists from the midwest to the far east.

Practice B   Decide what words should be capitalized. Write them down.

> My favorite holiday is thanksgiving. every november family members   *1*
> from illinois, indiana, and Michigan travel to my parents' house to
> celebrate the best thursday of the year. While Mom and my aunts work
> on the dressing and mashed potatoes, my cousins and I watch football on
> the fox network. it has long been a tradition for the Detroit lions to play a   *5*
> home game every thanksgiving. By the time the game is finished, the food
> is ready and the feast is on. Turkey, gravy, and green-bean casserole—you
> can't beat thanksgiving.

INSIGHT

Different languages use capitalization differently. For example, German capitalizes not just proper nouns but all important nouns. Compare and contrast capitalization styles between your heritage language and English.

LO2 Advanced Capitalization

Sentences in Parentheses

Capitalize the first word in a sentence that is enclosed in parentheses if that sentence is not combined within another complete sentence.

My favorite designer is hosting a fashion show for her new collection.
(**N**ow I just need a ticket.)

NOTE: Do *not* capitalize a sentence that is enclosed in parentheses and is located in the middle of another sentence.

Rachel's cousin (his name is Carl) can't make it tonight.

Sentences Following Colons

Capitalize a complete sentence that follows a colon when that sentence is a formal statement, a quotation, or a sentence that you want to emphasize.

I would like to paraphrase Patrick Henry: Give me chocolate or give me death.

Salutation and Complimentary Closing

In a letter, capitalize the first and all major words of the salutation. Capitalize only the first word of the complimentary closing.

Dear Dr. Howard: **S**incerely yours,

Sections of the Country

Words that indicate sections of the country are proper nouns and should be capitalized; words that simply indicate directions are not proper nouns.

I'm thinking about moving to the **W**est **C**oast. *(section of country)*
I'm thinking about driving **west** to California. *(direction)*

Languages, Ethnic Groups, Nationalities, and Religions

Capitalize languages, ethnic groups, nationalities, religions, Supreme Beings, and holy books.

African	**N**avajo	**I**slam	**G**od	**A**llah
Jehovah	the **K**oran	**E**xodus		the **B**ible

Correcting Capitalization

Practice A   In each sentence below, capitalize the appropriate words.

1. The midwest region of the United States is made up of 12 states.

2. The bible and the koran are considered holy books.

3. The navajo indians of the southwest have significant populations in an area known as the Four Corners (arizona, new mexico, utah, and Colorado).

4. Mark Twain once said this about adversity: "it's not the size of the dog in the fight; it's the size of the fight in the dog."

5. My brother Phil is starting college today. (my mom finally has the house to herself.)

6. I'm a proud member of the latino community in Miami.

7. In Quebec, Canada, many citizens speak both english and french.

Practice B   Read the following paragraph. Then capitalize the appropriate words.

> I ate the best seafood of my life at a new england restaurant. The   *1*
> small, coastal restaurant in Massachusetts features fresh seafood from
> the atlantic ocean. I ordered the maine lobster, and I have one impression:
> it was awesome. If you have never tried fresh lobster before, I highly
> recommend it. You won't be disappointed. (now I need to figure out when I   *5*
> can go back.)

Practice C   Decide what words should be capitalized. Write them down.

tomorrow   hanukah   wednesday   bank   frisbee

u.s. bank   flying disc   russia   tree

INSIGHT

Do not capitalize words used to indicate direction or position.

Turn **south** at the stop sign. *(South refers to direction.)*

The **South** is known for its great Cajun food. *(South refers to a region of the country.)*

LO3 Other Capitalization Rules I

Titles

Capitalize the first word of a title, the last word, and every word in between except articles *(a, an, the)*, short prepositions, *to* in an infinitive, and coordinating conjunctions. Follow this rule for titles of books, newspapers, magazines, poems, plays, songs, articles, films, works of art, and stories.

The Curious Case of Benjamin Button	*New York Times*
"Cry Me a River"	"Cashing in on Kids"
A Midsummer Night's Dream	*The Da Vinci Code*

Organizations

Capitalize the name of an organization or a team and its members.

American Indian Movement	Democratic Party
Lance Armstrong Foundation	Indiana Pacers
Susan G. Komen for the Cure	Boston Red Sox

Abbreviations

Capitalize abbreviations of titles and organizations.

M.D.   Ph.D.   NAACP   C.E.   B.C.E.   GPA

Letters

Capitalize letters used to indicate a form or shape.

U-turn   I-beam   V-shaped   T-shirt

INSIGHT ————————————————

Note that the American Psychological Association has a different style for capitalizing the titles of smaller works. Be sure you know the style required for a specific class.

Correcting Capitalization

Practice A   In the sentences below, capitalize the appropriate words.

1. I'm stopping by the gas station to pick up the sunday *Chicago tribune*.
2. The Los Angeles lakers play in the staples center.
3. At the next stoplight, you will need to take a u-turn.
4. My favorite author is Malcolm Gladwell, who wrote the best-sellers *blink* and *The tipping point*.
5. How many times have you heard the song "I got a feeling" by the Black-eyed peas?
6. The American cancer society raises money for cancer research.
7. I was happy to improve my gpa from 3.1 to 3.4 last semester.
8. Where did you buy that Seattle mariners t-shirt?
9. The doctor charted the growth of the tumor using an s-curve.
10. The man read a copy of *gq* magazine in New York City's central park.
11. Jill was promoted to chief operating officer (ceo) this july.

Practice B   Read the paragraph below. Then write down the words that need to be capitalized.

On our way to the Kansas city royals game, my friend Ted and I got   *1*

in an argument over our favorite music. He likes coldplay, while I prefer

radiohead. His favorite song is "Vida la viva." My favorite is "Fake plastic

trees." But as we argued about the merits of each band, we completely

missed our exit to the stadium. Ted suggested we perform a u-turn.   *5*

Instead, I used my gps to find a new route. Luckily, we made it to the

ballpark in time to grab a hot dog and coke before the opening pitch.

LO4 Other Capitalization Rules II

Words Used as Names

Capitalize words like *father, mother, uncle, senator,* and *professor* only when they are parts of titles that include a personal name or when they are substitutes for proper nouns (especially in direct address).

Hello, **S**enator Feingold. (*Senator* is part of the name.)

It's good to meet you, **S**enator. (*Senator* is a substitute for the name.)

Our **senator** is an environmentalist.

Who was your chemistry **professor** last quarter?

I had **P**rofessor **W**illiams for Chemistry 101.

Good morning, **P**rofessor.

NOTE: To test whether a word is being substituted for a proper noun, simply read the sentence with a proper noun in place of the word. If the proper noun fits in the sentence, the word being tested should be capitalized. Usually the word is not capitalized if it follows a possessive—*my, his, our, your,* and so on.

Did **D**ad (Brad) pack the stereo in the trailer? (*Brad* works in the sentence.)

Did your **dad** (Brad) pack the stereo in the trailer?
(*Brad* does not work in the sentence; the word *dad* follows *your.*)

Titles of Courses

Words such as *technology, history,* and *science* are proper nouns when they are included in the titles of specific courses; they are common nouns when they name a field of study.

Who teaches **A**rt **H**istory 202? (title of a specific course)

Professor Bunker loves teaching **history.** (a field of study)

Internet and E-Mail

The words *Internet* and *World Wide Web* are capitalized because they are considered proper nouns. When your writing includes a Web address (URL), capitalize any letters that the site's owner does (on printed materials or on the site itself).

When doing research on the **I**nternet, be sure to record each site's **W**eb address (URL) and each contact's **e-mail** address.

Correcting Capitalization

Practice A In each sentence below, capitalize the appropriate words.

1. I met mayor Greg Ballard by chance today at the daily brew coffee shop.

2. When I was a freshman, I studied the history of roman art in art history 101.

3. Ever since I gained wireless access to the internet, I've spent hours each day on YouTube.

4. Let's hope dad can make it in time for our tee time.

5. In a speech to his constituents, congressman Paul Ryan called for fiscal responsibility.

6. My favorite class this semester is advanced forensics 332 with dr. Charles Wendell, a well-known professor.

7. My uncle Brad has no clue how to navigate the world wide web.

8. Elizabeth attended the Wayne State University senior Banquet.

9. In searching for exercise routines, Jack bookmarked a web address (url) for *men's health* magazine.

10. You will need to contact commissioner Sheffield for permission.

Practice B Read the paragraph below. Then write down the words that need to be capitalized.

Before Steve Jobs became ceo of apple Inc. and the brainchild behind   *1*

Macintosh, he attended high school in the San Francisco bay Area, a

region that is famously known as silicon valley. Jobs enrolled at Reed

College in portland, Oregon, but dropped out after the first semester to

return home to co-create apple. At the same time, other tech innovators   *5*

flooded the area to create companies such as Hewlett-packard and Intel. It

is also here where internet giants google and Yahoo! were founded. Today

Silicon valley remains a region of technological innovation.

LO5 Real-World Application

Correct   In the following basic letter, capitalize the appropriate words. Then lowercase the words that shouldn't be capitalized. If a letter is capitalized and shouldn't be, put a lowercase editing mark through the letter.

Ball State university Volunteer Center
7711 S. Hampton drive
Muncie, IN 47302
July, 5 2010

Mr. Ryan Orlovich
Muncie parks Department
1800 Grant Street
Muncie, IN 47302

Dear superintendent Orlovich:

Last Saturday, the Ball State volunteer center committee met to discuss new volunteer opportunities for the upcoming semester. We are interested in putting together a service event at big oak park for the incoming Freshmen.

We would like to get in contact with someone from your department to set up a time and date for the event. We would prefer the event to take place between thursday, August 23, and Sunday, August 26. Also, we hope to design t-shirts for the volunteers and were wondering if your office knew of any sponsors who might be interested in funding this expenditure.

When you have time, please contact me by phone at 317-555-3980 or E-mail at ehenderson@bs23u.edu. (you may also e-mail the office at bsuvolunteerism@bs23u.edu.)

Yours Truly,

Liz Henderson

Liz Henderson

BSU Volunteer President

Special Challenge   Write a sentence that includes a colon followed by another sentence you want to emphasize.

22

Comma

> "The writer who neglects punctuation, or mispunctuates, is liable to be misunderstood for the want of merely a comma."
>
> —Edgar Allan Poe

Commas divide sentences into smaller sections so that they may be read more easily and more precisely. They also show which words belong together and which line up in parallel. Of all the punctuation marks, commas are used most frequently—and oftentimes incorrectly.

This chapter will guide you in the conventional use of commas. Understanding correct comma usage is an important step in becoming a college-level writer. Applying these rules will make your writing clearer and easier to follow.

Learning Outcomes

LO1 Use commas in compound sentences.

LO2 Use commas with introductory phrases and equal adjectives.

LO3 Use commas between items in a series.

LO4 Use commas with appositives and nonrestrictive modifiers.

LO5 Use commas in real-world writing.

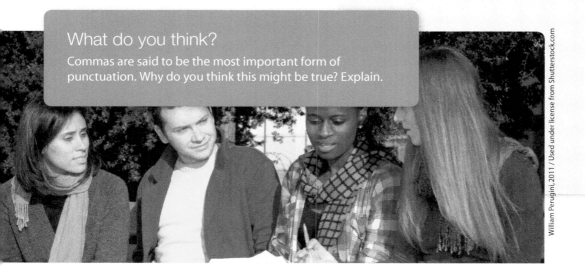

What do you think?

Commas are said to be the most important form of punctuation. Why do you think this might be true? Explain.

William Perugini, 2011 / Used under license from Shutterstock.com

LO1 In Compound Sentences and After Introductory Clauses

The following principles will guide the use of commas in your writing.

In Compound Sentences

Use a comma before the coordinating conjunction *(and, but, or, nor, for, yet, so)* in a compound sentence.

Heath Ledger completed his brilliant portrayal as the Joker in *The Dark Knight*, **but** he died before the film was released.

NOTE: Do not confuse a compound verb with a compound sentence.

Ledger's Joker became instantly iconic and won him the Oscar for best supporting actor. *(compound verb)*

His death resulted from the abuse of prescription drugs, but it was ruled an accident. *(compound sentence)*

After Introductory Clauses

Use a comma after most introductory clauses.

Although Charlemagne was a great patron of learning, he never learned to write properly. (adverb dependent clause)

When the clause follows the independent clause and is not essential to the meaning of the sentence, use a comma. This comma use generally applies to clauses beginning with *even though, although, while,* or some other conjunction expressing a contrast.

Charlemagne never learned to write properly, **even though he continued to practice.**

NOTE: A comma is *not* used if the dependent clause following the independent clause is needed.

CONSIDER THE TRAITS

Make sure to use both a comma and a coordinating conjunction in a compound sentence, or you will create a comma splice or a run-on.

Correcting Comma Errors

Correct For each sentence below, add a comma before the coordinating conjunction *(and, but, or, nor, for, so, yet)* if the clause on each side could stand alone as a sentence. Write "correct" if the conjunction separates word groups that can't stand alone.

1. I was sick of sitting around on the couch so I drove over to the driving range.   _____

2. Her cell phone rang but she decided against answering it.   _____

3. Maria downloaded some new music and imported it on her iPod.   _____

4. I wanted to finish my assignment but I couldn't turn away from the *House* marathon.   _____

5. Should I put a down payment on a new car or should I save my money for a new apartment?   _____

6. Kelly is studying frog populations in the rain forest and she hopes to publish her work.   _____

7. Ryan wanted to make a new style of chili but he lost the recipe.   _____

8. Trisha was looking forward to the baseball game but it got rained out.   _____

Correct For each sentence below, add a comma after any introductory clauses. If no comma is needed, write "correct" next to the sentence.

1. While Becca prefers grilled salmon Mia's favorite food is sushi.   _____

2. Although the water conditions were perfect I couldn't catch a wave to save my life.   _____

3. Perhaps I should rethink my major because I don't enjoy the classes.   _____

4. Even though the Cubs haven't won a World Series since 1901 I still cheer for them.   _____

5. While *American Idol* is popular in America *Britain's Got Talent* is the craze in England.   _____

LO2 With Introductory Words and Equal Adjectives

After Introductory Phrases

Use a comma after introductory phrases.

In spite of his friend's prodding, Jared decided to stay home and study.

A comma is usually omitted if the phrase follows an independent clause.

Jared decided to stay home and study **in spite of his friend's prodding.**

You may omit a comma after a short (four or fewer words) introductory phrase unless it is needed to ensure clarity.

At 10:32 p. m. he would quit and go to sleep.

To Separate Adjectives

Use commas to separate adjectives that equally modify the same noun. Notice in the examples below that no comma separates the last adjective from the noun.

You should exercise regularly and follow a **sensible, healthful** diet.

A good diet is one that includes lots of **high-protein, low-fat** foods.

To Determine Equal Modifiers

To determine whether adjectives modify a noun equally, use these two tests.

1. Reverse the order of the adjectives; if the sentence is clear, the adjectives modify equally. (In the example below, *hot* and *crowded* can be switched, but *short* and *coffee* cannot.)

   Matt was tired of working in the **hot, crowded** lab and decided to take a **short coffee** break.

2. Insert *and* between the adjectives; if the sentence reads well, use a comma when *and* is omitted. (The word *and* can be inserted between *hot* and *crowded,* but *and* does not make sense between *short* and *coffee.*)

Correcting Comma Errors

Correct If a comma is needed after the introductory phrase, write the words before and after the comma, with it between them. If no comma is needed, write "correct."

1. Before you can receive your diploma you will need to pay your unpaid parking tickets.
   _____

2. At Central Perk Ross, Rachel, and the gang sipped coffee and exchanged barbs.
   _____

3. In accordance with state law Hanna decided against sending a text message while driving on the interstate.
   _____

4. On the other hand pursuing the wrong type of adrenaline high can be destructive.
   _____

5. After handing in her paper Eva felt a great wave of relief.
   _____

6. Eva felt a great wave of relief after handing in her paper.
   _____

7. Based on his primary research Andy came up with a preliminary hypothesis.
   _____

8. To save a few dollars Stephanie rode her bike to work.
   _____

Correct For each sentence below, determine whether or not a comma is needed to separate the adjectives that modify the same noun. Add any needed commas. Write "no" next to the sentence if a comma is not needed.

1. The **long difficult** exam took a lot out of me.
   _____

2. Last night I went to a **fun graduation** party.
   _____

3. A good concert includes many **memorable hair-raising** moments.
   _____

4. A **thoughtful considerate** friend goes an extra mile to make you smile.
   _____

5. I could really use a **relaxing back** massage.
   _____

6. When dressing for skiing, consider wearing a **thick well-insulated** jacket.
   _____

Steve Mann, 2011 / Used under license from Shutterstock.com

LO3 Between Items in a Series and Other Uses

Between Items in Series

Use commas to separate individual words, phrases, or clauses in a series. (A series contains at least three items.)

Many college students must balance studying with **taking care of a family, working, getting exercise, and finding time to relax.**

Do not use commas when all the items are connected with *or, nor,* or *and.*

Hmm ... should I study **or** do laundry **or** go out?

To Set Off Transitional Expressions

Use a comma to set off conjunctive adverbs and transitional phrases.

Handwriting is not, **as a matter of fact,** easy to improve upon later in life; **however,** it can be done if you are determined enough.

If a transitional expression blends smoothly with the rest of the sentence, it does not need to be set off.

If you are **in fact** coming, I'll see you there.

To Set Off Dialogue

Use commas to set off the words of the speaker from the rest of the sentence. Do not use a comma before an indirect quotation.

"Never be afraid to ask for help," advised Ms. Kane

"With the evidence that we now have," Professor Thom said, **"many scientists believe there could be life on Mars."**

To Enclose Explanatory Words

Use commas to enclose an explanatory word or phrase.

Time management, **according to many professionals,** is an important skill that should be taught in college.

Correcting Comma Errors

Correct Indicate where commas are needed. Write the words before and after the comma, showing the comma between them.

1. I'm looking forward to graduation summer vacation and moving into a new apartment.

2. A new strain of virus according to biologists could cause future outbreaks of poultry disease.

3. "To confine our attention to terrestrial matters would be to limit the human spirit" said Stephen Hawking.

4. I need you to pick up two jars of peanut butter, a half-gallon of skim milk and snacks for the party.

5. I enjoy live music; however I don't like big crowds.

6. "With all the advancements in technology" Sara said, "you'd think we would have invented a quicker toaster by now."

7. Eighty percent of states as a matter of fact are in financial trouble.

8. We can meet up at either the library the student union or memorial hall.

9. The difference between perseverance and obstinacy according to Henry Ward Beecher is that one comes from strong will, and the other from a strong won't.

10. Chicago, Detroit and Indianapolis are the most-populated cities in the Midwest.

Correct Indicate where commas are needed. Write the line number and the words before and after the comma, showing the comma between them.

> The Erie Canal is a man-made waterway that connects the Atlantic   *1*
> Ocean to Lake Erie. It was the first transportation system to connect the
> eastern seaboard and the Great Lakes was faster than carts pulled by
> animals and significantly cut transportation time. "The opening of the
> Erie Canal to New York in 1825 stimulated other cities on the Atlantic   *5*
> seaboard to put themselves into closer commercial touch with the West"
> said John Moody. Since the 1990s the canal is mostly home to recreational
> traffic; however some cargo is still transported down the waterway.

LO4 With Appositives and Other Word Groups

To Set Off Some Appositives

A specific kind of explanatory word or phrase called an *appositive* identifies or renames a preceding noun or pronoun.

Albert Einstein, **the famous mathematician and physicist,** developed the theory of relativity.

Do not use commas if the appositive is important to the basic meaning of the sentence.

The famous physicist **Albert Einstein** developed the theory of relativity.

With Some Clauses and Phrases

Use commas to enclose phrases or clauses that add information that is not necessary to the basic meaning of the sentence. For example, if the clause or phrase (in boldface) were left out of the two examples below, the meaning of the sentences would remain clear. Therefore, commas are used to set off the information.

The locker rooms in Swain Hall, **which were painted and updated last summer,** give professors a place to shower. (nonrestrictive clause)

Work-study programs, **offered on many campuses,** give students the opportunity to earn tuition money. (nonrestrictive phrase)

Do not use commas to set off necessary clauses and phrases, which add information that the reader needs to understand the sentence.

Only the professors **who run at noon** use the locker rooms. (necessary clause)

Using "That" or "Which"

Use *that* to introduce necessary clauses; use *which* to introduce unnecessary clauses.

Campus jobs **that are funded by the university** are awarded to students only. (necessary)

The cafeteria, **which is run by an independent contractor,** can hire nonstudents. (unnecessary)

Correcting Comma Errors

Correct Indicate where commas are needed in the following sentences. If no commas are needed, write "correct."

1. John D. Rockefeller the famous American philanthropist and oil executive is sometimes referred to as the richest person in history.

   _____

2. The new library which is scheduled to open in July will include three different computer labs.

   _____

3. The renowned trumpeter Louis Armstrong sang the song "What a Wonderful World."

   _____

4. Kansas City along with Memphis, Tennessee is known for its delicious barbecue.

   _____

5. Judge Sonya Sotomayer the first Hispanic Supreme Court justice was confirmed into office in 2009.

   _____

6. The book *The Notebook* which was later adapted into a movie was written by Nicolas Sparks.

   _____

Write The following sentences contain clauses using *that.* Rewrite the sentences with clauses using *which,* and insert commas correctly. You may need to reword some parts.

1. The road construction that delayed traffic yesterday should be completed by the end of the week.

   _____

   _____

2. The homework that Dr. Grant assigned yesterday will consume the next two weeks of my life.

   _____

   _____

3. The earplugs that we bought before the race made the deafening noise more bearable.

   _____

   _____

Vocabulary

appositive
a noun or noun phrase that renames
another noun right beside it

LO5 Real-World Application

Correct   Indicate where commas are needed in the following e-mail message. Write the line number and the words before and after the comma, showing it between them.

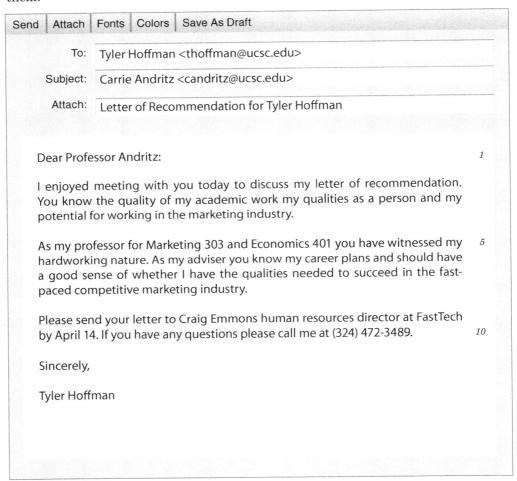

| Send | Attach | Fonts | Colors | Save As Draft |

To: Tyler Hoffman <thoffman@ucsc.edu>

Subject: Carrie Andritz <candritz@ucsc.edu>

Attach: Letter of Recommendation for Tyler Hoffman

Dear Professor Andritz: *1*

I enjoyed meeting with you today to discuss my letter of recommendation. You know the quality of my academic work my qualities as a person and my potential for working in the marketing industry.

As my professor for Marketing 303 and Economics 401 you have witnessed my   *5*
hardworking nature. As my adviser you know my career plans and should have a good sense of whether I have the qualities needed to succeed in the fast-paced competitive marketing industry.

Please send your letter to Craig Emmons human resources director at FastTech by April 14. If you have any questions please call me at (324) 472-3489.   *10*

Sincerely,

Tyler Hoffman

CONSIDER THE WORKPLACE ──────────────────────

Correct comma use is critical for clear business communication.

23

> "A fine quotation is a diamond on the finger of a man of wit, and a pebble in the hand of a fool."
>
> —Joseph Roux

Quotation Marks and Italics

Much of the time, language flows from us as naturally as breathing. We think; we speak; someone hears and responds—all without consciously thinking about the words.

Sometimes, however, we have need to note a word as a word, to call attention to a phrase in a special sense, to use an apt or time-honored quotation from someone else, or to mark the title of a work. In such cases, quotation marks and italics allow us to indicate this special use of language.

Learning Outcomes

LO1 Understand the use of quotation marks.

LO2 Understand the use of italics.

LO3 Apply quotation marks and italics in a real-world document.

What do you think?

Study the image and quotation. What makes the gemstones in the photo valuable? In what way does this relate to the Joseph Roux quotation?

Tom Mc Nemar, 2011 / Used under license from Shutterstock.com

LO1 Quotation Marks

To Punctuate Titles (Smaller Works)

Use quotation marks to enclose the titles of smaller works, including speeches, short stories, songs, poems, episodes of audio or video programs, chapters or sections of books, unpublished works, and articles from magazines, journals, newspapers, or encyclopedias.

Speech:	"The Cause Endures"
Song:	"Head Like a Hole"
Short Story:	"Dark They Were, and Golden Eyed"
Magazine Article:	"The Moral Life of Babies"
Chapter in a Book:	"Queen Mab"
Television Episode:	"The Girl Who Was Death"
Encyclopedia Article:	"Cetacean"

Placement of Periods and Commas

When quoted words end in a period or comma, always place that punctuation inside the quotation marks.

"If you want to catch the train," Grace said, "you must leave now."

Placement of Semicolons and Colons

When a quotation is followed by a semicolon or colon, always place that punctuation outside the quotation marks.

I finally read "Heart of Darkness"; it is amazingly well written!

Placement of Exclamation Points and Question Marks

If an exclamation point or a question mark is part of the quotation, place it inside the quotation marks. Otherwise, place it outside.

Marcello asked me, "Are you going to the Dodge Poetry Festival?" What could I reply except, "Yes, indeed"?

For Special Words

Quotation marks can be used (1) to show that a word is being referred to as the word itself; (2) to indicate that it is jargon, slang, or a coined term; or (3) to show that it is used in an ironic or sarcastic sense.

(1) Somehow, the term "cool" has survived decades.
(2) The band has a "wicked awesome" sound.
(3) I would describe the taste of this casserole as "swampy."

Using Quotation Marks

Correct   For the following sentences, insert quotation marks where needed.

1. Kamala loves to listen to the song I Take Time, over and over and over.
2. Ray Bradbury's short story A Sound of Thunder has been republished many times.
3. Fast Company published an article today called How Google Wave Got Its Groove Back.
4. Angelo told Arlena, I have a guy who can fix that fender.
5. Arlena asked, How much will it cost me?
6. Was she thinking, This car is driving me into bankruptcy?
7. This is the message of the article Tracking the Science of Commitment: Couples that enhance one another have an easier time remaining committed.
8. I love the article Tall Tales About Being Short; it challenged my preconceptions about the effect of height on a person's life.
9. How many examples of the word aardvark can you find on this page?
10. Is anyone else here tired of hearing about his bling bling?

Write   Write a sentence that indicates the actual meaning of each sentence below.

1. Hoyt's great Dane "skipped" across the floor and "settled" its bulk across his lap.

2. Our baked goods are always "fresh."

3. And so began another "wonderful" day of marching through a "fairyland" of bugs.

LO2 Italics

To Punctuate Titles (Larger Works)

Use italics to indicate the titles of larger works, including newspapers, magazines, journals, pamphlets, books, plays, films, radio and television programs, movies, ballets, operas, long musical compositions, CD's, DVD's, software programs, and legal cases, as well as the names of ships, trains, aircraft, and spacecraft.

Magazine: *Wired*

Play: *Night of the Iguana*

Film: *Bladerunner*

Book: *Moby Dick*

Newspaper: *Washington Post*

Journal: *Journal of Sound & Vibration*

Software Program: *Paint Shop Pro*

Television Program: *The Prisoner*

For a Word, Letter, or Number Referred to as Itself

Use italics (or quotation marks) to show that a word, letter, or number is being referred to as itself. If a definition follows a word used in this way, place that definition in quotation marks.

The word *tornado* comes to English from the Spanish *tronar,* which means "to thunder."

I can't read your writing; is this supposed to be a *P* or an *R*?

For Foreign Words

Use italics to indicate a word that is being borrowed from a foreign language.

Je ne sais pas is a French phrase that many English speakers use as a fancy way of saying "I don't know what."

For Technical Terms

Use italics to introduce a technical term for the first time in a piece of writing. After that, the term may be used without italics.

The heart's *sternocostal* surface—facing toward the joining of sternum and ribs—holds the heart's primary natural pacemaker. If this sternocostal node fails, a lower, secondary node can function in its place.

NOTE: If a technical term is being used within an organization or a field of study where it is common, it may be used without italics even the first time in a piece of writing.

Using Italics

Correct   For the following sentences, underline words that should be in italics.

1. I almost couldn't finish Stephenie Meyer's second book, New Moon, because of its deep emotion.

2. What is your favorite part of the movie Avatar?

3. The Spanish say duende to describe a transcendent, creative passion.

4. Was the aircraft carrier Enterprise named after the vessel from the Star Trek series or the other way around?

5. You might use the term bonhomie to describe our relationship.

6. One thing I love about the MS Word program is its "Track Changes" feature.

7. In this course, we will use the term noetics as an indication of deep-felt self-awareness, beyond mere consciousness.

8. How am I supposed to compete at Scrabble when all I have is an X and a 7.

9. Wait, that's not a 7; it's an L.

10. That, ladies and gentleman, is what we in show business call a finale!

Write   Write three sentences, each demonstrating your understanding of one or more rules for using italics.

1. _____

_____

_____

2. _____

_____

_____

3. _____

_____

_____

LO3 Real-World Application

Practice In the following business letter, underline any words that should be italicized and add quotation marks where needed.

Brideshead Publishing
1012 Broadway
New York, New York 10011

May 13, 2010   *1*

Neva Konen
4004 W. Obleness Parkway
Hollenshead, New Hampshire 03305

Dear Neva Konen: *5*

Thank you for your recent novel submission entitled A Time of Dimly Perceived Wonders, which I read with great interest. The setting is richly portrayed, and the main characters are at the same time both mysterious and familiar, conveying a certain je ne sais quas about themselves. For example, although his words land strangely on my ear, still I am overwhelmed with feelings of kinship for Anibal when he cries out, I could've et 'em up   *10* right there 'n' then! Similarly, when at the end Kandis softly croons the words of Come One, Come All, to the Family Reunion, I feel I'm being called home myself, although I've never actually seen the Appalachians.

While I greatly enjoyed the novel, and it would certainly receive an "A" in my Creative Writing Seminar at Midtown College, I do have a few concerns. For one thing, the title   *15* seems long and somewhat vague; I'd recommend Foggy Mountain Memories, instead. Also, it seems unnecessary to print the full text of Abraham Lincoln's Gettysburg Address and Martin Luther King, Jr.'s, I Have a Dream speech in the chapter entitled A Few Words of Hope. Modern readers are certainly familiar with both speeches. It should be enough to merely include a few phrases, such as Four score and seven years ago, and Let   *20* freedom ring from Lookout Mountain of Tennessee.

If you are willing to accept changes such as these, I believe we can work together to make your novel a commercial success. Please review the enclosed contract and return it to me at your earliest convenience.

Sincerely,   *25*

Christene Kaley

Christene Kaley

24

"If the English language made any sense,
a catastrophe would be an apostrophe with fur."
—Doug Larson

Other Punctuation

You may be surprised to discover that the words *catastrophe* and *apostrophe* have something in common. Both come from the Greek word for "turn." An apostrophe simply turns away, but a catastrophe overturns.

Sometimes the use of apostrophes becomes a catastrophe. Apostrophes shouldn't be used to form plurals of words. Their main use is to form possessives and contractions. The rules and activities in this chapter will help you understand their usage and avoid an apostrophe catastrophe.

This chapter also provides guidelines for the rules and correct usage of semicolons, colons, hyphens, and dashes.

Learning Outcomes

LO1 Use apostrophes for contractions and possessives.

LO2 Use semicolons and colons correctly.

LO3 Understand hyphen use.

LO4 Use dashes well.

LO5 Apply apostrophes in real-world documents.

LO6 Apply punctuation in real-world documents.

What do you think?

Why do you think *apostrophe* comes from the word "to turn away?"

Gary James Calder, 2011 / Used under license from Shutterstock.com

LO1 Contractions and Possessives

Apostrophes are used primarily to show that a letter or number has been left out, or that a noun is possessive.

Contractions

When one or more letters are left out of a word, use an apostrophe to form the contraction.

don't	he'd	would've
(*o* is left out)	(*woul* is left out)	(*ha* is left out)

INSIGHT

Pronoun possessives *do not use* apostrophes: *its, whose, hers, his, ours*

Missing Characters

Use an apostrophe to signal when one or more characters are left out.

class of '16	rock 'n' roll	good mornin'
(*20* is left out)	(*a* and *d* are left out)	(*g* is left out)

Possessives

Form possessives of singular nouns by adding an apostrophe and an *s*.

Sharla's pen	the man's coat	*The Pilgrim's Progress*

Singular Noun Ending In *s* (One Syllable)

Form the possessive by adding an apostrophe and an *s*.

the boss's idea	the lass's purse	the bass's teeth

Singular Noun Ending In *s* (Two Or More Syllables)

Form the possessive by adding an apostrophe and an *s*—or by adding just an apostrophe.

Kansas's plains	*or*	Kansas' plains

Plural Noun Ending In *s*

Form the possessive by adding just an apostrophe.

the bosses' preference	the Smiths' home
the girl's ball	the girls' ball
(*girl* is the owner)	(*girls* are the owners)

INSIGHT

The word before the apostrophe is the owner.

Plural Noun Not Ending In *s*

Form the possessive by adding an apostrophe and an *s*.

the children's toys	the women's room

Forming Contractions and Possessives

Write   For each contraction below, write the words that formed the contraction. For each set of words, write the contraction that would be formed.

1. they're _____
2. you've _____
3. Charlie is _____
4. wouldn't _____
5. we have _____

6. have not _____
7. I would _____
8. I had _____
9. won't _____
10. will not _____

Rewrite   Rework the following sentences, replacing the "of" phrases with possessives using apostrophes.

1. The idea of my friend is a good one.

   _____

2. I found the flyer of the orchestra.

   _____

3. The foundation of the government is democracy.

   _____

4. He washed the jerseys of the team.

   _____

5. I went to the house of the Kings.

   _____

6. The plan of the managers worked well.

   _____

7. I like the classic albums of Kiss.

   _____

8. I graded the assignment of Ross.

   _____

9. The pastries of the chef were delicious.

   _____

10. The books of the children covered the floor.

    _____

Vocabulary

contraction
word formed by joining two words, leaving out one or more letters (indicated by an apostrophe)

LO2 Semicolons and Colons

Semicolons and colons have specific uses in writing.

Semicolon

A semicolon can be called a soft period. Use the semicolon to join two sentences that are closely related.

The job market is improving; it's time to apply again.

Before a Conjunctive Adverb

Often, the second sentence will begin with a conjunctive adverb *(also, besides, however, instead, meanwhile, therefore),* which signals the relationship between the sentences. Place a semicolon before the conjunctive adverb, and place a comma after it.

I looked for work for two months; however, the market is better now.

With Series

Use a semicolon to separate items in a series if any of the items already include commas.

I should check online ads, headhunting services, and position announcements; compile a list of job openings; create a résumé, an e-résumé, and a cover letter; and apply, requesting an interview.

Colon

The main use of a colon is to introduce an example or a list.

I've forgotten one other possibility: social networking.
I'll plan to use the following: LinkedIn, Twitter, and Facebook.

After Salutations

In business documents, use a colon after salutations and in memo headings.

Dear Mr. Ortez: To: Lynne Jones

Times and Ratios

Use a colon to separate hours, minutes, and seconds. Also use a colon between the numbers in a ratio.

7:35 p.m.   6:15 a.m.   The student-teacher ratio is 30:1.

Using Semicolons and Colons

`Correct` Add semicolons and commas as needed in the sentences below.

1. Searching for a job is nerve-wracking however it's also about possibilities.

2. Don't think about rejections think about where you could be working.

3. Each résumé you send is a fishing line then you wait for a nibble.

4. Put out dozens of lines also give yourself time.

5. Make sure that you have a strong résumé e-résumé and cover letter that you consult social networks local newspapers and friends and that you keep your spirits up.

6. It doesn't cost much to send out résumés therefore send out many.

7. Job searching can feel lonely and frustrating rely on friends and family to help you through.

8. Ask people if you can use them as references don't provide the list of references until requested.

9. When you interview, wear professional clothing show up at the right place at the right time and armed with any information you need and be confident.

10. Try to enjoy the process it is the gateway to your future.

`Correct` Add colons where needed in the sentences below.

1. Use your social resources contacts, references, and organizations.

2. Call for an appointment between 9 00 a.m. and 4 00 p.m.

3. Remember a response rate of 1 10 is good for résumés submitted.

4. Politely start your cover letter with a salutation "Dear Mrs. Baker."

5. For an interview, remember these three keys Be punctual, be polite, and be professional.

6. Here's one last piece of advice Be yourself.

Vocabulary

semicolon
a punctuation mark (;) that connects sentences and separates items in some series

colon
a punctuation mark (:) that introduces an example or list and has other special uses

salutation
the formal greeting in a letter; the line starting with "Dear"

LO3 Hyphens

A hyphen joins words to each other or to letters to form compounds.

Compound Nouns

Use hyphens to create compound nouns.

city-state   fail-safe   fact-check   one-liner   mother-in-law

Compound Adjectives

Use hyphens to create compound adjectives that appear before the noun. If the adjective appears after, it usually is not hyphenated.

peer-reviewed article   an article that was peer reviewed

ready-made solution   a solution that is ready made

NOTE: Don't hyphenate a compound made from an -ly adverb and an adjective, or a compound that ends with a single letter.

newly acquired songs (ly adverb)   grade B plywood (ending with a letter)

Compound Numbers

Use hyphens for compound numbers from twenty-one to ninety-nine. Also use hyphens for numbers in a fraction and other number compounds.

twenty-two   fifty-fifty   three-quarters   seven thirty-seconds

With Letters

Use a hyphen to join a letter to a word that follows it.

L-bracket   U-shaped   T-shirt   O-ring   G-rated   x-ray

With Common Elements

Use hyphens to show that two or more words share a common element included in only the final term.

We offer low-, middle-, and high-coverage plans.

Using Hyphens

Correct   Rewrite the following sentences. Add hyphens as needed.

1. The secretary treasurer recorded the vote as four five.

2. We had to x ray twenty one people today.

3. Cut each board at seven and three sixteenths inches.

4. The statistics on low , middle , and high income households are ready.

5. A double insulated wire should be used for high voltage applications.

6. The x axis shows months and the y axis shows dollar amounts.

7. The tax rate table shows I should pay twenty eight cents.

8. My mother in law thinks I am quite a fine son in law.

9. The L bracket measured eleven sixteenths by twenty seven thirty seconds.

Vocabulary

hyphen
a short, horizontal line (-) used to form compound words

compound noun
a noun made of two or more

words, often hyphenated or spelled closed

compound adjective
an adjective made of two or more words, hyphenated

before the noun but not afterward

compound numbers
two-word numbers from twenty-one to ninety-nine

LO4 Dashes

Unlike the hyphen, the **dash** does more to separate words than to join them together. A dash is indicated by two hyphens with no spacing before or after. Most word-processing programs convert two hyphens into a dash.

For Emphasis

Use a dash instead of a colon if you want to emphasize a word, phrase, clause, or series.

Ice cream—it's what life is about.

I love two things about ice cream—making it and eating it.

Ice cream is my favorite dessert—cold, sweet, and flavorful.

To Set Off a Series

Use a dash to set off a series of items.

Rocky road, moose tracks, and chocolate-chip cookie dough—these are my favorite flavors.

Neapolitan ice cream—chocolate, strawberry, and vanilla—is my sister's favorite.

With Nonessential Elements

Use a dash to set off explanations, examples, and definitions, especially when these elements already include commas.

Ice milk—which, as you might guess, is made of milk instead of cream—provides a light alternative.

To Show Interrupted Speech

Use a dash to show that a speaker has been interrupted or has started and stopped while speaking.

"Could you help me crank this—"

"I've got to get more salt before—"

"It'll freeze up if you don't—Just give me a hand, please."

Using Dashes

Correct In the sentences below, add a dash where needed.

1. Which dessert would you prefer brownies, apple pie, or ice cream?
2. I love the triple brownie surprise a brownie with vanilla and chocolate ice cream covered in hot fudge.
3. Ice cream it's what's for dinner.
4. "Could I have a taste of " "You want to try some of " "I want to try um could I try the pistachio?"
5. Bananas, ice cream, peanuts, and fudge these are the ingredients of a banana-split sundae.
6. Making ice cream at home takes a long time and a lot of muscle!
7. An electric ice-cream maker which replaced arm power with a cranking motor makes the job easier but less fun.
8. Nothing tastes better than the first taste of freshly made ice cream nothing except perhaps the next taste.
9. Don't eat too quickly brain-freeze.
10. A danger of ice cream I'll risk it every time.

Correct Write your own sentence, correctly using dashes for each of the situations indicated below:

1. For emphasis:

   _____

2. To set off a series:

   _____

3. With nonessential elements:

   _____

Vocabulary

dash
long horizontal line that separates words, creating emphasis.

LO5 Real-World Application

Correct The following letter sounds too informal because it contains too many contractions. For any contractions you find, write the line number and full form of the word. Also, if you find any errors with apostrophes, write the line number and show the correct punctuation.

 **Hanford Building**
Supply Company, Inc.

5821 North Fairheights Road
Milsap, CA 94218
Ph: 567-555-1908

June 1, 2011   *1*

Account: 4879003

Mr. Robert Burnside, Controller
Circuit Electronic's Company
4900 Gorham Road   *5*
Mountain View, CA 94040-1093

Dear Mr. Burnside:

This letter's a reminder that your account's past due (presently 60 days).

As of today, we haven't yet received your payment of $1,806.00, originally due March
31. I've enclosed the March 1 invoice. It's for the mitered flange's that you ordered   *10*
January 10 and that we shipped January 28.

You've been a valued customer, Mr. Burnside, and Hanford appreciate's your business. We've enclosed a postage-paid envelope for your convenience.

If there's a problem, please call (567-555-1908, ext. 227) or e-mail me
(marta@hanford.comm). As alway's, we look forward to serving you.   *15*

Sincerely,

Marta Ramones

Marta Ramones'
Billing Department

Enclosures 2

LO6 Real-World Application

Correct Rewrite the following e-mail message, and insert semicolons, colons, hyphens, and dashes where necessary.

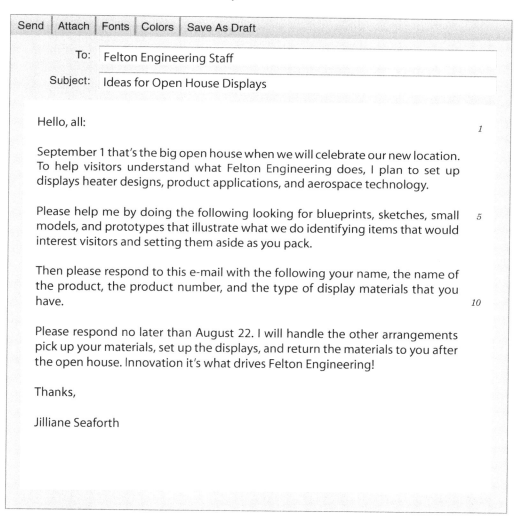

| Send | Attach | Fonts | Colors | Save As Draft |

To: Felton Engineering Staff

Subject: Ideas for Open House Displays

Hello, all:

September 1 that's the big open house when we will celebrate our new location. To help visitors understand what Felton Engineering does, I plan to set up displays heater designs, product applications, and aerospace technology.

Please help me by doing the following looking for blueprints, sketches, small models, and prototypes that illustrate what we do identifying items that would interest visitors and setting them aside as you pack.

Then please respond to this e-mail with the following your name, the name of the product, the product number, and the type of display materials that you have.

Please respond no later than August 22. I will handle the other arrangements pick up your materials, set up the displays, and return the materials to you after the open house. Innovation it's what drives Felton Engineering!

Thanks,

Jilliane Seaforth

1

5

10

Appendix and Glossary

Additional Readings
Citing Sources of Information: Using
    MLA and APA Styles
Proofreading and Correction Symbols
Understanding Assignments
Understanding the Reading Process
Understanding the Writing Process
Using the Traits for Reading and Writing
Understanding the Structure
    of Paragraphs and Essays
Understanding Strong Writing
Using Graphic Organizers
Reading for the Main Idea
Using a Peer Review Sheet
Using Standard English
Understanding Word Parts
Glossary

Additional Readings

Read the following personal narrative from Geoffrey Canada's book *FistStickKnifeGun*, a memoir about growing up in the middle of urban violence. Use the reading process to help you fully appreciate and understand the text.

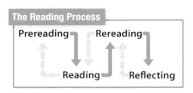

About the Author

Geoffrey Canada spent his early years in the South Bronx amid violence, poverty, and broken families. Later, in high school, he lived with an aunt in Long Island and, eventually, earned undergraduate and graduate degrees. He now serves as CEO and president of the Harlem Children's Zone, an organization that helps students in Harlem graduate from high school and college. *FistStickKnifeGun* is his first book.

Codes of Conduct

Down the block from us was a playground. It was nearby and we didn't have to cross the street to get there. We were close in age. My oldest brother, Daniel, was six, next came John who was five, I was four, and my brother Reuben was two. Reuben and I were unable to go to the playground by ourselves because we were too young. But from time to time my two oldest brothers would go there together and play.   5

I remember them coming inside one afternoon having just come back from the playground. There was great excitement in the air. My mother noticed right away and asked, "Where's John's jacket?"

My brother responded, "This boy . . . this boy he took my jacket."   10

Well, we all figured that was the end of that. My mother would have to go and get the jacket back. But the questioning continued. "What do you mean, he took your jacket?"

"I was playing on the sliding board and I took my jacket off and left it on the bench, and this boy he tried to take it. And I said it was my jacket,   15 and he said he was gonna take it. And he took it. And I tried to take it back, and he pushed me and said he was gonna beat me up."

To my mind John's explanation was clear and convincing; this case was closed. I was stunned when my mother turned to my older brother, Daniel, and said, "And what did you do when this boy was taking your   20 brother's jacket?"

Daniel looked shocked. What did he have to do with this? And we all recognized the edge in my mother's voice. Daniel was being accused of something and none of us knew what it was.

Daniel answered, "I didn't do nuthin; I told Johnny not to take his jacket off. I told him."

My mother exploded, "You let somebody take your brother's jacket and you did nothing? That's your younger brother. You can't let people just take your things. You know I don't have money for another jacket. You better not ever do this again. Now you go back there and get your brother's jacket."

My mouth was hanging open. I couldn't believe it. What was my mother talking about, go back and get it? Dan and Johnny were the same size. If the boy was gonna beat up John, he certainly could beat up Dan. We wrestled all the time and occasionally hit one another in anger, but none of us knew how to fight. We were all equally incompetent when it came to fighting. So it made no sense to me. If my mother hadn't had that look in her eye, I would have protested. Even at four years old I knew this wasn't fair. But I also knew that look in my mother's eye. A look that signified a line not to be crossed.

My brother Dan was in shock. He felt the same way I did. He tried to protest. "Ma, I can't beat that boy. It's not my jacket. I can't get it. I can't."

My mother gave him her ultimatum. "You go out there and get your brother's jacket or when you get back I'm going to give you a beating that will be ten times as bad as what that little thief could do to you. And John, you go with him. Both of you better bring that jacket back here."

The tears began to flow. Both John and Dan were crying. My mother ordered them out. Dan had this look on his face that I had seen before. A stern determination showed through his tears. For the first time I didn't want to go with my brothers to the park. I waited a long ten minutes and then, to my surprise, John and Dan triumphantly strolled into the apartment. Dan had John's jacket in his hand.

From *Fist, Stick, Knife, Gun: A Personal History of Violence in America*, pages 4-6. Boston: Beacon Press, 1995. Permission conveyed through Copyright Clearance Center.

Vocabulary Practice

Explain or define the following words in the narrative by using context clues and your understanding of word parts. List the words or word parts that help you define each term.

- edge (line 23)
- incompetent (line 36)
- ultimatum (line 43)

Read Read the narrative, noting how the writer created effective opening and closing parts. Also note how he developed his ideas in the middle part. Are all of the details arranged chronologically? Does the writer include any personal thoughts and feelings about the experience?

Remembering Gramps

Opening paragraph

It was sometime after eight o'clock on a Saturday morning *1* when I received the call about my grandfather's death. I was already awake, cracking eggs into a skillet, when my cell phone buzzed on the countertop. A little early for a phone call, I thought. It was my mom. "Are you awake?" she asked, her *5* voice cracking. Sensing her distress, I asked, "What's wrong?" She told me my grandfather had suffered a stroke during the night and didn't make it.

Middle paragraph 1

After talking through the funeral plans, I wobbled over to my cushy, leather couch and stared blankly at the circulating *10* blades on the ceiling fan. Memories of my grandfather spun around in my head, like the time he taught me how to throw a curveball, and the fishing trip we took together on the Gulf Coast, and the day he poured me a Coke, but instead mistakenly handed me his glass of bourbon and ice. *15*

Middle paragraph 2

Of course, those were old memories. By the time I reached college, Grandpa wasn't as active anymore. Tired and overworked from his years of hard labor at the steel yard, his back eventually gave out and his joints swelled up with arthritis. He lived alone in the modest two-bedroom home he *20* built for my grandmother after they married. But even after she was gone, he never lost the sparkle in his brown eyes. Nor did he lose his sense of humor, punctuated by a deep baritone laugh.

Closing paragraph

And so I sat there, staring at the ceiling and reminiscing *25* about Grandpa. Sure, I had a lump in my throat, and tears filled my eyes; but I felt thankful for the times we had together and hopeful that one day I could be as good a grandfather as he had been to me. I owed him that much—and so much more.

Read Read the following essay from *FOCUS on College and Career Success* in which Constance Staley and Steve Staley explore the concept of emotional intelligence.

About the Authors

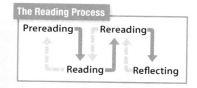

Constance Staley is a professor at the University of Colorado, Colorado Springs. During her time in the classroom, she has worked with thousands of students, helping them prepare for and succeed in college. *FOCUS on College* and *Career Success* puts in one place all of the valuable advice that she has shared with students over the years.

Steve Staley is dean of academics and professor of management and humanities at Colorado Technical University. He has also taught at the Air Force Academy, the Naval War College, and the University of Colorado, and has been an Air Force instructor pilot and served as director of corporate communications and educational development in a high-tech firm.

What Is Emotional Intelligence?

Many experts believe that intelligence takes many forms. Rather than a narrow definition of intelligence, they believe in Multiple Intelligences: Linguistic, Logical-Mathematical, Spatial, Kinesthetic, Musical, Interpersonal, Intrapersonal, and Naturalistic. Emotional intelligence may well be a combination, at least in part, of intrapersonal and interpersonal intelligences. 5

Emotional intelligence is a set of skills that determines how well you cope with the demands and pressures you face every day. How well do you understand yourself, empathize with others, draw on your inner resources, and encourage the same qualities in people you care about? Emotional 10 intelligence involves having people skills, a positive outlook, and the capacity to adapt to change. Emotional intelligence can propel you through difficult situations.

The bottom line? New research links emotional intelligence to college success, and learning about the impact of emotional intelligence in the first 15 year of college helps students stay in school.

As you read about the five scales of emotional intelligence, begin thinking about yourself in these areas. As each scale is introduced, ask yourself whether you agree or disagree with the sample statement from a well-known emotional intelligence instrument as it pertains to you.   *20*

Intrapersonal Skills (Self-Awareness)

"It's hard for me to understand the way I feel." Agree or disagree?
Are you in tune with your emotions? Do you fully realize when you're anxious, depressed, or thrilled? Or do you just generally feel up or down? Are you aware of layers of emotions . . . ?   *25*

Interpersonal Skills (Relating to Others)

"I'm sensitive to the feelings of others." Agree or disagree?
Are you aware of others' emotions and needs? Do you communicate with sensitivity and work to build positive relationships? Are you a good listener . . . ?   *30*

Stress Management Skills

"I feel that it's hard for me to control my anxiety." Agree or disagree?
Can you productively manage your emotions so that they work *for* you and not *against* you? Can you control destructive emotions? Can you work well under pressure . . . ?   *35*

Adaptability Skills

"When trying to solve a problem, I look at each possibility and then decide on the best way." Agree or disagree?
Are you flexible? Do you cope well when things don't go according to plan? Can you switch to a new plan when you need to? Do you manage change effectively . . . ?   *40*

General Mood

"I generally expect things will turn out all right, despite setbacks from time to time." Agree or disagree?
Are you optimistic and positive most of the time? Do you feel happy   *45*
and content with yourself, with others, and your life in general? Are you energetic and self-motivated . . . ?

Emotional intelligence affects every part of our lives. For example, researchers study related concepts: "hardiness," "resilience," and "learned optimism." Some people are more resistant to stress and illness. Hardy,   *50*
resilient, optimistic people are confident, committed to what they're doing, feel greater control over their lives, and see hurdles as challenges. Emotional intelligence is part of the reason why.

Vocabulary

hardiness
able to withstand hardship

resilience
the ability to recover quickly

Read Read the following process essay from Dave Ellis's book *Becoming a Master Student*. In this essay, the author provides directions for creating and using "to-do" lists to help you manage your daily tasks. Remember to use the reading process to help you fully appreciate the text.

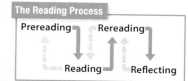

About the Author

Dave Ellis is an author, an educator, a workshop leader, and a lecturer. His book *Becoming a Master Student* is a best seller in its 13th edition, and it is used by students in the United States and in several other countries. He has co-authored other books on subjects such as human effectiveness and career planning.

The ABC Daily To-Do List

One advantage of keeping a daily to-do list is that you don't have to remember what to do next. It's on the list. A typical day in the life of a student is full of separate, often unrelated tasks—reading, attending lectures, reviewing notes, working at a job, writing papers, researching special projects, running errands. It's easy to forget an important task on a busy day. When that task is written down, you don't have to rely on your memory.

The following steps present one method for creating and using to-do lists. This method involves ranking each item on your list according to three levels of importance—A, B, and C. Experiment with these steps, modify them as you see fit, and invent new techniques that work for you.

Step 1 Brainstorm tasks

To get started, list all of the tasks you want to get done tomorrow. Each task will become an item on a to-do list. Don't worry about putting the entries in order or scheduling them yet. Just list everything you want to accomplish on a sheet of paper or planning calendar, or in a special notebook. . . .

Step 2 Estimate time

For each task you wrote down in Step 1, estimate how long it will take you to complete it. This can be tricky. If you allow too little time, you end up feeling rushed. If you allow too much time, you become less productive. For now, give it your best guess. If you are unsure, overestimate rather than underestimate how long it will take you for each task. . . .

Add up the time needed to complete all your to-do items. Also add up the number of unscheduled hours in your day. Then compare the two totals. The power of this step is that you can spot overload in advance. If you have 8 hours' worth of to-do items but only 4 unscheduled hours, that's a potential problem. To solve it, proceed to Step 3.

Step 3 Rate each task by priority

To prevent over scheduling, decide which to-do items are the most   *30*
important, given the time you have available. One suggestion for making
this decision comes from the book *How to Get Control of Your Time and
Your Life* by Alan Lakein: Simply label each task A, B, or C. . . . [The A's
are the most critical, then the B's followed by the C's.]

Once you've labeled the items on your to-do list, schedule time for all of   *35*
the A's. The B's and C's can be done randomly during the day when you are
in between tasks and are not yet ready to start the next A.

Step 4 Cross off tasks

Keep your to-do list with you at all times. Cross off activities when you
finish them, and add new ones when you think of them. If you're using 3x5   *40*
note cards, you can toss away or recycle the cards with completed items.
Crossing off tasks and releasing cards can be fun—a visible reward for
your diligence. This step fosters a sense of accomplishment.

Step 5 Evaluate

At the end of the day, evaluate your performance. Look for A priorities   *45*
you didn't complete. Look for items that repeatedly turn up as B's or C's
on your list and never seem to get done. Consider changing them to A's or
dropping them altogether. Similarly, you might consider changing an A
that didn't get done to a B or C priority. When you're done evaluating, start
on tomorrow's to-do list. . . .   *50*

Keep in mind the power of planning a whole week or even 2 weeks
in advance. Planning in this way can make it easier to put activities
in context and see how your daily goals relate to your long-term goals.
Weekly planning can also free you from feeling that you have to polish off
your whole to-do list in 1 day. Instead, you can spread tasks out over the   *55*
whole week.

In any case, make starting your own to-do list an A priority.

From ELLIS. *Becoming a Master Student,* 13E. ©2011 Wadsworth, a part of Cengage Learning, Inc.
Reproduced by permission. www.cengage.com/permissions

Vocabulary Practice

Explain or define the following words in the essay by using context clues and your
understanding of word parts. Also list the clues or word parts that help you define each
term.

- productive (line 21)
- fosters (line 43)
- priority (line 49)

liseykina, 2011 / Used under license from Shutterstock.com

Read   Read the following essay, noting how the writer created effective opening and closing parts and arranged the causes and effects of the topic.

Herbivore, Carnivore, or Omnivore?

Opening paragraph

Thesis statement

"We've spent thousands of years getting to the top of the food chain, so why go back to eating leaves?" That's what people sometimes ask vegans and vegetarians, wondering why anyone would choose that kind of diet. Vegetarians may choose a meat-free diet for different reasons, but their diet has the same basic benefits.

Middle paragraph: Causes

Every vegetarian is unique, with unique reasons for eating what they eat. Many see animals as more than meat—creatures with intelligence and feelings. These vegetarians don't like the idea of killing animals for food, especially not in the overcrowded and inhumane factory farms of today. Other vegetarians reject modern American eating habits, with too much meat and too few vegetables. The U.S. Department of Agriculture recommends that people "go lean on protein" and eat even less fat. However, the average American eats 16 percent of calories in proteins and 44 percent in fat. Vegetarians seek a better diet and a more sustainable lifestyle. And for some, it's just a matter of personal preference. They just would rather have a salad.

Middle paragraph: Effects

For most vegetarians, their choice has very positive effects. Vegetarians have to think about what they eat and where it comes from, and therefore they tend to eat better quality food and less of it. As a result, vegetarians are often slimmer than omnivores and less prone to arteriosclerosis and colon cancer—caused by fatty red meats. Vegetarians feel they live a more sustainable lifestyle, with less impact on the natural world. Still, vegans and vegetarians have their struggles. Many restaurants have meat in just about every dish, including soups and salads, making it a challenge to eat out. Ads and consumer culture also push vegetarians to eat meat. And vegetarians have to be careful to find proteins that can replace those that others get from eating meat.

Closing paragraph

The vegetarian lifestyle offers numerous physical and spiritual benefits to a person who chooses it. But the lifestyle isn't for everyone. People with poor impulse control will have a hard time resisting society's penchant for eating meat. Besides that, growing children and adolescents must be careful to get enough of the proteins and fats they need to keep growing. The vegetarian lifestyle doesn't work for everyone, but some people wouldn't have it any other way.

1

5

10

15

20

25

30

35

Citing Sources of Information

You must give credit to the sources of ideas or words that you use in your academic essays and reports. Doing so avoids *plagiarism,* which is using the words and thoughts of others without crediting them in your writing.

Academic research uses a number of different styles for citing sources. For example, the Modern Language Association (MLA) style is generally used for research in the humanities (literature, philosophy, and so on), and the American Psychological Association (APA) style is generally used for research in the social sciences (sociology, psychology, and so on). Check with your instructor before choosing a citation style.

Using MLA and APA Styles

Here are the basic guidelines for using the MLA and APA styles for crediting sources in the text of a research report.

Sources	MLA	APA
Work with one author	*Author name and page number* (Waye 27)	*Author name, year of publication, and page number* (Waye, 2008, p. 27)
Work with two (or three) authors	(Waye and Joniz 27)	(Waye & Joniz, 2008, p. 27)
Work with four (or five) authors	(Waye et al. 27)	(Waye, Joniz, Damik, & Martin, 2008, p. 27)
Work with six or more authors	(Waye et al. 27)	(Waye et al., 2008, p. 27)
Author identified within the sentence	According to Mariah Waye, fishery expert, wild salmon need human help (27).	According to Mariah Waye, fishery expert, wild salmon need human help (2008, p. 27).
Work with no author specified	*First main word(s) of the title and page number* ("Salmon in Crisis" 27)	*First main word(s) of the title, date, and page number.* ("Salmon in Crisis," 2008, p. 27)
Work with no page number specified (as in a Web page)	*Author name only (or first main word[s] of title if no author is specified)* (Waye)	*Author name only (or first main word[s] of title if no author is specified), and date* (Waye, 2008)

Citing Sources Within a Report

You can learn more about basic documentation by studying the passages below from a research report, demonstrating first the MLA style and then the APA style.

MLA Style

Source is cited in the sentence.

Title only; this Web site names no author.

According to the United States Consumer Product Safety Commission, almost 25,000 children ages five and under are treated in hospital emergency rooms each year as a result of shopping-cart injuries. The total number of injuries has, in fact, risen by more than 30 percent since 2000 ("Secure Children").

B. Potential Injuries

Four authors

Shopping-cart injuries include cuts, bruises, fractures, internal injuries, and head injuries—even skull fractures. In fact, children have died as a result of shopping-cart falls (Smith et al. 161). For the sake of our customers, Jonesville Home Mart needs to take steps to ensure shopping-cart safety. . . .

C. Solutions

Single author

A solution to this problem comes from a sister store in Anchorage, which has made safety its motto (Clepper 47). Like this store, Jonesville . . .

APA Style

Online material with no page numbers specified

According to the United States Consumer Product Safety Commission, almost 25,000 children ages five and under are treated in hospital emergency rooms each year as a result of shopping-cart injuries (2009). The total number of injuries has, in fact, risen by more than 30 percent since 1985 ("Secure Children," 2009).

B. Potential Injuries

Four authors

Shopping-cart injuries include cuts, bruises, fractures, internal injuries, and head injuries—even skull fractures. In fact, children have died as a result of shopping-cart falls (Smith, Dietrich, Garcia, & Shields, 2010, p. 161). For the sake of our customers, Jonesville Home Mart needs to take steps to ensure shopping-cart safety.

C. Solutions

Single author

A solution to this problem comes from a sister store in Anchorage, which has made safety its motto (Clepper, 2010, p. 47). Like this store, Jonesville . . .

Creating a Source List

At the end of your report, you must list your sources (either a works-cited list or a reference list) so that your reader can locate them. In both the MLA and APA formats, any source listed must also be cited in your paper, and any source cited in your paper must appear in the source list.

What to Include

Whether your sources are books, magazine articles, pamphlets, or Web sites, the citations should include all of the following elements that are available:

1. **Author name(s)**
2. **Title** (When including two parts of a publication, list the smaller part first.)
   - "Book chapter" / *Book title*
   - "Magazine article" / *Magazine title*
   - "Web-site article" / *Web-site title*
3. **Publication facts** (the date, the place of publication, the publisher; or appropriate Web information)

How MLA and APA Styles Differ

	Author	Title	Publication Facts
MLA	Give the name as it appears on the title page.	Capitalize all important words.	Place the date after the publication information.
	Waye, Mariah S. *Environmental Watch: Salmon in Danger.* New York: Pudding Press, 2010.		
APA	Use initials for the first and middle names.	Capitalize only the first word in a title, the first word in a subtitle, and any proper nouns. Capitalize titles of periodicals normally.	Place the date after the author's name.
	Waye, M. S. (2010). *Environmental watch: Salmon in danger.* New York, NY: Pudding Press.		

Vocabulary

works-cited list
list of sources prepared according to MLA style

reference list
list of sources prepared according to APA style

MLA Style

Magazine article

Web article

Article, four authors

Web site (2009 is the publication date; 2010 is the date it was viewed)

Works Cited

Clepper, Irene. "Safety First: Alaska Retailer Attracts Customers with Safe-and-Sound Seminars." *Playthings* 97 (2010): 46-47. Print.

"Secure Children Properly in Shopping Carts." Texas Medical Center, 2009. Web. 22 Sept. 2010.

Smith, Gary A., et al. "Injuries to Children Related to Shopping Carts." *Pediatrics* 97 (2010): 161-65. Print.

United States. Consumer Product Safety Commission. "Shopping Cart Injuries: Victims Five Years Old and Younger." 8 Oct. 2009. Web. 22 Sept. 2010.

APA Style (for the same sources)

References

Clepper, I. (2010). Safety first: Alaska retailer attracts customers with safe-and-sound seminars. *Playthings, 97,* 46-47.

Secure children properly in shopping carts. (2009). Retrieved September 22, 2010, from http://www.tmc.edu/health_briefs/06_15_00-shoppingcart.html

Smith, G. A., Dietrich, A., Garcia, T., & Shields, B. (2010). Injuries to children related to shopping carts. *Pediatrics, 97,* 161-165.

United States Consumer Product Safety Commission. (2009, October 8). Shopping cart injuries: Victims five years old and younger. Retrieved September 22, 2010, from http://www.cpsc.gov/LIBRARY/shopcart.html

Proofreading and Correction Symbols

ab	do not abbreviate	∧	insert (word/s left out)
ad	incorrect adjective	⌅	begin paragraph
adv	incorrect adverb	‖	not parallel
agr	agreement problem	omit	omitted word
ambig	ambiguous wording	p	punctuation
appr	inappropriate language	∧	insert comma
aud	unclear audience	?	questionable idea
avoid	this should be avoided	pass	ineffective use of passive voice
awk	awkward expression		
cap (≡)	capitalize	pro ref	pronoun reference
case	error in case	ramb	rambling sentence
cf	comma fault	red	redundant
⬭	check this out	rep	unnecessary repetition
choppy	choppy style	RO	run-on sentence
coord	faulty coordination	shift	shift in tense/person
cs	comma splice	show	show, don't tell
d	diction	sp	spelling
details	add details	ss	sentence structure
dev	inadequate development	stet	let it stand
dm	dangling modifier	sub	faulty subordination
d neg	double negative	support	add evidence
doc	incorrect or incomplete documentation	t	wrong verb tense
		thesis	thesis unclear or missing
frag	sentence fragment		
gen	be more specific	℘	delete
gram	grammatical error	trans	weak transition
inc	incomplete construction	TS	topic sentence
inf	too informal	u	usage/mixed pair
irr	irregular verb error	vary	add variety
ital	italics (underscore)	voice	inconsistent voice
lc (✗)	use lowercase	w	wordy
logic	not logical	wc	word choice
mm	misplaced modifier	wo	word order
ms	manuscript form	x	find and correct error
nc	not clear	#	insert space
nonst	nonstandard language	⌒	close up space
num	error in use of numbers	⌄	insert apostrophe

Understanding Assignments

You can use the STRAP strategy to analyze your writing and reading assignments. The strategy consists of answering questions about these five features: _subject, type, role, audience,_ and _purpose._ Once you answer the questions, you'll be ready to get to work. This chart shows how the strategy works:

For Reading Assignments		For Writing Assignments
What specific topic does the reading address?	**S**ubject	What specific topic should I write about?
What form (_essay, text chapter, article_) does the reading take?	**T**ype	What form of writing (_essay, article_) will I use?
What position (_student, responder, concerned individual_) does the writer assume?	**R**ole	What position (_student, citizen, employee_) should I assume?
Who is the intended reader?	**A**udience	Who is the intended reader?
What is the goal of the material?	**P**urpose	What is the goal (_to inform, to persuade_) of the writing?

Understanding the Reading Process

When reading academic texts, be sure to use the **reading process** to gain a full understanding of the material. This graphic shows the reading process in action. The arrows show how you may move back and forth between the steps.

The Reading Process

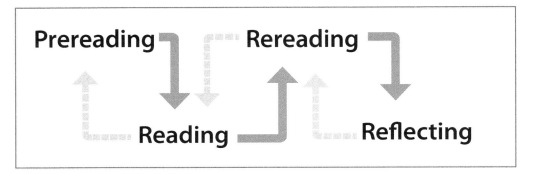

Key Terms to Remember

To use the reading process, you must understand each step in the process.

- **Prereading**—Becoming familiar with the text by reviewing the title, headings, etc.
- **Reading**—Read the text once for a basic understanding, using a reading strategy such as note taking
- **Rereading**—Complete additional readings as needed until you have a clear understanding of the material
- **Reflecting**—Evaluate your reading experience: *What have you learned? What questions to you still have?*

Understanding the Writing Process

When completing a writing assignment, be sure to use the writing process to help you do your best work. This graphic shows the writing process in action. The arrows show how you may move back and forth between the steps.

The Writing Process

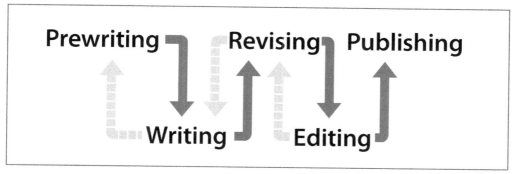

Key Terms to Remember

To use the writing process, you must understand each step in the process.

- **Prewriting**—Starting the process by analyzing the assignment, selecting a topic, gathering details, and finding a focus
- **Writing**—Writing a first draft using your prewriting as a guide
- **Revising**—Improving the content of a first draft
- **Editing**—Checking for style, grammar, mechanics, and spelling
- **Publishing**—Preparing your writing to share or submit

Using the Traits for Reading and Writing

The **traits** identify the key elements of written language. The traits help you to know what to look for when analyzing reading material. They also help you to know what to consider in your own writing.

The Traits of Written Language

Read to identify . . .	The Traits	Write to shape . . .
▪ the topic. ▪ the thesis (main point). ▪ the key supporting details.	**Ideas**	▪ a thesis or focus. ▪ your thoughts on the topic. ▪ effective supporting details.
▪ the quality of the beginning, middle, and ending parts. ▪ the organization of the supporting details.	**Organization**	▪ an effective beginning, middle, and ending. ▪ a logical, clear presentation of your supporting details.
▪ the level of the writer's interest in and knowledge about the topic.	**Voice**	▪ a voice that sounds interesting, honest, and knowledgeable.
▪ the quality of the words. (Are they interesting and clear?)	**Word Choice**	▪ words that are specific, clear, and fitting for the assignment.
▪ the effectiveness of the sentences. (Do they flow smoothly, and are they clear?)	**Sentence Fluency**	▪ smooth-reading, clear, and accurate sentences.
▪ to what degree the writing follows conventions (and why or why not).	**Conventions**	▪ paragraphs or essays that follow the conventions or rules.

Key Terms to Remember

To use the traits, you must understand what they mean.

- **Ideas**—The main point and supporting details
- **Organization**—The arrangement of the ideas
- **Voice**—The personality or tone of the writing
- **Word choice**—The words in writing
- **Sentences**—The sentences in writing
- **Conventions**—The rules governing correctness in writing

Understanding the Structure of Paragraphs and Essays

Paragraphs and essays follow a three-part structure. Knowing the purpose of each part will help you understand reading assignments and develop your own writing.

Three-Part Structure

Paragraph Structure

Topic Sentence
- Names the topic and focus

Body Sentences
- Provide supporting sentences
- Follows a pattern of organization

Closing Sentence
- Wraps up the paragraph

Essay Structure

Opening Part
- Introduces the topic
- Provides background information
- Identifies the main point or thesis

Middle Part
- Supports or develops the main point
- Follows one or more patterns of organization

Closing Part
- Summarizes the key ideas
- Restates the thesis
- Provides final thoughts or analysis

Understanding Strong Writing

The checklist below serves as a guide to strong writing. Your writing will be clear and effective when it can "pass" each point. This checklist is especially helpful during revising, when you are deciding how to improve your writing.

A Guide to Strong Writing

Ideas

☐ 1. Does an interesting and relevant topic serve as a starting point for the writing?

☐ 2. Is the writing focused, addressing a specific feeling about or a specific part of the topic? (Check the thesis statement.)

☐ 3. Are there enough specific ideas, details, and examples to support the thesis?

☐ 4. Overall, is the writing interesting and informative?

Organization

☐ 5. Does the writing form a meaningful whole—with opening, middle, and closing parts?

☐ 6. Does the writing follow a logical pattern of organization?

☐ 7. Do transitions connect ideas and help the writing flow?

Voice

☐ 8. Does the writer sound informed about and interested in the topic?

☐ 9. Does the writer sound sincere and genuine?

Word Choice

☐ 10. Does the word choice clearly fit the purpose and the audience?

☐ 11. Does the writing include specific nouns and verbs?

Sentence Fluency

☐ 12. Are the sentences clear, and do they flow smoothly?

☐ 13. Are the sentences varied in their beginnings and length?

Conventions

☐ 14. Does your writing follow the rules of the language?

Using Graphic Organizers

Consider the graphic organizers below to help you map out your thinking for reading and writing.

Sample Graphic Organizers

Time Line Use for personal narratives to list actions or events in the order they occurred.

Subject: _____

1 ── _____
2 ── _____
3 ── _____
4 ── _____

Line Diagram Use to collect and organize details for informational essays.

Cause-Effect Organizer Use to collect and organize details for cause-effect essays.

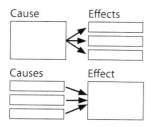

Evaluation Chart Use to collect supporting details for essays of evaluation.

Subject: _____

Points to Evaluate	Supporting Details
1	
2	
3	
4	

Process Diagram Use to collect details for science-related writing, such as the steps in a process.

Topic: _____

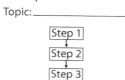

Venn Diagram Use to collect details to compare and contrast two topics.

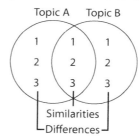

Problem-Solution Web Use to map out problem-solution essays.

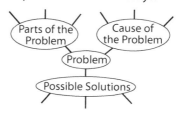

Cluster Use to collect details for informational essays.

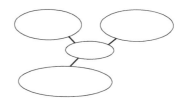

Reading for the Main Idea

Follow the steps below to help you identify the main idea or thesis in an essay, an article, or a chapter. In paragraphs, you usually need to look no further than the first sentence.

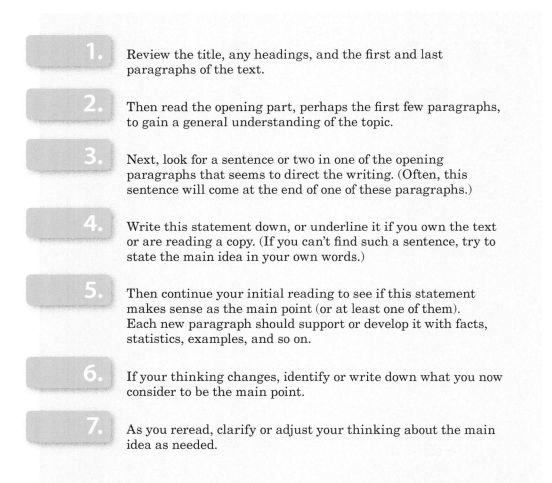

1. Review the title, any headings, and the first and last paragraphs of the text.

2. Then read the opening part, perhaps the first few paragraphs, to gain a general understanding of the topic.

3. Next, look for a sentence or two in one of the opening paragraphs that seems to direct the writing. (Often, this sentence will come at the end of one of these paragraphs.)

4. Write this statement down, or underline it if you own the text or are reading a copy. (If you can't find such a sentence, try to state the main idea in your own words.)

5. Then continue your initial reading to see if this statement makes sense as the main point (or at least one of them). Each new paragraph should support or develop it with facts, statistics, examples, and so on.

6. If your thinking changes, identify or write down what you now consider to be the main point.

7. As you reread, clarify or adjust your thinking about the main idea as needed.

Using a Peer Review Sheet

Sharing your writing at various stages is important, but it is especially important when you review and revise a first draft. The feedback that you receive will help you change and improve your essay.

Peer Review Sheet

Essay title: _____

Writer: _____

Reviewer: _____

1. Which part of the essay seems to work best—opening, middle, or closing? Why?

   _____

   _____

2. Which part of the essay needs work—opening, middle, or closing? Why?

   _____

   _____

3. Do the middle paragraphs clearly present each step of the process? Explain.

   _____

   _____

4. Do you understand the process after reading the essay?

   _____

   _____

5. Identify a phrase or two that shows the writer's level of interest.

   _____

   _____

Using Standard English

Standard English (SE) is English that is considered appropriate for school, business, and government. You have been learning SE throughout your years in school. The chart that follows shows the basic differences between non-Standard English (NS) and SE.

Differences in . . .	NS	SE
1. Expressing plurals after numbers	10 mile	10 miles
2. Expressing habitual action	He always be early.	He always is early.
3. Expressing ownership	My friend car . . .	My friend's car . . .
4. Expressing the third-person singular verb	The customer ask . . .	The customer asks . . .
5. Expressing negatives	She doesn't never . . .	She doesn't ever . . .
6. Using reflexive pronouns	He sees hisself . . .	He sees himself . . .
7. Using demonstrative adjectives	Them reports are . . .	Those reports are . . .
8. Using forms of *do*	He done it.	He did it.
9. Avoiding double subjects	My manager he . . .	My manager . . .
10. Using *a* or *an*	I need new laptop. She had angry caller.	I need a new laptop. She had an angry caller.
11. Using the past tense of verbs	Carl finish his . . .	Carl finished his . . .
12. Using *isn't* or *aren't* versus *ain't*	The company ain't . . .	The company isn't . . .

Understanding Word Parts

The next nine pages include common prefixes, suffixes, and roots. Many of our words are made up of combinations of these word parts.

Prefixes

Prefixes are those "word parts" that come *before* the root words (*pre* = before). Depending upon its meaning, a prefix changes the intent, or sense, of the base word. As a skilled reader, you will want to know the meanings of the most common prefixes and then watch for them when you read.

a, an [not, without] amoral (without a sense of moral responsibility), atypical, atom (not cuttable), apathy (without feeling), anesthesia (without sensation)

ab, abs, a [from, away] abnormal, abduct, absent, avert (turn away)

acro [high] acropolis (high city), acrobat, acronym, acrophobia (fear of height)

ambi, amb [both, around] ambidextrous (skilled with both hands), ambiguous, amble

amphi [both] amphibious (living on both land and water), amphitheater

ante [before] antedate, anteroom, antebellum, antecedent (happening before)

anti, ant [against] anticommunist, antidote, anticlimax, antacid

be [on, away] bedeck, belabor, bequest, bestow, beloved

bene, bon [well] benefit, benefactor, benevolent, benediction, bonanza, bonus

bi, bis, bin [both, double, twice] bicycle, biweekly, bilateral, biscuit, binoculars

by [side, close, near] bypass, bystander, by-product, bylaw, byline

cata [down, against] catalog, catapult, catastrophe, cataclysm

cerebro [brain] cerebral, cerebrum, cerebellum

circum, circ [around] circumference, circumnavigate, circumspect, circular

co, con, col, com [together, with] copilot, conspire, collect, compose

coni [dust] coniosis (disease that comes from inhaling dust)

contra, counter [against] controversy, contradict, counterpart

de [from, down] demote, depress, degrade, deject, deprive

deca [ten] decade, decathlon, decapod (10 feet)

di [two, twice] divide, dilemma, dilute, dioxide, dipole, ditto

dia [through, between] diameter, diagonal, diagram, dialogue (speech between people)

dis, dif [apart, away, reverse] dismiss, distort, distinguish, diffuse

dys [badly, ill] dyspepsia (digesting badly), dystrophy, dysentery

em, en [in, into] embrace, enslave

epi [upon] epidermis (upon the skin, outer layer of skin), epitaph, epithet

eu [well] eulogize (speak well of, praise), euphony, euphemism, euphoria

ex, e, ec, ef [out] expel (drive out), ex-mayor, exorcism, eject, eccentric (out of the center position), efflux, effluent

extra, extro [beyond, outside] extraordinary (beyond the ordinary), extrovert, extracurricular

for [away or off] forswear (to renounce an oath)

fore [before in time] forecast, foretell (to tell beforehand), foreshadow

hemi, demi, semi [half] hemisphere, demitasse, semicircle (half of a circle)

hex [six] hexameter, hexagon

homo [man] Homo sapiens, homicide (killing man)

hyper [over, above] hypersensitive (overly sensitive), hyperactive

hypo [under] hypodermic (under the skin), hypothesis

il, ir, in, im [not] illegal, irregular, incorrect, immoral

in, il, im [into] inject, inside, illuminate, illustrate, impose, implant, imprison

infra [beneath] infrared, infrasonic

inter [between] intercollegiate, interfere, intervene, interrupt (break between)

intra [within] intramural, intravenous (within the veins)

intro [into, inward] introduce, introvert (turn inward)

macro [large, excessive] macrodent (having large teeth), macrocosm

mal [badly, poorly] maladjusted, malady, malnutrition, malfunction

meta [beyond, after, with] metaphor, metamorphosis, metaphysical

mis [incorrect, bad] misuse, misprint

miso [hate] misanthrope, misogynist

mono [one] monoplane, monotone, monochrome, monocle

multi [many] multiply, multiform

neo [new] neopaganism, neoclassic, neophyte, neonatal

non [not] nontaxable (not taxed), nontoxic, nonexistent, nonsense

ob, of, op, oc [toward, against] obstruct, offend, oppose, occur

oct [eight] octagon, octameter, octave, octopus

paleo [ancient] paleoanthropology (pertaining to ancient humans), paleontology (study of ancient life-forms)

para [beside, almost] parasite (one who eats beside or at the table of another), paraphrase, paramedic, parallel, paradox

penta [five] pentagon (figure or building having five angles or sides), pentameter, pentathlon

per [throughout, completely] pervert (completely turn wrong, corrupt), perfect, perceive, permanent, persuade

peri [around] perimeter (measurement around an area), periphery, periscope, pericardium, period

poly [many] polygon (figure having many angles or sides), polygamy, polyglot, polychrome

post [after] postpone, postwar, postscript, posterity

pre [before] prewar, preview, precede, prevent, premonition

pro [forward, in favor of] project (throw forward), progress, promote, prohibition

pseudo [false] pseudonym (false or assumed name), pseudopodia

quad [four] quadruple (four times as much), quadriplegic, quadratic, quadrant

quint [five] quintuplet, quintuple, quintet, quintile

re [back, again] reclaim, revive, revoke, rejuvenate, retard, reject, return

retro [backward] retrospective (looking backward), retroactive, retrorocket

se [aside] seduce (lead aside), secede, secrete, segregate

self [by oneself] self-determination, self-employed, self-service, selfish

sesqui [one and a half] sesquicentennial (one and one-half centuries)

sex, sest [six] sexagenarian (sixty years old), sexennial, sextant, sextuplet, sestet

sub [under] submerge (put under), submarine, substitute, subsoil

suf, sug, sup, sus [from under] sufficient, suffer, suggest, support, suspend

super, supr [above, over, more] supervise, superman, supernatural, supreme

syn, sym, sys, syl [with, together] system, synthesis, synchronize (time together), synonym, sympathy, symphony, syllable

trans, tra [across, beyond] transoceanic, transmit (send across), transfusion, tradition

tri [three] tricycle, triangle, tripod, tristate

ultra [beyond, exceedingly] ultramodern, ultraviolet, ultraconservative

un [not, release] unfair, unnatural, unknown

under [beneath] underground, underlying

uni [one] unicycle, uniform, unify, universe, unique (one of a kind)

vice [in place of] vice president, viceroy, vice admiral

Numerical Prefixes

Prefix	Symbol	Multiples and Submultiples	Equivalent	Prefix	Symbol	Multiples and Submultiples	Equivalent
tera	T	10^{12}	trillionfold	centi	c	10^{-2}	hundredth part
giga	G	10^{9}	billionfold	milli	m	10^{-3}	thousandth part
mega	M	10^{6}	millionfold	micro	u	10^{-6}	millionth part
kilo	k	10^{3}	thousandfold	nano	n	10^{-9}	billionth part
hecto	h	10^{2}	hundredfold	pico	p	10^{-12}	trillionth part
deka	da	10	tenfold	femto	f	10^{-15}	quadrillionth part
deci	d	10^{-1}	tenth part	atto	a	10^{-18}	quintillionth part

Suffixes

Suffixes come at the end of a word. Very often a suffix will tell you what kind of word it is part of (noun, adverb, adjective, and so on). For example, words ending in *-ly* are usually adverbs.

able, ible [able, can do] capable, agreeable, edible, visible (can be seen)

ade [result of action] blockade (the result of a blocking action), lemonade

age [act of, state of, collection of] salvage (act of saving), storage, forage

al [relating to] sensual, gradual, manual, natural (relating to nature)

algia [pain] neuralgia (nerve pain)

an, ian [native of, relating to] African, Canadian, Floridian

ance, ancy [action, process, state] assistance, allowance, defiance, truancy

ant [performing, agent] assistant, servant

ary, ery, ory [relating to, quality, place where] dictionary, bravery, dormitory

ate [cause, make] liquidate, segregate (cause a group to be set aside)

cian [having a certain skill or art] musician, beautician, magician, physician

cule, ling [very small] molecule, ridicule, duckling (very small duck), sapling

cy [action, function] hesitancy, prophecy, normalcy (function in a normal way)

dom [quality, realm, office] freedom, kingdom, wisdom (quality of being wise)

ee [one who receives the action] employee, nominee (one who is nominated), refugee

en [made of, make] silken, frozen, oaken (made of oak), wooden, lighten

ence, ency [action, state of, quality] difference, conference, urgency

er, or [one who, that which] baker, miller, teacher, racer, amplifier, doctor

escent [in the process of] adolescent (in the process of becoming an adult), obsolescent, convalescent

ese [a native of, the language of] Japanese, Vietnamese, Portuguese

esis, osis [action, process, condition] genesis, hypnosis, neurosis, osmosis

ess [female] actress, goddess, lioness

et, ette [a small one, group] midget, octet, baronet, majorette

fic [making, causing] scientific, specific

ful [full of] frightful, careful, helpful

fy [make] fortify (make strong), simplify, amplify

hood [order, condition, quality] manhood, womanhood, brotherhood

ic [nature of, like] metallic (of the nature of metal), heroic, poetic, acidic

ice [condition, state, quality] justice, malice

id, ide [a thing connected with or belonging to] fluid, fluoride

ile [relating to, suited for, capable of] missile, juvenile, senile (related to being old)

ine [nature of] feminine, genuine, medicine

ion, sion, tion [act of, state of, result of] contagion, aversion, infection (state of being infected)

ish [origin, nature, resembling] foolish, Irish, clownish (resembling a clown)

ism [system, manner, condition, characteristic] heroism, alcoholism, Communism

ist [one who, that which] artist, dentist

ite [nature of, quality of, mineral product] Israelite, dynamite, graphite, sulfite

ity, ty [state of, quality] captivity, clarity

ive [causing, making] abusive (causing abuse), exhaustive

ize [make] emphasize, publicize, idolize

less [without] baseless, careless (without care), artless, fearless, helpless

ly [like, manner of] carelessly, quickly, forcefully, lovingly

ment [act of, state of, result] contentment, amendment (state of amending)

ness [state of] carelessness, kindness

oid [resembling] asteroid, spheroid, tabloid, anthropoid

ology [study, science, theory] biology, anthropology, geology, neurology

ous [full of, having] gracious, nervous, spacious, vivacious (full of life)

ship [office, state, quality, skill] friendship, authorship, dictatorship

some [like, apt, tending to] lonesome, threesome, gruesome

tude [state of, condition of] gratitude, multitude (condition of being many), aptitude

ure [state of, act, process, rank] culture, literature, rupture (state of being broken)

ward [in the direction of] eastward, forward, backward

y [inclined to, tend to] cheery, crafty, faulty

Roots

A *root* is a base upon which other words are built. Knowing the root of a difficult word can go a long way toward helping you figure out its meaning—even without a dictionary. For that reason, learning the following roots will be very valuable in all your classes.

acer, acid, acri [bitter, sour, sharp] acrid, acerbic, acidity (sourness), acrimony

acu [sharp] acute, acupuncture

ag, agi, ig, act [do, move, go] agent (doer), agenda (things to do), agitate, navigate (move by sea), ambiguous (going both ways), action

ali, allo, alter [other] alias (a person's other name), alibi, alien (from another place), alloy, alter (change to another form)

alt [high, deep] altimeter (a device for measuring heights), altitude

am, amor [love, liking] amiable, amorous, enamored

anni, annu, enni [year] anniversary, annually (yearly), centennial (occurring once in 100 years)

anthrop [man] anthropology (study of mankind), philanthropy (love of mankind), misanthrope (hater of mankind)

anti [old] antique, antiquated, antiquity

arch [chief, first, rule] archangel (chief angel), architect (chief worker), archaic (first, very early), monarchy (rule by one person), matriarchy (rule by the mother)

aster, astr [star] aster (star flower), asterisk, asteroid, astronomy (star law), astronaut (star traveler, space traveler)

aud, aus [hear, listen] audible (can be heard), auditorium, audio, audition, auditory, audience, ausculate

aug, auc [increase] augur, augment (add to; increase), auction

auto, aut [self] autograph (self-writing), automobile (self-moving vehicle), author, automatic (self-acting), autobiography

belli [war] rebellion, belligerent (warlike or hostile)

bibl [book] Bible, bibliography (list of books), bibliomania (craze for books), bibliophile (book lover)

bio [life] biology (study of life), biography, biopsy (cut living tissue for examination)

brev [short] abbreviate, brevity, brief

cad, cas [to fall] cadaver, cadence, caducous (falling off), cascade

calor [heat] calorie (a unit of heat), calorify (to make hot), caloric

cap, cip, cept [take] capable, capacity, capture, reciprocate, accept, except, concept

capit, capt [head] decapitate (to remove the head from), capital, captain, caption

carn [flesh] carnivorous (flesh eating), incarnate, reincarnation

caus, caut [burn, heat] caustic, cauterize (to make hot, to burn)

cause, cuse, cus [cause, motive] because, excuse (to attempt to remove the blame or cause), accusation

ced, ceed, cede, cess [move, yield, go, surrender] procedure, secede (move aside from), proceed (move forward), cede (yield), concede, intercede, precede, recede, success

centri [center] concentric, centrifugal, centripetal, eccentric (out of center)

chrom [color] chrome, chromosome (color body in genetics), chromosphere, monochrome (one color), polychrome

chron [time] chronological (in order of time), chronometer (time measured), chronicle (record of events in time), synchronize (make time with, set time together)

cide, cise [cut down, kill] suicide (killing of self), homicide (human killer), pesticide (pest killer), germicide (germ killer), insecticide, precise (cut exactly right), incision, scissors

cit [to call, start] incite, citation, cite

civ [citizen] civic (relating to a citizen), civil, civilian, civilization

clam, claim [cry out] exclamation, clamor, proclamation, reclamation, acclaim

clud, clus, claus [shut] include (to take in), conclude, claustrophobia (abnormal fear of being shut up, confined), recluse (one who shuts himself away from others)

cognosc, gnosi [know] recognize (to know again), incognito (not known), prognosis (forward knowing), diagnosis

cord, cor, cardi [heart] cordial (hearty, heartfelt), concord, discord, courage, encourage (put heart into), discourage (take heart out of), core, coronary, cardiac

corp [body] corporation (a legal body), corpse, corpulent

cosm [universe, world] cosmic, cosmos (the universe), cosmopolitan (world citizen), cosmonaut, microcosm, macrocosm

crat, cracy [rule, strength] democratic, autocracy

crea [create] creature (anything created), recreation, creation, creator

cred [believe] creed (statement of beliefs), credo (a creed), credence (belief), credit (belief, trust), credulous (believing too readily, easily deceived), incredible

cresc, cret, crease, cru [rise, grow] crescendo (growing in loudness or intensity), concrete (grown together, solidified), increase, decrease, accrue (to grow)

crit [separate, choose] critical, criterion (that which is used in choosing), hypocrite

cur, curs [run] concurrent, current (running or flowing), concur (run together, agree), incur (run into), recur, occur, precursor (forerunner), cursive

cura [care] curator, curative, manicure (caring for the hands)

cycl, cyclo [wheel, circular] Cyclops (a mythical giant with one eye in the middle of his forehead), unicycle, bicycle, cyclone (a wind blowing circularly, a tornado)

deca [ten] decade, decalogue, decathlon

dem [people] democracy (people-rule), demography (vital statistics of the people: deaths, births, and so on), epidemic (on or among the people)

dent, dont [tooth] dental (relating to teeth), denture, dentifrice, orthodontist

derm [skin] hypodermic (injected under the skin), dermatology (skin study), epidermis (outer layer of skin), taxidermy (arranging skin; mounting animals)

dict [say, speak] diction (how one speaks, what one says), dictionary, dictate, dictator, dictaphone, dictatorial, edict, predict, verdict, contradict, benediction

doc [teach] indoctrinate, document, doctrine

domin [master] dominate, dominion, predominant, domain

don [give] donate, condone

dorm [sleep] dormant, dormitory

dox [opinion, praise] doxy (belief, creed, or opinion), orthodox (having the correct, commonly accepted opinion), heterodox (differing opinion), paradox (contradictory)

drome [run, step] syndrome (run-together symptoms), hippodrome (a place where horses run)

duc, duct [lead] produce, induce (lead into, persuade), seduce (lead aside), reduce, aqueduct (water leader or channel), viaduct, conduct

dura [hard, lasting] durable, duration, endurance

dynam [power] dynamo (power producer), dynamic, dynamite, hydrodynamics

endo [within] endoral (within the mouth), endocardial (within the heart), endoskeletal

equi [equal] equinox, equilibrium

erg [work] energy, erg (unit of work), allergy, ergophobia (morbid fear of work), ergometer, ergonomic

fac, fact, fic, fect [do, make] factory (place where workers make goods of various kinds), fact (a thing done), manufacture, amplification, confection

fall, fals [deceive] fallacy, falsify

fer [bear, carry] ferry (carry by water), coniferous (bearing cones, as a pine tree), fertile (bearing richly), defer, infer, refer

fid, fide, feder [faith, trust] confidante, Fido, fidelity, confident, infidelity, infidel, federal, confederacy

fila, fili [thread] filament (a single thread or threadlike object), filibuster, filigree

fin [end, ended, finished] final, finite, finish, confine, fine, refine, define, finale

fix [attach] fix, fixation (the state of being attached), fixture, affix, prefix, suffix

flex, flect [bend] flex (bend), reflex (bending back), flexible, flexor (muscle for bending), inflexibility, reflect, deflect

flu, fluc, fluv [flowing] influence (to flow in), fluid, flue, flush, fluently, fluctuate (to wave in an unsteady motion)

form [form, shape] form, uniform, conform, deform, reform, perform, formative, formation, formal, formula

fort, forc [strong] fort, fortress (a strong place), fortify (make strong), forte (one's strong point), fortitude, enforce

fract, frag [break] fracture (a break), infraction, fragile (easy to break), fraction (result of breaking a whole into equal parts), refract (to break or bend)

gam [marriage] bigamy (two marriages), monogamy, polygamy (many spouses or marriages)

gastr(o) [stomach] gastric, gastronomic, gastritis (inflammation of the stomach)

gen [birth, race, produce] genesis (birth, beginning), genetics (study of heredity), eugenics (well born), genealogy (lineage by race, stock), generate, genetic

geo [earth] geometry (earth measurement), geography (earth writing), geocentric (earth centered), geology

germ [vital part] germination (to grow), germ (seed; living substance, as the germ of an idea), germane

gest [carry, bear] congest (bear together, clog), congestive (causing clogging), gestation

gloss, glot [tongue] glossary, polyglot (many tongues), epiglottis

glu, glo [lump, bond, glue] glue, agglutinate (make to hold in a bond), conglomerate (bond together)

grad, gress [step, go] grade (step, degree), gradual (step-by-step), graduate (make all the steps, finish a course), graduated (in steps or degrees), progress

graph, gram [write, written] graph, graphic (written, vivid), autograph (self-writing, signature), graphite (carbon used for writing), photography (light writing), phonograph (sound writing), diagram, bibliography, telegram

grat [pleasing] gratuity (mark of favor, a tip), congratulate (express pleasure over success), grateful, ingrate (not thankful) grav [heavy, weighty] grave, gravity, aggravate, gravitate

greg [herd, group, crowd] gregarian (belonging to a herd), congregation (a group functioning together), segregate (tending to group aside or apart)

helio [sun] heliograph (an instrument for using the sun's rays to send signals), heliotrope (a plant that turns to the sun)

hema, hemo [blood] hemorrhage (an outpouring or flowing of blood), hemoglobin, hemophilia

here, hes [stick] adhere, cohere, cohesion

hetero [different] heterogeneous (different in birth), heterosexual (with interest in the opposite sex)

homo [same] homogeneous (of same birth or kind), homonym (word with same pronunciation as another), homogenize

hum, human [earth, ground, man] humus, exhume (to take out of the ground), humane (compassion for other humans)

hydr, hydra, hydro [water] dehydrate, hydrant, hydraulic, hydraulics, hydrogen, hydrophobia (fear of water)

hypn [sleep] hypnosis, Hypnos (god of sleep), hypnotherapy (treatment of disease by hypnosis)

ignis [fire] ignite, igneous, ignition

ject [throw] deject, inject, project (throw forward), eject, object

join, junct [join] adjoining, enjoin (to lay an order upon, to command), juncture, conjunction, injunction

juven [young] juvenile, rejuvenate (to make young again)

lau, lav, lot, lut [wash] launder, lavatory, lotion, ablution (a washing away), dilute (to make a liquid thinner and weaker)

leg [law] legal (lawful; according to law), legislate (to enact a law), legislature, legitimize (make legal)

levi [light] alleviate (lighten a load), levitate, levity (light conversation; humor)

liber, liver [free] liberty (freedom), liberal, liberalize (to make more free), deliverance

liter [letters] literary (concerned with books and writing), literature, literal, alliteration, obliterate

loc, loco [place] locality, locale, location, allocate (to assign, to place), relocate (to put back into place), locomotion (act of moving from place to place)

log, logo, ogue, ology [word, study, speech] catalog, prologue, dialogue, logogram (a symbol representing a word), zoology (animal study), psychology (mind study)

loqu, locut [talk, speak] eloquent (speaking well and forcefully), soliloquy, locution, loquacious (talkative), colloquial (talking together; conversational or informal)

luc, lum, lus, lun [light] translucent (letting light come through), lumen (a unit of light), luminary (a heavenly body; someone who shines in his or her profession), luster (sparkle, shine), Luna (the moon goddess)

magn [great] magnify (make great, enlarge), magnificent, magnanimous (great of mind or spirit), magnate, magnitude, magnum

man [hand] manual, manage, manufacture, manacle, manicure, manifest, maneuver, emancipate

mand [command] mandatory (commanded), remand (order back), mandate

mania [madness] mania (insanity, craze), monomania (mania on one idea), kleptomania, pyromania (insane tendency to set fires), maniac

mar, mari, mer [sea, pool] marine (a soldier serving on shipboard), marsh (wetland, swamp), maritime (relating to the sea and navigation), mermaid (fabled sea creature, half fish, half woman)

matri [mother] maternal (relating to the mother), matrimony, matriarchate (rulership of women), matron

medi [half, middle, between, halfway] mediate (come between, intervene), medieval (pertaining to the Middle Ages), Mediterranean (lying between lands), mediocre, medium

mega [great, million] megaphone (great sound), megalopolis (great city; an extensive urban area including a number of cities), megacycle (a million cycles), megaton

mem [remember] memo (a reminder), commemoration (the act of remembering by a memorial or ceremony), memento, memoir, memorable

meter [measure] meter (a metric measure), voltameter (instrument to measure volts), barometer, thermometer

micro [small] microscope, microfilm, microcard, microwave, micrometer (device for measuring small distances), omicron, micron (a millionth of a meter), microbe (small living thing)

migra [wander] migrate (to wander), emigrate (one who leaves a country), immigrate (to come into the land)

mit, miss [send] emit (send out, give off), remit (send back, as money due), submit, admit, commit, permit, transmit (send across), omit, intermittent (sending between, at intervals), mission, missile

mob, mot, mov [move] mobile (capable of moving), motionless (without motion), motor, emotional (moved strongly by feelings), motivate, promotion, demote, movement

mon [warn, remind] monument (a reminder or memorial of a person or an event), admonish (warn), monitor, premonition (forewarning)

mor, mort [mortal, death] mortal (causing death or destined for death), immortal (not subject to death), mortality (rate of death), mortician (one who prepares the dead for burial), mortuary (place for the dead, a morgue)

morph [form] amorphous (with no form, shapeless), metamorphosis (a change of form, as a caterpillar into a butterfly), morphology

multi [many, much] multifold (folded many times), multilinguist (one who speaks many languages), multiped (an organism with many feet), multiply

nat, nasc [to be born, to spring forth] innate (inborn), natal, native, nativity, renascence (a rebirth, a revival)

neur [nerve] neuritis (inflammation of a nerve), neurology (study of nervous systems), neurologist (one who practices neurology), neural, neurosis, neurotic

nom [law, order] autonomy (self-law, self-government), astronomy, gastronomy (art or science of good eating), economy

nomen, nomin [name] nomenclature, nominate (name someone for an office)

nov [new] novel (new, strange, not formerly known), renovate (to make like new again), novice, nova, innovate

nox, noc [night] nocturnal, equinox (equal nights), noctilucent (shining by night)

numer [number] numeral (a figure expressing a number), numeration (act of counting), enumerate (count out, one by one), innumerable

omni [all, every] omnipotent (all-powerful), omniscient (all-knowing), omnipresent (present everywhere), omnivorous

onym [name] anonymous (without name), synonym, pseudonym (false name), antonym (name of opposite meaning)

oper [work] operate (to labor, function), cooperate (work together)

ortho [straight, correct] orthodox (of the correct or accepted opinion), orthodontist (tooth straightener), orthopedic (originally pertaining to straightening a child), unorthodox

pac [peace] pacifist (one for peace only; opposed to war), pacify (make peace, quiet), Pacific Ocean (peaceful ocean)

pan [all] panacea (cure-all), pandemonium (place of all the demons, wild disorder), pantheon (place of all the gods in mythology)

pater, patr [father] paternity (fatherhood, responsibility), patriarch (head of the tribe, family), patriot, patron (a wealthy person who supports as would a father)

path, pathy [feeling, suffering] pathos (feeling of pity, sorrow), sympathy, antipathy (feeling against), apathy (without feeling), empathy (feeling or identifying with another), telepathy (far feeling; thought transference)

ped, pod [foot] pedal (lever for a foot), impede (get the feet in a trap, hinder), pedestal (foot or base of a statue), pedestrian (foot traveler), centipede, tripod (three-footed support), podiatry (care of the feet), antipodes (opposite feet)

pedo [child] orthopedic, pedagogue (child leader; teacher), pediatrics (medical care of children)

pel, puls [drive, urge] compel, dispel, expel, repel, propel, pulse, impulse, pulsate, compulsory, expulsion, repulsive

pend, pens, pond [hang, weigh] pendant pendulum, suspend, appendage, pensive (weighing thought), ponderous

phil [love] philosophy (love of wisdom), philanthropy, philharmonic, bibliophile, Philadelphia (city of brotherly love)

phobia [fear] claustrophobia (fear of closed spaces), acrophobia (fear of high places), hydrophobia (fear of water)

phon [sound] phonograph, phonetic (pertaining to sound), symphony (sounds with or together)

photo [light] photograph (light-writing), photoelectric, photogenic (artistically suitable for being photographed), photosynthesis (action of light on chlorophyll to make carbohydrates)

plac [please] placid (calm, peaceful), placebo, placate, complacent

plu, plur, plus [more] plural (more than one), pluralist (a person who holds more than one office), plus (indicating that something more is to be added)

pneuma, pneumon [breath] pneumatic (pertaining to air, wind, or other gases), pneumonia (disease of the lungs)

pod (see ped)

poli [city] metropolis (mother city), police, politics, Indianapolis, Acropolis (high city, upper part of Athens), megalopolis

pon, pos, pound [place, put] postpone (put afterward), component, opponent (one put against), proponent, expose, impose, deposit, posture (how one places oneself), position, expound, impound

pop [people] population, populous (full of people), popular

port [carry] porter (one who carries), portable, transport (carry across), report, export, import, support, transportation

portion [part, share] portion (a part; a share, as a portion of pie), proportion (the relation of one share to others)

prehend [seize] comprehend (seize with the mind), apprehend (seize a criminal), comprehensive (seizing much, extensive)

prim, prime [first] primacy (state of being first in rank), prima donna (the first lady of opera), primitive (from the earliest or first time), primary, primal, primeval proto [first] prototype (the first model made), protocol, protagonist, protozoan

psych [mind, soul] psyche (soul, mind), psychiatry (healing of the mind), psychology, psychosis (serious mental disorder), psychotherapy (mind treatment), psychic

punct [point, dot] punctual (being exactly on time), punctuation, puncture, acupuncture

reg, recti [straighten] regiment, regular, regulate, rectify (make straight), correct, direction

ri, ridi, risi [laughter] deride (mock, jeer at), ridicule (laughter at the expense of another, mockery), ridiculous, derision

rog, roga [ask] prerogative (privilege; asking before), interrogation (questioning; the act of questioning), derogatory

rupt [break] rupture (break), interrupt (break into), abrupt (broken off), disrupt (break apart), erupt (break out), incorruptible (unable to be broken down)

sacr, sanc, secr [sacred] sacred, sanction, sacrosanct, consecrate, desecrate

salv, salu [safe, healthy] salvation (act of being saved), salvage, salutation

sat, satis [enough] satient (giving pleasure, satisfying), saturate, satisfy (to give pleasure to; to give as much as is needed)

sci [know] science (knowledge), conscious (knowing, aware), omniscient (knowing everything)

scope [see, watch] telescope, microscope, kaleidoscope (instrument for seeing beautiful forms), periscope, stethoscope

scrib, script [write] scribe (a writer), scribble, manuscript (written by hand), inscribe, describe, subscribe, prescribe

sed, sess, sid [sit] sediment (that which sits or settles out of a liquid), session (a sitting), obsession (an idea that sits stubbornly in the mind), possess, preside (sit before), president, reside, subside

sen [old] senior, senator, senile (old; showing the weakness of old age)

sent, sens [feel] sentiment (feeling), consent, resent, dissent, sentimental (having strong feeling or emotion), sense, sensation, sensitive, sensory, dissension

sequ, secu, sue [follow] sequence (following of one thing after another), sequel, consequence, subsequent, prosecute, consecutive (following in order), second (following "first"), ensue, pursue

serv [save, serve] servant, service, preserve, subservient, servitude, conserve,   reservation, deserve, conservation

sign, signi [sign, mark, seal] signal (a gesture or sign to call attention), signature (the mark of a person written in his or her own handwriting), design, insignia (distinguishing marks)

simil, simul [like, resembling] similar (resembling in many respects), assimilate (to make similar to), simile, simulate (pretend; put on an act to make a certain impression)

sist, sta, stit [stand] persist (stand firmly; unyielding; continue), assist (to stand by with help), circumstance, stamina (power to withstand, to endure), status (standing), state, static, stable, stationary, substitute (to stand in for another)

solus [alone] soliloquy, solitaire, solitude, solo

solv, solu [loosen] solvent (a loosener, a dissolver), solve, absolve (loosen from, free from), resolve, soluble, solution, resolution, resolute, dissolute (loosened morally)

somnus [sleep] insomnia (not being able to sleep), somnambulist (a sleepwalker)

soph [wise] sophomore (wise fool), philosophy (love of wisdom), sophisticated

spec, spect, spic [look] specimen (an example to look at, study), specific, aspect, spectator (one who looks), spectacle, speculate, inspect, respect, prospect, retrospective (looking backward), introspective, expect, conspicuous

sphere [ball, sphere] stratosphere (the upper portion of the atmosphere), hemisphere (half of the earth), spheroid

spir [breath] spirit (breath), conspire (breathe together; plot), inspire (breathe into), aspire (breathe toward), expire (breathe out; die), perspire, respiration

string, strict [draw tight] stringent (drawn tight; rigid), strict, restrict, constrict (draw tightly together), boa constrictor (snake that constricts its prey)

stru, struct [build] construe (build in the mind, interpret), structure, construct, instruct, obstruct, destruction, destroy

sume, sump [take, use, waste] consume (to use up), assume (to take; to use), sump pump (a pump that takes up water), presumption (to take or use before knowing all the facts)

tact, tang, tag, tig, ting [touch] contact, tactile, intangible (not able to be touched), intact (untouched, uninjured), tangible, contingency, contagious (able to transmit disease by touching), contiguous

tele [far] telephone (far sound), telegraph (far writing), television (far seeing), telephoto (far photography), telecast

tempo [time] tempo (rate of speed), temporary, extemporaneously, contemporary (those who live at the same time), pro tem (for the time being)

ten, tin, tain [hold] tenacious (holding fast), tenant, tenure, untenable, detention, content, pertinent, continent, obstinate, abstain, pertain, detain

tend, tent, tens [stretch, strain] tendency (a stretching; leaning), extend, intend, contend, pretend, superintend, tender, extent, tension (a stretching, strain), pretense terra [earth] terrain, terrarium, territory, terrestrial

test [to bear witness] testament (a will; bearing witness to someone's wishes), detest, attest (bear witness to), testimony

the, theo [God, a god] monotheism (belief in one god), polytheism (belief in many gods), atheism, theology

therm [heat] thermometer, therm (heat unit), thermal, thermostat, thermos, hypothermia (subnormal temperature)

thesis, thet [place, put] antithesis (place against), hypothesis (place under), synthesis (put together), epithet

tom [cut] atom (not cuttable; smallest particle of matter), appendectomy (cutting out an appendix), tonsillectomy, dichotomy (cutting in two; a division), anatomy (cutting, dissecting to study structure)

tort, tors [twist] torture (twisting to inflict pain), retort (twist back, reply sharply), extort (twist out), distort (twist out of shape), contort, torsion (act of twisting, as a torsion bar)

tox [poison] toxic (poisonous), intoxicate, antitoxin

tract, tra [draw, pull] tractor, attract, subtract, tractable (can be handled), abstract (to draw away), subtrahend (the number to be drawn away from another)

trib [pay, bestow] tribute (to pay honor to), contribute (to give money to a cause), attribute, retribution, tributary

turbo [disturb] turbulent, disturb, turbid, turmoil

typ [print] type, prototype (first print; model), typical, typography, typewriter, typology (study of types, symbols), typify

ultima [last] ultimate, ultimatum (the final or last offer that can be made)

uni [one] unicorn (a legendary creature with one horn), unify (make into one), university, unanimous, universal

vac [empty] vacate (to make empty), vacuum (a space entirely devoid of matter), evacuate (to remove troops or people), vacation, vacant

vale, vali, valu [strength, worth] valiant, equivalent (of equal worth), validity (truth; legal strength), evaluate (find out the value), value, valor (value; worth)

ven, vent [come] convene (come together, assemble), intervene (come between), venue, convenient, avenue, circumvent (come or go around), invent, prevent

ver, veri [true] very, aver (say to be true, affirm), verdict, verity (truth), verify (show to be true), verisimilitude

vert, vers [turn] avert (turn away), divert (turn aside, amuse), invert (turn over), introvert (turn inward), convertible, reverse (turn back), controversy (a turning against; a dispute), versatile (turning easily from one skill to another)

vic, vicis [change, substitute] vicarious, vicar, vicissitude

vict, vinc [conquer] victor (conqueror, winner), evict (conquer out, expel), convict (prove guilty), convince (conquer mentally, persuade), invincible (not conquerable)

vid, vis [see] video, television, evident, provide, providence, visible, revise, supervise (oversee), vista, visit, vision

viv, vita, vivi [alive, life] revive (make live again), survive (live beyond, outlive), vivid, vivacious (full of life), vitality

voc [call] vocation (a calling), avocation (occupation not one's calling), convocation (a calling together), invocation, vocal

vol [will] malevolent, benevolent (one of goodwill), volunteer, volition

volcan, vulcan [fire] volcano (a mountain erupting fiery lava), volcanize (to undergo volcanic heat), Vulcan (Roman god of fire)

volvo [turn about, roll] revolve, voluminous (winding), voluble (easily turned about or around), convolution (a twisting)

vor [eat greedily] voracious, carnivorous (flesh eating), herbivorous (plant eating), omnivorous (eating everything), devour

zo [animal] zoo (short for zoological garden), zoology (study of animal life), zodiac (circle of animal constellations), zoomorphism (being in the form of an animal), protozoa (one-celled animals)

The Human Body

capit	head	gastro	stomach	osteo	bone
card	heart	glos	tongue	ped	foot
corp	body	hema	blood	pneuma	breathe
dent	tooth	man	hand	psych	mind
derm	skin	neur	nerve	spir	breath

Glossary

A

abstract
something that can't be sensed (seen, heard, etc.); a feeling or idea

abstract nouns
nouns referring to ideas or conditions that cannot be sensed

academic sentences
usually longer sentences with multiple layers of meaning; reveal careful thought on the part of the writer

academic voice
the tone or style used in most textbooks and professional journals; formal and serious

action verb
word functioning as a verb that expresses action

active voice
the voice created when a subject is acting

adjective
a word that modifies a noun or pronoun

adjective phrase or clause
a dependent clause functioning as an adjective

adverb
word that modifies a verb, an adjective, an adverb, or a whole sentence

adverb clause
a dependent clause functioning as an adverb

agree in number
when subject and verb are both singular or both plural

ambiguous
unclear or confusing

annotate
to add comments or make notes in a text

antecedent
the noun or pronoun that a pronoun refers to or replaces

APA
American Psychological Association; provides documentation guidelines for the social sciences

appositive
a noun or non phrase that renames another noun right beside it; usually set off by commas

apostrophe
a punctuation mark (') used to show that a letter or number has been left out or that a word is possessive

argumentation
a discussion or course of reasoning aimed at demonstrating truth or falsehood; relies on logic and sound reasoning

article
common noun markers (*a, an,* or *the*)

audience
the intended reader of a text

auxiliary verbs
helping verbs used with the main verb to indicate tense and other things

B

base word (root)
the word part or base upon which other words are built (help is the base for the word helpful)

"be" verb
forms of the verb "be" (*is, are, was, were*); function as linking verbs

C

causal connection
the link between the causes and effects of a topic; usually identified in the thesis statement

causes
the reasons for an action or a condition

chronological
organized by time

citations
sources referred to in research; occur within the text and in a listing at the end of the report

claim
the position or thesis developed in an argument essay

classification
the act of arranging or organizing according to classes or categories

closing
the final part of writing; a closing sentence in a paragraph, a closing paragraph (or two) in an essay

cluster
a strategy to generate ideas graphically; used to select topics and to gather details about a topic

colon
a punctuation mark (:) that introduces an example or list

comma splice
a sentence error that occurs when two sentences are connected with only a comma

common noun
a general noun, not capitalized

comparison-contrast
showing how two or more subjects are similar and different

complete predicate
the predicate with modifiers and objects

complete subject
the subject with modifiers

complex sentences
a sentence with an independent and dependent clause

compound adjective
an adjective made of two more words, hyphenated before the noun, but not afterward (*ready-made meals*)

compound-complex sentences
a sentence with two or more independent clauses and one or more dependent clauses

compound noun
noun made up of two or more words (*editor in chief*)

compound predicate
two or more predicates joined by *and* or *or*

compound sentence
two or more simple sentences joined with a coordinating conjunction that share the same verb

compound subject
two or more subjects connected by *and* or *or*

concrete nouns
nouns referring to something that can be sensed

conjunction
word or word group that joins parts of a sentence

content
the ideas and meaning developed in a piece of writing

context
the part of a text that surrounds a particular word; helps determine the word's meaning

contraction
word formed by joining two words, leaving out one or more letters (indicated by an apostrophe)

conventions
the rules governing the standard use of the language

coordinating conjunctions
conjunction that joins grammatically equal parts

correlative conjunctions
pair of conjunctions that stress the equality of the parts that are joined

count nouns
nouns that name things that can be counted (*pens, votes, people*)

counterarguments
opposing positions or arguments

cycle chart
a graphic organizer that identifies the steps in a recurring process

D

dangling modifiers
a modifying word, phrase, or clause that appears to modify the wrong word

dash
long horizontal line (—) that separates words or ideas, creating emphasis

declarative sentence
a sentence that express a basic statement

deductive thinking
following a thesis (main idea) with supporting reasons, examples, and facts

definite article
the word *the*

definition
the formal statement or explanation of a meaning of a word

delayed subject
a subject that appears after the verb

demonstrative adjective
a demonstrative pronoun (*this, that, those*) used as an adjective

dependent clause
a group of words with a subject and verb that does not express a complete thought

description
the creation of an image of a person, place, thing, or idea

dialogue
conversation between two or more people

direct object
a word that follows a transitive verb

documentation guidelines
rules to follow for giving credit for the ideas of others used in a report; MLA and APA provide two common sets of documentation rules

double negative
the nonstandard use of two negatives to express a single negative idea (*I hardly can't sleep*)

double preposition
the nonstandard use of two prepositions together (*off of*)

double subject
error created by following a subject with a pronoun

E

editing
checking revised writing for style, grammar, punctuation, capitalization, and spelling errors

effects
circumstances brought about by a cause or an action

essay
a short piece of writing that uses facts and details to support a claim (thesis)

example
details that demonstrate or show something

exclamation mark
a punctuation mark (!) used at the end of an exclamatory sentence or a word that indicates strong emotion

exclamatory sentence
a sentence that expresses strong emotion

F

feminine
female

first draft
a first attempt to develop writing

focus
a particular part or feeling about topic that is emphasized in a piece of writing; usually expressed in a thesis statement

formal English
a serious, straightforward style used in most academic writing; objective (sticks to the facts)

fragment
a group of words that does not express a complete thought

freewriting
a prewriting strategy involving rapid, nonstop writing; helps in selecting a topic and gathering details about it

future tense
verb tense indicating that action will happen later

G

gathering grid
a graphic organizer used to identify or gather different types of defining details

gender
masculine, feminine, neuter, or indefinite

gerund
a verb form that ends in *ing* and is used as a noun

graphic organizers
clusters, lists, charts, and other visuals that help writers explore and arrange ideas

H

helping (auxiliary) verb
verbs that work with a main verb to form different tenses and so on

hyphen
a short, horizontal line (-) used to form compound words (*in-service*)

I

ideas
the first and main trait of writing; includes the main idea plus supporting details

idiom
a common expression whose meaning is different from its literal meaning (*hit the roof*)

illogical
without logic; senseless, false, or untrue

illustration
the act of clarifying or explaining in writing

implied subject
the word you assumed to begin command sentences

indefinite article
the words *a* or *an*

indefinite adjective
an indefinite pronoun (*man, much, some*) used as an adjective

indefinite pronoun
a pronoun such as *someone* or *everything* that does not refer to a specific person or thing

independent clause
a group of words with a subject and verb that expresses a complete thought

indirect object
a word that comes between a transitive verb and a direct object

inductive thinking
presenting specific details first and concluding with the thesis (main point)

inferences
a logical conclusion that can be made about something that is not actually said or stated in a text

infinitive
a verb form that begins with *to* and can used as a noun (or as an adjective or adverb)

informal English
a relaxed style used in most personal essays; subjective (contains the writer's thoughts and feelings)

interrogative sentence
a sentence that asks a question

italics
a special type style like *this* used to identify titles of books moves, etc.; functions the same as underlining

items in a series
three or more words, phrases, or clauses that are grammatically the same; set off by commas

interjection
a word or phrase that expresses strong emotion

intransitive verb
action verb that does not transfer action to a direct object

irregular verb
a verb in which the principal parts are different words (*give, gave, given*)

K

KWL
a reading strategy, identifying what the reader knows, wants to learn, and eventually learns

L

levels of detail
details that contain differing levels of clarifying support

line diagram
a graphic organizer used to identify the main idea and examples in writing

linking verb
verb that connects the subject with a noun or another word; "be" verbs (*is, are, was, were*) are linking verbs

listing
a strategy used to gather ideas for writing

M

main idea (main point)
the idea that is developed in a piece of writing

masculine
male

misplaced modifier
a modifying word, phrase, or clause that has been placed incorrectly in a sentence

MLA
Modern Language Association; provides documentation guidelines for use in the humanities (literature, history, philosophy, etc.)

N

narration
the sharing of a story; a personal narrative shares a true story

neuter
neither male nor female

nominative case
used as a subject or a subject complement

noncount noun
nouns that name things that cannot be counted (*ice, plastic, sunshine*)

noun
a word that names a person, place, thing, or idea

noun clause
a dependent clause that functions as a noun

noun phrase
a noun plus its modifiers

number
singular or plural

O

objective
sticking to the facts; uninfluenced by personal feelings

objective case
used as a direct object, an indirect object, or an object of a preposition

organization
the second important trait; deals with the arranged of ideas

organized list
an outline-like graphic used to keep track of the information in a report and other forms of writing; customized for personal use

outline
an orderly graphic representation of ideas, following specific rules for arrangement

P

paragraph
a distinct division of writing containing a topic sentence, body sentences, and a closing sentence; usually develops one specific topic

paraphrase
a form of summary writing with explanations and interpretations; may be as long or longer than the source text

participle
verbal ending in *ing* or *ed* and functioning as an adjective

passive voice
the voice created when a subject is being acted upon

past tense
verb tense indicating that action happened earlier

perfect tense
verb tense that expresses completed action

person
whether the pronoun is speaking, being spoken to, or being spoken about

personal voice
sounds informal and somewhat relaxed; subjective (including the writer's thoughts and feelings)

persuasion
a form of discourse attempting to convince a audience; may appeal to emotion as well as logic

phrase
a group of words that lacks a subject or predicate or both

plagiarism
using the words and thoughts of others without crediting them; intellectual stealing

plot
the different parts of a story that create suspense

plural
referring to more than one thing

points of comparison
the special elements or features used to make a comparison (size, strength, appearance, etc.)

possessive
used to show ownership

predicate
the part of the sentence that tells or asks something about the subject

predicate adjective
adjective that appears after a linking verb

prefix
word parts that come before the base word (*un* is a prefix in *unwind*)

prepositional phrase
a group of words with a preposition, an object, and any modifiers

prereading
becoming familiar with a text by reviewing the title, heading, etc.

present tense
verb tense indicating that action is happening now

prewriting
starting the writing process by analyzing the assignment, selecting a topic, gathering details, and finding a focus

primary sources
information collected directly, such as through firsthand experiences

process
a series of actions, steps, or changes bringing about a result

progressive tense
verb tense that expresses ongoing action

pronoun
word that takes the place of a noun or another pronoun

proper adjective
an adjective based on the name of a specific person, place, thing, or idea; capitalized

proper noun
the specific name of a person, place, thing, or idea; capitalized

publishing
preparing writing to share or submit

purpose
the reason for writing (to inform, to entertain, to persuade, etc.)

Q

question mark
a punctuation mark (?) used an the end of an interrogative sentence (question)

quotation
the specific thoughts or words of other people used in writing

quotation marks
punctuation marks (" ") that set off certain titles, special words, and the exact words spoken by someone

R

rambling sentence
a sentence error that occurs when a long series of separate ideas are connected by one connecting word after another

reading
the second step in the reading process; getting a basic understanding of the text

reading process
a process helping a reader gain a full understanding of a text

rereading
part of the reading process; consists of additional readings and analysis after the first reading

research report
a carefully planned form of informational writing, ranging in length from two or three pages on up

revising
improving the content of a first draft

relative clause
a dependent group of words beginning with a relative pronoun and a verb

relative pronoun
a word—that, which, who, whom—that introduces a relative clause

root (base word)
the word part (base) upon which other words are built (*help* is the base in *helpful*)

run-on sentence
a sentence error when two sentences are joined without punctuation or a connecting word

S

satiric voice
the use of humor, fake praise, or sarcasm (ridicule) to make fun of someone or something

secondary sources
information gained through reading what others have learned about a topic

semicolon
a punctuation mark (;) that connects sentences and separates items in some series

sensory details
specific sights, sounds, smells, textures, and tastes

sentences
the thoughts that carry the meaning in discourse; one of the key traits

sequencing
the following of one thing after another

shift in person
when first, second, and/or third person are improperly mixed in a sentence

shift in tense
more than one verb tense improperly used in a sentence

simple predicate
the verb and any helping verbs without modifiers or objects

simple sentence
a complete thought (containing a subject and a verb)

simple subject
the subject without any modifiers

singular
referring to one thing

spatial
organization related to location; often used in descriptions

SQ3R
a reading strategy consisting of survey, question, read, recite, and review

Standard English
English considered appropriate for school, business, and government

story line
the parts of a plot or story; includes exposition, rising action, climax, and resolution

STRAP strategy
a strategy to analyze writing and writing assignments

subject
the part of a sentence that tells who or what the sentence is about

subject complement
as word that follows a linking verb and renames or describes the subject

subjective
including a writer's personal thoughts and feelings

subordinate clause
word group that begins with a subordinating conjunction and has a subject and verb but can't stand alone as a sentence

subordinating conjunction
word or word groups that connects clauses of different importance

summarizing
the process of presenting the core of a text in a condensed form

suffix
a word part coming after a base word (*ful* is a suffix in *healthful*)

T

T-chart
A graphic organizer used to list causes and effects

tense
tell whether the action (verb) happens in the past, present, future, etc.

thesis statement
the statement of the main idea or focus of an essay; usually appears early in the text (often at the end of the first paragraph)

time line
a graphic organizer used to list ideas or events in chronological order

topic sentence
the statement of the main idea in a paragraph

transitions
words and phrases that link ideas in writing

transitive verb
action verb that transfers action to a direct object

traits
the main elements or features in writing; includes ideas, organization, voice, word choice, sentences, and conventions

U

usage error
using the wrong word (*they're* instead of *their*)

V

Venn diagram
a graphic organizer (two intersecting circles) used to identify similarities and differences for comparative writing

verb
A word that expresses action or a state of being

verb phrase
the main verb and any auxiliary verbs

verbal
a construction formed from a verb but functioning as a noun, adjective, or adverb (gerund, participle, or infinitive)

voice
the personality or tone in a piece of writing; one of the traits

W

word choice
the choice of words in a piece of writing; one of the traits

writing (the first draft)
the first attempt to develop a piece of writing; one of the steps in the writing process

writing process
a series of steps to follow to develop a piece of writing; includes prewriting, writing, revising, editing, and publishing